Mechanizing Proof

Inside Technology
edited by Wiebe E. Bijker, W. Bernard Carlson, and Trevor Pinch

Mechanizing Proof
Computing, Risk, and Trust

Donald MacKenzie

The MIT Press
Cambridge, Massachusetts
London, England

This book was set in Sabon by Achorn Graphic Services, Inc. on the Miles 33 system and was printed and bound in the United States of America.

Library of Congress Cataloging-in-Publication Data

MacKenzie, Donald A.
  Mechanizing proof : computing, risk, and trust / Donald A. MacKenzie.
    p. cm. — (Inside technology)
  Includes bibliographical references and index.
  ISBN 0-262-13393-8 (HC : alk. paper)
  1. Computer systems—Reliability. 2. Computers and civilization. I. Title.
  II. Series.

QA76.76.R44 M36   2001
004′.2′1—dc21
                                                              2001018687

Contents

9

Machines, Proofs, and Cultures   299

to Caroline

Acknowledgments

The work upon which this book is based was made possible by a series of generous research grants: the U.K. Economic and Social Research Council (especially grant R000234031, Studies in the Sociology of Proof, but also grant R00029008, and the Council's Programme on Information and Communication Technologies); the Joint Committee of that Council and the Science and Engineering Research Council (grant GR/ H74452); the U.K. Safety Critical Systems Research Programme (GR/ J58619); and the Engineering and Physical Sciences Research Council (EPSRC; GR/L37953). The final stages of the writing were supported by EPSRC's grant (GR/N13999) to DIRC, the Interdisciplinary Research Collaboration on the Dependability of Computer-Based Systems.

These grants supported several coworkers without whose help I could not have written the book, especially Eloína Peláez (whose Ph.D. thesis, drawn on heavily in chapter 2, first sparked my interest in the topic), Maggie Tierney, Tony Dale (who conducted the majority of the interviews drawn on here), and Garrel Pottinger (whose interviews form the basis for chapter 5, and who has kindly allowed me in that chapter to draw upon material from an earlier joint article). Further background interviews were conducted by Dave Aspinall, Savitri Maharaj, Claudio Russo, and Colin Smart. This large body of interview material was transcribed by Antoinette Butler, Jean Goldring, and (with exceptional dedication and skill) Dominic Watt. Moyra Forrest gathered literally hundreds of (sometimes obscure) primary sources, and Barbara Silander heroically word-processed several drafts of the text as well as turning my rough sketches into neat figures. Much of this work was done in Edinburgh University's Research Centre for Social Sciences, with the unstinting support of its directors, Frank Bechhofer and, especially, Robin Williams. My colleagues in the Department of Sociology shouldered the burden when the research grants permitted me time free of teaching and administration, and the Department of the History of Science, Harvard University, provided a friendly home during part of the writing. My warm thanks to all.

The research also would not have been possible without the support and assistance of many members of the communities whose work is studied here. Several of them became fellow investigators in the grants listed above: Stuart Anderson, Alan Bundy, and Bernard Carré played particularly active roles. I am deeply grateful for other forms of help I received from Kenneth Appel, Wiebe Bijker, David Bloor, Bob Boyer, Alan Bundy, Bob Constable, Edsger W. Dijkstra, Moritz Epple, Rudolf Fritsch, Susan Gerhart, Mike Gordon, Wolfgang Haken, John Harrison, Pat Hayes, Tony Hoare, Cliff Jones, Roger Jones, Martin Kusch, Leslie Lamport, Carl Landwehr, Mike Mahoney, Ursula Martin, John McLean, Richard DeMillo, Robin Milner, J Strother Moore, Trevor Pinch, Randy Pollack, Dag Prawitz, Andrew Ranicki, Neil Robertson, Alan Robinson, John Rushby, Don Sannella, Richard Schwartz, Natarajan Shankar, Rob Shostak, Herbert Simon, Keith Stenning, Colin Stirling, Edward Swart, Sherry Turkle, Sam Valentine, Martina Weiss, and Tim Williamson. Many of those on this list read drafts of sections of the book or of chapters of it; a few even read the entire draft. Their comments helped me improve it greatly. Since I did not always take their advice, however, and since many sections were rewritten comprehensively after I received comments, responsibility for the remaining mistakes and errors of interpretation is mine alone.

Having coworkers who did so much of the interviewing meant that I was able to avoid being away from home too often, but writing a book demands concentration that is not always easily compatible with family life. Above all I am grateful to my family, Caroline, Alice, and Iain, who shared with me all the ups and downs of the decade that this research took.

The early sections of chapter 2 draw upon my chapter in *Systems, Experts, and Computers: The Systems Approach in Management and Engineering, World War II and After*, eds. Agatha C. Hughes and Thomas P. Hughes (Cambridge, Mass.: MIT Press, 2000). Chapters 3 and 8 draw upon my article "The Automation of Proof: A Historical and Sociological Exploration," *IEEE Annals of the History of Computing* 17(3) (1995): 7–29; an earlier version of chapter 4 appeared as "Slaying the Kraken: The Sociohistory of a Mathematical Proof," *Social Studies of Science* 29 (1999): 7–60; chapter 5 draws upon sections (drafted originally by me) of my joint article with Garrel Pottinger, "Mathematics, Technology, and

Trust: Formal Verification, Computer Security, and the U.S. Military,'' *IEEE Annals of the History of Computing* 19(3) (1997): 41–59. I am grateful to the copyright holders for permission to use this material here.

I also thank all those who provided me with or permitted me to reproduce illustrations, in particular the American Mathematical Society, Kenneth Appel, Barry Boehm, Doug Bonin, Randal Bryant, Edsger W. Dijkstra, the Charles Stark Draper Laboratory, the Grand Hotel Sonnenbichl, Wolfgang Haken, Tom Hales, the Institute of Electrical and Electronics Engineers, John Koch, Leonard LaPadula, Daryl McCullough, the National Aeronautics and Space Administration, Peter Naur, the George C. Page Museum, Penguin Books, Roger R. Schell, Scientific American, Inc., Herbert A. Simon, Springer-Verlag, and Willis H. Ware.

1

Knowing Computers

Of all the technologies bequeathed to us by the twentieth century, one above all saturates our lives and our imaginations: the digital computer. In little more than half a century, the computer has moved from rarity to ubiquity. In the rich, Euro-American, world—and to a growing extent beyond it as well—computers now play an essential part in work, education, travel, communication, leisure, finance, retail, health care, and the preparation and the conduct of war. Increasingly, computing is to be found in devices that do not look like computers as one ordinarily thinks of them: in engines, consumer products, mobile telephones, and in the very fabric of buildings.

The benefits brought by all this computerization are clear and compelling, but it also brings with it dependence. Human safety, the integrity of the financial system, the functioning of utilities and other services, and even national security all depend upon computing. Fittingly, the twentieth century's end was marked both by an upsurge of enthusiasm for computing and by a wave of fear about it: the huge soon-to-be-reversed rise in the prices of the stock of the "dotcom" Internet companies and the widespread worries about the "millennium bug," the Y2K (year 2000) date change problem.

How can we know that the computing upon which we depend is dependable? This is one aspect of a question of some generality: how do we know the properties of artifacts? The academic field of the social studies of science and technology (a diverse set of specialisms that examine the social nature of the content of science and technology and their relations to the wider society) has for several decades been asking how we know the properties of the natural world.[1] The corresponding question for the properties of artifacts is much less often asked; surprisingly so, given that a good part of recent sociological interest in technology derives ultimately from the sociology of scientific knowledge.[2]

Asking the question specifically for computers—how do we know the properties of computers and of the programs that run on them?—is of particular interest because it highlights another issue that sociological work on science has not addressed as much as it might: deductive knowledge.

Sources of knowledge, whether of the properties of the natural world or of those of artifacts, can usefully be classified into three broad categories:

- induction—we learn the properties by observation, experiment, and (especially in the case of artifacts) testing and use;

- authority—people whom we trust tell us what the properties are; and

- deduction—we infer the properties from other beliefs, for example by deducing them from theories or models.[3]

Social studies of science have focused primarily on the first of these processes, induction, and on its relations to the other two: on the dependence of induction upon communal authority[4] and interpersonal trust;[5] and on the interweaving of induction and deductive, theoretical knowledge.[6]

Deduction itself has seldom been the focus of attention: the sociology of mathematics is sparse by comparison with the sociology of the natural sciences; the sociology of formal logic is almost nonexistent.[7] At the core of mathematics and formal logic is deductive proof. That propositions in these fields can be proved, not simply justified empirically, is at the heart of their claim to provide "harder," more secure, knowledge than the natural sciences. Yet deductive proof, for all its consequent centrality, has attracted remarkably little detailed attention from the sociology of science, the work of David Bloor and Eric Livingston aside.[8] In the social studies of science more widely, the single best treatment of proof remains one that is now forty years old, by the philosopher Imre Lakatos in the 1961 Ph.D. thesis that became the book *Proofs and Refutations* (see chapter 4).[9] Indeed, it has often been assumed that there is nothing sociological that can be said about proof, which is ordinarily taken to be an absolute matter. I encountered that presumption more than once at the start of this research. Even the founder of the modern sociology of knowledge, Karl Mannheim, excluded mathematics and logic from the potential scope of its analyses.[10]

Asking how we know the properties of computer systems (of hardware and/or of software) directly raises the question of deductive knowledge and of proof. An influential current of thinking within computer science has argued that inductive knowledge of computer systems is inadequate, especially in contexts in which those systems are critical to human safety or security. The number of combinations of possible inputs and internal states of a computer system of any complexity is enormously large. In consequence it will seldom be feasible, even with the most highly automated testing, to exercise each and every state of a system to check for errors and the underlying design faults or "bugs" that may have caused them.[11] As computer scientist Edsger W. Dijkstra famously put it in 1969, "Program testing can be used to show the presence of bugs, but never to show their absence!"[12] Even extensive computer use can offer no guarantees, because bugs may lurk for years before becoming manifest as a system failure.

Authority on its own is also a problematic source of knowledge of the properties of computer systems. In complex, modern societies trust is typically not just an interpersonal matter, but a structural, occupational one. Certain occupations, for example, are designated "professions," with formal controls over membership (typically dependent upon passing professional examinations), norms requiring consideration of the public good (not merely of self-interest), mechanisms for the disciplining and possible expulsion of incompetent or deviant members, the capacity to take legal action against outsiders who claim professional status, and so on. Although many computer hardware designers are members of the established profession of electrical and electronic engineering, software development is only partially professionalized. Since the late 1960s, there have been calls for "software engineering" (see chapter 2), but by the 1990s it was still illegal, in forty-eight states of the United States, to describe oneself as a "software engineer," because it was not a recognized engineering profession.[13]

With induction criticized and authority weak, the key alternative or supplementary source of knowledge of the properties of computer systems has therefore often been seen as being deductive proof. Consider the analogy with geometry.[14] A mathematician does not seek to demonstrate the correctness of Pythagoras's theorem[15] by drawing triangles and measuring them: since there are infinitely many possible right-angled triangles, the task would be endless, just as the exhaustive testing of a computer system is, effectively, infeasible. Instead, the mathematician seeks a proof: an argument that demonstrates that the theorem must hold in all cases. If one could, first, construct a faithful mathematical representation of what a program or hardware design was intended to do (in the terminology of computing, construct a "formal specification"), and, second, construct a mathematical representation of the actual program or hardware design, then perhaps one could prove deductively that the program or design was a correct implementation of its specification. It would not be a proof that the program or design was in an absolute sense "correct" or "dependable," because the specification might not capture what was required for safety, security, or some other desired property, and because an actual physical computer system might not behave in accordance with even the most detailed mathematical model of it. All of those involved in the field would acknowledge that these are questions beyond the scope of purely deductive reasoning.[16] Nevertheless, "formal verification" (as the application of deductive proof to programs or to hardware designs is called) has appeared to many within computer science to be potentially a vital way of determining whether specifications have been implemented correctly, and thus a vital source of knowledge of the properties of computer systems.

The Computer and Proof

Formal verification is proof about computers. Closely related, but distinct, is the use of computers in proof. There are at least three motivations for this use. First, proofs about computer hardware designs or about programs are often highly intricate. Many of those who sought such proofs therefore turned to the computer to help conduct them. Mechanized proofs, they reasoned, would be easier, more dependable, and less subject to human wishful thinking than proofs conducted using the traditional mathematicians' tools of pencil and paper. This would be especially true in an area where proofs might be complicated rather than conceptually deep and in which mistakes could have fatal real-world consequences. Second, some mathematicians also found the computer to be a necessary proof tool in pure mathematics. Chapter 4 examines the most famous instance of such use: the 1976 computer-assisted solution of the long unsolved four-color problem: how to prove that four colors suffice to color in any map drawn upon a plane such that countries that share a border are given different colors. A third source of interest in using computers in proofs is artificial intelligence. What is often claimed to be the first artificial-intelligence program was designed to prove theorems in propositional logic (see chapter 3), and automated theorem proving has remained an important technical topic in artificial intelligence ever since. Underneath the more glamorous applications of artificial intelligence, such as robotics, are often "inference engines" based upon theorem proving.

Although the theorems they prove would not be regarded by mathematicians as interesting or challenging, more sophisticated mechanized provers (far broader in their scope than the ad hoc programs used in the four-color proof) have been used to solve problems that human mathematicians found intractable, such as the 1996 solution of the Robbins problem, an open question in Boolean algebra (see chapter 3). Automated theorem proving, therefore, raises the question of whether there is a sense in which a computer can be an artificial mathematician. To the proponents of artificial intelligence this has been an attractive possibility; to its opponents it is a repugnant one.

Historical Sociology

The topic of this book is the interrelations of computing, risk, and proof. It is neither a technical nor a philosophical treatment of them, but rather a historical sociology. The historical aspect is the more straightforward. What this book seeks to do is to describe salient features of the interrelations between computing and proof as they have evolved from the 1950s onward. Relevant archival material is still sparse, so I have used two main bodies of evidence. First is the technical literature of computer science and of artificial intelligence, which offers the central documentary record of the evolving thinking of the relevant technical communities. Second is an extensive series of "oral history" interviews with the main participants. Interview data must be treated with caution: interviewees' memories are fallible, and they may wish a particular version of events to be accepted. As far as possible, therefore, I have tried to use written sources to document factual assertions, using interviews primarily as evidence of interviewees' opinions and beliefs.

Even in this role, interviews are an imperfect source (interviewees' opinions may change through time in ways they may not wish to acknowledge or of which they may even be unaware). Nevertheless, they add an important dimension to what would otherwise be the overabstract and disembodied history that would result from the use of the technical literature alone. The interviews were conducted under conditions of confidentiality, but they were tape-recorded and transcribed, and intended quotations were sent to interviewees for review and permission to publish.[17] In many cases, points made in interview were then elaborated in further exchanges, especially by electronic mail.

The result, I hope, is accurate narrative history. Nevertheless, it is selective history: I have not attempted comprehensive accounts of the development of the various technical specialisms bearing upon computing, risk, and proof.[18] I have focused upon episodes, issues, and debates that appeared to be particularly interesting from the viewpoint of my twin concerns: the nature of knowledge of the properties of computer systems and the nature of deductive proof. I see these not just as technical matters (though plainly they are that) but as sociological questions, issues for the social studies of science and technology.

Since the social studies of science (less so those of technology) have recently become controversial in the debate called the "science wars,"[19] some preliminary remarks on the sociological aspect of the approach taken here are also necessary. Although some of the diverse strands that make up social studies of science can rightly be classified as criticism of science (not just in the literary, but in the everyday meaning of "criticism"), that is emphatically not true of the kind of historical sociology pursued here. To investigate the variety of meanings of mathematical proof, for example, is simply to inquire, not to denigrate. The fundamental point—almost always missed in "science wars" debates—is that the analysis of science, technology, and mathematics is not a zero-sum game in which the greater the weight of social influence the less the weight of empirical input or other aspects of what used to be called "internal" factors, such as intellectual consistency and rigor.[20] For example, that modern mathematicians do not usually work in isolation, but as members of specialist mathematical communities, deeply affecting each other's work, has surely the typical effect of improving the mathematics they generate. That kind of social influence, which arises from the way in which science and mathematics are conducted within communities, is in no sense in tension with empirical input or with matters such as consistency. In an appropriate community with an appropriate orientation, social processes surely generate rigor rather than undermine it.

Nor should one assume a priori the existence of a zero-sum trade-off when social influence arises from outside the scientific community. In a sense, most of this book is a study of social influence of that second kind, of the effects upon deductive knowledge of the desire to be able reliably to predict the behavior of computer systems upon which human life and security depend. Those effects, I would argue and I think this book demonstrates, have in general been beneficial intellectually as well as practically. Concern for safety or security does not diminish concern for rigor or for intellectual consistency; it increases it.

Another cross-disciplinary matter is raised by the historical sociology of science or technology: technical accuracy. Writing about disciplines that are not one's own is an error-prone activity, and its difficulty is increased when these disciplines are mathematical and one is trying to describe developments in them in a way that is accessible to the non-mathematical reader. The healthiest attitude is to accept that one will make mistakes and to seek the help of one's technical colleagues in eradicating them. Although I am extremely grateful to those who have assisted in this, I have no illusions that what remains will be beyond criticism. I welcome any errors here of any kind being pointed out; I only ask the "science wars" critic not simply to indulge in facile cross-disciplinary point scoring, but to concentrate attention on the main themes and arguments of the book.

Risk, Trust, and the Sociology of Proof

From a sociological viewpoint, the question of one's knowledge of computer-system dependability blends in to a more general issue: risk and trust in the societies of "high modernity." (The term is drawn from the sociologist Anthony Giddens.[21] It is preferable to the more voguish "postmodernity," which tends to exaggerate the discontinuities between the present and the recent past, sometimes on the basis of sloppily impressionistic analyses.) One of the most striking features of the politics of high modernity is the salient place in it of issues of technological risk.

Measured by life expectancy, today's Euro-American world is uniquely safe. We have learned to protect ourselves against natural hazards such as earthquake, flood and storm; famine is for us a distant memory; and epidemic infections (the great killers of premodernity) have largely been eliminated or, at worst, controlled. Patently, however, members of these societies do not always feel safe. The issue of whether the cattle disease BSE (bovine spongiform encephalopathy, or "mad cow disease") could be transmitted to human beings played a significant part in British politics in the 1990s. Debates over the safety of chemical pesticides, of nuclear power, and, most recently, of genetically modified organisms have raged internationally, often involving political direct action and significant impact upon the industries involved.

Among the most influential commentators on the politics of risk in high modernity has been the German sociologist Ulrich Beck.[22] "[S]ooner or later in the continuity of modernization," wrote Beck, "the social positions and conflicts of a 'wealth-distributing' society begin to be joined by those of a 'risk-distributing' society." Previous forms of societies had their dangers, but the "hazards in those days assaulted the nose or the eyes and were thus perceptible to the senses, while the risks of civilization today typically escape perception." The layperson's senses are no guide to whether BSE poses risks to human beings, or whether genetically modified foodstuffs are safe. On questions such as these, the layperson must turn to others, and in the process risks can "be changed, magnified, dramatized or minimized within knowledge. . . . [T]he mass media and the scientific and legal professions in charge of defining risks become key social and political positions. . . . Knowledge gains a new political significance. Accordingly the political potential of the risk society must be elaborated and analyzed in a sociological theory of the origin and diffusion of knowledge about risks."[23]

Despite the pervasive high-modern concern with technological risk, in only one episode has fear of the computer become widespread: the Y2K problem. In the United States especially there were many predictions and a substantial amount of popular fear that the "millennium bug" would seriously disrupt utilities and other essential parts of the infrastructure of high modernity. These concerns turned out to be misplaced, and in retrospect it is easy to mock them and to question whether the large sums spent on checking for and eliminating the "bug" were justified (worldwide spending is said to have totaled as much as $400 billion, though much of this sum represents system replacement and upgrading desirable on other grounds).[24]

The episode highlights, however, both the dependence of high-modern societies upon computing and the difficulty of forming a judgment on the risks posed by that dependence. However small or large Y2K dangers might have been in the absence of the effort to detect and to correct them, political and business leaders throughout most of the Euro-American world judged the effort essential: not knowing how computer systems would behave was intolerable. The Y2K problem was, furthermore, in a sense an easy case: one in which the possible underlying fault (the vulnerability of two-digit representations of the year to a century change) was clear, even though immense effort was needed to be sure what its effects would be. More typically, those involved in issues of computer-system dependability will be trying to judge the trustworthiness of a system that may be vulnerable to any number of faults, including design faults or "bugs" in its software. Even though this is an issue scarcely ever discussed in the burgeoning literature on "risk society,"[25] it is an archetypal case of the phenomenon described by Beck: an invisible potential danger, the seriousness of which the layperson's unaided senses cannot judge.

Reliance upon experts is an inevitable aspect of high modernity. Particular experts, including those regarded by the scientific community as the appropriate experts, may be disbelieved (a sense that the public authority of science has declined may well be one factor fueling the passions of the science wars), but, without turning one's back entirely on high modernity, that distrust cannot be generalized to rejection of cognitive authority of all kinds. Disbelief in one set of experts' knowledge claims is often belief in those of others, in those of environmental groups such as Greenpeace, for example, rather than in those of biotechnology companies such as Monsanto. The sociologist Brian Wynne and others have pointed out that lay thinking about scientific and technological matters is often more sophisticated and less ignorant than commonly believed,[26] but one should not exaggerate the possibility of cognitive "direct democracy." In a complex society, engaged in many complex activities, no one can be an expert in everything. Outside the necessarily narrow domains in which one has expertise, one can at best choose wisely in whom or in what to trust and find an appropriate balance between blind faith and self-defeating scepticism.

Among those within the social studies of science who have written most interestingly on the problems of trust are the historians Theodore Porter and Steven Shapin. The question addressed by Porter is how "to account for the prestige and power of quantitative methods in the modern world," not just in science but in areas such as actuarial work, accountancy, cost-benefit analysis, and social policy more generally. Although formal verification in computer science differs in important ways from these applications of quantitative methods, Porter's analysis of them is worth considering because it suggests a trade-off between mathematicization and trust. In traditional communities "face-to-face interactions typically obviated the need for formal structures of objectivity.... [U]ntil the eighteenth century, measurements even of land or grain volume were never intended to be purely mechanical, but normally involved an explicit judgment of quality. In a small-scale and unstandardized world, bargaining over measures caused no more inconvenience than bargaining over prices."

As *Gemeinschaft* (community) becomes modernity's *Gesellschaft* (society), however, face-to-face solutions are no longer viable. Modernity's "trust in numbers" is a substitute for absent trust in people, argues Porter: "reliance on numbers and quantitative manipulation minimizes the need for intimate knowledge and personal trust." Mathematics is suited to this role because it is "highly structured and rule-bound," a "language of rules, the kind of language even a thing as stupid as a computer can use."[27] Porter's analysis nicely captures the vastly increased importance of quantification and of standardization in modernity. (Indeed, one reason for scepticism about broad-brush notions of "post modernity" is that apparent departures from uniformity often rest upon deeper standardization, and quantification's significance has grown rather than declined in recent years.) Furthermore, Porter's is an account wholly compatible with standard sociological analyses of modernity such as that of Anthony Giddens, who sees modernity as involving "disembedding mechanisms" in which trust shifts from local, face-to-face relationships to delocalized, abstract systems. In driving, flying or even simply entering a building, one implicitly trusts that others—automobile engineers, pilots, air traffic controllers, structural engineers, building inspectors—have done or will do their job properly. But this trust is not confidence in specific, individual people: those on whose expertise we depend are frequently strangers to us. Instead, says Giddens, what we trust are "systems of technical accomplishment or professional expertise,"[28] not particular, personally known people.

Steven Shapin, however, offers a perspective subtly different from Porter's or Giddens's. He does not deny that much of the everyday experience of high modernity involves trust in anonymous, abstract "systems of expertise," but he also argues that "within communities of practitioners, for example within the communities of scientific knowledge-producers . . . it is far from obvious that the world of familiarity, face-to-face interaction, and virtue is indeed lost." Gentlemanly codes "linking truth to honor . . . were adapted and transferred to provide substantial practical solutions to problems of credibility in seventeenth-century English science." Nor should one assume, Shapin argues, that they offered only a temporary solution: even the scientists of high modernity "know so much about the natural world by knowing so much about whom they can trust."[29] Although given its sharpest formulation by Shapin, this is a widely-shared conclusion in social studies of science. Porter, for example, acknowledges that, at least within secure, high-status scientific communities, knowledge is still often produced and assessed in informal, nonstandardized ways.[30]

The subjects of Shapin's historical work, however, would not have agreed fully with his conclusion that "no practice has accomplished the rejection of testimony and authority and . . . no cultural practice recognizable as such could do so. . . . In securing our knowledge we rely upon others, and we cannot dispense with that reliance."[31] The early modern scientific thinkers discussed by Shapin were sharply aware of the necessary reliance in the natural sciences upon honest testimony and upon skillful experimentation. Thomas Hobbes, one of the two key protagonists of Shapin and Schaffer's earlier *Leviathan and the Air-Pump,* saw empirical, experimental knowledge as inadequate on those and other grounds. Hobbes saw in mathematics, specifically in geometry, however, a model of reasoning that was in contrast sure, incontrovertible and not dependent upon the dangerous testimony of others. Although Hobbes's opponent, Robert Boyle, had a quite different, much more positive view of the knowledge produced by experiment and by trustworthy testimony, he too noted that "In pure mathematicks, he, that can demonstrate well, may be sure of the truth of a conclusion, without consulting experience about it." Even Boyle, the great founder of the modern "experimental life," thus conceded that mathematics was, in Shapin's words, "the highest grade of knowledge." If one's goal were "uncontroverted certainty and confidence in one's knowledge, the culture of pure mathematics possessed the means to satisfy that goal."[32]

It is, indeed, easy to see why deductive, mathematical knowledge was and is granted a status not enjoyed by empirical, inductive, or testimony-based knowledge. Anyone who has been exposed to mathematical proof, at even an elementary level, knows the feeling of compulsion that proof can induce. Given the premises, a proof shows that the conclusion must follow, and that a proof compels is, at least apparently, not a matter of trust at all. Paraphrasing Hobbes, but largely expressing his own view as well, Porter comments that geometrical, or more generally mathematical, reasoning is "solid demonstration, which brings its own evidence with it and depends on nothing more than writing on paper."[33]

Is deductive proof therefore an exception to Shapin's claim that "the identification of trustworthy agents is necessary to the constitution of any body of knowledge?"[34] Does deductive proof yield a form of knowledge in which the individual is self-sufficient? The problem with this apparently common-sense conclusion is the difficulty for the isolated individual of distinguishing between being right and believing one is right. Although the point has many ramifications,[35] a basic issue was pointed out nearly three centuries ago by David Hume. "There is no Algebraist nor Mathematician so expert in his science, as to place entire confidence in any truth immediately upon his discovery of it," wrote Hume. "Every time he runs over his proof, his confidence encreases; but still more by the approbation of his friends; and is rais'd to its utmost perfection by the universal assent and applauses of the learned world."[36] Those who have wanted more than personal, subjective conviction of the correctness of a proof have, traditionally, had to turn to others' assessments of it. To anticipate an argument discussed in chapter 6, the "social processes" of the mathematical community sift putative proofs, thereby achieving a rigor that the individual mathematician cannot know for sure he or she possesses.

Yet the human community is now not the only "trustworthy agent" to which to turn: it has been joined by the machine. The mechanization of proof has produced automated systems that check whether a sequence of formulae expressed in sufficient detail in appropriate formalism has the syntactic structure that makes it a formal proof, in other words that check whether each formula in the sequence is generated from previous formulae by application of the rules of inference of the formal system in question. Some systems, furthermore, even have a limited capability to find such proofs for themselves. Modernity's "trust in numbers" can, it appears, lead back to a grounding not in trust in people, but trust in machines.

That the pursuit of objectivity may lead back literally to an object is a conclusion that some may find reassuring, but others disturbing.[37] As Sherry Turkle pointed out, the computer is an "evocative object." Previously, "animals, . . . seemed our nearest neighbors in the known universe. Computers, with their interactivity, their psychology, with whatever fragments of intelligence they have, now bid for this place." The computer is an "object-to-think-with," in particular to think about what it is to be human.[38] As sociologist of science Harry Collins has pointed out, artificial intelligence is in a sense an experiment in the sociology of knowledge.[39] If genuine "artificial experts" are possible, then, since no current machine (not even a neural network) learns by socialization in the way human experts appear to learn, there may be something wrong with the sociological view of expertise. The relationship between the computer and proof has the practical importance outlined above, but it has this intellectual importance as well. If machines can prove, does it mean that proof is not social?

The mechanization of proof is also of interest because of the light it throws upon nonmechanized deduction. Until the advent of formal, machine-implemented mathematics, there was a single dominant ideal type of deductive proof: proof as conducted by skilled human mathematicians. Although even that ideal type was not unitary—the contrast between different forms of human proving offers fascinating, if still underexplored, material for the social studies of mathematics[40]—it has now been joined by another ideal type: machine proof. There are now two "cultures of proving."[41] Mostly, they exist independently of each other, in different institutional locations, and only seldom is there overt conflict between them. But the existence of each reveals the contingency of the other.

This book examines the historical sociology of machine proof: ordinary, human-conducted, mathematical proof is discussed only in passing (mainly in chapters 4 and 9). I hope, however, that the contrast between the two forms of proving will lead colleagues in the social studies of science to be more curious about ordinary mathematical proof, indeed about mathematics. *Pace* Porter, mathematics, at least the mathematics of human research mathematicians, is not entirely "the kind of language even a thing as stupid as a computer can use." The mechanization of proof, to date, has largely been the mechanization of philosophy's ideal of formal proof (a sequence of formulae in which each formula is deduced from previous formulae by syntactic, "mechanical," inference rules), not proof as it is ordinarily conducted by human mathematicians. Indirectly, therefore, the mechanization of proof shows the need for the development of an analysis of mathematical proof that is better, as an empirical description of what mathematicians actually do, than philosophy's ideal type. As the concluding chapter suggests, there is reason to think that such an analysis will have to have a strong sociological component.[42]

Synopsis of the Book

Although I have tried to keep this book as nontechnical as possible, some of the passages in the chapters that follow will be demanding for the nonspecialist. The reader, therefore, may wish to skip particular passages or even particular chapters while still following the overall narrative. To facilitate this process, the remainder of this chapter gives a reasonably extensive summary of each of the chapters that follow.

Chapter 2 begins with the issue of dependability. Almost as soon as computers began to be used to control critical systems, the potential for disaster appeared. The chapter documents the main features of an awareness emerging in the 1960s that, despite the enormous strides being made in computer hardware, software production remained slow, expensive, and bug-ridden. This awareness crystallized in October 1968 at a NATO conference held at Garmisch in the Bavarian Alps. A "software crisis" was diagnosed there, and "software engineering" was proposed as its solution.[43] The latter had two broad strands, not always compatible: an emphasis on the "practical disciplines" to be found in other areas of engineering, and an emphasis on the "theoretical foundations" of computer science, especially on its foundations in mathematics and in logic. The chapter discusses the evolution of testing, as an empirical, inductive route to knowledge of the properties of computer systems, but it focuses mainly upon those who sought deductive knowledge of those properties, such as the Dutch computer scientist Edsger W. Dijkstra. Dijkstra hoped that the mountain sunshine of Garmisch represented "the end of the Middle Ages" of programming. He was the most outspoken of a group of computer scientists attempting to subject the computer to the rigor of mathematics and logic: others included the American computer scientist and artificial intelligence pioneer, John McCarthy; the Danish computer scientist, Peter Naur; the American, Robert W. Floyd; and the Briton, Tony Hoare.

Chapter 2 also outlines the first stirrings within computer science of Hume's issue: how does one know that a claimed proof is correct? There were two broad responses to the possibility of erroneous proofs. First was that of Harlan D. Mills, director of software engineering at a key site of the development of critical software: IBM's Federal Systems Division. Mills wanted programmers to prove mathematically that their programs were correct implementations of the specifications they were given, but he saw proof as a human activity that could lead only to "subjective conviction." The second response—the dominant one, at least in academic computer science—was to turn to the computer itself to alleviate the difficulty and error-proneness of the production of proofs. By 1969 the first automated system for applying proof to programs was constructed by Floyd's student, James King.

The automation of mathematical proof, however, did not begin with King's system. Chapter 3 returns to 1956 and to the iconic moment, often taken as the beginning of artificial intelligence, when Herbert Simon declared that he and his colleague Allen Newell had "invented a thinking machine." That machine—first a human simulation of a computer program and then an actual program—proved theorems in propositional logic. Simon's work in artificial intelligence interwove with his social science, especially with his critique of economists' hyperrationalistic view of human beings. In developing the "Logic Theory Machine," Simon studied how human beings like himself found proofs. To the logicians becoming interested in automated theorem proving, however, Simon and Newell's search for human-like "heuristics" was misguided and amateurish. For Hao Wang, one of those logicians, the attraction of computers was not that they were potentially intelligent machines but that they were "persistent plodders." Deep in the history of logic lay the search by the philosopher Gottfried Leibniz for a universal scientific language and logical calculus that would make it possible to "judge immediately whether propositions presented to us are proved . . . with the guidance of symbols alone, by a sure and truly analytical method."[44] In the centuries after Leibniz, human logicians had gradually accumulated the formal systems necessary for machine-like deductive inference; the computer offered them the means of turning these systems into technological reality, and to seek to make their operation human-like was, to the logicians, at best a distraction. In 1963, this strand of automated theorem proving reached its epitome in the development by philosopher and computer scientist Alan Robinson of the single most important technique of automated deduction: resolution, an explicitly "machine-oriented" rather than "human-oriented" form of inference.

Chapter 3 also describes other debates about computers, mathematics and artificial intelligence. Philosopher J. R. Lucas and mathematician Roger Penrose, the first an opponent of "mechanism," the second of artificial intelligence, argued that Gödel's famous incompleteness theorems showed that human minds could know mathematical truths that machines could not prove. From the side of artificial intelligence, Douglas B. Lenat sought to develop an "automated mathematician" (AM), which, he claimed, was able on its own to "rediscover" important parts of human mathematics. Lenat's system not only reopened the divide between artificial intelligence and formal logic (Wang described Lenat's thesis on AM as "baffling"), but also sparked fierce critique from within artificial intelligence.

Chapter 4 turns from computer science and artificial intelligence to mathematics itself. The most celebrated use of a computer to prove a mathematical theorem was the 1976 proof of the four-color conjecture by mathematician Wolfgang Haken and mathematical logician Kenneth Appel. First proposed in 1852, the conjecture can be understood by a young child, but a century of work by human mathematicians had not led to a proof that survived scrutiny. Appel and Haken's solution raised the issue of whether a partially computerized demonstration such as theirs was a proof at all. Opinions on that point differed sharply. The members of what Harry Collins calls the core set,[45] those mathematicians attempting a similar proof using similar computerized means, accepted the mechanized part of Appel and Haken's analysis as almost certainly correct, and they focused their doubts on the complicated human reasoning involved. Other mathematicians, however, focused their unease on Appel and Haken's use of computers. It was, one commented, as if they had simply consulted an oracle, and oracles were not mathematics.

Chapter 5 returns to the issue of dependability and to the dominant practical concern driving proof about computers: the vulnerability to intrusion of computer systems containing information critical to national security. Here, one encounters the two most important organizations that have influenced the development of computer proof: the U.S. Department of Defense's Advanced Research Projects Agency (ARPA) and the more powerful, but also more secretive, National Security Agency (NSA). For many years, NSA's very existence was not usually acknowledged. From the 1960s on, NSA and some other military agencies began to be concerned about computer security. Early experiments were unfailingly worrying: all serious attempts to circumvent the controls of the "time-sharing" computer systems entering service in the late 1960s succeeded.

In response, key ideas of computer security began to be formulated, such as the notion of a "security kernel" that any security-relevant request by user programs had to invoke. Drawing upon the "general system theory" then current in the work of von Bertalanffy and others, David Elliott Bell and Leonard J. LaPadula of the defense think tank, the MITRE Corporation, developed in the early 1970s the paradigmatic model of what, mathematically, "security" meant. A way forward then appeared clear: develop a security kernel that could be proved to implement the Bell-LaPadula model. Much of the financial support in the United States for the development of automated theorem provers arose from the desire of ARPA and NSA for mechanical proofs of security of this kind, and the 1970s' projects trying to prove the security of operating systems, of kernels, and of computer networks were the first real-world applications of proof to computer systems.

Applying the Bell-LaPadula model in practice was more complicated than it appeared in theory, and system developers found that they had to allow "trusted subjects" to violate the model's rules and to analyze "covert channels" not represented in the model. Bureaucratic turf wars and clashes of culture (such as between ARPA's relative openness and NSA's secrecy) also took their toll. By 1983, a stable set of *Trusted Computer System Evaluation Criteria* (universally known from the color of the covers of the document containing them as the "orange book") emerged, which demanded deductive proof that the detailed specification of the most highly secure systems (those in the orange book's highest, A1, category) correctly implemented a mathematical model of security like that put forward by Bell and LaPadula. Successful efforts to meet A1 criteria were, however, few. A vicious circle of high costs, limited markets, and long development and evaluation times set in. Furthermore, 1986 brought an apparent bombshell: the claim by computer security specialist John McLean of the U.S. Naval Research Laboratory that the Bell-LaPadula model was flawed: it allowed a hypothetical "System Z" that was patently insecure. The variety of responses to System Z, and the "dialectical" development of models of computer security that sought to block the insecurities permitted by earlier models, are reminiscent of Imre Lakatos's classic account of proving.[46] At stake, however, was not just a mathematical theorem, but arguably the authority of NSA and even the national security of the United States.

Chapter 6 turns to the two most prominent general attacks on the application of computerized proof to software. The first came in the 1970s from two young computer scientists, Richard A. DeMillo and Richard J. Lipton, and from Alan J. Perlis, one of the founders of American computer science. DeMillo, Lipton, and Perlis claimed that "proofs" of computer programs performed by automated theorem provers were quite different from proofs within mathematics. A real proof, they asserted, was not a chain of formal logical inferences of the kind that a computer could perform, but an argument that a human being could understand, check, accept, reject, modify, and use in other contexts. A computer-produced verification, thousands of lines long and readable only by its originator, could not be subject to these social processes and in consequence was not a genuine proof. To practitioners who had felt criticized by advocates of the mathematicization of computing, the attack by DeMillo, Lipton, and Perlis was welcome puncturing of what they took to be a theorists' bubble. To Edsger W. Dijkstra, in contrast, the attack was "a political pamphlet from the Middle Ages." Dijkstra was computer science's great rationalist, a man who describes himself as "a happy victim of the Enlightenment."[47] As the years went by, indeed, Dijkstra's views came to differ even more sharply from those of DeMillo, Lipton, and Perlis. He was no longer prepared to accept proof as ordinarily conducted by mathematicians as the model for computer scientists to emulate. Even mathematicians carried the taint of the Middle Ages: they were a "guild." They "would rather continue to believe that the Dream of

Leibniz is an unrealistic illusion."[48] Computer science, in contrast, showed the way to proofs more rigorous, more formal, than those of ordinary mathematics.

Chapter 6 also describes the quite different attack on the application of proof to computer programs launched in 1988 by the philosopher, James H. Fetzer. Though Fetzer's conclusion was as hostile to "program proof" as DeMillo, Lipton, and Perlis's, his reasoning was quite different. He rejected their sociological view of proof and in so doing returned to philosophical orthodoxy: for Fetzer, the canonical notion of proof was formal proof, and the validity of its logical inferences was not affected by whether they were conducted by a human being or by a machine. Instead, Fetzer argued that "the very idea" of "program proof" was what philosophers call a category mistake. A program was a causal entity that affected the behavior of a computer, which was a physical machine; "proof" was part of the formal, abstract, nonphysical world of mathematics and of logic. The presence or absence of "social processes" was mere contingency: what doomed program proof, claimed Fetzer, was that it was a self-contradictory notion.

Chapter 7 discusses how the relationship between proof and the real, physical world has played out not at the level of philosophical debate but in practice. It begins with the first major project in which proof was applied to a system in which the dominant concern was not security but human safety: an experimental aircraft control system called Software Implemented Fault Tolerance (SIFT). Though now largely forgotten, SIFT was the most prominent verification project in the world in the late 1970s and early 1980s. To SIFT's sophisticated design were applied some of the subtlest ideas of computer science, notably about what computer scientist Leslie Lamport called "Byzantine" faults, most easily conceived of by thinking of a system component, such as a clock, as being actively malicious. SIFT, and the clock convergence algorithm that was embodied in it, represent a kind of historical loop. Historian of physics Peter Galison has suggested that Einstein's theory of relativity may have been inspired in part by reflections on the technological problem of synchronizing geographically separate clocks.[49] Lamport, fascinated by time and its treatment in Einsteinian physics, returned the problem of synchronization from the realm of physics to that of technology. SIFT's ambitious design made the application of proof to it even harder than in the early security projects. A 1983 peer review of the SIFT proof work, intended largely to evaluate DeMillo, Lipton, and Perlis's critique of program proving, became, instead, a sharp internecine dispute among those committed to formal verification.

The overt debate in the peer review concerned the achievements of the SIFT proof work and how these had been reported. The SIFT project, however, also generated a divergence of greater long-term significance. Two participants in the early phases of the SIFT verification, Robert S. Boyer and J Strother Moore, took on what appeared to be a small task: applying proof to the fourteen lines of program that implemented the SIFT "dispatcher," lines written not in a high-level programming language but in assembly language, closer to the operations of the physical machine. Attempting to verify these lines of code, Boyer and Moore began to see a flaw in the entire enterprise of program proof as it was then practiced. It implicitly assumed, they suggested, that it was a "god," not a machine, that implemented programs. They began to believe that proof needed to be driven downwards, towards the hardware: verified programs needed verified machines to implement them. Chapter 7 describes the effort to produce such a machine and also discusses the controversy (described elsewhere)[50] over whether the claim of proof for a different, British-designed, microprocessor was justified. The chapter ends by briefly describing the form in which a version of proof (a highly automated form called model checking) has broken through from research to widespread industrial adoption.

Chapter 8 moves from the applications of mechanized proof to its key tools: automated theorem provers, in particular those systems designed not as exercises in artificial intelligence but to be controlled by a human being and used in practical verification tasks. The development of several of these provers is described to provide the basis for a discussion of what it means to use such a prover to perform a proof. One issue is the fact that different provers embody different formal logics. Another arises because theorem provers are themselves computer programs of some complexity. Alan Robinson, developer of resolution, has taken that latter fact as indicating a vicious regress undermining the entire enterprise of formal verification. Those most centrally involved do not accept that conclusion, and their different responses to the possibility that theorem-proving programs contain bugs are described.

A further matter discussed in chapter 8 is explicitly one of social trust. Among the most popular theorem provers, especially in Europe, is a family of systems that protect the validity of the inferences they perform by building a "firewall" (implemented by what computer scientists call "type checking") around formulae of a particular type: axioms and those formulae constructed from axioms by the mechanical rules of logical inference that the system implements. To proponents of systems of this kind, the firewall around the type "theorem" makes their use highly rigorous. The most widely used such system, Higher Order Logic (HOL), however, permits a user simply to assert a theorem by using the facility known as mk_thm. In the academic world from which HOL came, users were implicitly trusted not to abuse mk_thm. As HOL entered the world of security-critical computing, however, that trust could no longer be taken for granted. The malicious demon of the philosophy of mathematics became personified in the fear that among those performing an apparent proof might be a hostile agent. In the world of security, mk_thm became not a facility, as it had been in the academic world, but a loophole that had to be closed.

In chapter 9 the threads of the book are pulled together. The history of computer-related accidents is reviewed, and the question is asked why software-based systems appear to have killed relatively few people despite software's dependability problems. That is the most central aspect of what, in recognition of the man who pointed it out, I call the Hoare paradox: the fact that, without use of the proofs that Tony Hoare and his colleagues advocated, the practical record of software systems is better, for example, than had been feared at Garmisch. There are a variety of possible explanations, of which the most interesting from the viewpoint of this book are, first, the successful "moral entrepreneurship" of Hoare and many of his colleagues in alerting technical audiences to software's dangers (and in so doing reducing those dangers), and, second, that inductive and authority-based forms of knowledge of the properties of computer systems appear more effective, in sociotechnical practice, than, for example, the abstract statistical analysis of induction might suggest. In particular, it appears as if they may work to produce knowledge of people—of trustworthy system developers—as well as knowledge of the artifacts those people produce.

Chapter 9 then turns to cultures of proving. In the cleanroom, "proof" is explicitly intersubjective and need not be mathematical in form; for Dijkstra and those influenced by him, it must be formal, but need not be mechanical. The two central cultures of proving, however, are that of formal, mechanized proof and that of ordinary mathematics. Although the intellectual roots of the former lie within logic (a discipline to a significant extent separate from mathematics), its key practical underpinning has become the desire for mechanization, not for formality per se. The resultant culture, however, is not homogeneous. Different theorem provers implement different formal logics in ways that often differ significantly, and "investments" in developing these often complex programs, and in learning to use them effectively, tend to divide the culture of mechanized proof into distinct, albeit interacting, subcultures.

The book ends by discussing what the proving machines discussed in this book do not do. They simulate, at most, an individual mathematician operating within a given formal system. They neither modify formal systems nor choose between them. Nor, even within a given formal system, do their operations serve as the ultimate criterion of correctness, as the theorem-proving "bugs" discussed in chapter 8 demonstrate: they can be identified as causes of error, rather than as sources of valid, novel deductions, because normativity—the capacity to distinguish between "getting something right or wrong"[51]—remains vested in collective human judgment. It is we who allow, or disallow, machine operations as constituting proofs. Mechanized provers can be a vital aid to the fallible individual computer system developer and, perhaps, eventually to the individual mathematician as well, but they are no substitute for the human collectivity.

2

Boardwalks across the Tar Pit

It was only twenty minutes, but it seemed an eternity. On October 5, 1960, the president of IBM, Thomas J. Watson, Jr., and two other business leaders were being shown round the North American Air Defense headquarters at Colorado Springs. They were in the war room, where officers sat at their desks facing huge plastic display boards depicting Eurasia and North America. Above the map of Eurasia was an alarm level indicator directly connected to the radars and computer system of the missile early warning station at Thule, Greenland.

One of the visitors later recalled that "we were told that if No. 1 flashed, it meant only routine objects in the air. If two flashed, it meant there were a few more unidentified objects, but nothing suspicious. And so on. If five flashed, it was highly probable that objects in the air were moving toward America. In other words, an attack was likely." As they watched, the numbers started to rise. When they reached "4," senior officers started to run into the room. As "5" flashed, the visitors were hustled out of the war room into an office. They could do nothing but wait. "Our first thoughts were of our families. . . . They weren't with us and we couldn't reach them. It was a rather hopeless feeling."[1]

Flying 18,000 feet over Minnesota, General Laurence S. Kuter, commander-in-chief of the North American Air Defense Command (NORAD), was returning to Colorado Springs in his C-118. It was his command airplane, and his deputy, Canadian Air Marshal C. Roy Slemon, was able to reach him quickly. Years later, Kuter could still remember their conversation. "Chief," said Slemon, "this is a hot one. We have a lot of signals on BMEWS," the Ballistic Missile Early Warning System. Recalled Kuter: "I listened . . . as BMEWS recorded multiple missile launches from a general area in Siberia, and this was pretty hair raising. . . . [T]he indicators were all over the BMEWS scope. This could be a major missile launch against North America from Siberia. . . . Roy [Slemon] had the Joint Chiefs on an open telephone line." Kuter listened, his staff sergeant working frantically to keep him in contact with Colorado Springs, as Slemon talked on the telephone hot lines to the duty officers in the war rooms in Washington, D.C., Ottawa and Omaha, Nebraska, headquarters of the Strategic Air Command, which had the responsibility of launching nuclear retaliation against the kind of attack that BMEWS was reporting. "Everything was exceedingly tense for a matter of many minutes, perhaps 20 minutes, beyond the time of impact of what might have been those first missiles."[2]

On the ground in Colorado Springs, the NORAD Battle Staff faced a puzzling conflict of information. Alarm level 5 meant 99.9 percent certainty that a ballistic missile attack had been launched. If that were true, ellipses should be forming on the war room's display map of North America and should start to shrink, indicating the targets of the attack. Yet no ellipses were forming, and the "minutes-to-go" indicator showed nothing. Slemon turned to NORAD's chief of intelligence, Harris Hull, and asked him, "Where is Khrushchev?" "In New York City," answered Hull: Khrushchev was attending the General Assembly of the United Nations. Slemon decided that the Soviet Union was unlikely to attack the United States while its leader was in New York. It was characteristically human reasoning: it might have been fallible, but it helped reassure Slemon. Hull told him that the intelligence services had no reason to think an attack was imminent. Slemon also knew that BMEWS had been operational for only four days and was still being "run-in."[3]

Later that day, those involved gradually pieced together what had happened. What the radars in Greenland had detected was the moon rising over Norway. Apparently, no one involved in BMEWS's development had realized that its powerful radars, designed to detect objects up to 3,000 miles distant, would receive echoes from one almost a quarter of a million miles away. The BMEWS system software, designed to track fast-rising missiles, was thoroughly fooled by the slow-rising, far distant, moon. As radar echoes bounced back again and again, the BMEWS software interpreted them as sightings of multiple objects, not multiple sightings of the same object, and the consequent impression of a massive, continually growing missile attack was reinforced by the reflections from the moon of the radar beam's sidelobes.[4]

No Hiding Place

Reported worldwide, the October 1960 nuclear false alarm was a dramatic warning of the possible dangers of computerized systems. Human beings, however, had remained "in the loop" and, properly distrustful of the computerized system, had exercised their common sense in overruling it. Two years later, on July 22, 1962, an error in a computerized system, this time with no human being directly in the loop, caused the loss at Cape Canaveral of the United States's first interplanetary space probe, Mariner, destined for Venus. Hardware on the probe's Atlas booster rocket failed, leaving the booster under the control of a ground-based radar system, which fed data into a program that issued correction signals to the rocket. A bar had been missed out from above one of the symbols in the handwritten equations implemented in the requisite software. As a result, a calculation that should have been done using "smoothed" velocity data (the missing bar indicated averaging) was performed using raw data. The computer system attempted to compensate for the fluctuations in this raw data, but in doing so it made the rocket, which had been rising normally, start to move "on an erratic and potentially dangerous course, and the range safety officer . . . ordered it destroyed."[5]

That a small matter like a missing bar over a single symbol could lead to disaster would come as no surprise to any computer programmer. In computing's earliest days, the dominant problem had been getting what now looks like primitive hardware—processors built out of vacuum tubes and memories constructed from mercury delay lines or electrostatic storage tubes—to perform adequately. As soon as the early machines started to work, however, the difficulty of programming them began to become apparent. For example, Maurice Wilkes designed Cambridge University's Electronic Delay Storage Automatic Calculator (EDSAC), which began working in May 1949, and he went on to coauthor one of the first textbooks of computer programming. Years later he recalled the moment, perhaps no more than a month after he started to use EDSAC, when he realized the full difficulty of programming. The machine was on the top floor of the Cambridge computer laboratory, and the tape-punching machines used in programming were on the floor below. The stairs between the two became all too familiar to Wilkes as he edited and reedited programs to get them to run. On the stairs, one day, "the realization came over me with full force that a good part of the remainder of my life was going to be spent in finding errors in my own programs."[6]

As IBM's Fred Brooks was to write, the programmer had the joy of working "only slightly removed from pure thought-stuff," yet thought-stuff that, run on a computer, produced, almost magically, real, visible effects. Unfortunately, "[t]he computer resembles the magic of legend in this respect, too. If one character, one pause, of the incantation is not strictly in proper form, the magic doesn't work. Human beings are not accustomed to being perfect, and few areas of human activity demand it." The hardest part about learning to program was not the unfamiliar terms and syntax of a programming language: it was, concluded Brooks "[a]djusting to the requirement for perfection."[7]

To some, the need for perfection constituted programming's very appeal. A twenty-one-year-old Dutch student, Edsger W. Dijkstra, visited Cambridge for three weeks in 1951 to learn from Wilkes and his colleagues David Wheeler and Stanley Gill how to program EDSAC; Dijkstra had done well in his exams, and his father paid for him to take Wilkes's course as a reward. After returning to the Netherlands, Dijkstra started to work at the Mathematical Center in Amsterdam, another early computer site. He found he had to choose between programming and his original intention, to become a theoretical physicist. He chose programming because he thought the intellectual challenge to be greater. In physics, "you studied physical phenomena, and you get incomplete data, and must make your guesses. And if those guesses turn out not to be quite right you can always excuse yourself. You can hide yourself behind the unfathomed complexity of nature. However, if in programming . . . the program has a bug, you've done it yourself. . . . There you are with a finite number of zeroes and ones. There's really nowhere to hide." It was "the cruelty of the job" that drew him to programming, said Dijkstra.[8]

The "cruelty" of the programmer's job was at its peak when others might pay with their lives for the programmer's mistakes. The Apollo missions to the moon are an early example of "software"—a term coming into use in the computer industry by the end of the 1950s[9]—becoming safety critical. Computers onboard the Command Module and Lunar Module (see figure 2.1) performed crucial navigation tasks, including guiding the lunar landing.[10] These computers were among the first to use the silicon integrated circuits that, in the 1960s, started to replace the transistors that earlier had displaced vacuum tubes. Programs for them were written at the Massachusetts Institute of Technology (MIT) Instrumentation Laboratory, and a ground-based computer turned

Figure 2.1
The Apollo Lunar Module control panel. Lower central is the DSKY, the simple display and keyboard via which the astronauts operated the Lunar Module's computer. The hand controls for giving manual steering instructions to the computer are beside the DSKY. Courtesy Charles Stark Draper Laboratory, photograph number 53158.

Figure 2.2
Apollo computer core-rope module. Courtesy Charles Stark Draper Laboratory, photograph number 40261.

these programs into the onboard computers' machine language, the binary digits (zeroes and ones) that controlled their operations. These binary digits were then hard-wired into the onboard computers' memories in "core ropes" (figure 2.2), formed by wires threaded through tiny magnetic cores shaped like little ceramic "doughnuts."[11]

"The effort needed for the software design" for the Apollo mission "turned out to be grossly underestimated," wrote David G. Hoag, who directed MIT's work on Apollo navigation and control. Around 1,400 person years of work were eventually devoted to the task. The mathematicians and systems engineers at the Instrumentation Laboratory, and the programmers from industry to whom they had increasingly to turn for help, made immense efforts to ensure that the programs they wrote for the onboard computers were correct. They wrote another, independent, suite of programs to simulate an entire mission to the moon. The much bigger computers available on the ground could run both this "environment simulator" and a simulation of the onboard computers. The onboard programs could then be tested, before being fabricated into "ropes," by comparing the results of the two simulations.[12]

The result was not perfection, but it was workable. As Eldon Hall, in charge of the development of the Apollo onboard computer systems, put it: "Missions flew with program errors that were thoroughly documented, and the effects were understood before the mission. No *unknown* programming errors were discovered during a mission."[13] J Strother Moore, who worked on the mission simulator, commented that "when the thing actually flew the control panel was just littered with pieces of paper . . . [I]t wasn't as neat as it is in the photographs."[14]

The most serious incident took place just before the first moon landing in July 1969. Six minutes before the Apollo 11 Lunar Module was due to land, its computer began to produce overload alarms. Its software was designed to respond to an overload by prioritizing critical tasks, but a serious overload condition would endanger even these. Mission controllers in Houston, Texas, however, judged correctly as it turned out that the computer was still capable of performing its critical tasks and so they let the mission continue.[15] A second problem then intervened. The computerized guidance system relied upon a mathematical model of the moon's gravitational field, which was in error in the vicinity of the landing site, and as a result of this and an earlier navigation system error the computer was bringing the Lunar Module down in an area of dangerously big boulders. To begin with, the astronauts, distracted by the computer alarms, did not notice. Then, a mere 400 feet above the moon's surface, astronaut Neil Armstrong acted, suspending the descent while he used the manual controls (see figure 2.1) to instruct the computer to steer the spacecraft clear of the boulders to a safe place to land. It was a "dangerous maneuver," says Eldon Hall, but it succeeded. The first human beings to land on the moon did so safely, albeit with only "twenty-four seconds' worth of fuel left."[16]

The System Grows

Programs for early computers such as Wilkes's EDSAC, and those wired into Apollo's core ropes, were typically short. Vastly greater problems were encountered as much longer and more complex programs began to be written from the mid-1950s on. The first truly large-scale software system was the Semiautomatic Ground Environment (SAGE) air defense system, intended to integrate into a single system the previously separate, manually controlled defenses of North America. SAGE's origins go back to another early computer, MIT's "Whirlwind."[17] As early as April 1951, a combination of Whirlwind and the early warning radar at Hanscom Air Force Base, Massachusetts, demonstrated the capacity to track an incoming aircraft and to guide a fighter to intercept it, and an expanded system linking several radars in the Cape Cod area to Whirlwind was providing data by March 1953.[18] The Cape Cod system "worked—surprisingly well—less than a year after it was undertaken," wrote J. C. R. Licklider, an MIT electrical engineering professor who went on to become director of the celebrated Information Processing Techniques Office in the Department of Defense's Advanced Research Projects Agency.

What happened subsequently was therefore a shock: "The SAGE system was to be essentially a scaled-up and replicated Cape Cod system, hence easy to estimate and schedule. Yet the number of man-years of programming required was underestimated by six thousand at a time when there were only about a thousand programmers in the world."[19] A frantic recruitment effort was needed. "Street-car conductors, undertakers . . . school teachers, curtain cleaners," and many others with only rudimentary backgrounds in mathematics were hired, given a few weeks training, and set to work writing programs for SAGE that eventually added up to over a million lines.[20]

Two particular difficulties, later found to be pervasive in other contexts,[21] caused the SAGE software task to grow far beyond initial expectations. First, the system specification was not stable. The bomber threat evolved, and the weapons and procedures to meet it changed too. Of SAGE's eventual 700 to 800 programmers and systems analysts (who made up more than half of the total programming workforce in the U.S.) 400 "were continuously modifying SAGE and attempting to control the orderly implementation of myriad changes."[22] Second, it turned out to be impossible to use a standard "turn-key" software solution, and considerable programming effort was needed to fit the particularities of different air defense sites and the demands of their commanders. Much of the remainder of SAGE's programming workforce was deployed in the field handling these local exigencies. Even after an installation became operational, the System Development Corporation, which was responsible for SAGE software, had to leave a team of eight programmers at each site to correct mistakes and to update programs.[23]

By 1961 all the sites were declared "operationally ready," but, even in the late 1960s, the operators in some SAGE installations were to be found using "makeshift plastic overlays on the cathode-ray displays" and "the 'scope watchers were bypassing the elaborate electronics—operating more or less in the same 'manual mode' used in World War II."[24] Robert Everett, who headed the division of the MIT Lincoln Laboratory responsible for the overall system design and testing of SAGE, summed up the experience:

When we all began to work on SAGE, we believed our own myths about software—that one can do anything with software on a general-purpose computer; that software is easy to write, test, and maintain; that it is easily replicated, doesn't wear out, and is not subject to transient errors. We had a lot to learn.[25]

Even the mighty IBM, in the 1960s by far the dominant company in the computer industry, experienced trauma, especially with the development of the operating system for the machines in its famous System/360 series, which revolutionized the computer industry by replacing IBM's previous range of incompatible computers with a single series of machines. The common architecture of this series was intended to make it possible to run a program written for one machine on any other, subject only to the constraints of memory and of input-output capability. This ambitious endeavor called for great sophistication in operating systems, the suites of programs that have overall control of a computer and its peripheral devices, performing basic "housekeeping" tasks and permitting users' programs to be run. Like SAGE, the System/360 operating system, OS/360, grew to comprise over a million lines of program. At the time of peak effort, over 1,000 people worked on it, and in total IBM may have spent as much as $500 million (an enormous sum in the 1960s) on System/360 software. That was well in excess of the original budget, and OS/360 was an embarrassing year late in delivery. It was bug-ridden, and though corrections were made in subsequent releases, these modifications themselves introduced new problems: "Each new release of OS/ 360 contains roughly 1,000 new software errors."[26]

As pressure mounted, leading figures in the OS/360 effort succumbed to stress-related illness. Some had to leave their jobs with, in the words of three IBM insiders, "their usefulness temporarily impaired. The cost to IBM of the System/360 programming support is, in fact, best reckoned in terms of the toll it took of people: the managers who struggled to make and keep commitments to top management and to customers, and the programmers who worked long hours over a period of years, against obstacles of every sort, to deliver working programs of unprecedented complexity. Many in both groups left, victims of a variety of stresses ranging from technological to physical."[27]

Figure 2.3
Rancho la Brea tar pits. Detail of drawing by David P. Willoughby from mural by Charles R. Knight, courtesy George C. Page museum. Willoughby's drawing of Knight's mural was used by Frederick P. Brooks, Jr., as the frontispiece of *The Mythical Man-Month: Essays on Software Engineering* (Reading, Mass.: Addison-Wesley, 1975).

Frederick P. Brooks, Jr., manager of OS/360 during its design phase, warned that a "tar pit" (figure 2.3) lay in wait for the developers of large software systems: "No scene from prehistory is quite so vivid as that of the mortal struggles of great beasts in the tar pits. In the mind's eye one sees dinosaurs, mammoths and sabertoothed tigers struggling against the grip of the tar. The fiercer the struggle, the more entangling the tar, and no beast is so strong or so skillful but that he ultimately sinks. Large-system programming has over the past decade been such a tar pit."[28] For example, when a project began to slip behind schedule, extra personnel would typically be devoted to it. "Like dousing a fire with gasoline, this makes matters worse, much worse": experienced programmers had to spend time training novices; work had to be repartitioned, again costing time; more time had to be devoted to communication and to system testing.[29]

In the early days of computing, hardware had been expensive and software, in comparison, cheap. When programmer Barry Boehm joined defense contractor General Dynamics in 1955, his boss took him to the computer room and pointed out that while he was being paid $2 an hour, the corporation was paying $600 an hour for the machine.[30] By 1966, however, the cost to IBM of software development for System/360

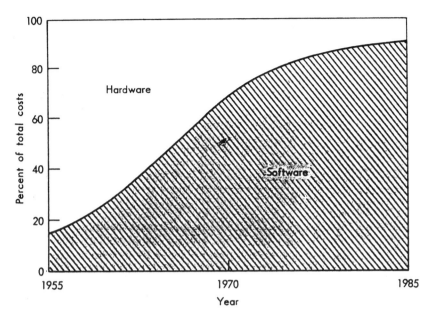

Figure 2.4
Hardware/software cost trends, as analyzed by Barry Boehm, "Software and Its Impact: A Quantitative Assessment," *Datamation* 19(5) (May 1973): 48–59, at p. 49.

was roughly equivalent to that of hardware development.[31] By the late 1960s, reported Boehm, the U.S. Air Force was beginning to spend more on software than on computer hardware,[32] and it began to be argued that the trend would intensify, a claim summarized in 1973 by Boehm in a famous, often-copied graph extrapolating the Air Force data (see figure 2.4). The empirical accuracy of the prediction is dubious and very sensitive to how costs are measured,[33] but there is no doubt that by the late 1960s the costs of software were becoming a salient concern.

Certainly, programming as an occupation had expanded remarkably. There are no reliable figures for the number of programmers in the early 1950s (most people who wrote programs did so as part of jobs with quite different titles), but Licklider's estimate, quoted above, of 1,000 worldwide, though perhaps an underestimate, is probably of the right order of magnitude.[34] By 1970, the U.S. Census recorded a quarter of a million programmers and computer systems analysts.[35] At one level, this massive increase was simply a marker of the astonishing success of the digital computer and of its rapid incorporation into the military, economic, organizational, and scientific infrastructure of the industrialized world. At another level, however, some computer-industry insiders had become convinced that there were pervasive, deep flaws in much of what these legions of programmers were producing.

The Software Crisis

The breadth and depth of the problems of software development were the focus of what was to become one of the most famous of all computer science conferences, the meeting on "software engineering" held in October 1968 at Garmisch-Partenkirchen, a resort nestling beneath the mountains of the Bavarian Alps. The idea for the conference had come most centrally from a leading German computer scientist, Professor Fritz Bauer of the Technische Hochschule München. Bauer was not the only one to coin the term "software engineering"—Douglas Ross of the MIT Servomechanisms Laboratory proposed a course on the subject in January 1968[36]—but the choice of the term as the conference's title greatly increased the salience of the idea that, in Bauer's words:

The time has arrived to switch from home-made software to manufactured software, from tinkering to engineering—twelve years after a similar transition has taken place in the computer hardware field. . . . It is high time to take this step. The use of computers has reached the stage that software production . . . has become a bottleneck for further expansion.[37]

Early in 1967, the U.S. representative on the NATO Science Committee, Nobel Laureate I. I. Rabi, "expressed deep concern about delays in delivering operating systems and other software for recently acquired large computers." The German representative on the committee asked Bauer for advice, and in the autumn of 1967 a small study group was set up. Late that November, Bauer met the Danish member of the study group, H. J. Helms, and, recalled Bauer, "we discussed the so-called 'software crisis.' " Bauer had already "mentioned in a provocative way that it was 'software engineering' that was needed," and at a meeting of the group in December 1967 he was commissioned to organize a conference on the topic, which he proceeded to do with the assistance of Helms and the group's French member, Professor L. Bolliet.[38] It was an invitation-only meeting, with invitees drawn from universities, IBM and other computer manufacturers, the emerging "software houses," and a small number of government and industrial organizations using computers. The British computer scientist, John Buxton, recalled: "The invita-

Figure 2.5
Garmisch and the peaks of the Wetterstein range from the Hotel Sonnenbichl.
Photograph courtesy Grand Hotel Sonnenbichl.

tion list was carefully contrived. . . . [I]t was done by the organizing committee specifically trying to pick the leading figures in their country. . . . [T]hey were all the top names."[39]

The meeting was held in the Hotel Sonnenbichl on the outskirts of Garmisch. The vista from its windows and terrace unrolled across the little town to the towering mountains (figure 2.5).[40] The keynote speech opening the conference was given by Alan Perlis of Carnegie Mellon University in Pittsburgh, a leading figure in U.S. computer science. "Our goal this week," Perlis told the small, select group of participants, "is the conversion of mushyware to firmware, to transmute our products from jello to crystals."[41] Buxton recalled the tone being set by frank admissions in an after-dinner talk on the first evening by Robert S. Barton, who had played a leading role in the development of Burroughs's innovative B-5000 computer. Barton told participants, "that we were all guilty, essentially, of concealing the fact that big pieces of software were increasingly disaster areas." The confessional atmosphere—"everybody else just chimed in and said: 'Yes!' "[42]—created an unusual degree of rapport and openness, remembered by those involved for many years afterward. "We undoubtedly produce software by backward techniques," said Doug McIlroy of the Bell Telephone Laboratories. "We undoubtedly get the short end of the stick in confrontations with hardware people because they are the industrialists and we are the crofters."[43]

To some of those involved, the situation was bad enough to merit being called a "software crisis."[44] Not all agreed. Some Garmisch participants pointed to the large number of computer installations that appeared to work perfectly satisfactorily. K. Kolence, of Boole and Babbage Inc., commented:

I do not like the use of the word "crisis." It's a very emotional word. The basic problem is that certain classes of system are placing demands on us which are beyond our capabilities and our theories and methods of design and production at this time. There are many areas where there is no such thing as a crisis—sort routines, payroll applications, for example. It is large systems that are encountering great difficulties. We should not expect the production of such systems to be easy.

MIT's Douglas Ross countered:

It makes no difference if my legs, arms, brain and digestive track are in fine working condition if I am at the moment suffering from a heart attack. I am still very much in a crisis.[45]

One of the most influential of the participants at Garmisch was Edsger W. Dijkstra, whose wholehearted embrace of the "cruelty" of programming had made him one of the rising stars of computer science. David Gries, a student of Bauer's who was himself to become a leading computer scientist, was particularly struck during the Garmisch meeting by Dijkstra's habit of "pacing up and down during his discussions, which were punctuated by audible silence."[46] Dijkstra had an emerging reputation both as a theorist and as a system designer: the operating system he designed for the computer center at his university, the Technische Hoogeschool Eindhoven, was celebrated for its simplicity and its elegance.[47] To Dijkstra, the Garmisch conference was a liberating experience. The acknowledgment, by an influential group of scientists and practitioners, of deep problems in software development justified the rigorous mathematical approach to software development that Dijkstra embraced. For him, even the early autumn weather symbolized the step forward that had been made: "The meeting in Garmisch Partenkirchen was very exciting. For me it was the end of the Middle Ages. It was very sunny."[48]

"Software Engineering"?

There was general agreement at Garmisch that "software engineering" was needed. But what was it? As an analogy, an aspiration, a slogan, few would have disagreed, but it remained an empty box awaiting content. Consensus around the slogan largely evaporated when it came to deciding more concretely what software engineering should consist of. The report of the Garmisch meeting noted that "The phrase 'software engineering' was chosen deliberately" by the study group that set up the meeting because it was "provocative in implying the need for software manufacture to be based on the types of theoretical foundations and practical disciplines, that are traditional in the established branches of engineering."[49] That formulation, however, immediately indicated the potential for radically different emphases on the relative importance of "practical disciplines" and "theoretical foundations." It would be too simple to portray this as a split between industry and academia—if nothing else, there was too much movement between firms and universities for individuals to be fitted easily into that dichotomy—but tensions lying beneath Garmisch's apparent consensus quickly became evident.[50]

At Garmisch, at least one industrial participant already privately believed that the notion of a "software crisis" was an exaggeration that theorists had constructed to justify their work.[51] When, a year after Garmisch, a second NATO Conference on Software Engineering was convened in Rome, such divides became much more open. The Rome conference "just never clicked"; it "was a disaster"; it was "bad-tempered," with most participants leaving with "an enormous sensation of disillusionment."[52] The evident tensions and apparent lack of communication led to an extra session devoted to the relations between theory and practice. Discussion was led by computer scientist Christopher Strachey of Oxford University, who referred openly to the complaints of participants from industry who "felt that they were invited here like a lot of monkeys to be looked at by the theoreticians," while theoreticians felt "they were here but not being allowed to say anything."[53]

Perhaps the most immediately promising way of giving content to the idea of "software engineering" was structured programming. At its most basic, pointed out its leading proponent, Edsger W. Dijkstra, structured programming was simply an exemplification of the age-old maxim, *divide et impera,* "divide and rule." A complex mathematical proof, for example, is typically built up out of lemmas: "subtheorems," each with its own proof, which when combined together give structure to what would otherwise be an overlong, difficult to grasp, proof of a theorem. A complex programming task, Dijkstra argued, had similarly to be divided into subtasks each of which "is implemented independently of how it is going to be used and is used independently of how it has been implemented."[54] Structured programming as the idea of "divide and rule" was neither new nor especially controversial.[55] Two elaborations of the idea, however, one "technical" and the other "social," did provoke opposition.

The first was that structured programming was understood by its proponents to rule out use of one of the most popular of programming instructions: the **go to** instruction. **Go to** made it possible for a programmer to command a "jump" from any line in a program to any other. It was pragmatically useful, but, to its critics, "too much an invitation to make a mess of one's program," for example by leaving or entering subroutines at arbitrary points and thus vitiating the effort to build programs systematically out of clearly delineated, discrete subcomponents.[56] "I have concluded that adherence to rigid sequencing decisions is essential," Dijkstra told the Rome conference. "[W]hen programs for a sequential computer are expressed as a linear sequence of basic symbols of a programming language, sequencing should be controlled by alternative, conditional and repetitive clauses and procedure calls, rather than by statements [**go to**] transferring control to labelled points."[57] **Go to** had been criticized as early as 1963 by Peter Naur, a leading figure in the development of ALGOL, a programming language particularly influenced by ideas from theoretical computer science. To Naur, excessive use of **go to** was inconsistent with the ideals of rigor and careful structuring that inspired the language: it was not "good ALGOL style"; it was "ugly . . . inelegant and uneconomical."[58]

The most famous attack on **go to,** however, was mounted by Dijkstra in a 1968 letter in the leading U.S. computer journal, the *Communications of the Association for Computing Machinery.* While Naur had complained only of excessive use of **go to,** Dijkstra was "convinced that the **go to** statement should be abolished from all 'higher level' programming languages." For Dijkstra, it was vital that the correspondence between the program, "spread out in text space," and the computing process, "spread out in time," that was taking place under the program's control, should be as simple and as clear-cut as possible. Arbitrary **go to** jumps sabotaged this goal.[59] Dijkstra's attack on the "harmful" **go to** statement attracted great attention. John R. Rice of Purdue University wrote to the editor of the *Communications* that he was "taken aback" by Dijkstra's "emotional" attack on "an obviously useful and desirable statement. . . . How many poor, innocent, novice programmers will feel guilty when their sinful use of **go to** is flailed in this letter?"[60]

Also controversial was what appeared to be the second—social—corollary of structured programming. Structured programming became linked to the idea of "chief programmer teams," a "new managerial approach to production programming," according to F. Terry Baker and Harlan D. Mills of IBM. In this approach, the experienced and highly skilled person who was designated "chief programmer" drew up the overall design of a software system and broke it down into smaller modules. He or she was shadowed by a "backup programmer," who was able to step into the chief's role should the latter move to a different company or project. The remaining programmers in the team, typically numbering between three and five, were responsible for writing the modules assigned to them by the chief programmer, and had to do their work according to a set of structured programming standards developed by IBM. These programmers were in their turn relieved of clerical activities by a programming secretary who was responsible for keypunching and for the management of the large amount of paperwork that was generated.[61]

Supporters of the idea of chief programmer teams compared them to the cooperation of a surgical team in an operating theater, an unthreatening, even a flattering, analogy.[62] Others, however, hoped or feared that the true organizational analog of structured programming was the factory. Historian of technology Michael S. Mahoney diagnoses "beneath much American thinking about software engineering the images and language of the machine shop." McIlroy, for example, whose comparison of software production to crofting is quoted above, went on at Garmisch to call for "mass production" of software: there did not exist for software, he complained, "manufacturers of standard parts, much less catalogues of standard parts. One may not order parts to individual specifications of size, ruggedness, speed, capacity, precision or character set."[63]

To others, however, the mass production of software was a threatening, undesirable goal. By 1977 sociologist Philip Kraft feared that the "routinization of computer programming" was well under way, and its key tool, deployed by managers in search of greater profits, was structured programming. Just as the division of labor in the manufacturing of physical goods permitted the parceling out of subtasks to cheaper, less skilled workers, so structured programming, said Kraft, "has become the software manager's answer to the assembly line . . . a standardized product made in a standardized way by people who do the same limited tasks over and over without knowing how they fit into a larger undertaking." The highly skilled chief programmer still conceptualized, but his or her subordinates simply executed, programming individual modules in a routinized way, and their work had become, in Kraft's view, at best semiskilled.[64]

Kraft's analysis of the deskilling of programming was an exaggeration, as Andrew Friedman's later, detailed study of the history of software development has shown. Managers adopting the ideas of structured programming may have hoped that they would increase direct management control over both programming and programmers, and some of the latter may have feared that outcome. Kraft's book was based in good part on interviews with programmers. The reality, however, was much less dramatic. Often, "structured programming" meant in practice nothing more than breaking programs up into modules of strictly limited length, indenting the text of a program so as to make its structure apparent, and perhaps banning **go tos**; there were only token attempts at standardization or routinization. Competent programmers and systems analysts remained in short supply, and thus readily could move to another job if they disliked their work; such evidence as exists suggests they retained levels of job satisfaction far above those of routine clerical workers. Indeed, they often expressed a preference for staying in technical work rather than being promoted to become managers. Rather than resisting structured methods, some programmers adopted them without any management pressure to do so, because they saw them as skill-enhancing, not skill-reducing.[65]

Furthermore, as Kraft acknowledged, the intellectual originators of structured programming, notably Dijkstra, had not wished to see programming deskilled.[66] Dijkstra recoiled at the analogy of the factory. When asked his profession, he was proud to declare himself simply a "programmer": for him, programming was intrinsically a demanding activity.[67] The translation of structured programming into IBM's chief programmer teams was abhorrent to him: "Since IBM stole the term 'structured programming' I don't use it anymore myself." The discipline needed for successful programming was not organizational and managerial, in Dijkstra's opinion, but intellectual. He recalled presenting this view in a lecture at IBM's British development laboratory at Hursley Park. Because of the bright light from his overhead projector, he could see only the front rows of the audience, who were "absolutely unresponsive: I felt as if I were addressing an audience of puppets made from chewing gum." But when he had finished and the lights in the room were turned up he was surprised by enthusiastic applause from the previously unseen back rows: "It then turned out that I had had a very mixed audience, delighted programmers in the back rows and in the front rows their managers who were extremely annoyed at my performance: by openly displaying the amount of 'invention' involved, I had presented the programming task as even more 'unmanageable' than they already feared."[68]

IBM's Harlan Mills, originator and key proponent of the idea of the chief programmer team, became a particular butt of Dijkstra's criticism. At a conference on software engineering education, one manager made the mistake of saying to Dijkstra, "So you are the world expert on structured programming and chief programmer teams." Then, said Dijkstra, "I knew I was out in the wilderness and politely refused to be associated with Harlan D. Mills."[69]

Testing and Review

In the years after the 1968 Garmisch meeting, the software crisis "eased" somewhat, concluded Andrew Friedman.[70] The continuing rapid increase in the power of computer hardware, and its declining relative cost, meant that in many contexts the developers of software could follow the dictates of structured programming without having to worry too much about their cost in inefficient use of hardware resources.[71] Both individuals and organizations grew more experienced; a number of technical systems to support aspects of software development emerged; and standard "packaged" solutions to key tasks, such as database management, became available. Much of software development came to involve modifying, and adding features to, existing systems rather than producing entirely new ones. In consequence, by the 1980s the programming team on a typical project was much smaller than the 800 people working on SAGE, so reducing the managerial demands.[72]

But no panacea was found. Building large systems from scratch remained risky, and the development of software for the direct control of systems in what practitioners call "real time" (for example, the control systems of aircraft or spacecraft, where a delayed command can be as dangerous as an erroneous one) remained a difficult task. Robert L. Glass of Boeing wrote in 1980:

The literature may picture modern methodologies, but the real-time practitioners are still coaxing along their antique products and using machine language and patching to hold them together. The result is a product that usually works, but not always; a product that may be very economical, if the developers are skilled, but may on the other hand cost a fortune; a product that is virtually unschedulable; and a product whose quality is intimately tied to the skill of the software mechanic. The result can be satisfying and satisfactory; but when it is bad, it is very bad.[73]

By 1987 it was clear to Frederick P. Brooks, Jr., who had diagnosed the existence of the "tar pit," that there was "no silver bullet," no single technical or organizational solution to the difficulties of software development.[74] Between the mid-1950s and the start of the 1980s, "hardware prices have dropped by a factor of a thousand, while software—still regarded as more an art than a science—costs little less than it did when [the System Development Corporation] built SAGE,"[75] and the resultant systems were still far from entirely dependable.

With no sure way of preventing mistakes in the writing of software, detecting those mistakes remained crucial. Testing was, therefore, the focus of considerable effort. For real-time systems, for example, environmental simulators like that developed in the 1960s for Apollo were "almost universally used" by 1980.[76] Testing, long seen primarily as part of the informal practice of "debugging"—"There are no rules of testing," wrote Fred Gruenberger in 1968[77]—gradually became a focus of systematic attention in its own right.

In 1972 opening what was, as far as I am aware, the first conference devoted to program testing, its organizer, William C. Hetzel, commented: "At the base of our testing problems is that there is currently no established discipline to act as a foundation."[78] Gruenberger complained to the meeting that program testing "is all art, and . . . demands a form of low cunning on the part of the programmer."[79] During the 1970s, several important papers helped to clarify ways of making testing more systematic, for example by striving to ensure that testing exercises all the control-flow paths through a program.[80] This work was drawn upon in the first textbook devoted exclusively to program testing, which appeared in 1979. The book's title, *The Art of Software Testing*, however, together with much of its content, implied a continuing vital role for the testers' experience and skill. An apparently inevitable part of real-world testing was what the textbook admitted to be the "intuitive" process of "error guessing."[81]

The two most important general attempts to change testing from an "art" to a "science" were reliability growth modeling and random testing. The former attempted to systematize, and to give an empirical justification for, the practitioner's intuitive sense that the dependability of a program improves as errors are detected and corrected. The key early work was done at TRW, the corporation responsible, for example, for the management of the U.S. ICBM program.[82] In reliability growth modeling (as in conventional software development), a program is tested until it fails. The design fault causing the failure is found and corrected, and the program is tested until it again fails; and the process is then continued through many iterations. The difference from conventional debugging is that the times between failures, or some other measure of the extent of testing, are entered into a mathematical model (the reliability growth model) derived from previous experience of similar development processes, until the model indicates a sufficiently low failure probability (or, equivalently, a sufficiently long expected mean time between failures). It was widely agreed that reliability growth modeling was a useful tool in the management of software development, but there were worries about whether there would always be strong enough similarities between the past development processes, on the basis of which the model had been constructed, and the current one.

Concerns were also expressed about the potential for the correction of bugs to reduce dependability (by introducing new mistakes) rather than to increase it. Critics argued that "for safety-critical applications one must treat each modification of the program as a new program. Because even small changes can have major effects, we should consider data obtained from previous versions of the program to be irrelevant."[83] Furthermore, in practice extremely large amounts of failure-free testing were found to be needed to use reliability growth modeling to justify claims of very low probabilities of failure.[84]

The second main approach to making testing a "science" was random testing. This was a more radical departure from existing practice in that the "common sense" approach to testing had been a highly focused, purposive search for the test cases most likely to reveal design faults. In random testing, test cases are selected from the domain of possible inputs to a system by an impersonal mechanism with known statistical properties, such as a random number generator.[85] One advantage of random over purposive testing was that the former was easier to automate, and its advocates suggested that it was not inferior as a means of finding bugs.[86] The other dominant advantage was that randomness permitted the application of the theory of probability to the results of testing. Instead of what critics saw as the mere empirical curve-fitting of reliability growth modeling, random testing could draw upon the credibility of well-established theories of statistical inference.[87]

Although it was straightforward to produce an algorithm to generate random test cases from a distribution of input cases, there was no algorithm for ensuring that the latter distribution was realistic (that is, representative of what would be met in use). Instead, "[d]eep knowledge and experience with the application area will be needed to determine the distribution from which the test cases should be drawn."[88] Furthermore, the theory of random testing had a feature that appeared suspicious to some. The theory treated programs as "black boxes," the internal structure of which (below the level at which testing was being conducted)[89] was irrelevant. In particular, the size of the program being tested did not enter into the equations, derived from classical statistical theory, governing the inferences to be made on the basis of testing. These formulae therefore predict "exactly the same reliability for a 10-line program computing roots of a quadratic equation as for a 100,000-line accounting system, if each is tested with the same number of points. The result seems intuitively wrong."[90]

Even if this aspect of the theory of random testing was set aside, there was again the problem that large amounts of failure-free testing were found to be needed to justify confidence in very low probabilities of failure. For example, two NASA computer scientists calculated that under realistic conditions (with, for example, only a modest number of systems available for testing in parallel), the sort of failure rate demanded for life-critical avionic systems required infeasible quantities of testing: "to quantify 10^{-8}/h[our] failure rate requires more than 10^8 h[ours] of testing,"[91] and 10^8 hours is over 11,000 years. Theirs was an application of standard, "frequentist" statistical theory, but the alternative Bayesian approach (in which statistical inference is seen as the modification, by experience, of prior beliefs) yielded scarcely more optimistic results: "Unless the Bayesian brings extremely strong prior beliefs to the problem . . . both approaches will generally give results that agree to within an order of magnitude." For example, "if we require a median time to failure of 10^6, and are only prepared to test for 10^3, we essentially need to *start* with the belief in the 10^6 median."[92]

These problems are in practice exacerbated by the fact that wholly automated testing—and clearly automation is necessary if large amounts of testing are contemplated—is, in some cases, difficult or impossible. One fundamental issue is what those involved sometimes call the "oracle" problem: the need for an independent criterion against which to judge the correctness of the responses of the system being tested.[93] The difficulty is that if a reliable, efficient way of calculating correct responses already exists, then a new system would not be needed, while if it does not exist, one may have to rely on slow "pseudooracles," such as expert human judgment of the correctness of response. In addition, the construction of suitable test inputs may also be hard to automate and may therefore be slow. The consequence of this sort of problem, when combined with the above statistical issues, was that practicable amounts of testing usually fell far short of what was agreed to be needed to justify claims of high reliability. Two nuclear industry regulators noted in 1991 that "we are not aware of anyone yet having achieved an effective test demonstration at the 10^{-4} level [1 failure per 10,000 demands]."[94]

Above all it was difficult to use testing credibly to claim the complete absence of program design faults. How could that be claimed without having tested a system exhaustively, which even the advocates of testing generally admitted would usually be infeasible, given the huge numbers of tests needed? The pithiest formulation of the point came from Dijkstra who told the 1969 Rome conference, in words quoted in chapter 1, that "Program testing can be used to show the presence of bugs, but never to show their absence!"[95] Another version of the same point came in 1984 from computer scientist Dick Hamlet:

. . . those who today use defect-detection methods claim a connection between those methods and confidence in the tested software, but the argument seems to be the following:

I've searched hard for defects in this program, found a lot of them, and repaired them. I can't find any more, so I'm confident there aren't any.

Consider the fishing analogy:

I've caught a lot of fish in this lake, but I fished all day today without a bite, so there aren't any more.

Quantitatively, the fishing argument is much the better one: a day's fishing probes far more of a large lake than a year's testing does of the input domain of even a trivial program.[96]

Testing was not the only way, however, to find mistakes in programs. Like testing, an obvious alternative was long practiced but only began to be systematized in the 1970s: program review. In 1976 Michael Fagan described the systematic inspection procedures he and his coworkers had for the previous three years been using within IBM to replace earlier, looser design and program "walk-throughs." The latter, for example, were typically led by the person responsible for the design and program, while Fagan's inspections were planned and led by a "moderator," who was usually from a different project to "preserve objectivity," and who was trained to do the job systematically. People have to be "taught or prompted to find errors effectively," wrote Fagan, so "it is prudent to condition them to seek the high-occurrence, high-cost error types." Checklists of "clues" suggesting the presence of such mistakes were provided, and mistakes found were carefully recorded. If more than 5 percent of a design or program had to be altered to remove these mistakes, a complete reinspection was deemed necessary; otherwise, moderators could check the work themselves or reconvene the inspection team to look at the reworked parts.[97]

Fagan's systematic inspection and review techniques, or modifications of them, were widely adopted and found to be remarkably effective in detecting errors. In some organizations, for example, inspection found a sufficiently high proportion of mistakes in individual program components that the expense of separately testing those components was held no longer to be justified.[98] Nevertheless, the success of the techniques plainly depended upon the skill, dedication, and even the "personal sensitivity" and "tact" of the moderator and the willing involvement of the developer of the design or program. The moderator's objectivity was an explicitly human objectivity: the distance that came from having no personal stake in the design or program being tested. Fagan was clear that the quality of the human relations involved mattered. He was emphatic that the results of inspection "must be counted for the programmer's use and benefit: *they should not under any circumstances be used for programmer performance appraisal*. To use them "negatively against programmers" would be "to 'kill the goose that lays the golden eggs.'" Even the plain human fatigue of the inspection team had to be kept in mind: inspection sessions should last "no more than two hours at a time."[99]

Deduction

Review techniques, then, explicitly returned the issue of software dependability to a question of human dependability. In a sense the same was true for test-based, inductive knowledge, for with exhaustive testing infeasible, and random testing unable to justify failure probabilities low enough for the most critical applications, much depended on the testers' human skill in discovering errors. The major remaining alternative[100] is, as noted in chapter 1, deduction, not the informal deduction of Fagan-style review but more formal deductive reasoning, using the techniques of mathematics and of logic to generate knowledge of computer systems.

To the uninitiated, computer programs had always looked like mathematics, but there was a sense in which the analogy was superficial. In the 1960s there was no complete, well-defined mathematical interpretation of the instructions in most programming languages: no formal semantics, as a computer scientist would put it. A programming language had of course to have a well-defined syntax—a set of rules governing how symbols should be combined—so that a computer could process it, and in 1960 the syntax of the programming language ALGOL was, famously, defined formally using a notation originally developed by IBM's John Backus and improved by the Danish computer scientist Peter Naur.

The development and standardization of ALGOL was an important part of the process by which a self-consciously "mathematicizing" community within computer science came into being. ALGOL, in good part European in inspiration, was seen by its proponents as more elegant and more supportive of good, structured programming than other early languages such as FORTRAN (originally closely associated with IBM and widely used for "number-crunching" in physics and engineering) and COBOL, which was to become pervasive in commercial data processing.[101] Even ALGOL, however, lacked a formal semantics: in 1960, when the attempt was also made to define ALGOL's semantics, symbolism was largely abandoned in favor of ordinary English.[102] Experienced programmers believed they "knew" perfectly well what the instructions of ALGOL, FORTRAN, or COBOL "meant." Finding an adequate mathematical formalism, however, within which to express the semantics of programming languages was a far from trivial task, one which was to occupy many computer science researchers from the 1960s onward.[103]

The development of formal semantics is intimately related to the central concern here: the development of formal program verification (the application of deductive proof to show that the text of programs corresponded to their specifications). Although fragmentary remarks and work by the computer pioneers John von Neumann and Alan Turing prefigure the application of proof to the computer,[104] it was only in the 1960s that sustained interest in formal verification of computer programs began to emerge. A key early statement of its desirability came in 1962 from John McCarthy. Born in Boston in 1927, McCarthy was awarded his Ph.D. in mathematics by Princeton University in 1951. During the 1950s, he became one of the pioneers of artificial intelligence, popularizing (and, indeed, probably coining) the term and organizing what is generally regarded as its founding conference, held in 1956 at Dartmouth College in New Hampshire, where McCarthy then taught. He joined MIT in 1958, and he and Marvin Minsky directed the renowned MIT Artificial Intelligence Laboratory until McCarthy moved to Stanford University in 1962.[105]

McCarthy's 1962 paper, "Towards a Mathematical Science of Computation," called for computer science to become more like mathematical physics. "In a mathematical science," wrote McCarthy, "it is possible to deduce from the basic assumptions, the important properties of the entities treated by the science. Thus, from Newton's law of gravitation and his laws of motion, one can deduce that the planetary orbits obey Kepler's laws." Existing directions of research were, in McCarthy's view, inadequate to the task of mathematicizing computer science. For example, those approaches that analyzed computers as finite automata (abstract machines that have only a finite number of states) were of great theoretical interest. Research on finite automata interacted, as historian Michael Mahoney pointed out, with the work of theoretical linguists, notably of Noam Chomsky. As McCarthy put it, however, "anyone who waits for an IBM 7090 to repeat a state, solely because it is a finite automaton, is in for a very long wait." In Mahoney's words, real computers were "intractably large finite state machine[s]." What was needed, said McCarthy, was a more adequate mathematical theory of computation that would make it possible "to prove that given procedures solved given problems." Achievement of such a goal would be a major step forward: "It should be possible almost to eliminate debugging. . . . Instead of debugging a program, one should prove that it meets its specifications, and this proof should be checked by a computer program."[106]

In McCarthy's research, however, the application of proof to computer programs played second fiddle to his primary interest in developing a logical formalism to express common-sense reasoning, though by 1962 he had already designed PC, a "proof-checking system" based upon his LISP programming language. In 1966 he and graduate student James Painter described their proof, by hand, of the correctness of a compiler, an algorithm for translating simple arithmetic expressions (the only operation allowed was addition) into a rudimentary machine language.[107] By then others had joined the pursuit of the goal of program proof: the Danish computer scientist, Peter Naur; Robert W. Floyd, of the Carnegie Institute of Technology (which was about to become Carnegie Mellon University); and the British computer scientist, Tony Hoare. During the mid-1960s, all began work in the area independently and gradually became aware of what each other had done.[108]

First to publish was Peter Naur. Originally an astronomer, Naur was drawn into computing via its applications to that subject and eventually became a full-time computer scientist in the Regnecentralen, the computer research and development institute of the Danish Academy of Technical Sciences. Naur was the editor of the 1960 report on the syntax and semantics of ALGOL (his work with Backus's formalism was so influential that the latter is now often called Backus-Naur Form) and co-editor of the report on the Garmisch "software engineering" meeting. He began his 1966 paper, "Proof of Algorithms by General Snapshots," by blaming "a large share of the unreliability and the attendant lack of over-all effectiveness of programs as they are used to-day," on the failure of programmers to use "systematic proof procedures." His route to such proofs, "snapshots," are statements of the values of a set of variables at successive points in the execution of a program. Naur gave as an example a program to find the largest of N numbers. Let the numbers be $A[1]$, $\ldots$, $A[N]$. The goal is to find R, which is the value of the greatest of these; that is the value of $A[r]$, where for $1 \leq i \leq N$, $A[i] \leq A[r]$. ($\leq$ is the mathematical symbol for "less than or equal to.")

Naur proposed the simple ALGOL 60 program shown in figure 2.6 and added the "snapshots," also shown in figure 2.6, which were "instantaneous, and therefore static, picture[s] of the development of the process." He then showed that each successive snapshot followed from the effects of execution of the program on the state of affairs described by preceding snapshots, and the resultant proof of the final snapshot "establishes the correctness of the algorithm."[109]

There was a minimum of formality in Naur's snapshots and in his proof: both were mixtures of ordinary mathematical notation and English rather than expressions in a formal system. He was a central member of the influential group of "mathematicizers" within computer science, but the mathematics he sought to apply was ordinary informal mathematics, not formal mathematical logic. Naur, indeed, was later to become an explicit critic of excessive formalism, with its "neglect of informal precision." "Even in the most formalized mathematical argument," he wrote in 1982, "the justification of each argument step in terms of a rule of inference must finally rest with the author's intuitive, informal acceptance that the rule applies and has been used correctly."[110]

PROGRAM 1

Greatest number

```
r := 1;
for i := 2 step 1 until N do
  if A[i] > A[r] then r := i;
R := A[r];
```

PROGRAM 2

Greatest number, with snapshots

comment *General Snapshot* 1: $1 \leq N$;
$r := 1$;
comment *General Snapshot* 2: $1 \leq N, r = 1$;
for $i := 2$ step 1 until N do
   begin comment *General Snapshot* 3: $2 \leq i \leq N, 1 \leq r \leq i-1,$
   $A[r]$ *is the greatest among the elements* $A[1], A[2], \ldots, A[i-1]$;
   if $A[i] > A[r]$ then $r := i$;
   comment *General Snapshot* 4: $2 \leq i \leq N, 1 \leq r \leq i$, $A[r]$ *is the greatest*
   among the elements $A[1], A[2], \ldots, A[i]$;
   end;
comment *General Snapshot* 5: $1 \leq r \leq N$, $A[r]$ *is the greatest among the*
elements $A[1], A[2], \ldots, A[N]$;
$R := A[r]$;
comment *General Snapshot* 6: R *is the greatest value of any element,*
$A[1], A[2], \ldots, A[N]$;

Figure 2.6
A "greatest number" program, and the same program annotated with Naur's "snapshots." From Peter Naur, "Proof of Algorithms by General Snapshots," *BIT* 6 (1996): 310–316, at pp. 311 and 313. This paper is reprinted in Naur, *Computing: A Human Activity* (New York and Reading, Mass.: ACM Press/Addison-Wesley, 1992), 329–335, and in *Program Verification: Fundamental Issues in Computer Science*, eds. T. R. Colburn, J. H. Fetzer and T. L. Rankin (Dordrecht: Kluwer, 1993), 57–64. Assignment is indicated by := , so the first line of the program can be read as "r is assigned the value 1."

His background in astronomy, as an "empirical scientist," as he puts it, meant that he regarded the question of the relationship of a mathematical model to the reality being described as far more important than the question, "to which logic can be applied," of whether one mathematical model corresponded to another.[111] He saw computer science as what he called "datalogy," the "science of the nature and use of data," and the chair at Copenhagen University to which he was appointed in 1969 was given that title.[112]

More formal, and (perhaps in consequence)[113] more influential than Naur's proposal, was a paper by Robert Floyd presented to the same 1966 conference as McCarthy and Painter's compiler proof, which was funded by the same source, the U.S. Department of Defense's Advanced Research Projects Agency. The first of Floyd's twin goals was the same as Naur's: to prove properties of programs. Floyd used the symbols of formal, mathematical logic to construct propositions (similar to Naur's less formal snapshots) that were asserted to hold whenever the flow of control through a program took the corresponding path through its flowchart.

So, for example, the first annotation in figure 2.7 states that the number n is a member of the set of positive integers. The command in the first square box on the flow chart assigns the value 1 to the variable i, and the next annotation states that n is a member of the set of positive integers and $i = 1$. Although such transitions might appear intuitively obvious, Floyd's first aim in giving a formal, symbolic interpretation to programming language commands such as assignment was formal verification. He sought the capacity to construct a proof, in a formal deductive system with appropriate axioms and rules of inference, that if "the initial values of the program variables" satisfied formally stated initial conditions, then "the final values on completion" would always correspond to the formal statement of the desired result. Floyd's second goal was expressed in the title of his paper: "Assigning Meanings to Programs." A formal, logical interpretation of the commands in a programming language gave a formal semantics of the language: a rigorous interpretation of what its commands "meant," independently of how they might be implemented in any particular computer. "Establishing standards of rigor for proofs about programs in [a] language," was, for Floyd, not just an end in itself but also a way of ensuring "that the semantics of a programming language may be defined independently of all processors for that language."[114]

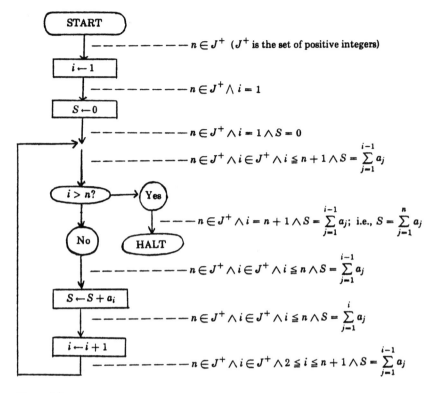

Figure 2.7
Flowchart of program to compute the sum of *n* numbers. ∈ means "is a member of"; ∧ means "and"; Σ means "sum of." From Robert W. Floyd, "Assigning Meanings to Programs," in *Mathematical Aspects of Computer Science: Proceedings of Symposia in Applied Mathematics, Vol. 19* (Providence, R.I.: American Mathematical Society, 1967), 19–32, at p. 20.

The goal of a formal semantics also inspired Tony Hoare. Born in 1934, C. A. R. Hoare—Tony is the abbreviation of his second name, Antony—graduated in Ancient Greats (Latin, Greek, Philosophy, and Ancient History) from Oxford University in 1956. While at Oxford, he also pursued extracurricular interests in the theory of probability and in mathematical logic, studying the latter on his own and then with the philosopher John Lucas (whose 1959 use of Gödel's incompleteness theorems to attack "mechanism" is discussed in chapter 3). Conscripted into the Royal Navy after his graduation, Hoare took the opportunity to study Russian, gaining an interpreter's qualification, and then spent a year at Moscow State University, attending lectures by the famous probability theorist A. N. Kolmogorov. At the end of his stay in Moscow, Hoare was asked to be an interpreter at an industrial exhibition. One of the exhibitors was the British firm Elliott Brothers, and Hoare was fascinated by the computer they had on display. The obviously talented young man was invited to come and talk to the company about a job on his return to Britain.[115]

In 1961 Hoare, now working for Elliott Brothers, attended a course on ALGOL 60 taught by Naur, Dijkstra, and the British computer scientist Peter Landin. The course was a revelation. During it Hoare suddenly realized how to use ALGOL's elegant features to implement a new, fast sorting algorithm that he had thought up. Hoare's Quicksort, published in 1962, began to establish his reputation as a computer scientist. Hoare also set to work implementing ALGOL 60 on Elliott's new computer, the Elliott 803. His academic, philosophical background and practical experiences combined in a fascination with programming languages and a sense of the desirability of program proof. Checking the properties of a program by testing alone resembled too strongly, wrote Hoare, the obviously inadequate attempt to prove a mathematical theorem "by showing that it is true of the first thousand numbers" one thought of. Without a formal semantics of programming languages, however, proofs about programs had to rely upon a merely "intuitive understanding of the meaning of the program itself."

Hoare became unhappy with "operational" approaches to programming language semantics "that specified the effect of each command" on an abstract, mathematical model of a computer. Hoare felt "that such a definition must incorporate a number of fairly arbitrary representation decisions and would not be much simpler in principle than an implementation of the language for a real machine." Instead, Hoare began to advocate, in a privately circulated December 1967 typescript, defining a programming language by a set of axioms, which "express exactly the properties which must be displayed by every implementation of the language." Such axioms would be the foundation of program proofs and would greatly facilitate language standardization.[116]

In 1968 Hoare was appointed Professor of Computer Science at the Queen's University, Belfast, and while unpacking his papers on arrival in Northern Ireland he turned again to a mimeographed draft of Floyd's paper, which he had earlier set aside because he "thought it was beyond me." Hoare suddenly realized that Floyd had shown the way to develop the axiomatic semantics that he sought. He quickly wrote up his ideas as a paper for the *Communications of the Association for Computing Machinery.*

This 1969 article, "An Axiomatic Basis for Computer Programming," became the most important manifesto of formal verification. Hoare wrote:

Computer programming is an exact science in that all the properties of a program and all the consequences of executing it in any given environment can, in principle, be found out from the text of the program itself by means of purely deductive reasoning. Deductive reasoning involves the application of valid rules of inference to sets of valid axioms. It is therefore desirable and interesting to elucidate the axioms and rules of inference which underlie our reasoning about computer programs.[117]

Hoare's approach applied directly to the text of programs rather than to their flow charts. "The most important property of a program," wrote Hoare, "is whether it accomplishes the intentions of its user." If those intentions could be specified formally as a description of the result, R, of execution of a program Q, then a program's "correctness" could be expressed in general terms as the theorem:

$P \{Q\} R.$

In other words, if the assertion P (which Hoare called a "precondition") is true before Q is executed, then the "postcondition" R will be true after it terminates.[118] This notation ("Hoare triples" as it was later to be called)[119] enabled Hoare to give axiomatic definitions of program language commands that were similar to Floyd's but easier to follow. For example, take the case of the assignment statement:

$x := f$

in a programming language without side effects in the evaluation of expressions.[120] This can be read as "x is assigned the value f": x is the label of a variable; f is an expression in the programming language, possibly but not necessarily containing x. Hoare's "axiom of assignment" is:

$P_0 \{x := f\} P$

where "P_0 is obtained from P by substituting f for all occurrences of x." As Hoare explained, this means that any assertion true of x after the assignment must have been true of f before it. Hoare also used his notation to formulate axioms defining iteration (**while** B **do** S in ALGOL 60), a "rule of composition," expressing the effect of executing commands in sequence, and "rules of consequence" permitting formal, logical deduction. He also noted, as had Floyd, that his axioms and rules "give no basis for a proof that a program successfully terminates"—it might, for example, loop endlessly—though, unlike Floyd, he did not believe that, in general, proofs of termination were worthwhile. One could simply prove that a program would give a correct result if it terminated and rely upon the computer system running the program to abandon its execution if it ran for too long.[121]

Of equal importance to the technical apparatus provided in Hoare's paper was what he was later to call his "sales explanation of the philosophical reasons why the approach was promising."[122] Although Hoare was not a participant in the Garmisch meeting at which the "software crisis" had been diagnosed, he was at the subsequent Rome conference, and his industrial experience had made him sharply aware of the practical problems of software development. In particular, Hoare had been responsible for a new suite of software for the Elliott 503 computer. Promotion to assistant chief engineer diverted his attention from this project until it failed to meet its March 1965 delivery date. Further delays, and deep problems with the ALGOL compiler, eventually led to its cancellation.

At a subsequent meeting with Elliott's customers, the embarrassed Hoare found them unsurprised at the fiasco: "Over lunch our customers were kind to try to comfort me. They had realized long ago that software for the original specification could never have been delivered, and even if it had been, they would not have known how to use its sophisticated features, and anyway many such large projects get canceled before delivery." "Two thirds (or more)" of the cost of software projects, Hoare wrote in his 1969 paper, was typically absorbed by detecting and removing programming mistakes. Furthermore, "the cost of error in certain types of program may be almost incalculable—a lost spacecraft, a collapsed building, a crashed aeroplane, or a world war." (He was to comment elsewhere that an "unreliable programming language generating unreliable programs constitutes a far greater risk to our environment and to our society than unsafe cars, toxic pesticides, or accidents at nuclear power stations.") So "the practice of program proving is not only a theoretical pursuit" but a potential solution to three of the major problems of software development: "reliability" (achieving failure-free programs); "documentation" (recording what a program and its subroutines were intended to do); and "compatibility" (identifying "machine-dependent" features of a program that would prevent it running successfully on different computers).[123]

Mills, Management, and Mathematics

Fred Brooks, whose dramatic image of the "tar pit" awaiting software developers was quoted above, was emphatic that despair was not inevitable: "boardwalks across the tar" could be constructed.[124] Hoare's 1969 paper presented formal verification—"[p]roofs of [p]rogram [c]orrectness"—as the key to such a boardwalk.[125] It was not the only candidate for this role, however, and a wide variety of others were proposed: new programming languages; a range of structured methods; different views of the software "life cycle"; a variety of management techniques; computerized systems for easing the programmer's task; and so on.[126] Furthermore, the state-of-the-art of formal verification in the 1960s was scarcely such as to inspire confidence in the pragmatically motivated software manager.

University of Wisconsin computer scientist Ralph L. London, an important contributor to early work on program proofs, described the three main weaknesses of the field as it stood at the end of the 1960s. First, such proofs as existed almost all "dealt with illustrative examples rather than with realistic computer programs." Second, the elaborate proofs that computer scientists had painstakingly produced by hand might be at least as hard to grasp and to check as the original programs. In London's words: "It is always possible that reading and verifying a correctness proof may be no easier than dealing with the original program and hence there is no gain—no increased confidence in the correctness or understanding of the program." Third: "There is also always the danger of errors in a correctness proof just as there is in usual mathematics proofs."[127] That last was no mere abstract possibility. In 1976 Susan Gerhart of Duke University and Lawrence Yelowitz of the University of Pittsburgh produced a list of mistakes in published specifications, programs, and claimed program proofs. The list was embarrassing, but that program proofs should sometimes be in error, they pointed out, was scarcely surprising, given that mathematicians themselves made mistakes in proofs.[128]

One response to the limitations of program proof described by London was to seek to move from proofs of "toy" programs to real, industrial examples, seeking to gain proof's benefits while explicitly accepting that knowledge gained by deductive proof rested upon the dependability of the human beings performing and assessing the proof. That was the response of Dijkstra's bête noire, IBM's Harlan D. Mills. Mills saw his goal in using mathematics as transforming programming from "an instinctive, intuitive process to a more systematic, constructive process that can be taught and shared by intelligent people in a professional activity."[129] Mills (1919–1996) received his Ph.D. in mathematics from Iowa State University in 1952, joined IBM in 1964, and rose to become director of software engineering and technology in IBM's Federal Systems Division, which developed software for SAGE, the Apollo and Space Shuttle programs, the Safeguard Anti-Ballistic Missile System, air-traffic control systems, and many other civil and defense applications. Within the division, Mills built up a distinctive approach to software development that by the mid-1980s was being called the "cleanroom," by analogy with the aseptic, dust-free environments within which silicon chips and pharmaceuticals are produced.

Mathematics and management were interwoven intimately in Mills's approach. For example, he helped undercut opposition within IBM to structured, **go to**-less programming by drawing upon a theorem by Corrado Böhm and Giuseppe Jacopini which implied that any program could be written without **go to**s.[130] Mills translated the Böhm-Jacopini theorem into a form more "valuable to management" as a "structure theorem, which established the existence of a structured program for any problem that permitted a flow chartable solution."[131] Any programmer claiming to need to use **go to**s, or seeking in other ways to escape the constraints of structured programming, could then be met by a manager confident that such violations of good practice were unnecessary. Programmers could not credibly claim that problems were "too difficult to be solved with a structured program": the structure theorem could be drawn upon to show such a claim to be false.[132]

As Kraft might have predicted, mathematics was being used as a tool of management, undermining programmers' autonomy. The tasks that programmers were left with, however, after the discipline of structured programming had been imposed, were far from routine. Mills's cleanroom demanded more, not less, from its programmers; in particular, it expected them to be able to write programs free from mistakes and to prove mathematically that they had done so, rather than to attempt to show it by empirical testing.

"There is an old myth about programming today, and there is a new reality," wrote Mills and his IBM colleagues, Richard C. Linger and Bernard I. Witt in 1979. "The old myth is that programming must be an error prone, cut-and-try process of frustration and anxiety. . . . [T]he new reality is that ordinary programmers, with ordinary care, can learn to write programs which are error free from their inception." The keys were the application of structured programming and of mathematics. Not only was it possible to write correct programs; it was also possible to know that one had written a correct program: "proofs of program correctness" were possible.[133] Central to Mills's viewpoint was to think of a program as a mathematical function transforming inputs into outputs. For an unstructured program—a "spaghetti program," as Mills put it— the function would typically be hopelessly complicated and rigorous reasoning about it infeasible. But a structured program could be thought of as "a function rule that uses simpler functions." Conceiving of programs as hierarchies of mathematical functions made it possible to demonstrate mathematically that, for every input permitted by the program's specification, the program would produce the correct output.[134]

What was most distinctive about Mills's approach was his view of proof, of what it meant mathematically to demonstrate that a program was a correct implementation of its specification. Any mathematical proof, said Mills, Linger, and Witt, was "an agenda for a repeatable experiment," designed to produce a "subjective conviction . . . that a given logical hypothesis leads to a given logical conclusion. . . . The proof may consist of a single claim, 'It is obvious,' or a sequence of such claims for a succession of intermediate conclusions, each of which may serve as a hypothesis for a later conclusion. But in the final analysis no other claim less than 'It is obvious,' is possible, because if one starts to explain why 'It is obvious,' the explanation must lead finally to a new subsequence of such claims, 'It is obvious,' and so on." Mathematical notation was a great practical convenience, but played no essential role in proof, "except in its effect on the person who is the experimental subject." What constituted "convincing proof" depended on who that person was. That mathematics led only to "subjective convictions" was not a fault, because that was "the only kind of reasoned conviction possible."[135]

One aspect of this use of "proof" in the cleanroom was the postponement of empirical testing to as late in the software development process as possible. Once a system was completed, it was tested as a whole, using inputs designed to simulate how it would be used in practice, but individual subprograms were not tested: their developers were forbidden even from testing them privately. Instead, program modules were subject to "team verification" processes of review. Top-level designs, and eventually program text, would be scrutinized in detail by development team members along with the putative proofs that the designs or programs were correct implementations of their specifications.[136] In cleanroom practice, therefore, the goal of "proof" was to convince first oneself, then one's fellow team members, that designs and programs were correct. "[A]greement that a proof is correct and the actual correctness of the proof are two quite independent things," conceded Mills and his IBM colleagues. "People still make mistakes doing mathematical reasoning, because people are fallible. But they make fewer mistakes, and they can check each other's work, to let even fewer mistakes through. The result is enough added precision in reasoning and communication to change programming from a cut-and-try ad hoc process to an orderly technical process."[137]

The systems produced by cleanroom techniques at the Federal Systems Division were not, in general, entirely free of "bugs," merely less prone to them than systems produced in the traditional manner. Traditional software development methods typically generated around fifty errors per 1,000 lines of code (program text), claimed Mills, 90 percent of which were painstakingly and expensively removed in debugging, leaving around five errors per 1,000 lines in completed systems. Cleanroom code emerged from "proof" with typically fewer than five errors per 1,000 lines, nearly all of which were removed when systems as a whole were tested.[138]

As with the earlier Apollo work, the product of the cleanroom was not perfection but workability. The flight-control software for the space shuttle, for example, largely developed by the Federal Systems Division, manifested an embarrassing bug that caused the first launch in 1981 to be postponed, and the procedures for maintaining and upgrading the flight-control software were later to be criticized by a review panel of computer scientists. But the software successfully flew the shuttle (it played no role in the 1986 Challenger disaster), and IBM claimed an "error rate of .1 errors per thousand lines of code detected after release." The achievement was expensive—the code cost NASA $1,000 per line—but in the light of the fears expressed at Garmisch, its dependability was no mean achievement.[139]

Automating Program Proof

In cleanroom proof, "[t]he level of rigor employed is a business decision based on risks and rewards," and proof usually took the form of "verbal proofs in team reviews."[140] To some proponents of testing, the claims made for the cleanroom were an affront,[141] and to those computer scientists, especially in academia, committed to formal deductive proof the cleanroom's informal, often verbal, proofs were unsatisfactory.[142] But was written proof any better? Proofs conducted by hand, especially the intricate, tedious proofs that program verification often required, were error prone. Dijkstra was one of the few to argue that hand-produced proofs about computer systems could be dependable: "Over the last ten years [to 1993] I have derived thousands of formal proofs. All have been written down and seen by others. One mistake has been discovered, by myself six days after I had written the thing."[143] The majority opinion in computer science rapidly turned to the conclusion that the automation of proof was the best solution to the problems of proof conducted by hand. The machine itself was to be used to rectify the fallibility of human deduction.

As noted, McCarthy had called in 1962 for program proofs to be checked by computer; he even envisaged the eventual use of proof-checking programs, with at least a limited capacity to construct the details of proofs, within mathematics itself.[144] In 1967 Floyd too suggested the use of the computer to construct the proofs needed for formal verification. He put forward the notion of what he called a "verifying compiler," illustrating the need for it with the cartoon in figure 2.8. Into the compiler would be fed programs annotated with comments as in figure 2.7. The compiler would attempt to prove that the comments were valid, that is, that the program would do what it should. If it could not do so, "what remained unproven would be displayed to the programmer as theorems necessary for the validity of his comments. He might then in-

Figure 2.8
Why a "verifying compiler" was needed. From Robert W. Floyd, "The Verifying Compiler," in *Carnegie Mellon University Annual Report* (Pittsburgh, Penn.: Carnegie Mellon University, 1967), 18–19, at p. 18.

teractively assist the machine in finding proofs for these theorems."[145] Floyd's was simply a proposal for such a compiler, but an actual automated system for program verification, the first of its kind, was constructed by Floyd's student, James Cornelius King, and described in his 1969 thesis.

King presented his work as "a first step" towards Floyd's "verifying compiler." He wrote a suite of programs for an IBM 360 computer designed to verify programs (written in a simple programming language) to perform integer arithmetic. King added to these programs annotations akin to those in figure 2.7 and the programs and annotations were then processed by a "verification condition generator," which transformed the annotations into formulae submitted to an automated theorem prover (a program of the type discussed in chapter 3), which set to work to prove them. The most challenging proof described in King's thesis was of a program to raise an integer to an integral power, and King noted that his work "has been extremely modest." Nevertheless, he wrote, "One can dream of routinely using a verifying compiler as an everyday tool. . . . We only hope that, indeed, this has been a first step of a progression which will allow this dream to come to fruition."[146]

Floyd and King were not alone in the dream of automated program proof: by the early 1970s, it was a "hot topic" in computer science in the United States. It was also quickly to move into a fateful alliance with national security interests, an embrace that is the subject of chapter 5. Before turning to the further development of mechanized verification, however, it is necessary to examine the history of its key tools, automated theorem provers. Many of those who worked on these provers also had a dream, an even more ambitious one: artificial intelligence, which is the topic of chapter 3.

3

Artificial Mathematicians?

Pittsburgh, Pennsylvania, January 1956. Before long, its mills and blast furnaces would become silent and cold, but Pittsburgh was still a steel town. At the Carnegie Institute of Technology, however, a new technology was being born. Edward A. Feigenbaum, later to become one of the leaders of the new field, was then an undergraduate senior, taking a course in Carnegie's Graduate School of Industrial Administration taught by one of the school's professors, Herbert Simon. "Just after Christmas vacation," recalled Feigenbaum, "Simon came into the classroom and said, 'Over Christmas Allen Newell and I invented a thinking machine.'"[1]

Among the features that made the "thinking machine" remarkable was that its coinventor was a social scientist. Born in Milwaukee in 1916, Herbert Simon studied political science at the University of Chicago, gaining his B.A. in 1936 and his Ph.D. in 1943, at a time when Chicago led the move away from political theory to the empirical, behavioral study of politics.[2] By 1956 Simon was well known as an organizational theorist (*Administrative Behavior*, the 1947 book based upon his Ph.D. thesis, was a classic of the field) and on his way to becoming one of the twentieth century's most influential social scientists. He attacked as unrealistic the model of human beings held by most economists. Orthodox economic theory posited a view of human beings as possessing a stable set of preferences, complete (or almost complete) information, and an unlimited capacity to calculate which course of action was best. The task Simon set himself as a social scientist was to replace these assumptions with a model of rational behavior that was compatible with the limited information-processing capacities of real human beings and with how those human beings were observed to behave, especially as members of large organizations. "It is impossible," Simon wrote in 1947, "for the behavior of a single, isolated individual to reach any high degree of rationality. The number of alternatives he must explore is so great, the information he would need to evaluate them so vast that even an approximation to objective rationality is hard to conceive."[3]

Simon's development of the view of human beings as possessing only "bounded," not complete, rationality was productive enough eventually to earn him the 1978 Nobel Prize in Economics. This viewpoint, however, was exemplified in his work in computer science as well as in social science. The crucial moment in forging the connection came in 1952, when Simon was appointed a consultant to the Santa Monica defense think tank, the RAND Corporation. There, he came into contact with the emerging world of digital computing. His career in administrative science had involved work with punched-card machines, which by World War II were commonplace in large organizations in the United States, and during the war he began to hear rumors about the emergence of digital computers.

His interest was further piqued by reading Edmund Berkeley's 1949 popular account of the early computers, *Giant Brains, or Machines that Think*. To accompany the book, Berkeley sold "a little toy do-it-yourself computer . . . constructed of nothing more than batteries and wires, which could be 'programmed' by rewiring to do a variety of tasks." Buying and experimenting with one of these, Simon "got some hands-on feel for the way computers did their work."[4] Reading Berkeley and also Norbert Wiener's work in cybernetics, Simon became intrigued by the thought that, as he put it in 1950, "the computing machine is in fact a 'brain,' exhibiting many of the simpler characteristics of the human brain." Even a simple servomechanism like a thermostat "has a purpose . . . and . . . strives to accomplish that purpose. . . . If it were alive, we would say that it exhibited rationality and intelligence."[5]

At RAND, Simon came into contact with computers more flexible than punched-card machines and more powerful by far than Berkeley's toy. "If imagination and technique make a scientist," said Simon, "we must also add dollars," and, via its link to the U.S. Air Force, RAND had dollars aplenty. It was building its own digital computer, the Johnniac (named after computer pioneer John von Neumann), and it also bought from IBM the machine on which Simon learned to program: the 701 or "defense calculator," IBM's first full-blown stored-program electronic digital computer.

The scale of RAND's resources was indicated by the fact that its System Research Laboratory had constructed an entire simulated air-defense station to study how to improve the efficiency with which its personnel performed tasks such as diagnosing which radar echoes demanded the launch of an interceptor aircraft. Imitation radar maps for the simulation were produced by an IBM card-programmed electronic calculator (a precursor to the digital computer), using a method devised by Allen Newell and J. C. (Cliff) Shaw of RAND. Simon was struck by the fact that Newell's and Shaw's simulation "was generating not numbers," as most computer applications did, "but locations, points on a two-dimensional map." The example began to make more concrete Simon's evolving view that "[c]omputers . . . could be general symbol systems, capable of processing symbols of any kind—numerical or not."[6]

The RAND connection also provided Simon with his key collaborators, programmer Cliff Shaw and, especially, Allen Newell. Newell had come to RAND in 1950 from an undergraduate physics major at Stanford University and a year of graduate work in mathematics at Princeton. Like Simon, he became fascinated by possible nonnumerical applications of computers, and in 1955 he persuaded RAND to second him to Pittsburgh to gain his Ph.D. under Simon's supervision. The original plan was for Newell to develop a computer program to play chess. Every Saturday Newell and Simon met, the former bringing the technical insights from computing, the latter drawing upon his knowledge of "human problem solving." As their discussion broadened beyond chess, Simon began to think about how human beings solved geometry problems, and he convinced himself that "we could program a machine to solve such problems." In October 1955 he and Newell began to work toward that goal. By November, however, their attention moved to formal logic because, unlike in geometry, problems in logic could readily be formulated and solved in purely symbolic form without recourse to diagrams and to visual representation.[7]

As a student at Chicago, Simon had taken part in seminars with the philosopher Rudolph Carnap, attended visiting lectures by Bertrand Russell, and read the philosophical and logical work of Carnap, Russell, Wittgenstein, and Tarski. On a mid-1930s' birthday or Christmas list, Simon put a request for a copy of the three volumes of Whitehead and Russell's *Principia Mathematica,* their ambitious attempt to give mathematics a secure grounding solely in logical principles. Simon's parents bought him the *Principia* and it was still on his bookshelves two decades later when he needed a source for problems in formal logic.[8] Simon refreshed his memory of logic by working through the section of the *Principia* on propositional logic, the relatively elementary part of formal, symbolic logic that deals with how propositions (statements that assert something) are combined by "logical connectives" such as ∧ ("and"), ∨ ("or"), ¬ ("not"), and → ("if . . . then," "implies"). Suppose, for example, *p* represents the proposition "it is raining," and *q* represents the proposition "it is cold," then we can represent "it is raining, and it is cold" as *p* ∧ *q*.

Gradually, Simon began to develop a rule-of-thumb for finding proofs of the *Principia*'s propositional-logic theorems: a heuristic, as he and Newell began to call it. (The term "heuristic" had been popularized by one of Newell's Stanford professors, George Polya, in his widely read *How to Solve It,* a compendium of "tricks of the trade" and habits of thought to aid problem solving in mathematics.[9]) Newell and Simon worked to "sharpen" Simon's heuristic so that it could be implemented by computer, while Newell collaborated by teletype with Cliff Shaw at RAND on the development of a programming language to permit flexible handling of the data structures generated in symbolic problem solving. By the middle of December 1955, Simon had a clear enough notion of the requisite heuristic that he "succeeded in simulating by hand (in literal imitation of a computer program) the first proof."[10] The "thinking machine" that Simon described to his class at the start of 1956 was thus still a simulated rather than a real machine. Newell and Shaw worked on its implementation on RAND's Johnniac, and Newell and Simon wrote out on index cards, in English, the rules for the program's subroutines and the *Principia*'s axioms of propositional logic. On "a dark winter evening," in January 1956, they gathered Simon's wife Dorothea, their three children, and some graduate students. "To each member of the group, we gave one of the cards, so that each person became, in effect, a component of the computer program—a subroutine that performs some special function, or a component of its memory. It was the task of each participant to execute his or her subroutine, or to provide the contents of his or her memory," whenever called upon by the overall program.[11]

In August 1956 the simulated machine became a real one. Written in Newell and Shaw's information processing language and running on RAND's Johnniac, the Logic Theory Machine, as they called their program, produced its first full proof, of the *Principia*'s first theorem in propositional logic (theorem 2.01): that if a proposition *p* implies its negation, ¬*p*, then *p* is false. Newell, Shaw, and Simon provided their program with the five axioms of propositional logic and three rules of inference shown in figure 3.1. They then gave it theorem 2.01 and its successors from the *Principia* and set it to find proofs. One way of doing

Axioms:

p, *q*, and *r* are propositions.

$(p \lor p) \to p$	(1.2)
$p \to (q \lor p)$	(1.3)
$(p \lor q) \to (q \lor p)$	(1.4)
$[p \lor (q \lor r)] \to [q \lor (p \lor r)]$	(1.5)
$(p \to q) \to [(r \lor p) \to (r \lor q)]$	(1.6)

Rules of inference:

1) Rule of substitution. "[A]ny expression may be substituted for any variable in any theorem, provided the substitution is made throughout the theorem wherever that variable appears."

2) Rule of replacement. A logical connective "can be replaced by its definition, and *vice versa.*" Thus in the logical system of the *Principia*, $p \to q$ means $(\neg p) \lor q$, and one of these expressions can be replaced by the other.

3) Rule of detachment (*modus ponens*). If A and $A \to B$ are theorems, B is a theorem.

Proof of theorem 2.01

$(p \to \neg p) \to \neg p$ \qquad (theorem 2.01, to be proved)

1) $(A \lor A) \to A$	(axiom 1.2)
2) $(\neg A \lor \neg A) \to \neg A$	(subs. of $\neg A$ for A)
3) $(A \to \neg A) \to \neg A$	(repl. of "$\lor$" with "$\to$")
4) $(p \to \neg p) \to \neg p$	(subs. of p for A; QED).

Figure 3.1
The Logic Theory Machine's axioms, rules of inference, and proof of theorem 2.01 of the *Principia*. From A. Newell, J. C. Shaw, and H. A. Simon, "Empirical Explorations of the Logic Theory Machine: A Case Study in Heuristic," *Proceedings of the Western Joint Computer Conference, 1957*, 218–240, at p. 219. $\lor$ is the symbol for "or"; $\to$ for "implies"; $\neg$ for "not."

so would have been to start from the five axioms and systematically apply the rules of inference to construct all possible sequences of valid logical deductions: the "British Museum Algorithm," as Newell, Shaw, and Simon called it. As well as being hopelessly inefficient, however, such an approach would not have been a step toward their goal. The Logic Theory Machine "was devised to learn how it is possible to solve difficult problems such as proving mathematical theorems, discovering scientific laws from data, playing chess, or understanding the meaning of English prose." Just as Simon the social scientist had rejected the economist's overrational model of human beings, so the Logic Theory Machine's designers were "not interested in methods that guarantee solutions, but which require vast amounts of computation. Rather, we wish to understand how a mathematician, for example, is able to prove a theorem even though he does not know when he starts how, or if, he is going to succeed."[12]

The Logic Theory Machine began with the theorem to be proved, and searched for a direct "one-step" proof of it by substitution of variables and/or replacement of logical connectives in an axiom or in a previously proved theorem. (Theorem 2.01 is a case where a "one-step" proof is available: although, when written out as in figure 3.1, it occupies more than one line, no operation other than substitution or replacement is involved.) If no one-step proof could be found, then the program looked for a two-step proof by searching for subgoals: formulae from which the desired result could be proved either by *modus ponens* (see figure 3.1) or by "chaining."[13] Proofs of these subgoals by substitution or replacement were then sought; if that search failed, *modus ponens* and chaining were again applied to subgoals to create "subsubgoals," and a three-step proof sought; and, at least in principle, so on iteratively.

In practice, however, the Logic Theory Machine found only very short proofs: three steps at most.[14] This was in part because of the limited capacity of the Johnniac (the machine's main memory consisted of only 4,096 words, with a further 10,000 usable words on a magnetized drum),[15] but more profoundly it resulted from the relatively unselective search for a proof. Subgoals, for example, were considered simply in the order in which they were generated, with no attempt at a heuristic "guess" as to which was most likely to yield a proof. As the number of steps in a proof increased, the amount of search required to find it grew extremely rapidly. Right at the start of automated theorem proving, its central problem had appeared: the "combinatorial explosion,"[16] the exponential (or worse) increase in the necessary search space as the number of steps in a proof increases.

The Logic Theory Machine's ponderously systematic approach to theorem proving might not have been as good a simulation of human intelligence as Newell, Shaw, and Simon would have wished, but they clearly intended it as a first step in that direction: that was what Simon meant by describing it as a "thinking machine." Although they preferred the term "complex information processing," their work was a contribution to the nascent field that John McCarthy (see chapter 2) was beginning to call "artificial intelligence." In 1956 McCarthy, Marvin Minsky (who was to set up the Artificial Intelligence Laboratory at MIT), Nathaniel Rochester of IBM, and Claude Shannon of the Bell Telephone Laboratories organized the first meeting of the new field, a summer workshop at McCarthy's college, Dartmouth, beside the Connecticut River in New Hampshire. Alone among the invitees to Dartmouth, Newell and Simon were able to bring with them the printouts of a working program.[17]

After the Logic Theory Machine, Newell and Simon moved away from automated theorem proving, in the first instance to work on what they called the "general problem solver," an ambitious attempt to extract, from human beings' accounts of the mental processes of problem solving, the necessary elements of a reasoning system that could be applied to a wide variety of intelligent tasks. The general problem solver epitomized, more clearly than the Logic Theory Machine, Newell and Simon's central conviction: that the study of the heuristics employed by human beings, with their "bounded rationality," was the central resource for the development of artificial intelligence.[18]

The other founders of artificial intelligence, notably John McCarthy and Marvin Minsky, were less convinced, believing that machines could be made intelligent in ways that differed from how human beings solved problems.[19] Even at the beginnings of the new field, too, there were tensions over intellectual credit. There was, for example, dispute over who should report on the Dartmouth summer workshop to the September 1956 meeting of the Institute of Radio Engineers. In the end, McCarthy gave a general account of the workshop, and Newell and Simon separately described the Logic Theory Machine.[20]

The most direct successor to the Logic Theory Machine was the Geometry Machine, developed by Herbert Gelernter and his colleagues J. R. Hansen and Donald Loveland at the IBM Research Center in Poughkeepsie, New York. The task was assigned to Gelernter by Nathaniel

Rochester, designer of the IBM 701 computer and one of the organizers of the Dartmouth workshop. Newell and Simon had toyed with the idea of a geometry theorem prover, and during the Dartmouth meeting Marvin Minsky "sketched out the heuristic search procedure" for such a prover and simulated by hand how it might find a proof of an elementary theorem of Euclidean geometry: that the angles at the base of an isosceles triangle (that is, a triangle with two sides of equal length) are equal. Although it was later found to be well-known, the proof "was new and elegant to the participants."[21]

Developing the Geometry Machine, Gelernter and his colleagues found that the expression of geometric problems in the form of diagrams—the issue that had deterred Newell and Simon—provided a simple, effective way of restricting the search for a proof. With the technology of the time, diagrams could not be scanned directly by a computer, so Gelernter and his colleagues translated them into a series of coordinates of points. As the program (which was implemented on an IBM 704 computer, successor to the 701) generated subgoals, it did not seek a proof of each of them indiscriminately, as the Logic Theory Machine had done. Instead, it ignored those subgoal expressions that were not valid in the diagram and concentrated on searching for a proof of those subgoals that were valid. The resulting heavily pruned search was remarkably successful: the Geometry Machine "found solutions to a large number of problems taken from high-school textbooks and final examinations in plane geometry."[22]

Automated Theorem Proving and the Logicians

In the development of the Geometry and Logic Theory Machines, commitment to the general project of "artificial intelligence" was clear. Algorithms that were guaranteed always to find a proof were rejected not simply on the grounds of their claimed inefficiency, but because the goal was to find heuristic procedures akin to those of human problem solving. The validity of the elementary theorems of propositional logic proved by the Logic Theory Machine, for example, could easily have been decided by the well-known method of truth tables, in which all possible combinations of truth values of a formula's component propositions are examined (see figure 3.2). But an approach that did not throw light upon human problem solving would not have satisfied Simon and Newell. As Simon put it: "it would be nice to have a good theorem-proving

Disjunction (∨, "or"):

p	q	p∨q
T	T	T
T	F	T
F	T	T
F	F	F

Implication (→, "implies"):

p	q	p→q
T	T	T
T	F	F
F	T	T
F	F	T

Theorem 2.01 of the *Principia:*

p	¬p	p→¬p	(p→¬p)→¬p
T	F	F	T
F	T	T	T

Figure 3.2
Truth tables for disjunction, implication, and theorem 2.01 of the *Principia.*
T = true; F = false. A formula that, like theorem 2.01, is true for all assignments
of truth values to its component propositions is called a "tautology."

program, but that was not our central interest. Our central interest is:
How does the human mind manage to do these things?"[23]

The goal of understanding human problem solving and going on to
build intelligent machines was, however, by no means universal among
the early developers of automated theorem provers. Those whose background was in mathematical logic could find computers attractive for
quite the opposite reason: not because they were potentially intelligent,
but because they were "persistent plodders," as the logician Hao Wang
put it in 1960.[24] Twentieth century logicians were, in a sense, the intellectual descendants of Gottfried Leibniz (1646–1716), who had proposed
the development of a formal system that would reduce reasoning to calculation, enabling the validity of arguments to be checked without reference to the content being reasoned about.[25] With such a system "men
of good will desiring to settle a controversy on any subject whatsoever"
could simply "take their pens in their hands" and say "let us calculate."[26]

Leibniz left behind him only fragments of such a system, but his successors such as Augustus De Morgan (1806–71), George Boole (1815–64), and Gottlob Frege (1848–1925) proposed formalisms that were later developed into modern symbolic logic.[27] Symbolic logic separated the formal structure of deductive argument from the meaning of the terms used in such argument, and some of the more elementary ideas involved were occasionally implemented in simple machines.[28] The advent of the digital computer, however, promised a far more thorough going mechanization of Leibniz's dream. As Wang wrote, it was "as though logicians had worked with the fiction of man as a persistent and unimaginative beast who can only follow rules blindly, and then the fiction found its incarnation in the machine."[29]

Logicians quickly became aware of the Logic Theory and Geometry Machines, notably via a five-week Summer Institute for Symbolic Logic held at Cornell University in 1957, at which Gelernter described his work. During the summer school, the logician Abraham Robinson responded with a talk asking whether mathematical logic could "do more than provide a notation for the detailed formulation of a proof on computer?" It was clear that the automation of mathematical proof would require not just propositional logic (dealing with how propositions are combined by logical connectives) but also predicate logic, with its predicates, quantifiers, and functions. (A predicate is an expression used to assert a property of some entity or entities. For instance, "is a prime number"[30] is an example of a predicate. Quantifiers are symbols that denote the "quantity" of entities for which a property is asserted as holding, allowing, for instance, the true proposition "there exists an integer which is a prime number" to be distinguished from the false proposition "all integers are prime numbers." The two standard quantifiers are the existential quantifier, $\exists$, "there exists," and the universal quantifier, $\forall$, "for all.")

Predicate logic was powerful and expressive, but the automation of predicate-logic proofs was a far harder problem than the automation of proofs in propositional logic. Robinson suggested that a way forward might be the use of a key idea of modern logic, the Herbrand procedure, in which the search for a proof of a theorem in first-order[31] predicate logic is reduced to checking the validity of an everexpanding set of propositional logic formulae until one is found that yields a proof of the theorem.[32] Robinson noted that "the generation" of this "infinite sequence of particular instances . . . can be easily systematized (and hence programmed)." A systematic search of this kind might still be infeasible on "a contemporary computer," but Robinson sketched a suggestion for making it more discriminating. He did not, however, himself turn to practical work on automated proving,[33] but as other logicians did so they found rich resources within their discipline.

The first contributions of logicians to automated theorem proving focused on automating "decision procedures"—algorithms,[34] such as the method of truth tables in the case of propositional logic, that will determine, in a finite number of steps, whether or not an arbitrary formula in a given mathematical domain is a theorem—for those restricted parts of mathematics and logic where such procedures were known to exist. (Classic work in the 1930s by Alonzo Church and by Alan Turing had showed that there could be no decision procedure for full predicate logic or for the entirety of mathematics.) The first effort to automate a decision procedure predated the Logic Theory Machine. Mojzesz Presburger had shown in 1929 that a restricted fragment of arithmetic, involving only the addition of integers, was decidable: in other words, a decision procedure for it existed.[35] In 1954 the mathematical logician Martin Davis implemented Presburger's decision procedure on the original "Johnniac" at the Princeton Institute for Advanced Study, and he described this work to the 1957 Cornell Summer Institute.[36] Given the limitations of the Johnniac, and the fact that Presburger's procedure is demanding of computational resources, Davis's program could, however, handle only simple theorems: "Its great triumph was to prove that the sum of two even numbers is even."[37]

Another early user of decision procedures was Hao Wang, whose work contrasts directly with Newell, Shaw, and Simon's Logic Theory Machine.[38] Born in 1920 in Tsinan, China, Wang moved to the United States after World War II, receiving his Ph.D. from Harvard in 1948. Election to Harvard's Society of Fellows and a junior faculty position in its Department of Philosophy followed. Nevertheless, "[a]round the beginning of 1953," wrote Wang, "I became dissatisfied with philosophy (as seen at Harvard) and, for other reasons, I also wanted to do something more obviously useful." In a 1954 article he talked of the formal logician as an "intellectual outcaste [sic]," valued neither by mathematicians nor by philosophers. He began to see the computer as a potential remedy for this uncomfortable situation, as offering logicians what they were otherwise "often hard put to give," a "very convincing justification of their occupation and preoccupation." In particular, the computer provided an answer to the "common complaint among mathematicians" that logicians' concern with formalizing proof was "pointless hairsplitting." The computer was "a home for the obsessive formal precision of (the older parts of) mathematical logic which mathematicians tend to find irrelevant and worse, pedestrian and perhaps a hindrance to creativity." While still pursuing his academic career (he moved to Oxford University as Reader in the Philosophy of Mathematics in 1956), Wang began to seek practical involvement in computing. Appointment as a "research engineer" at the Burroughs Corporation in 1953–54 was disappointing: "I was not permitted to use the only local computer and was even discouraged from taking a course for electronics technicians."[39]

In the summer of 1958, however, Wang finally got access to a computer (an IBM 704), via the logician Bradford Dunham of the IBM Poughkeepsie Research Laboratory. "It was an enjoyable long summer (owing to the fact that Oxford begins school only late in October)," wrote Wang. He learned to program and implemented a decision procedure that could handle all of the *Principia*'s theorems in propositional logic. The following summer, Wang implemented a decision procedure for a decidable fragment of first-order predicate logic.[40]

Wang's decision procedures were vastly more efficient than the Logic Theory Machine's heuristic. By the end of the summer of 1958, Wang's programs had proved all the propositional logic theorems from the *Principia* proved by the Logic Theory Machine, using less than thirty seconds of central processing time in total, and had begun to prove theorems in a restricted but still significant domain of predicate logic. (To Wang's surprise, he found that all the predicate-logic theorems in the *Principia* fell into the fragment of that logic for which he had implemented the decision procedure.) These successes revealed "a fundamental inadequacy" in Newell, Shaw, and Simon's approach, Wang wrote:

There is no need to kill a chicken with a butcher's knife. Yet the net impression is that Newell-Shaw-Simon failed even to kill the chicken with their butcher's knife. They do not wish to use standard algorithms such as the method of truth tables. . . . [But] to argue the superiority of "heuristic" over algorithmic methods by choosing a particularly inefficient algorithm [the "British Museum" algorithm, indiscriminately constructing sequences of deductions] seems hardly just.[41]

Herbert Simon did not agree:

I remember explaining to him [Wang] on several occasions that he was in a different business than we were. . . . We were trying to understand how human beings do it. . . . Everything we know about human beings suggests that the reason they are able to do interesting things is heuristic search. Occasionally things that human beings do that way, we can bludgeon through on a computer, but why go that way?[42]

Other logicians, however, shared Wang's criticism of Simon's approach. Bradford Dunham and two colleagues at IBM argued that an "average clerical worker," by rote use of known decision procedures such as truth tables, could "validate in a matter of hours" all the propositional-logic theorems in the *Principia*. They developed a mechanized equivalent of this clerk, a "nonheuristic" computer program broadly analogous to Wang's, which "disposed of" all these theorems "in approximately two minutes." Claims of the inferiority of algorithmic techniques were mere "loose talk," they asserted.[43] Similarly, the Dutch philosopher and logician Evert Beth wrote:

Newell and Simon . . . and Gelernter . . . seem to think of using those heuristic devices which are often applied by human beings in finding a proof or solving a problem. It seems not unfair to draw a comparison between such devices and certain tricks which one resorts to in mental computation. A number of these tricks may be of sufficient importance to be taken into account in designing a computer, or, perhaps, rather in programming a specific problem. But many tricks, helpful though they may be in mental computation, will be devoid of any value with a view to computational machinery.[44]

Logicians like Wang, Dunham, and Beth felt that the efforts of the pioneers of artificial intelligence were amateurish—"unprofessional," as Wang later put it.[45] They were convinced that symbolic logic provided better routes to the mechanization of proof. Logicians also knew, however, that to fulfil logic's promise they had to go beyond implementing decision procedures for limited domains and build a theorem prover for full first-order predicate logic, for which, as Church and Turing had shown, no decision procedure existed. That logic was powerful enough to allow the expression of much of mathematics, so a prover for it was potentially an enormous contribution to the automation of mathematical proof. Wang's sights were clearly set on such a theorem prover, and he was not alone. In Sweden, Dag Prawitz devised a predicate-logic proof procedure that was implemented on a Facit EDB computer in 1957–58 by Håkan Prawitz and Neri Voghera.[46] The logician Paul Gilmore joined IBM's Thomas J. Watson Research Center as a staff mathematician in 1958, and by April 1959 he too had written a first-order predicate-logic theorem prover, for the IBM 704.[47]

This first generation of predicate-logic theorem provers, however, had sharp practical limitations. Procedures that must eventually find a proof if one exists were of little use if "eventually" was in practice so long that limitations on run-time or on computer memory meant that only elementary theorems could be proved. Gilmore described how his prover was quickly crippled by the combinatorial explosion, and Prawitz and his colleagues also admitted that the power of their program was limited.[48] Pat Hayes, later to become a leading figure in artificial intelligence, recalled working with an early predicate-logic prover and "realising that the instances it needed, to prove some simple lemma, were several million steps in its future, and feeling helpless at the problem of how to order the instances in some suitable way."[49]

The early predicate-logic theorem provers split the process of searching for a proof essentially into two parts: first, generating an everexpanding set of propositional-logic formulae by substitution of one expression for another (that is the process the inefficiency of which dismayed Hayes); and second, checking the satisfiability or the validity of the resultant formulae.[50] If either part of the process could be made more efficient, then perhaps the limitations of the first-generation provers could be circumvented. Dag Prawitz focused on improving the first part of the process of predicate-logic theorem proving: generating substitution instances. "The different effective proof procedures for the predicate calculus of first order . . . consist simply in generating certain expressions . . . until one is found which is a proof . . . of the formula to be proved," wrote Prawitz. The first predicate-logic provers generated substitution instances "essentially [at] random" in this search. Prawitz showed how to restrict the process so that it generated only instances that could be used to construct a proof, "in other words a method which makes only such substitutions that are of some real use in finding a proof."[51]

A junior member of the Philosophy Department at Princeton University, Hilary Putnam, who was to become a famous name in late twentieth-century philosophy, focused on the second part of the process. Putnam had broad interests in how thinking about computers could throw light on traditional philosophical topics such as the mind-body problem,[52] but he was also interested in theorem proving and knew that the standard techniques for checking the satisfiability or the validity of formulae in propositional logic, such as the truth-table method (figure 3.2), were inefficient. Putnam approached Martin Davis, who had by then moved from Princeton to the Rensselaer Polytechnic Institute, to ask him to collaborate. It was too late in the year to gain funding for their work from the usual funding agencies, but, as Davis recollected, "someone suggested that we go to an agency I'd never heard of at that time . . . the National Security Agency [see chapter 5]. And it turned out that they were interested, but they said: 'Forget this theorem proving—what we're interested in is good algorithms for propositional calculus.' "[53]

Davis and Putnam spent the summer of 1958 studying such algorithms, and they developed what has become known as the Davis-Putnam procedure for checking the satisfiability of formulae in the propositional calculus, which involved putting the formula into a particular standard form and systematically applying three simple rules.[54] As the results of Wang's and Gilmore's work became known, Davis and Putnam argued that their new procedure repaired one of the main sources of inefficiency in the early predicate-logic provers. Although they did not immediately implement their procedure on a computer, they noted that "a formula on which Gilmore's routine for the IBM 704 causes the machine to compute for 21 minutes without obtaining a result was worked successfully by *hand computation* using the present method in 30 minutes."[55]

Resolution

Because Prawitz's work and the Davis-Putnam procedure addressed different sources of inefficiency in the early predicate-logic provers, it is not surprising that more than one person working within the "logicians'" approach to theorem proving should have sought, in Martin Davis's words, "to combine [their] virtues." Davis developed a method for "mating" formulae (involving what came to be called "unification": see below) and then applying the Davis-Putnam rules. The method was implemented in 1962 by Doug McIlroy of the Bell Telephone Laboratories.[56] In parallel with this work, however, a new entrant to the field of automated theorem proving, John Alan Robinson, developed a subtly different way of achieving the same goal. Instead of first unifying and then applying the Davis-Putnam rules, Robinson found a way of directly fusing the two steps into a single, powerful rule of deductive inference that was to become the paradigmatic technique of automated proving: resolution.

Born in Yorkshire in 1930, Alan Robinson came to the United States in 1952 with a classics degree from Cambridge University. He studied philosophy at the University of Oregon and at Princeton, receiving his Ph.D. from the latter in 1956. "Disillusioned with philosophy," he went to work as an operations research analyst for the chemical giant Du Pont, where he learned programming and taught himself mathematics.[57] After four years with Du Pont, Robinson returned to philosophy via a postdoctoral fellowship at the University of Pittsburgh, but he kept up his involvement in computing by spending a series of summers as a visiting researcher at the Atomic Energy Commission's Argonne National Laboratory in Illinois.

Argonne's primary mission was research on nuclear reactors, but the director of its Applied Mathematics Division, William F. Miller, had a broad conception of his role. He "was thinking a great deal about 'what could be automated' including data analysis, control of experiments, aids to theory development, design automation, and aids to programming," and was "much influenced" by the codeveloper of the Logic Theory Machine, Allen Newell.[58]

Miller pointed Alan Robinson in the direction of theorem proving. He showed him Davis and Putnam's as yet unmechanized propositional logic procedure, and suggested that he use his programming skills to implement it on the Argonne IBM 704. (Putnam had served as the supervisor of Robinson's Princeton thesis, but that had been on the philosophy of David Hume, not on theorem proving.) Robinson implemented the Davis-Putnam procedure in FORTRAN, the programming language that was rapidly coming to dominate scientific computing at sites like Argonne. "I spent the summer [of 1961] happily . . . running this thing. Yes, it worked just like they [Davis and Putnam] said. However, the examples that one would like to try next blew it up, and we ran into the combinatorial explosion of the instantiation, 'try all the instances, enumerate all the instances.' So I learnt that summer that that was not exactly an elegant way to go." Robinson, however, was finding his summer work at Argonne more fascinating than the philosophy that he began to teach at Rice University in 1961. "The work at Argonne really was dominating my life, because I started looking at other ways to go in this first-order proof procedure stuff, and stumbled across the work of Prawitz, who was the one who reached for some form of unification, calculating instances rather than trying them all." In his second summer at Argonne, Robinson programmed Prawitz's procedure, again using FORTRAN.[59]

Like Davis, Robinson came to the conclusion that the way forward was to bring together Prawitz's work and the Davis-Putnam procedure. Robinson knew of Davis's attempt to do so, and in November 1962 he wrote that "it does not yet seem clear just how Davis will proceed, and one awaits with great interest reports of his further researches along these lines."[60] In his third summer at Argonne in 1963, however, Robinson found his own way of linking Prawitz's approach and the Davis-Putnam procedure: resolution. The basic idea was to employ only one inference rule: the resolution principle. Setting aside some complications,[61] suppose one has two formulae $A \vee p$ ("A or p") and $B \vee \neg p$ ("B or not-p"). The resolution principle allows one to deduce from the two formulae the "resolvent," $A \vee B$ ("A or B").[62]

Of course, pairs of formulae will not usually have the convenient form that makes the principle directly applicable, so the resolution method involves "unification," in other words making substitutions to make the principle applicable: this is where Prawitz's work was relevant. A resolution theorem prover is provided by its human users with the axioms of the field of mathematics in question and with the negation of the conjecture whose proof is sought. (Like most of the early predicate-logic provers, a resolution prover does not seek a direct proof, but "assumes" the negation of the conjecture and seeks to generate a contradiction.) The theorem prover systematically resolves pairs of formulae until a contradiction, and thus a proof of the original conjecture, is reached. Robinson showed that if the conjecture is indeed a theorem, this procedure must (in principle) terminate and a proof will thus be found. There was, therefore, no need for any other rule of inference and so no need for choices between rules that would add to the explosion of the search space.

The gain in mechanical efficiency provided by resolution brought a cost in opacity to human beings. Robinson described resolution as a "machine-oriented" rather than a "human-oriented" form of inference:

Traditionally, a single step in a deduction has been required, for pragmatic and psychological reasons, to be simple enough, broadly speaking, to be apprehended as correct by a human being in a single intellectual act. No doubt this custom originated in the desire that each single step of a deduction should be indubitable, even though the deduction as a whole may consist of a long chain of such steps.

The extensive searching needed when inference steps were small and humanly comprehensible, Robinson argued, contributed greatly to the combinatorial explosion that dogged theorem provers. By comparison, resolution was far more complex but therefore more powerful: it "condones single inferences which are often beyond the ability of the human to grasp (other than discursively)," but greatly reduced the amount of searching needed. Since resolution was designed to be implemented on a computer, Robinson felt that the fact that it was hard for human beings to follow resolution inferences did not matter, but the gain in efficiency did.[63]

Resolution and Artificial Intelligence

In September 1963 Alan Robinson submitted a paper describing resolution to the *Journal of the Association for Computing Machinery*. It languished unread on the desk of a referee for a year and so did not appear until

1965, but even before then word began to spread. "I . . . got a phone call from Marvin Minsky," recalled Robinson. By then, Minsky, head of MIT's Artificial Intelligence Laboratory, was an acknowledged leader of the field. For Robinson, being phoned by him was "like being called by the Queen. . . . Minsky said, 'Yes, I've got your paper here on resolution. . . . I want to ask your permission to use it in a seminar.' "[64]

The 1964 phone call from Minsky was the beginning of a surge of intense interest in Robinson's new technique. Resolution greatly increased the potential power of predicate-logic theorem provers. Robinson's early work was rapidly elaborated: by himself; by others at Argonne; at Stanford University, where John McCarthy used his LISP (list-processing) programming language to write and to test a resolution theorem prover, taking, to Alan Robinson's amazement, only a few hours to do so; at the University of Edinburgh, where the enthusiasm for resolution of Bernard Meltzer, a Reader in Electrical Engineering, who had spent some summer months with Robinson, played an important part in establishing what became the Department of Artificial Intelligence; and elsewhere.[65]

In its original version, resolution required formulae to be presented in what is called "clausal form,"[66] and formalisms alternative to clausal form were now investigated. Resolution was generalized from pairs of clauses to arbitrarily large sets of clauses. Strategies were formulated for optimizing the order in which clauses were resolved, and ways were found to increase the efficiency with which equality was handled. (Human mathematicians have a finely tuned intuitive understanding of how to handle the substitution of "equals for equals," but adding axioms governing equality to predicate logic greatly increases the search spaces of resolution theorem provers.) By 1978 one of the contributors to the development of resolution, Gelernter's collaborator Donald Loveland, was able to include twenty-five different variants of the technique in his textbook of automated theorem proving.[67]

The "resolution boom"[68] in the latter half of the 1960s was based on more than an interest in automated theorem proving: it was intimately bound to the fortunes of artificial intelligence. Predicate logic was a general system for formal reasoning, not one specific to mathematics. If human knowledge could successfully be expressed in predicate logic, and if resolution provided efficient automated theorem provers for that logic, then the general problem of artificial intelligence would be well on the way to solution, and furthermore would have essentially a unitary solution: resolution could "be used as a universal problem solver."[69] As long as these two preconditions appeared plausible, the two approaches discussed here—artificial intelligence and formal, symbolic logic—appeared to converge rather than to diverge as they had in the 1950s. Alan Robinson was invited to join the editorial board of the former field's leading journal, *Artificial Intelligence.* When, for example, he came to spend a sabbatical with the artificial intelligence group at Edinburgh, "[h]e sort of brought resolution with him, and blew everybody's mind. . . . [W]e were all terribly excited,"[70] reported Pat Hayes, then a member of the group. "[T]he core ideas of resolution" formed "a new way to think about the *process* of doing logic . . . and . . . suddenly enabled us to see how to do all kinds of things."[71]

The plausibility of the preconditions of resolution's centrality to artificial intelligence was, however, precarious. Among the early pioneers of artificial intelligence, the most prominent proponent of the use of formal logic was John McCarthy, who from 1962 headed the Artificial Intelligence Laboratory at Stanford University.[72] A program could be said to have "common sense," McCarthy wrote in 1959, "if it automatically deduces for itself a sufficiently wide class of immediate consequences of anything it is told and what it already knows." McCarthy believed that predicate logic, perhaps suitably extended, could satisfactorily express such knowledge and permit such deductions.[73] But not all of the field's leaders were convinced.

Criticism coalesced around McCarthy's former colleague at MIT, Marvin Minsky, who argued vigorously that formal logic was inadequate for the representation of knowledge required by any general approach to artificial intelligence. In particular, the MIT group believed that resolution was an overly uniform approach to deduction. As a general proof procedure for predicate logic, resolution did not make use of domain-specific knowledge: for example, the specificities of particular areas of mathematics were represented only through the presence of the axioms of each field. As Minsky's MIT colleague, Seymour Papert put it, "as long as your methods are supposed to be good for proving everything, they're not likely to be good for proving anything." More generally, predicate logic itself was, the MIT group believed, an overly static and rigid framework for representing knowledge. When humans solve problems, said Papert, they "draw on very disparate [knowledge], not necessarily coherent and so not representable in strictly logical form."[74]

The MIT group believed it better to embody knowledge in procedures than in predicate logic. "Even such a simple statement as: 'If there are no cars coming, cross the road' . . . is more naturally transcribed as:

'Look left, look right, if you haven't seen a car, cross,' " rather than as a predicate logic formula, they wrote in a 1971 proposal to the key sponsor of artificial intelligence in the United States, the Department of Defense's Advanced Research Projects Agency. Imagine, they went on caustically, a theorem prover "trying to prove by resolution or other logical principles that no car is coming!"[75] Pat Hayes recalled the impact of a visit from Papert to Edinburgh, which had become the "heart of [artificial intelligence's] Logicland," according to Papert's MIT colleague, Carl Hewitt.[76]

Papert eloquently voiced his critique of the resolution approach dominant at Edinburgh, "and at least one person upped sticks and left because of Papert."[77] Nor, furthermore, was the Edinburgh group united. Hayes was inspired by McCarthy's dream of drawing upon logic to find ways of representing human knowledge and performing commonsense inferences, but others in the Edinburgh group appeared to Hayes to see theorem proving far too narrowly, as an end in itself, rather than as a contribution to a more general vision of artificial intelligence.[78] They therefore tended to stand aside in what Hayes describes as the "bitter civil war" that developed within artificial intelligence between "logicists" (such as McCarthy, his Stanford colleague Cordell Green, and Hayes) and "proceduralists" (such as Minsky and Papert).

Within artificial intelligence, the two camps acquired the labels of "neats" (logicists) and "scruffies" (proceduralists).[79] Some in the latter camp did not even accept that theorem proving was an acceptable topic for conferences on artificial intelligence.[80] The "scruffies" appeared in practice to win the early skirmishes in this civil war—they appeared, said Hayes, "to have won a battle for the heart and soul of the subject," including, crucially, the sympathies of the Advanced Research Projects Agency, the only major source of funding in the United States[81]—and interest in automated theorem proving suffered accordingly. In the 1970s, furthermore, the focus of many of those within artificial intelligence most strongly influenced by logic was no longer primarily on theorem proving, per se, but on the burgeoning new field of logic programming.

Central to its evolution was the collaboration between Robert Kowalski, a logician in the artificial intelligence group at Edinburgh, and Alain Colmerauer of the Université d'Aix Marseille. Colmerauer "was a computer scientist who combined practical achievements with sound contributions to their theory," wrote Kowalski, while he himself "was a logician at heart," who had been attracted to logic by the hope that it might resolve the "difficult philosophical problems" that had troubled him during his adolescence at a Jesuit high school, and "who suffered a faint revulsion for programming and everything else to do with computers."[82] Their idea—also Hayes's[83]—was to use predicate logic as a programming language. For example, in the language PROLOG ("PROgrammation en LOGique"), developed by Colmerauer and his Marseille colleague Philippe Roussel, problems are stated as goal clauses or theorems, which the system then seeks to prove, using a resolution theorem prover. The requisite theorem prover, however, does not have to be a powerful one: many practical PROLOG programs require only limited search.[84] Though PROLOG did not displace McCarthy's LISP as the programming language of choice in artificial intelligence in the United States, it was widely used in Europe and in Japan. Minsky, who remained a critic of logic-based approaches, was later to blame the failure of Japan's widely touted "Fifth Generation" program for the development of artificial intelligence on its adoption of PROLOG.[85]

That PROLOG placed limited demands on its theorem prover was fortunate, because the early resolution-based provers were in practice disappointing. This, at least as much as the "scruffy" critique of logic and of theorem proving, led the resolution "boom" of the late 1960s to turn to "bust" by the early 1970s. The problem was that while resolution ameliorated the combinatorial explosion, it did not eliminate it: although there was only one inference rule, the choices between different uses of it still caused the search space to grow rapidly. Resolution-based provers of the period still got bogged down in the search for proofs beyond quite modest lengths. So, for example, when the applied mathematician Sir James Lighthill reviewed progress in artificial intelligence on behalf of the U.K. Science Research Council early in 1972, he was told by "[t]hose most involved" that "this is particularly an area where hopes have been disappointed through the power of the combinatorial explosion in rapidly cancelling out any advantages from increase in computer power."[86]

Complexity

In 1971 a far-reaching theoretical analysis of automated theorem proving began to intensify the pessimism caused by experience of the practical limitations of resolution provers. During the late 1950s and 1960s, researchers such as Michael Rabin, Juris Hartmanis, and Richard Stearns began to develop the modern form of what has become known as "complexity theory." This involves a systematic attempt to define the "hardness" of different computational problems by specifying a function of the length of input that gives an upper bound to the number of steps required to solve a problem.[87]

Consider, for example, the problem of checking a formula in propositional logic for validity or tautologyhood (see figure 3.2): the input length here is the number, n, of elementary propositions in the formula. If the upper bound on the number of steps needed to find a solution to a problem is a polynomial function of the input length (that is, a function containing terms in n, n^2, n^3, and so on), complexity theorists regard that procedure as computationally feasible. If, on the other hand, the bound on the number of steps is an exponential function of the input length, then the procedure is seen as infeasible. The method of truth tables falls into the latter category. If a formula contains one elementary proposition (as in figure 3.2), a truth table with two rows is needed; if there are two elementary propositions, 2^2 or 4 rows are needed; three elementary propositions demand 2^3 or 8 rows; and n elementary propositions demand a truth table with 2^n rows. For only modest values of n, 2^n becomes impracticably large; the "combinatorial explosion" sets in.

Although the early developers of automated provers never provided a systematic analysis of the complexity of theorem-proving procedures, they certainly were attentive to the issue: it was, for example, one of the motivations for the work of Davis and Putnam. In 1971, however, Steven Cook, who had been one of Wang's students at Harvard, came up with a result that was profoundly disturbing from the point of view of automated proving. Cook showed that if the problem of determining whether a formula in propositional logic was a tautology had a "polynomial time" solution (that is, could be solved in a number of steps that was a polynomial function of input length), then so too did a host of other "hard" problems. Cook, in other words, defined what was later to be called the class of "*NP*-complete" problems.

If one could guess a correct solution to such a problem (such as an assignment of truth values that makes a propositional-logic formula false), it can be checked in polynomial time, but the only known deterministic solutions to an *NP*-complete problem are exponential functions, rather than polynomial functions, of the length of input. The set is "complete," in the sense that any of these problems is convertible into any other, and so if any one of them belongs to P (the set of problems that have a polynomial-time deterministic solution), they all do.[88] Since most automated theorem provers—certainly all resolution provers—were based ultimately on checking the tautologyhood or satisfiability[89] of formulae in propositional logic, the conclusion that these problems were *NP*-complete was a depressing one.

Cook's analysis left open the possibility that $NP = P$, in other words that an algorithm might be found that made all the hard, *NP*-complete, problems tractable. Subsequent researchers have also been unable to find an acceptable proof either that $NP = P$ or $NP \neq P$. Indeed, the issue is often seen as *the* outstanding theoretical problem in computer science, the analog of the great, long unsolved, mathematical problems such as the four-color problem (discussed in chapter 4) or Fermat's last theorem. Nevertheless, the instincts of nearly all computer scientists are that $NP \neq P$.[90] That would imply that no clever algorithm will ever be found that solves *NP*-complete problems in polynomial time. The conclusion was a depressing one from the point of view of automated theorem proving, because it suggested that the combinatorial explosion that dogged resolution provers was an intrinsic feature of what they were trying to do, rather than a problem that future research could solve.

Furthermore, research in complexity theory building upon that of Cook suggested that other automated theorem-proving procedures were not necessarily any better than resolution from the point of view of complexity. In 1974 Michael Fischer and Michael Rabin showed that the decision problem in Presburger arithmetic (the problem with which Martin Davis had begun the logicians' contributions to the practical automation of proof) was worse than exponential. Rabin described this and other complexity-theory results in a 1974 lecture on "Theoretical Impediments to Artificial Intelligence":

Experience and experiment have shown that . . . theorem proving programs are not effective in any but the simplest, sometimes hand-tailored cases. On most sentences presented to the program as exercises, the computation does not terminate by reason of running out of time or out of memory space, or often both.

The above results . . . point to the possibility that this bad behavior of theorem proving programs is inherent.

Although Rabin also had a solution to propose—the development of a different, "probabilistic" approach to proof, in which one was prepared to accept a very small probability that a theorem might be false—the "theorem-proving people" in Rabin's audience "were extremely worried. They were afraid—they told me so—of the impact this would have on the funding agencies. . . . [P]eople lined up in front of the microphones to direct questions to me. All they wanted was to elicit a statement that this wasn't the end of the world."[91] Some of them may have shared the confident belief later expressed by Robert S. Boyer and J Strother Moore that, since the complexity of theorem proving did not prevent human beings from proving difficult theorems, it implied no inherent limit upon machines, but only made automated proving "more interesting."[92] By 1974, however, said Hayes, "theorem proving folk . . . felt themselves to be intellectual refugees" within artificial intelligence. They feared that Rabin's analysis would be "seized upon by their enemies as a technical approval of their erstwhile purely rhetorical attacks."[93]

Theorem Proving after Resolution

The crisis of the early 1970s was not "the end of the world" for automated theorem proving, but the salience of the topic within artificial intelligence declined rapidly. A key role in preventing it from being eclipsed altogether was played by Woodrow Wilson Bledsoe. Born in Oklahoma in 1921, Bledsoe served in World War II as a captain in the U.S. Army Corps of Engineers, before taking his Ph.D. in mathematics from the University of California at Berkeley. By the late 1950s he was the manager of the systems analysis department of the Sandia nuclear weapons laboratory in Albuquerque, New Mexico. His developing interest in artificial intelligence caused him to leave Sandia in 1960 to help found one of the earliest commercial firms in the field, Panoramic Research Inc. From 1966 on he pursued this work at the University of Texas at Austin. In his 1985 presidential address to the American Association for Artificial Intelligence, he recalled:

Twenty-five years ago I had a dream. . . . I dreamed of a special kind of computer, which had eyes and ears and arms and legs, in addition to its "brain." . . . [M]y dream was filled with the wild excitement of seeing a machine act like a human being, at least in many ways. . . . When I awoke from this day-dream, I found that we didn't have these things, but we did have some remarkable computers, even then, so I decided then and there to quit my job and set about spending the rest of my life helping to bring this dream to reality. . . . Recently a reporter asked me, "Why do you scientists do AI [artificial intelligence] research?" My answer, "Well certainly not for money, though I wouldn't mind being rich. It goes deeper, to a *yearning* we have to make machines act in some fundamental ways like people."[94]

Bledsoe's early research in automated theorem proving was on resolution and on a new decision procedure for Presburger arithmetic, but, like others in the early 1970s, he was sharply disappointed with the limitations of resolution provers. He responded, however, not by abandoning theorem proving, but by devoting himself to the development of what he called "nonresolution" theorem proving, a more "human-like" approach: "The word 'knowledge' is a key to much of this modern theorem proving. Somehow we want to use the knowledge accumulated by humans over the last few thousand years, to help direct the *search* for proofs."[95]

Like the MIT group, Bledsoe believed that resolution was an overly uniform proof procedure. He was impressed by the new procedural programming languages, such as PLANNER, developed by Carl Hewitt of the MIT group,[96] which were designed to facilitate domain-specific inference procedures. Furthermore, Bledsoe felt that much of the legacy of formal logic was inappropriate to "human-like" automated theorem proof. Inference rules should be "natural," he argued.[97] Logicians had typically been concerned to restrict to a minimum the number of inference rules employed in logical systems. That simplified proofs of "theorems *about* logics,"[98] but Bledsoe did not want to prove theorems about logics: he wanted to design systems that proved mathematical theorems in a way at least loosely analogous to how human mathematicians did it. In particular, unlike the logicians, who prized the completeness[99] of formal systems, Bledsoe was unconcerned if the proof procedures he used were incomplete as long as they yielded more natural and more powerful proofs.

Like Herbert Simon and Allen Newell, Bledsoe believed that the development of appropriate heuristics was essential. His first efforts in this direction, reported in 1971, were in the mathematical theory of sets. He developed heuristics (some general, some specifically designed for set theory) the effect of which "is to break the theorem [to be proved] into parts which are easier to prove." When resolution was used, it was "relegated to the job it does best, proving relatively easy assertions."[100] He tested out his theorem prover on theorems from a set-theory textbook written by his mathematics Ph.D. supervisor, A. P. Morse.[101]

In at least one case, Bledsoe's system found a proof that was, he believed, "more direct and natural" than Morse's: the new heuristics "reduced [the theorem] to its *essence*," and the automated system "acted 'humanlike' in getting to the 'nub of the problem.' "[102] Soon Bledsoe abandoned resolution altogether in favor of a "rather natural" procedure for handling deductions in predicate logic "which we believe is faster and easier to use (though not complete)" and which "bears a closer resemblance to the proof techniques of the mathematician than does resolution."[103] The new procedure, together with a "limit heuristic" specifically designed to aid proofs in calculus, and routines for algebraic simplification and for solving linear inequalities, produced a theorem prover that could prove many theorems of elementary calculus, an area in which existing resolution provers had had little success.

In its focus on "humanlike" inferences, Bledsoe's work can be seen as a continuation of the original, artificial intelligence, goals of Simon, Newell, and Gelernter. In contrast, the theorem-proving group at the Argonne National Laboratory, the location of Alan Robinson's development of resolution, favored the same trade-off as Robinson had: more powerful automated inference, at the cost of performing that inference in ways unlike those used by human beings. They were, quite consciously, not swayed by the priorities dominant in artificial intelligence: "our approach to the automation of reasoning differs sharply from approaches one often finds in artificial intelligence; indeed, our paradigm relies on types of reasoning and other procedures that are *not* easily or naturally applied by a person."[104] Even as Alan Robinson worked on resolution, others at Argonne (notably George Robinson, who was no relation) were working on broadly similar lines[105] and they continued to do so. For example, Larry Wos and George Robinson developed the new resolution-style proof procedures of "demodulation" and "paramodulation,"[106] and increasingly sophisticated strategies were developed for guiding resolution provers' search processes.

Allied to this conceptual work were practical improvements (focusing on matters such as indexing, and the storage and retrieval of clauses), and a growing understanding of how to tune a resolution prover for particular problems, for example, by altering the weights governing search strategies. Even a "logically irrelevant" matter such as the order in which axioms are entered into the system was found to influence whether a given theorem could be proved, because it affected the order in which clauses were considered. For several years, the Argonne group—whose main systems were AURA (AUtomated Reasoning Assistant) and OTTER, developed by William McCune—attracted little attention, working as it was in a tradition that had widely been deemed a failure.

At the end of the 1970s and in the early 1980s, however, the group's dedicated theoretical and practical work started to pay off, as the Argonne provers began to be applied successfully, not just to theorems for which proofs were already known, but to the proof of open conjectures in several specialized fields of mathematics (conjectures that human mathematicians had formed but which they had been unable themselves to prove). In 1996 this work even reached the pages of the *New York Times,* when William McCune of Argonne used an equational logic theorem prover to solve the Robbins problem, a six-decade-old open question in Boolean algebra. The final, successful search for a proof required large amounts of computer time—it "took about 8 days on a RS/6000 processor"—and drew upon Argonne work on the problem that stretched back to 1979.[107]

Minds and Machines

Although the Argonne group's provers made no attempt to mimic human problem solving, the reportage of their success with the Robbins problem was inexorably drawn to reconstruct a link to artificial intelligence. "Brute Computers Show Flash of Reasoning Power," was how the *Times* headlined the work: "The achievement would have been called creative if a human had done it."[108] The connection between automated theorem proving and artificial intelligence was forged, rhetorically, from the earliest years of the latter field. To the proponents of artificial intelligence, the Logic Theory Machine "gave the first justification to the claim that artificial intelligence was a science."[109]

In a 1958 article that was a celebrated manifesto for their "heuristic problem solving" form of artificial intelligence, Simon and Newell made four predictions of what would be accomplished within the next ten years: that "a digital computer will be the world's chess champion, unless the rules bar it from competition"; that "a digital computer will discover and prove an important new mathematical theorem"; that "a digital computer will write music that will be accepted by critics as possessing considerable aesthetic value"; and that "most theories in psychology will take the form of computer programs, or of qualitative statements about the characteristics of computer programs."[110]

The goal of mechanizing aspects of what many took to be the essence of humanness meant that artificial intelligence was a controversial field from its earliest years on. Given the ambition and the salience of Simon and Newell's predictions for the new field, its critics quickly focused on the slowness of progress toward their four milestones. The closest that the second of the predictions—automated discovery and proof of an important theorem—came to fulfillment, within Simon and Newell's allotted time span, was in 1966 when a group of researchers at the Applied Logic Corporation in Princeton, New Jersey, was developing a series of systems they called SAM, or semiautomated mathematics.[111]

In 1966 this group was using the fifth of these systems, "SAM V," implemented on a time-sharing PDP-6 computer, to construct proofs of theorems from a 1965 article by Robert Bumcrot in the area of modern algebra known as lattice theory.[112] The mathematician using SAM V realized that the system had proved an intermediate result that yielded "as an immediate consequence" the proof of a conjecture Bumcrot had posited but not proved. Some generosity was required, however, to see "SAM's lemma" as an important theorem, and the SAM system was an interactive one in which a human user provided detailed guidance to theorem proving. On its own, its developers admitted, it "was not capable of recognizing the value of all the consequences of many of the proven formulas": the human user had to do that.[113]

Two interpretations of the failure of Simon and Newell's predictions were possible. Artificial intelligence could simply be a more difficult goal than had been assumed at the start of the field; or it could be an impossible one, a contradiction in terms. Naturally, artificial intelligence's critics tended to the second of these interpretations. The best-known of these critics, the philosopher Hubert L. Dreyfus, did little more than touch upon automated theorem proving in his critique. He mocked an inflated claim made by W. Ross Ashby, author of *Design for a Brain,* for Minsky's proof of the theorem that the angles at the base of an isosceles triangle are equal (a proof mistakenly attributed by Ashby to the Geometry Machine), and he also noted the superior efficiency of Wang's nonheuristic theorem-proving program compared to the Logic Theory Machine.[114]

A more fundamental line of critique of automated theorem proving, which posited an inherent limit upon what any machine could ever do, focused on Kurt Gödel's famous incompleteness theorems.[115] Put loosely, Gödel showed in 1931 that any consistent formal system capable of encompassing arithmetic must be incomplete.[116] By the device now called "Gödel numbering," he established a mapping between the formulas of the formal system, S, and the integers, and thus a mapping between "metamathematical" statements about S and arithmetical propositions. He then constructed a formula A within S that, in effect, asserted its own unprovability within S. Gödel then showed that either the provability within S of A, or the provability of not-A, would demonstrate that S was inconsistent;[117] so if S is consistent, neither A nor not-A is provable within S. Since the unprovability of A within S means in effect that what A asserts is true, S contains a true but unprovable formula. Nor could the situation be rescued by adding A to the axioms of S: Gödel's procedure could then be applied to the enlarged system to generate a further true but formally unprovable formula; addition of that formula to the axioms generates another unprovable formula; and so on. Any finite consistent formal system encompassing arithmetic must contain a true proposition not provable within the system.

Gödel's work was a serious blow to the then influential competitor to Russell and Whitehead's logicism: the "formalist" program spearheaded by the German mathematician David Hilbert. Hilbert, in part spurred by the challenge from the "intuitionist" mathematician L. E. J. Brouwer (see chapter 8), hoped for "finitistic" proofs of the consistency of formalized mathematics. Gödel's second incompleteness theorem, however, a corollary of the first, showed that the consistency of S could not be proved within S.[118] If a formal system capable of encompassing arithmetic is consistent, then the fact of its consistency cannot be proved within the system.

Gödel's theorems were striking, even startling, results, and his proofs involved a new, complicated form of reasoning. Though there were doubters, notably the German mathematician Ernst Zermelo, Gödel's reasoning was accepted, and indeed refined, by those who had most to lose, the key figures of formalism: David Hilbert and his students Paul Bernays and John von Neumann. By the end of the 1930s, "serious opposition to Gödel's work, at least within the community of logicians" had been stilled.[119] What Gödel's incompleteness theorems implied for the philosophy of mathematics, however, remained controversial. Gödel himself became an adherent to the venerable Platonist viewpoint, according to which mathematical entities are quasi-objects that exist in a nonempirical realm of ideas, and, in a 1967 letter to Hao Wang, he suggested that his success in reaching the incompleteness theorems could be attributed to his philosophical convictions.[120]

With the exception of some of the systems based on decision procedures, the computerized theorem provers discussed in this chapter automated formal, symbol-manipulating proof of the kind whose limitations Gödel had diagnosed. Even the Logic Theory Machine's proofs were of this kind: the search for a proof might be guided by a heuristic, but the proof itself was formal. It is not surprising, therefore, that it struck several people that Gödel's theorems could be turned not just against formalism but against artificial intelligence. Could a machine grasp the "informal"[121] reasoning, outside of system S, by which human beings convince themselves that the Gödel sentence A, though unprovable within S, is true? Did Gödel's incompleteness theorems not show that a computer, implementing proof in a formal system, was indeed, in Wang's words, a "persistent plodder," not a "thinking machine"? Might humans have insights into the apparently Platonic realm of mathematical truth that will forever be denied to machines?

That Gödel's incompleteness theorem refuted the reduction of minds to machines was argued in 1959 by the Oxford philosopher John Lucas. "Gödel's Theorem seems to me to prove that Mechanism is false," said Lucas. He did not claim this to be an original conclusion—"almost every mathematical logician I have put the matter to has confessed to similar thoughts"—but Lucas sought to set out the "whole argument . . . with all objections fully stated and properly met." According to Lucas, "it is of the essence of being a machine, that it should be a concrete instantiation of a formal system." Gödel had shown that a consistent formal system capable of encompassing arithmetic must contain a formula that was "unprovable-in-the-system." Given any machine capable of arithmetic, there must therefore be a formula which the machine cannot prove; however, "we [human beings] can see [the formula] to be true. It follows that no machine can be a complete or adequate model of the mind, that minds are essentially different from machines."[122]

How could human beings "see" the truth of a theorem that could not be proved within a given formal system? The answer, suggested Lucas, lay in the fact that human beings, unlike "inanimate objects," were "self-conscious." The unprovable formula was "self-referring": it was, in effect, the statement that "This formula is unprovable-in-this-system." No machine could "see" the truth of this self-referring formula, because "[t]he machine is being asked a question about its own processes. We are asking it to be self-conscious, and say what things it can and cannot do." On the other hand, "a conscious being can be aware of itself." From "mechanist determinism" a most undesirable consequence had appeared to flow: "that we must look on human beings as determined automata and not as autonomous moral agents." His Gödelian argument, it appeared to Lucas, had banished this "bogey." He had shown "mechanical models of the mind" and "explanations in purely mechanist terms" to be inadequate: "no scientific inquiry can ever exhaust the infinite variety of the human mind."[123]

Lucas did not refer explicitly to artificial intelligence, which was only nascent when he wrote. Thirty years later, however, the Gödelian argument against mechanism was taken up again by Roger Penrose, Rouse Ball Professor of Mathematics at Oxford University, in a best-selling 1989 attack on artificial intelligence, *The Emperor's New Mind*. "[B]y the very way that [the unprovable Gödel formula] is constructed we [human beings] can *see,*" wrote Penrose, "using our insight and understand[ing] about what the symbols in the formal system are supposed to mean, that the [unprovable] Gödel proposition is actually *true!* This tells us that the very concepts of truth, meaning, and mathematical insight cannot be encapsulated within any formalist scheme." This result, Penrose claimed, was "not just bad news for the formalists," and support for his own Platonist view of mathematics. "It is bad news for strong-AI [artificial intelligence], as well."[124]

Both Lucas's and Penrose's arguments sparked controversy. Lucas attracted criticism mainly from his fellow philosophers. Paul Benacerraf, for example, questioned whether machines were capable only of formal proof: might they not also be capable of an informal proof of the truth of the Gödel formula? Judson Webb argued that self-reference was an "epiphenomenon" of the particular way Gödel generated his undecidable formula, and Webb constructed another undecidable formula that did not say anything "about itself."[125] Penrose, too, was widely attacked. Martin Davis, for example, echoed a point made earlier by Benacerraf against Lucas: that to know the truth of the Gödel sentence one had to know that the formal system was consistent. The "true but unprovable Gödel sentence" can actually be "provided by an *algorithm,*" said Davis. "If *insight* is involved, it must be in convincing oneself that the given axioms are indeed consistent, since otherwise we will have no reason to believe that the Gödel sentence is true. But here things are quite murky: Great logicians (Frege, Curry, Church, Quine, Rosser) have managed to propose quite serious systems of logic which later have turned out to be inconsistent. 'Insight' didn't help." Penrose "thinks he knows he is consistent," added Pat Hayes and two colleagues, but, like any human being, "he will never be able to establish this, for he does not really know it. He only thinks he knows."[126]

The "computationalist thesis" of artificial intelligence—that human intelligence can be understood as computation—"accepts the limitations placed on us by Gödel," said Pat Hayes and his colleagues. Those limitations were incompatible only "with a kind of grandiose self-confidence that human thought has some kind of magical quality which resists rational description," and for Hayes and his colleagues that formulation described Platonist claims "that any mathematical statement which one proves can be known by direct mathematical intuition." Mathematics was a public, not a private, activity. If someone were to claim that "she could simply *see*" the truth or falsity of some mathematical result, "we would require the claimant to explain and justify this insight . . . and if she were unable to do so, it would not be regarded as having been mathematically established." The computationalist thesis did not claim that a particular computer program could reproduce all the methods available to the entire mathematical community, now and in the future. All it claimed was "that the theorems resulting from the correct methods of individual mathematicians can be reproduced by individual machines."[127]

Automating Mathematical Discovery

That what machines were simulating was the deductive processes of individual mathematicians is a point of some interest discussed in chapter 9. More usually, however, the debates sparked by the Gödelian attacks on "mechanism" and especially on artificial intelligence, like today's "science wars," are more interesting as indicators of cultural tensions than for their detailed content. Penrose's critique of artificial intelligence, for example, propelled him onto the best-seller lists, not the usual fate of authors discussing topics such as the λ-calculus (see chapter 8). The computer's Turklean status as "evocative object"[128] meant that whether or not it could become in any sense an artificial mathematician could never be simply a technical question.

The mechanization of proof did not exhaust the possibilities of automating what human mathematicians do. They also, for example, solve equations, differentiate and integrate, and manipulate algebraic expressions and matrices; especially in applied mathematics, these activities can sometimes become very complicated. The automation of these areas has been strikingly successful: from the early 1960s onward, a range of programs has become available that perform them, programs such as MACSYMA, MAPLE, and the currently widely used and well-known MATHEMATICA.[129] Impressive in their capabilities though these programs are, they did not spark Turklean issues about artificial intelligence. More likely to do that, because closer to a widely shared sense of what it was to be intelligent, was the automation of mathematical discovery. Mathematicians develop concepts, study the relationship between those concepts, and construct conjectures that might or might not be provable. A machine with a claim to be an artificial mathematician would not just have to be able to prove theorems, but, as indicated by Simon and Newell's second prediction for the future of artificial intelligence, also able to discover them.

The automation of mathematical discovery, however, has been the focus of much less activity than the automation of mathematical proof.

The former field has been dominated by a single system, Douglas B. Lenat's AM. "Originally," said Lenat, AM was the acronym of automated mathematician, "but somewhere in the 1974–75 time period I got enough humility to let it just be called AM."[130] A graduate student at Stanford University, Lenat received his Ph.D. for his work on AM in 1976.[131] Lenat provided AM with the definitions of 115 concepts, largely from set theory, which were "meant to be those possessed by young children (age 4, say)." No notion of number and no notion of proof were provided, but AM was given 250 heuristics to guide mathematical discovery: "rules of thumb" like "If f is an interesting function, consider its inverse," so that if the program discovered, for example, multiplication, it will be led to division. "AM is not supposed to be a model of a child," wrote Lenat. "[T]hough it possesses a child's ignorance of most concepts, AM is given a large body of sophisticated 'adult' heuristics."[132]

After providing AM with its initial concepts, heuristics, and rules for determining a concept's "worth" (involving considerations such as the ratio of examples of a concept to nonexamples of it), Lenat set the program loose to find out how much of mathematics it would discover for itself. "Most of the obvious set-theory relations . . . were eventually uncovered," wrote Lenat. "After this initial period of exploration, AM decided that 'equality' was worth generalizing, and thereby discovered the relation 'same-size-as.' 'Natural numbers' were based on this, and soon most simple arithmetic operations were defined." After defining multiplication, for example, AM's heuristics led it to investigate "the process of multiplying a number by itself: squaring." The heuristics then led it to the inverse of squaring and thus to the concept of square root. Investigation of numbers with minimal numbers of factors led it to "what we call primes." It "conjectured the fundamental theorem of arithmetic (unique factorization into primes) and Goldbach's conjecture (every even number greater than 2 is the sum of two primes)." AM also investigated concepts not part of the normal corpus of human mathematics, such as "maximally divisible numbers": those numbers such that any number smaller than them has a smaller number of divisors.[133]

AM aroused considerable interest on the Stanford campus. Computer scientist Donald Knuth, for example, "used to pore through the outputs of AM as if he were going through Babylonian or Aztec scrolls or hieroglyphics—looking for things that I and the system didn't realize were valuable," said Lenat. George Polya (popularizer of the notion of heuristics), then in his late 80s, told Lenat that AM's investigation of maximally divisible numbers reminded him of "something the student of a friend of mine once did." Polya's friend turned out to be the great number theorist G. H. Hardy (1877–1947), and his "student" the Indian mathematician Srinivasa Ramanujan (1889–1920), who, equipped with little more than the beginnings of a college education and a single textbook, produced in isolation a remarkable set of conjectures of which some were, in Hardy's words, "familiar," some "scarcely possible to believe," some "definitively false." Lenat liked the connection. "[P]erhaps a more faithful image" of AM than the child, he wrote, "is that of Ramanujan, a brilliant modern mathematician who received a very poor education, and was forced to rederive much of known number theory all by himself. Incidentally, Ramanujan never did master the concept of formal proof."[134]

In the divide between artificial intelligence's "neats" and "scruffies," AM was an archetypal scruffy program. The term is not pejorative: human thinking, after all, can be seen as typically scruffy rather than logically neat, and in the words of Lenat's fellow Stanford Ph.D. student, Randall Davis, "the whole idea behind AM was to recapture the spirit of mathematics as it's actually done, not as it's recast later in clean proofs and logical formalisms."[135] AM was "a large LISP program," wrote Lenat, with "the usual battery of customized functions . . . hacks and . . . bugs."[136] Lenat's effort also resonated down the divide that separated artificial intelligence from logic. The Stanford geneticist and Nobel laureate Joshua Lederberg had developed an interest in artificial intelligence, collaborating with Edward Feigenbaum (the student witness to Simon's announcement of his development of the "thinking machine") in the construction of DENDRAL, an early "expert system" for determining the structure of organic molecules from the results of mass spectroscopy.[137] Lederberg sent Hao Wang a copy of Lenat's thesis. The logician was no more impressed by AM than he had been by the Logic Theory Machine. "I found [Lenat's thesis] thoroughly unwieldy," wrote Wang, "and could not see how one might further build on such a baffling foundation."[138]

In England at the University of Kent, two computer scientists with an interest in artificial intelligence, Keith Hanna and Graeme Ritchie, decided to reimplement AM, believing it to be an appropriate application on which to test ideas of distributed, parallel computing with which Hanna was working. They found they could not find a clear enough specification of what the program was intended to do and abandoned the effort.[139] They came to share Wang's criticism of Lenat, broadening it into a critique of the way such work in artificial intelligence was reported.

Ritchie and Hanna conceded that AM was "a substantial piece of work in AI [artificial intelligence], and seems to contain a large amount of originality, creativity and detailed effort," and they accepted that Lenat, "has attempted (more than most other workers in AI) to render his program available to public assessment, both by making it available for running and by supplying . . . detailed appendices in his thesis." Nevertheless, Ritchie and Hanna argued that even with "this unusual level of documentation," the theoretical content of AM was unclear, like that of many "large impressive-looking" AI programs. The crucial point in AM's process of automated mathematical discovery was when it moved from set-theoretic concepts to develop the notion of number. "[M]ost of the later 'discoveries' depend on this one," said Ritchie and Hanna: "if numbers are not found, AM cannot go on to further triumphs." They wrote, however, "it is possible to gain the impression that the successful 'discovery' [of numbers] was the result of various specially designed pieces of information, aimed at achieving this effect."[140]

Lenat was unmoved by Ritchie and Hanna's criticism of his program. He denied "[t]uning the system extensively (except to improve its use of space and time)." AM did indeed find the concept of natural number "all by itself," he said, although he and his colleague John Seely Brown conceded that "concepts such as 'Bag' and 'Set-Equality' took it halfway there to begin with."[141] More profoundly, Lenat and Brown felt that Lenat's critics misread what he was trying to do. Ritchie and Hanna "appear to treat Lenat's thesis as if it were a formal proof of a theorem, in which finding even the tiniest inconsistency or irregularity from the clean control structure claimed therein would 'refute' it." But, argued Lenat and Brown, "AI research is rarely like proving a theorem. The AM thesis is not making a formal claim about a provable property of a small, clean algorithm; AM is a demonstration that little more than a body of plausible heuristic rules is needed to adequately guide an 'explorer' in elementary mathematics theory formation."[142]

Just as Simon and Newell's Logic Theory Machine was only a staging post in their search for artificial intelligence, so Lenat moved on from the automation of mathematics to more general, intensely ambitious efforts, in his case eventually to Cyc, a long-term, also controversial, effort (heavily funded by a number of major corporations, such as Bellcore, DEC, and Kodak) to develop "a huge knowledge base, one that spans most of what humans call common sense."[143] Although others advanced Newell and Simon's early work in theorem proving, Lenat's work on the automation of mathematical discovery was not taken up widely.[144] AM remained an essentially isolated, controversial, demonstration that this, the most creative part of the mathematician's work, could be automated.

Missing Mathematicians

If the lack of attention to mathematical discovery is a "technical" absence from the history of the automation of mathematical proof, there is also a striking "social" absence: the small involvement of mainstream mathematicians. Leading figures within artificial intelligence contributed, as did prominent philosophers and logicians such as Wang, Davis, and Putnam. In contrast, few well-known mathematicians played a salient part in the history of automated proving. Penrose is a mathematician, as was Sir James Lighthill, Lucasian Professor of Applied Mathematics at Cambridge University, whose damning 1972 report on artificial intelligence famously suggested that "pseudomaternal" urges played their part, especially among male robot builders compensating "for lack of the female capability of giving birth to children."[145] Penrose and Lighthill, though, were critics of artificial intelligence, not developers of automated theorem provers.

In part the small contribution of career mathematicians to automated theorem proving was simply the result of the incapacity of fully automatic provers (at least until the successes of the Argonne systems) to handle theorems that a mathematician would consider challenging. Mathematicians also showed little interest, however, in the less highly automated but more capable "proof checkers." These are systems that are provided with a full (or nearly full) formal proof, constructed by a human being, and that check whether this proof is indeed a correct one. The most influential such system was AUTOMATH, developed in 1967–1968 at the Technische Hogeschool Eindhoven by N. G. de Bruijn and colleagues. AUTOMATH "is defined by a grammar, and every text written according to its rules is claimed to correspond to correct mathematics. . . . The rules are such that a computer can be instructed to check whether texts written in the language are correct."[146] For example, L. S. van Benthem Jutting, a student of de Bruijn, translated into AUTOMATH and automatically checked the proofs from Edmund Landau's text, *Grundlagen der Analysis*.[147]

Such achievements, however, aroused little enthusiasm among mathematicians. As two mathematicians commented: "The formalized counterpart of normal proof material is difficult to write down and can be very lengthy. . . . Mathematicians . . . are not really interested in doing this kind of thing."[148] Later analogues of AUTOMATH—a Polish-developed system called MIZAR, and QED, an ambitious American-led proposal for a giant computerized encyclopedia of formally, mechanically proved mathematics—appear likewise to have sparked only limited interest within the mainstream mathematical community.[149]

The difficulty and length of formal proofs are certainly a major cause of the absence of any widespread adoption by mathematicians of automated proof checkers. But are they the entirety of the explanation? In the latter half of the 1970s, computerized proof was catapulted to the center of mathematicians' attention by the partially automated proof of one of the most famous, indeed perhaps *the* most famous, unsolved mathematical problem: the four-color conjecture. The history of that proof, and the way it revealed many mathematicians' ambivalence about, and even hostility to, the use of computers in proof, is the subject of chapter 4.

4

Eden Defiled

To the observer, it "seemed like the perfect setting" for one of the climactic moments of twentieth-century mathematics. Packing the "elegant and old lecture hall" of the University of Toronto in August 1976 were the attendees at one of the high points of the mathematician's year, the summer meeting of the American Mathematical Society and Mathematical Association of America. The speaker was Wolfgang Haken of the University of Illinois, and from leaks to the press the audience already knew what he was going to announce: a proof of the famous four-color conjecture, that four colors suffice to color in any map drawn upon a plane in such a way that no countries that share a border are given the same color.

Every mathematician and many laypersons knew the conjecture: in the judgment of some, it was the "most fascinating unsolved problem of mathematics." Over the preceding century, many professional mathematicians and a host of amateurs had attempted to prove it. All had failed, some sacrificing their careers and perhaps even their sanity to the compulsive belief that the result, so simple to state, must be provable. "It is dangerous to work close to The Problem," wrote W. T. Tutte, one of the leaders of the field of mathematics to which the four-color conjecture belonged, graph theory. Yet Haken, and his collaborators Kenneth Appel and John Koch, had done just that and had succeeded: they had finally solved this notoriously "man-eating problem."[1]

No wonder, then, that the observer expected that when Haken had finished "the audience [would] erupt with a great ovation." Only "polite applause," however, greeted him. "[P]uzzled" by this "cool reception," the observer circulated among the audience, seeking the reason: "Mathematician after mathematician expressed uneasiness with a proof in which a computer played a major role." Many suggested—and the observer came to speculate they hoped—that "there might be an error buried in the hundreds of pages of computer print outs" that Haken and his colleagues had generated. Nor did the unease cease with the Toronto meeting. In 1982 Frank Bonsall, Professor of Mathematics at the University of Edinburgh, denied that computerized analysis should be considered mathematical proof:

> . . . if the solution involves computer verification of special cases . . . such a solution does not belong to mathematical science at all. . . . We cannot possibly achieve what I regard as the essential element of a proof—our own personal understanding—if part of the argument is hidden away in a box. . . . Perhaps no great harm is done, except for the waste of resources that would be better spent on live mathematicians, so long as we do not allow ourselves to be content with such quasi-proofs. We should regard them as merely a challenge to find a proper proof. . . . [L]et us avoid wasting those funds on pseudo mathematics with computers and use them instead to support a few real live mathematicians.

In 1990 Paul Halmos, one of the world's most distinguished mathematicians, told the summer meeting of the Mathematical Association of America: "We are still far from having a good proof of the Four Color Theorem. I hope as an article of faith that the computer missed the right concept and the right approach. . . . The present proof relies in effect on an Oracle, and I say down with Oracles! They are not mathematics." Appel and Haken remembered telling a mathematician friend of theirs in 1975 that they believed they could prove the four-color conjecture using a computer. The mathematician, they recalled, "exclaimed in horror, 'God would never permit the best proof of such a beautiful theorem to be so ugly.' " Even Appel and Haken could sympathize with the reaction: "When faced with such a proof even the fairest minded mathematician can be forgiven for wishing that it would just go away rather than being forced to think about the fact that an 'elegant' proof may never appear and thus our Eden is defiled."[2]

Origins

The four-color conjecture has its roots in the widespread convention in map-making of assigning different colors to adjacent districts or countries, so that their borders can be distinguished readily from other lines such as those indicating railways or rivers. Its attraction to mathematicians was not practical, however, but lay instead in its tantalizing combination of simplicity of statement and difficulty of solution. There is no evidence that mapmakers had sought to find the minimum number of colors that would suffice. Historian of mathematics Kenneth May finds no discussion of this topic in books on map-making, nor any tendency in practice to use only the minimum number of colors. Prior to printing, there was no reason to use only a minimum number of the colors available, while printers could overcome the constraints of a limited set of inks by "printing one color over another . . . hatching and shading."[3] May showed that the originator of the conjecture was a graduate of University College London, Francis Guthrie (1831–1899). From the college, Guthrie earned first a B.A. (in 1850) and then an Ll.B. (in 1852), before going to South Africa in 1861 to become Professor of Mathematics at Graaff-Reinet College and then at the South African College in Cape Town.[4]

Around 1852 while coloring a map of England, Guthrie guessed that, in De Morgan's words: "if a figure be anyhow divided, and the compartments differently coloured, so that figures with any portion of common boundary *line* are differently coloured—four colours may be wanted, but not more."[5] He easily showed that there were maps for which three colors are not enough (see figure 4.1), and he suspected that four were always enough, but could not find a proof "altogether satisfactory to himself."[6] He told his younger brother, Frederick Guthrie, also a University College student, and on October 23, 1852, Frederick put the conjecture to his professor, the well-known English mathematician Augustus De Morgan.

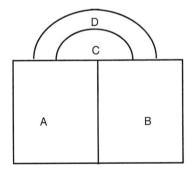

Figure 4.1
A map that cannot be colored with fewer than four colors. Based upon figure in Augustus De Morgan to William Rowan Hamilton, October 23, 1852. A copy of this letter can be found in Rudolf Fritsch and Gerda Fritsch, *The Four-Color Theorem: History, Topological Foundations, and Idea of Proof*, trans. Julie Peschke (New York: Springer, 1998), p. 7.

De Morgan was intrigued and quickly realized that the simplicity of the question hid difficult issues; he wrote that very day to the Irish mathematician, William Rowan Hamilton: "it is tricky work, and I am not sure of all convolutions."[7] De Morgan's letter failed to arouse Hamilton's interest: "I am not likely to attempt your 'quaternion of colours' very soon," he replied.[8] Sustained attention to the problem came only a quarter of a century later, when another leading English mathematician, Arthur Cayley, asked the membership of both the London Mathematical Society and the Royal Geographical Society whether anyone had solved it.[9] Cayley's 1878 query sparked considerable interest and prompted the publication, the following year, of the first claimed proof by Alfred Bray Kempe (1849–1922), a Cambridge Wrangler (first-class graduate in mathematics) and former student of Cayley's, who combined an interest in mathematics with a distinguished legal career.[10] It was the start of a hundred years of periodically intense interest in, and effort devoted to, the four-color conjecture.

Maps, Rubber Sheets, and Graphs

How might one prove that four colors suffice to color in any map drawn on a plane in such a way that no countries that share a border are the same color?[11] First, just what is a "map"? In the words of a modern textbook, it is "a partition of an (infinite) plane into finitely many countries that are divided from one another by borders and of which only one country is unbounded."[12] This is an extension of the everyday notion of map: it has become conventional to consider the region outside a map (in the everyday sense) to be another, unbounded, country. A second point is explicit even in De Morgan's first statement of the conjecture, sharing a border means sharing a border line. Countries that meet only at a single point are not considered to share a border (if they were, the map in figure 4.2 would require more than four colors).[13] Third, as Cayley pointed out, the conjecture can be true only for "countries" that are single, connected regions.[14] If a region that is made up of separate, disjoint parts is allowed to be a "country," then a counterexample, such as figure 4.3, is easy to construct.[15]

These last two qualifications excluded all readily constructable counterexamples to the four-color conjecture. As Cayley put it, "in any tolerably simple case it can be seen that four colours are sufficient."[16] Failing to find a counterexample proves nothing, however, because one can never rule out the possibility that some as yet unexamined, possibly

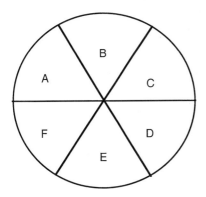

Figure 4.2
Sharing a border means sharing a border line. A and B share a border; A and C do not.

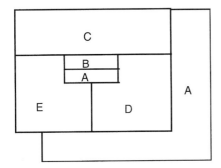

Figure 4.3
"Countries" must be connected regions; otherwise this figure is a counterexample to the four-color conjecture. If the two separate regions labeled "A" are allowed to be one country, this map requires five colors. If the two regions labeled "A" are treated as separate countries, then four colors suffice.

fiendishly complex, map might show the conjecture to be false. In April 1975 the columnist Martin Gardner successfully spoofed many readers of *Scientific American* by publishing, as part of an April Fool's joke, a map that he said was a counterexample to the four-color conjecture (see figure 4.4). It is not, yet the fact that four colors suffice is not obvious immediately: though hundreds of readers sent Gardner four-colorings of the map, many "said the task had taken days."[17]

From the point of view of coloring, the shapes of countries do not matter, only their relative position.[18] Imagine a map drawn upon a

Figure 4.4
Martin Gardner's "April Fool" map. From Gardner, "Mathematical Games," *Scientific American* 232 (April 1975): 126–133, at p. 128. ©1975 by *Scientific American,* Inc. All rights reserved.

rubber sheet (see figure 4.5). Continuously deforming the sheet, for example by stretching it, can radically change the shapes of countries, but the relationship of "neighborhood" between countries does not alter (for example, country D remains surrounded by the other three countries), and thus the coloring problem posed by the map is unchanged. Another important aspect of the problem, first noted by Kempe,[19] is that the four-color conjecture has what mathematicians call a "dual": a superficially quite different conjecture which, if true, implies the truth of the four-color conjecture, and vice versa. To construct the dual, imagine marking the capital city of every country in a map. If two countries have a common border, link up their capitals by a road or railway that does not go through any other country (see figure 4.6).[20]

If one then deletes the original borders one is left with what mathematicians call a graph. The capital cities are the "vertices" of the graph;

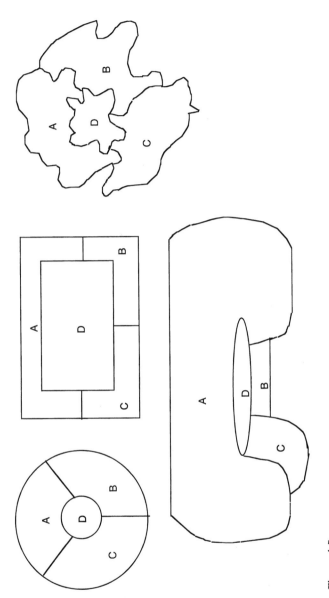

Figure 4.5
Drawing a map on a rubber sheet. All four maps present the same coloring problem: they are topologically identical.

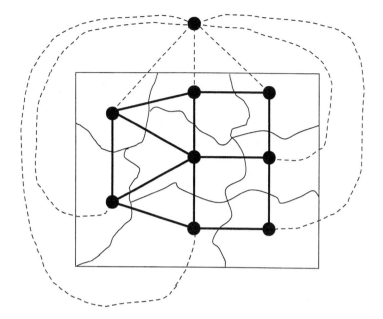

Figure 4.6
A map and its dual graph. The topmost vertex is the "capital" of the unbounded country. For simplicity, it and the lines connecting it to the capitals of its neighbors are omitted from figure 4.7.

the roads joining them are its "edges." Together, they form the graph corresponding to the original map. The map-coloring problem then becomes the "dual" problem of showing that four colors suffice to color the vertices of a planar graph (a graph that can be drawn on a plane without its edges meeting at any point other than a vertex) in such a way that no vertices connected by a single edge are the same color.

In itself, the graph-coloring problem is no more tractable than the map-coloring problem. The duality connects the map-coloring problem, however, to the wider field that has become known as "graph theory."[21] In 1813 the French mathematician, Augustin-Louis Cauchy, proved an important result about planar graphs.[22] A planar graph divides the region of the plane it occupies into a number of regions, which are called "faces." In modern graph theory it has become conventional to count the region surrounding the graph as a face; here Imre Lakatos's reconstruction of this work is followed and only the "internal" faces are counted. Call the number of vertices in a planar graph V, the number of edges E, and the number of faces F. Cauchy's conjecture, in Lakatos's

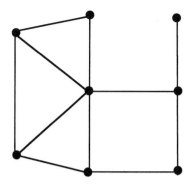

Figure 4.7
Excising an outside edge from the graph in figure 4.6. The number of vertices (V) is unchanged, but both the number of edges (E) and of faces (F) are reduced by one. So $V - E + F$ is unchanged.

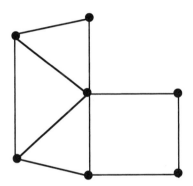

Figure 4.8
Excising a "dangling" vertex from figure 4.7. F is unchanged, but both V and E are reduced by one. So $V - E + F$ is unchanged.

reconstruction, was that $V - E + F = 1$. Inspection shows that this holds, for example, for the graph in figure 4.6.

Again, one cannot hope to *prove* Cauchy's conjecture just by inspecting graphs. A simple argument, however, (a simplification of Cauchy's since here the demands of brevity must outweigh those of historical accuracy) can be deployed to construct a proof. Start with an arbitrary planar graph. Removing an outside edge does not alter $V - E + F$ (figure 4.7); nor does removing a "dangling" vertex (figure 4.8). By progressively removing outside edges and dangling vertices, like a careful gardener pruning a bush, one can eventually reduce the graph to a solitary vertex. For this final graph, V is one, while both E and F are zero, so $V - E + F = 1$. Since $V - E + F$ was unchanged throughout the reduction process, $V - E + F = 1$ for the arbitrary graph with which this began.[23]

Polyhedra and Proof

Cauchy's work was to be drawn on in research on the four-color conjecture (see below), but he was working forty years before it was formulated, so clearly he did not have it in mind. Instead, his formula was a stage in his proof of another famous mathematical conjecture, Leonhard Euler's polyhedral formula, the main subject of Imre Lakatos's well-known study.[24] A polyhedron is a three-dimensional figure each of the faces of which is a polygon (a plane figure bounded by straight lines). Euler's conjecture was that the numbers of vertices (V), edges (E) and faces (F) of any polyhedron are related by $V - E + F = 2$. Euler sought to prove his conjecture by starting with an arbitrary polyhedron and excising tetrahedra (four-faced polyhedra) from it in such a way that $V - E + F$ is not changed, until left with a tetrahedron, for which $V = 4$, $E = 6$ and $F = 4$ (figure 4.9). Euler's proof was, however, later regarded as dubious: "it is not at all obvious that this slicing procedure can always be carried out, and it may give rise to 'degenerate' polyhedra for which the meaning of the formula is ambiguous."[25]

Cauchy's formula can be used, however, to construct a proof of Euler's conjecture. In Lakatos's words: "Let us imagine [an arbitrary] polyhedron to be hollow, with a surface made of thin rubber. If we cut out one of the faces, we can stretch the remaining surface flat . . . without tearing it."[26] The edges and vertices of the flattened polyhedron form a planar graph. (It is this connection to polyhedra that explains the use of the

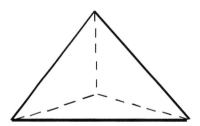

Figure 4.9
A tetrahedron.

terms "vertex," "edge," and "face" when talking about graphs.) The edges of the graph may be curved, but that does not matter since we are in the world of "rubber sheet geometry." Cauchy's theorem applies: $V - E + F = 1$. The original, arbitrary polyhedron had one more face (which was cut out) than the flattened one, so, for the former, $V - E + F = 2$. Cauchy had proved Euler's conjecture.

Or had he? The history of Euler's theorem is littered both with what Lakatos calls "local counterexamples," which refute a particular step in the proof, and with "global counterexamples": apparently polyhedral figures for which $V - E + F \neq 2$. To keep Euler's formula true, "polyhedron" can no longer be defined simply as a three-dimensional figure each of the faces of which is a polygon. That definition includes figures (for example with tunnels, cavities, and multiple structure) where $V - E + F \neq 2$. The meaning of apparently basic terms such as "edge" may have to be reconsidered. Even the apparently simplest part of the above proof of Euler's theorem—the proof of Cauchy's theorem for planar graphs—could be subject to this process. Some anomalous polyhedra, for example, stretch (after the removal of a face) into planar graphs that fall into two disconnected parts. "Pruning" such a graph leads eventually to two isolated vertices, not one, so one needs to make explicit that a "planar graph" here means "connected planar graph," in which it is possible to go from any vertex to any other via a path consisting of edges in the graph. Furthermore, one needs to add an additional condition to this simple proof of Cauchy's theorem: that, when pruning, the graph must be kept connected.

Mathematics, Lakatos concluded, should not be seen as a simple accumulation of clear-cut truths for which unquestionable proofs exist. Even mathematical concepts are "stretchable," and this is not a flaw: concepts "grow."[27] Mathematics is a creative process in which conjectures are formulated, attempts are made to prove them, counterexamples are perhaps found, and conjectures and proofs are subjected to criticism and improvement. To some extent Lakatos's conclusions hold also for the attempts to prove the four-color conjecture, as is shown by the first claimed proof by Kempe. Throughout the 1880s, his argument— which was, for example, carefully scrutinized and clarified by the associate editor of the journal in which he published[28]—appears to have been accepted universally as a proof of the four-color theorem. Cayley and others successfully proposed Kempe's election as a Fellow of the Royal Society, and he went on to become the society's vice-president and treasurer.[29] After more than a decade, however, Kempe's proof was rejected as fallacious.

Kempe's Proof and Heawood's Counterexample

Central to Kempe's claimed proof were the processes of reducing and developing maps, which he explained in terms of fastening or removing a "patch." Figure 4.10 shows an example of reduction; development is removing the patch to reveal the original map. By progressive patching, any map can be "reduced to a single district devoid of boundaries or points of concourse. The whole map is patched out."[30] By removing patches in reverse order, taking off first the last patch to be put on, the original, arbitrary, map can be developed step-by-step. Kempe's goal was to show that the process of development preserved "four-colorability." He wanted to prove that if at any stage in its development the map was four-colorable, then it was still four-colorable at the next stage of its development: that is, when the next patch was removed. Since the completely reduced single district was patently four-colorable (it is one-colorable), that would show that the original, arbitrary, map was four-colorable, and therefore that the four-color conjecture was true.

If the patch to be removed at a particular stage of development covers a country with one, two, or three neighbors, then development clearly preserves four-colorability, since the newly revealed country can simply be colored using a color not used for its neighbors. The difficult cases are countries with four and five neighbors. (Kempe showed by an argument using Cauchy's formula that every map has to contain a country with fewer than six neighbors,[31] so he was able to restrict himself to these cases.) Consider first the case of a country, X, with four neighbors—A, B, C, and D—each of which has been colored using a different color. (If fewer than four colors have been used for A, B, C, and D, then the coloring of X clearly poses no problem.) Here Kempe used the argument that has become known as the method of "Kempe chains" or "Kempe interchanges."[32]

Consider country A (colored, say, red) and country C (colored green). Either they are joined by a continuous chain of red and green countries (as in figure 4.11) or they are not. If they are not joined, one can change A's color to green by swapping the colors red and green in all the red-green countries joined to A. X can then be colored red, and four-colorability is preserved. If A and C are joined by a continuous red-green chain, then the swap does not work. In that case, however, (since one

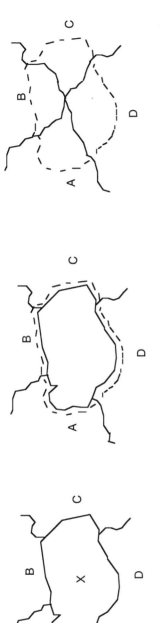

The original map segment

A patch (shown by the dotted line) is placed over country X

The borders of A, B, C and D are joined up on the patch. The "reduced" map has one less country.

Figure 4.10
An example of using a patch to "reduce" a map. In "development," the process is reversed by removing the patch.

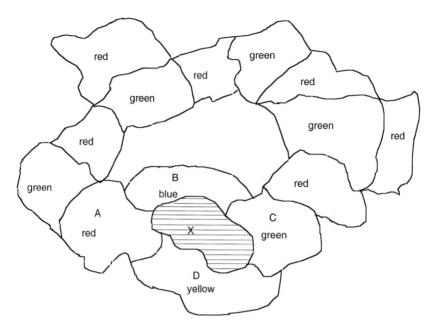

Figure 4.11
If A and C are joined by a continuous chain of red and green countries, B and
D cannot be joined by a continuous chain of blue and yellow countries.

is dealing with a map drawn on a plane) B and D obviously[33] cannot be
joined by a continuous blue-yellow chain (see figure 4.11). So one can
change B's color to yellow by swapping blue and yellow in all blue-yellow
countries joined to B. X can then be colored blue, so four-colorability
is again preserved.

But what about a country with five neighbors, A, B, C, D, and E (see,
for example, figure 4.12)? Can a similar argument be used to show that
colors can be swapped so that a color is left with which to color country
X? Kempe believed it could. It is worth quoting in full his discussion of
this case, since this is the point in Kempe's argument where Percy Heawood (1861–1955), a lecturer at Durham College (later Durham University), was able to construct a counterexample:

If A and C belong to different green and blue regions, interchanging the colours
in either, A and C become both green or both blue. If A and C belong to the
same green and blue region [that is, if there is a continuous green-blue chain
joining A and C], see if A and D belong to different yellow and blue regions; if
they do, interchanging the colours in either region, A and D become both yellow
or both blue. If A and C belong to the same green and blue region, and A and

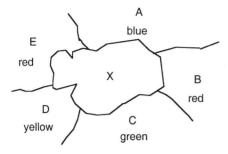

Figure 4.12
A country with five neighbors.

D belong to the same yellow and blue region, the two regions cut off B from E, so that the red and yellow region to which B belongs is different from that to which D and E belong, and the red and green region to which E belongs is different from that to which B and C belong. Thus, interchanging the colours in the red and yellow region to which B belongs, and in the red and green region to which E belongs, B becomes yellow and E green, A, C and D remaining unchanged. In each of the three cases the number of colours [of X's neighbors] is reduced to three.[34]

Heawood's counterexample is shown in figure 4.13:

Mr Kempe says—the transposition of colours throughout E's *red-green* and B's *red-yellow* regions will each remove a red, and what is required is done. If this were so, it would at once lead to a proof of the proposition in question [the four-colour conjecture]. . . . But, unfortunately, it is conceivable that though *either* transposition would remove a red, *both* may not remove both reds. Fig. [4.13] is an actual exemplification of this possibility.[35]

Figure 4.13 shows E's red-green region cross-hatched vertically, and B's red-yellow region horizontally. There is a border at which a green country of the former meets a yellow country of the latter. The two countries cannot both be colored red, preventing one from carrying out *both* the requisite swaps: "either transposition prevents the other from being of any avail . . . so that Mr. Kempe's proof does not hold, unless some modifications can be introduced into it to meet this case of failure."[36]

After Heawood

Kempe accepted that Heawood had refuted his proof of the four-color theorem; he himself reported Heawood's work to the London Mathematical Society, admitting that he "had not succeeded in remedying the

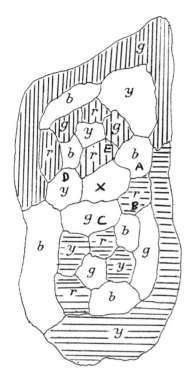

Figure 4.13
Heawood's counterexample to Kempe's proof. b = blue; g = green; r = red;
y = yellow. The X labeling the central country and the A, B, C, D, and E labeling
its five neighbors have been added, as has the cross-hatching. From plate accom-
panying P. J. Heawood, "Map-Color Theorem," *Quarterly Journal of Mathematics*
24 (1890): 332–339.

defect."[37] Neither was Heawood able to do the latter, although he was
"hooked," working on the problem almost until his death in 1955.[38] At
least two other claimed proofs were published—by mathematician and
physicist P. G. Tait and by Frederick Temple, Bishop of London (and
future Archbishop of Canterbury)—but they, likewise, did not stand up
to scrutiny.[39] Heawood's counterexample, however, was (in Lakatos's terminology) a local, not a global, counterexample: Heawood's map could
still be four-colored even though, as Kempe conceded, it showed his
proof to be erroneous.

Four responses to Heawood's refutation of Kempe's proof can be distinguished in subsequent mathematical work. One was to preserve the
main elements of that proof and to try to find a watertight way of han-

dling the specific, troublesome, case of the country with five neighbors. A second response was to reformulate Kempe's strategy for approaching the problem and to try to find a more complicated, but successful, way of implementing it. A third response was to abandon Kempe's approach altogether and to seek another, quite different, more powerful way of proving that four colors suffice. A final option was to conclude that the conjecture might be false and to try to find not a local but a global counterexample: a map that could not be four-colored.

The first response—trying to find a way of directly circumventing Heawood's counterexample—appears to have been abandoned relatively quickly, at least by "serious" professional mathematicians. It was, for example, not listed as an option when George Birkhoff, Professor of Mathematics at Harvard, reviewed plausible alternatives in 1913.[40] Birkhoff did take seriously the last of the above possibilities: that the conjecture might be false. The search for a counterexample that showed its falsity was, however, also a minority pursuit among professional mathematicians, though at least one important contributor to an understanding of the problem, Edward F. Moore of the University of Wisconsin, suspected that the conjecture might be false and produced maps that were deliberate challenges to the eventual main route to the proof.[41] Instead, most efforts concentrated on the second and third of the above options.

To most professional mathematicians, the third option, seeking a quite different approach, appeared most attractive, because the history of mathematics in the nineteenth and twentieth centuries seemed to show that "if you run into terrific complexities, do not go on, but look for more powerful means . . . stronger tools of higher mathematics."[42] The approach taken by Appel and Haken, however, followed the second option—the reformulation and improvement of Kempe's overall strategy[43]—which will be concentrated on here. No attempt will be made to give a full history; instead three key notions will be introduced to understand the later work: a "normal map," an "unavoidable set of configurations," and "reducibility."

A Normal Map

Let us begin with a "normal map": a map in which no bounded country entirely encloses another or others and in which there is no point at which more than three countries meet.[44] Any map can be modified into a normal map that requires as many colors. If, for example, more than three countries meet at a point, two of them cannot share a border. Consider, for instance, the case of four countries meeting at a point (figure 4.14). Suppose the shaded pair of countries share a border somewhere

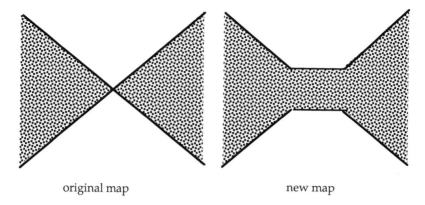

original map   new map

Figure 4.14
Merging two countries with no common border into one. Based upon figure in
Keith Devlin, *Mathematics: The New Golden Age* (London: Penguin, 1988), p. 165.

on the map. This prevents the unshaded pair from having a common
border (the situation is akin to the Kempe chain argument discussed
above). Similarly, if the unshaded pair have a common border, the
shaded pair cannot. Take two countries with no common border and
combine these into one, as in figure 4.14. If the new map can be colored
with N colors, then the original map can also be colored with N colors
by using the same color for the two countries that were combined. By
repeating this process, the map can be altered so that an original map
with more than three countries meeting at a point can be reduced to
one where no more than three meet at the point.

By processes of this kind, one can transform any map into a normal
map that requires as many colors. So to prove that four colors suffice
for any map, it is enough to prove that a normal map requiring five or
more colors is impossible. There is no great difficulty in showing that
six or more colors are never needed: that much can readily be salvaged
from Kempe's argument, even after Heawood's counterexample. Hence,
a proof of the four-color theorem can be constructed by showing the
impossibility of a "five-chromatic" normal map (that is, a normal map
that requires five colors). If there was a normal map that required five
colors, then there must be one with a minimum number of countries,
a "minimal normal five-chromatic map" ("minimal" here means that any
map with fewer countries could be colored with fewer than five colors).
If one can show that a minimal five-chromatic normal map cannot exist,
one has proved the four-color theorem.[45]

An Unavoidable Set of Configurations

So one is searching for a proof by reductio ad absurdum: the reformulated Kempe proof strategy is, in the words of Appel and Haken, to show "that postulating the existence of a minimal normal map requiring five colors leads to a contradiction."[46] Though this sounds different from Kempe's original argument, the latter can readily be restated in these terms and doing so introduces the notion of an "unavoidable set of configurations." Translated into the terminology of normal maps, Kempe had shown that any normal map must contain a country with fewer than six neighbors. This part of Kempe's argument survived Heawood's and later mathematicians' scrutiny: it is here that Euler's polyhedral formula is most directly drawn on in work on the four-color problem (a proof is in an endnote).[47] In Appel and Haken's words, Kempe thus demonstrated that the following set of configurations is unavoidable: "a country with two neighbors . . . a country with three neighbors . . . a country with four neighbors . . . and a country with five neighbors." At least one of these four configurations must be present.[48]

Reducibility

Where Heawood had demonstrated a flaw, however, was in Kempe's argument about *reducibility*. Phrased in terms of the reductio ad absurdum proof strategy, rather than in Kempe's original formulation, what is needed is to show that each of Kempe's unavoidable set of configurations can be reduced: if a five-chromatic normal map contained one of these configurations (as it must), then there would be a five-chromatic map with fewer countries. This would yield the requisite contradiction. There can be no minimal normal map requiring five colors, so there is no map requiring five colors. Unfortunately for Kempe's proof, Heawood's counterexample showed that he had failed to prove the reducibility of the case of a country with five neighbors. Kempe had found an unavoidable set of configurations, but one member of that set was not reducible. The minority tradition to which Appel and Haken's work belonged was the attempt to find an unavoidable set of configurations all of which were reducible, and therefore to complete the reductio ad absurdum proof of the four-color theorem. In the years following Heawood's refutation of Kempe's proof, it gradually became clear that an unavoidable, reducible set would have to be a much more complicated set of configurations than Kempe's, and it was this complication that was eventually to cause this approach to the proof of the four-color theorem to turn to the computer for assistance.

Heinrich Heesch

There is no immediately obvious way of automating the kinds of argument used by Kempe and by Heawood. Crucial steps that made it possible to automate the search for an unavoidable, reducible set of configurations were made by the German mathematician Heinrich Heesch (1906–1995). While an assistant to Hermann Weyl at Göttingen in the early 1930s, Heesch solved what is called the regular tiling problem: he provided a list of all the shapes of regular "tile" that can be used completely to tile the plane and proved that the list is exhaustive. At Göttingen one of Heesch's friends, Ernst Witt, thought he had solved the even more demanding four-color problem. Heesch went with Witt to show the solution to Richard Courant, who was about to leave Göttingen to travel to Berlin. They bought tickets to accompany him, and on the train journey presented Witt's solution. They could not convince Courant that it was a proof of the four-color conjecture, and as the chastened young men returned to Göttingen, Heesch indeed found an error in Witt's proof.[49]

Like Heawood before him, however, Heesch was hooked. His mathematical career, though, was in difficulties. He was not a supporter of the Nazi Party and was unwilling to ingratiate himself with the new regime, particularly disliking the work camps that the Nazis insisted had to be attended by those intending to become professors. For almost two decades, he combined private study of mathematics with work on industrial problems, until in 1955 he finally obtained a teaching post in mathematics at the Technische Universität Hannover. He began to become more and more convinced that the four-color conjecture could be proved by finding an unavoidable set of reducible configurations, even though the set might be extremely large. In 1947 and 1948 he presented his ideas at seminars at the Universities of Hamburg and Kiel. The latter was attended by the young Wolfgang Haken (then a student at Kiel), who recalled Heesch estimating that such a set of configurations might have as many as 10,000 members.[50]

One of Heesch's key contributions to the search for such a set was a method of showing the unavoidability of a set of configurations. The method is most easily thought of by way of an electrical analogy later suggested by Haken. Consider the "dual" form of the four-color conjecture discussed above: that is, the colorability of planar graphs. The part of Kempe's work that was accepted as correct showed that if the graph corresponded to a minimal five-chromatic map, then at least five edges must meet at each vertex of the graph. (A vertex at which fewer than five edges converge corresponds to a country with fewer than five neighbors and thus to a reducible configuration.) The analogy is to think of the planar graph as an electrical network and to imagine giving each vertex an electrical charge. If k edges meet at a vertex, then the vertex has "degree k" and it is given a charge of $6-k$. Vertices of degree 5 (corresponding to countries with five neighbors) thus have a charge of $+1$, vertices of degree 6 have no charge, vertices of degree 7 have charge -1, and so on. Euler's polyhedral formula then implies that the sum of the electrical charges over the entire network must be fixed and positive.[51]

Heesch's method can be thought of as shifting positive charge around the vertices in such a way that the total sum of charges over the network remains constant (taking the positive charge away from degree-five vertices is called "discharging" them). Although there are many complexities to discharging procedures, in Appel and Haken's words the key point is that: "Given a specified discharging procedure on an arbitrary graph, . . . it is possible to make a finite list of all the configurations that, after discharging is done, have vertices of positive charge." Since the network must have an overall positive charge, at least one member of this list must appear in any graph corresponding to a minimal five-chromatic normal map: the list is therefore an unavoidable set of configurations. (If one transfers no charge, only degree-five vertices are positive, corresponding to the unavoidability of Kempe's set of configurations.) Discharging algorithms, in other words, allow the systematic construction of unavoidable sets.[52]

Automating Reducibility

The first use of computers in attempts to prove the four-color theorem, however, was not in the construction of unavoidable sets, but in proofs of reducibility. Early in the twentieth century, proving even one configuration to be reducible was a considerable task. For example, a central result of George Birkhoff's 1913 paper systematizing the notion of "reducibility" was that the configuration shown in figure 4.15 was reducible.[53] Birkhoff's "diamond," as it was later to be called, is a relatively simple configuration. The size of configurations is conventionally measured by the "ring size": the number of countries in the simple closed path, the "ring," surrounding the configuration ($\alpha_1 - \alpha_6$ in figure 4.15). Birkhoff's diamond is a configuration of ring size 6; by the 1970s, configurations with ring sizes of 13, 14, and 15 were being analyzed.

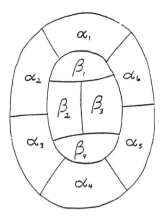

Figure 4.15
Birkhoff's "diamond." From George D. Birkhoff, "The Reducibility of Maps,"
American Journal of Mathematics 35 (1913): 115–128, at p. 125.

Gradually, reducibility proofs increased the so-called "Birkhoff number":
the lower bound on the number of countries in a five-chromatic map.
For example, Philip Franklin showed in 1922 that every map with fewer
than twenty-six countries was four-colorable. By 1968 Oystein Ore and
Joel Stemple showed that a five-chromatic map must contain at least
forty countries. But the detail was increasingly daunting: Ore and Stemple's paper could only outline the proofs involved, and they had to lodge
a separate manuscript laying them out in full in the library of the Yale
Mathematics Department.[54]

Furthermore, "Birkhoff number" proofs did not even approach the
complexity of a full proof of the four-color conjecture. As noted above,
Heesch estimated that an unavoidable set of reducible configurations
might have 10,000 members, and an entirely manual approach to proving the reducibility of thousands of configurations was, clearly, likely to
be infeasible. Heesch systematized the approaches to proving reducibility that had been developed in the half century since Birkhoff's paper,
christening them A-, B-, and C-reducibility, and, crucially, he added his
own method, D-reducibility (D-Reduzibilität), which was sufficiently algorithmic potentially to be implementable on a computer.[55] D-reducibility
applies to the four-color conjecture's graph-theory "dual." Demonstrating D-reducibility involves examining every possible four-coloring of
the vertices forming the ring of a configuration and showing that each
four-coloring of the ring can be extended after a finite number of

Kempe interchanges to a four-coloring of the vertices inside the ring.[56] (The entire graph of which the configuration is a part is, by assumption, a minimal five-chromatic graph, so the entire graph minus the vertices inside the ring is four-colorable. If every four-coloring of the ring can be extended to a four-coloring of the vertices inside the ring, then the entire graph is four-colorable, thus yielding the requisite contradiction.) The need for automation is shown by the fact that there are 199,291 nonequivalent colorings of a 14-ring, each of which has to be shown to be extendable to the vertices inside the ring.[57]

A program for determining D-reducibility was written by Karl Dürre (a Hannover graduate who was working as a mathematics teacher), in the programming language ALGOL 60, for the Control Data Corporation CDC 1604A computer at Hannover. In November 1965 Dürre's program confirmed the reducibility of the Birkhoff diamond and was then used to analyze configurations of ever-increasing complexities. The limitations of the 1604A, however, were quickly encountered. Because each of the different ways of coloring the ring vertices has to be considered, the run-time of a D-reducibility program rises approximately four-fold for each increment of one in the ring size. A 12-ring configuration took around six hours of computing time to analyze, and a 13-ring figure between sixteen and sixty-one hours.[58]

Heesch's and Dürre's work was the harbinger of a spate of interest in applying computers to the proof of the four-color conjecture. With potentially the need to analyze thousands of configurations, run-times of tens of hours on a single configuration were a daunting obstacle, especially in a period when personal computers did not yet exist, and when securing processing time on mainframe computers was hard and expensive. Failure of the D-reducibility program, however, did not demonstrate the irreducibility of the configuration, because it might still be possible to prove it reducible by other, more discriminating methods: Heesch successfully did this in several cases where Dürre's program had failed. The most important such method is what Heesch called "C-reducibility." It involves replacing the configuration with a different subgraph that has fewer vertices (the subgraph is called a "reducer") and generating the requisite contradiction by examining only a subset of the colorings of the ring.[59] C-reducibility is harder to automate than D-reducibility, since the number of possible reducers for a configuration of even modest size is huge; but if a suitable reducer can be found, it may be possible to show that a D-irreducible configuration is nonetheless C-reducible.

"A Blow against Computers"

The most direct way of overcoming the limitations of automated demonstrations of D-reducibility, however, was simply to find a more powerful computer. An initial approach by Heesch, via Wolfgang Haken, to use the University of Illinois supercomputer, ILLIAC IV, was unsuccessful: the controversial machine, with its massively parallel architecture, was too far from completion. John R. Pasta, head of the department of computer science of the University of Illinois, referred Heesch to Yoshio Shimamoto, chair of the applied mathematics department of the U.S. Atomic Energy Commission's Brookhaven Laboratory on Long Island. The commission was the world's single most important customer for high-performance computers, and Brookhaven had a Control Data 6600 designed by the famous supercomputer engineer Seymour Cray and widely acknowledged to be the fastest computer of its day. Shimamoto, by training a theoretical physicist, was himself interested in the four-color problem and had considered writing his own program to study reducibility. He was responsible for managing the Brookhaven computer center, and he was able to arrange for Heesch and Dürre to come there in 1968 and 1969, Heesch spending a year and Dürre nearly two years at Brookhaven.[60]

The Brookhaven 6600 was hugely more powerful than the Hannover 1604A. Configurations of ring size 14, which it was not feasible to analyse for D-reducibility on the latter, now became tractable. First, however, Dürre had to translate his program, originally written in Europe in ALGOL, into the FORTRAN dominant in scientific computing in the United States. After some testing, Dürre's new program worked satisfactorily, and large numbers of configurations were analyzed for reducibility.[61] Together with his earlier work, what Dürre did at Brookhaven won him his doctorate. The list of configurations his program showed to be D-reducible, however, still fell far short of an unavoidable set and therefore of a proof of the four-color conjecture. In August 1971 Heesch returned to Brookhaven to examine whether any of the configurations that Dürre's program had shown to be D-irreducible could be demonstrated to be C-reducible.

In mid-September, Haken too came to visit. Suddenly, however, the atmosphere was electrified not by the two mathematicians, but by the theoretical physicist Shimamoto. He had retained his interest in the four-color conjecture and, in the morning of September 30, during a long

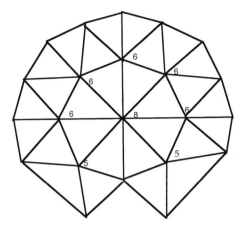

Figure 4.16
The "horseshoe" configuration which Dürre's program had apparently demon-strated to be D-reducible, shown here as its dual graph (with the degrees of some vertices added for clarity). It consists of a central degree-8 vertex surrounded by vertices of degrees 5, 6, 6, 6, 6, 6, 5, and a vertex (shown here as the bot-tommost of those surrounding the central vertex) the degree of which is unde-fined.

meeting with the chairs of other Brookhaven departments, he became bored and "started to 'play' with critical triangulations," building up the figure (4.16) that was to become known as the "horseshoe." Shimamoto's construction showed, directly and succinctly, that the D-reducibility of the horseshoe was incompatible with the existence of a five-chromatic normal map.[62] In other words, if the horseshoe was D-reducible, the four-color conjecture was proved.

As he was returning to his office, Shimamoto saw Heesch and Haken on their way to the cafeteria. He asked Heesch whether the horseshoe was indeed D-reducible. Heesch immediately recognized it as one of the 14-ring configurations that the program had shown to have this prop-erty.[63] It was a truly remarkable development: the enormously elaborate proof that Heesch was constructing could be set aside for a straight-forward, direct piece of reasoning based upon a single figure, or so it appeared.

It all depended, however, on the horseshoe genuinely being D-reducible. On this point, Shimamoto was duly cautious, writing that "In view of the importance of [the horseshoe configuration], plans are being made to write a completely new program to verify Heesch's result."[64]

The most immediate test, however, was to rerun the horseshoe through Dürre's program, which he had left behind at Brookhaven. Shimamoto, even though he directed the computer center, could not monopolize its computers, so he submitted the job to be run on a "time available" basis. When he went to check on it, he found that it had already taken more than an hour longer than that of the original run, so he "had the run terminated."[65] Dürre himself was brought over from Germany, as suspicions grew that the original computer result might be wrong. The printouts of the original run were no longer available, so there was no alternative but to redo the computation. Eventually the computer time was found to do this. Haken recalls that the 6600, ultrafast supercomputer as it was, ground on and on for twenty-six excruciating hours.[66] The machine finally generated the result that the horseshoe was not D-reducible. Despite much scrutiny and testing of the program, no mistake could be found: the deeply disappointing result stood.[67]

Because the records of the original run no longer exist, there is no way of knowing why it was in error. One possibility is that the horseshoe figure had been analyzed when Dürre's rewritten FORTRAN program was still being debugged, and it had ended up in the file of D-reducible figures erroneously and had not been removed.[68] Shimamoto himself was adamant that the two incompatible results were obtained by the use of the same program, and he suggested that the fault may have lain in the earlier "use of a newly installed second computer system before its operation was stable."[69]

Whatever the cause, the episode was more than a private disappointment to Shimamoto. Even as the computer reanalysis at Brookhaven proceeded, word of the apparent stunning breakthrough spread: "In October 1971 the combinatorial world was swept by the rumour that the notorious Four Colour Problem had at last been solved . . . with the help of a computer."[70] The mathematicians who scrutinized Shimamoto's reasoning could find no error. "To my great amazement I found out his theory was correct," recalled Haken.[71] Haken, indeed, gave seminars on it at the Princeton Institute for Advanced Study and at the University of Illinois, and he circulated a paper setting out Shimamoto's argument "clearly and in full logical detail." With that overall argument judged to be correct, "the burden of proof was not now on a few pages of close reasoning, but on a computer!"[72]

Among those whose interest was aroused were two mathematicians acknowledged as being among the leaders of graph theory: Hassler Whitney and William T. Tutte. Tutte wrote in December 1971: "The feeling is that the Four Colour Theorem ought not to have been provable like that,—'by brute force,' . . . I have wavered between belief and disbelief in Shimamoto's proof, but I have never liked it."[73] To Whitney and Tutte, the proof was too simple to be credible:

This method of proof was greeted by the present authors (independently) first with some misgivings and then with real skepticism. It seemed to both of us that if the proof was valid it implied the existence of a much simpler proof (to be obtained by confining one's attention to one small part of [the horseshoe]), and that this simpler proof would be so simple that its existence was incredible. . . . We found no essential flaw in Shimamoto's reasoning. . . . We therefore decided that the computer result must be wrong.

By theoretical reasoning, based upon "an analysis in depth" of D-reducibility, Whitney and Tutte concluded that "the deductions become incredible and are seen to constitute a proof by reductio ad absurdum that [the horseshoe] is not in fact D-reducible."[74]

The episode "was, of course, a blow against computers."[75] Memory of it among graph theorists contributed to the skepticism that met Appel and Haken's result. But Shimamoto's work, and Tutte and Whitney's involvement, contributed to the eventual solution by helping clarify the theory of D-reducibility and by increasing interest in what had hitherto been the esoteric topic of reducibility proofs. As Haken puts it: "Tutte and Whitney were the senior graph theorists of the time, and when those two write a joint paper on such an approach, then that stimulates many others to work on it too."[76]

A Plus for the Tenure System

Although Tutte remained skeptical,[77] a small but growing group of mathematicians felt that reducibility proofs offered a route to an overall proof of the four-color conjecture. Among those planning or implementing such an approach in the early 1970s were Heesch, Frank Allaire (of the University of Calgary), Edward Swart (of what was then the University of Rhodesia), and Frank Bernhart (son of an earlier contributor to work on the problem, Arthur Bernhart). Wolfgang Haken, the central figure in the finally successful solution of the problem, had been interested in it since his undergraduate days when he attended Heesch's seminar outlining what was to become the strategy of the Appel-Haken solution: the search for an unavoidable set of reducible configurations.

Haken's was by more recent standards an unusual mathematical education: "I am really not a mathematician. I could not pass any one of
those exams which are now required." At the University of Kiel immediately after World War II, the mathematics department was essentially
one person, Professor Karl-Heinrich Weise, who had to teach without
books. The university had been destroyed in the war, and though its
library's contents had been stored safely in underground bunkers, the
books had not yet been returned to the surface.[78] In a course on topology, the charismatic Weise introduced his students to the great unsolved
problems of the field: the four-color problem, the Poincaré conjecture,[79]
and the knot problem.[80] Those problems were to become the center of
Haken's academic life.

After completing his doctor's thesis in three-dimensional topology (it
gave some preliminary results of Haken's work on the knot problem),
Haken was unable to find an academic position, and he went to work
as a physicist for the electrical engineering company, Siemens. In the
time left over from his work for Siemens on microwave technology, Haken pursued the tantalizing goals of the open conjectures, in particular
the Poincaré conjecture and the knot problem. "I spent . . . I think, 13
years on the Poincaré conjecture, in abortive attempts to prove it. Once
I thought I had the proof . . . in '64, but that fell through . . . [it] depended on 200 cases, of which 198 worked out as I wanted, and 2 did
not." The knot problem, however, did eventually succumb to Haken's
hard work and determination: he solved it "with very, very elementary
means on which everybody else had given up." As with the four-color
conjecture, the majority of mathematicians had concluded that solving
the knot problem required more sophisticated methods, and Haken was
alone in his conviction that simple methods, applied with great care,
could generate a solution. He announced his solution at the International Congress of Mathematics in Amsterdam in 1954, but "people told
me I would have to write this up in all details. . . . I had a doctor's degree
in mathematics, but I was an outsider and an engineer then. And if such
a person announces a proof of an important mathematical problem nobody will even look at that if it is a short version. If it is written out in
all details, I was promised one would look at it. And so that took me
three years. . . . And then of course it was so long that nobody wanted
to read it." It was 1961 before Haken finally succeeded in having his
solution to the knot problem published in *Acta Mathematica*.[81]

This paper brought Haken to the University of Illinois at Urbana-
Champaign, because it impressed the Illinois mathematical logician, Wil-

liam W. Boone. Kurt Gödel's incompleteness theorems, discussed in chapter 3, had deeply influenced mathematical logic and had given rise to the suspicion that problems like the four-color conjecture and the knot problem might be unsolved because they were unsolvable (interestingly, topologists, in contrast, were confident that the knot problem was solvable).[82]

With the knot problem solved and the Poincaré conjecture remaining intractable, Haken pondered turning to the four-color conjecture. He remembered Heesch's 1948 talk on trying to solve the four-color problem by proving the reducibility of an unavoidable set of around 10,000 configurations. After over fifteen years, Haken thought, surely Heesch would have given up. He inquired, "and then I learnt 'No, he is still going,' and that fascinated me."[83] Haken invited Heesch to give a talk at the University of Illinois, and he tried to help him get access to the more powerful computers needed to advance his approach. At the start of the 1970s, Haken and Heesch collaborated in attempts to find discharging procedures that simplified the search for an unavoidable set of reducible configurations. Their collaboration "was interrupted in October 1971 when the work of Shimamoto was thought to have settled the Four Color Problem."[84]

After the failure of the apparent shortcut offered by Shimamoto's work, it again appeared clear that the problem was of daunting complexity, and Haken was put off using a computer in the search for a proof both by the limited power of then available computers (the computer experts he consulted told him that the problem was beyond the capacity of existing machines) and by the difficulty of obtaining the computer time necessary: "I am shy of the enormous political effort it requires to get computer time. At that time, using a big computer was something like $1,000 per hour and so this does not appeal to me."[85] In the 1960s and early 1970s, access to large amounts of computer time could indeed constitute a difficult obstacle. Heesch was stymied in Germany in part because, as a somewhat peripheral figure in the German mathematical community (he never attained the rank of full professor), he was unable to raise the research funding needed for enough time on a sufficiently powerful machine.[86]

Haken, however, had a student, Thomas W. Osgood, working on the four-color problem, and one of the members of Osgood's thesis committee, the Illinois mathematical logician Kenneth Appel, asked Haken "to give [a] talk in the logic seminar on that subject, so he could better understand Osgood's thesis." Haken gave his talk, explaining the difficulties with a computerized approach to the problem and concluding that, while in the future he might return to the problem, "right now I'm quitting."[87]

Appel, however, was intrigued. Unlike Haken, who had no background in computing, Appel was an experienced computer programmer, learning programming first in a 1956 computer course at the University of Michigan and then in a summer job at Douglas Aircraft. Subsequently, he wrote several large programs, often eschewing the emerging high-level programming languages like FORTRAN, choosing instead to go for the maximum efficiency to be gained by using more primitive assembly language. When he learned from Haken of the current state of work on the four-color conjecture, Appel told him: "I don't know of anything involving computers that can't be done; some things just take longer than others. Why don't we take a shot at it?"[88] Appel later reflected that their solution of the four-color problem was a "plus for the tenure system": had he not held a tenured post, he would not have been willing to invest as much time as he did in a task that might have been fruitless.[89]

It was the beginning of the most important collaboration of either of their lives. Despite Appel's optimism, it was clear both to him and to Haken that a "brute force solution," using only the methods then available for finding an unavoidable set and for determining reducibility, was infeasible, either with the computers of the early 1970s, or with those that were likely to become available in the near future. Haken had been impressed, however, by Heesch's apparently intuitive understanding of whether or not a configuration was likely to be reducible:

What fascinated me most was that Heesch looked at the configuration, and he either said, "No, there is no chance. That cannot be reducible," [or] he said, "But this one: that is certainly reducible." And I asked him, "How do you know? How can you tell?" "Well, I need two hours computer [time] . . ."[90]

From the results of Heesch's experience, later supported by theoretical analysis of irreducible configurations by Allaire, Swart, Frank Bernhart, and a Harvard Ph.D. student, Walter Stromquist,[91] Appel and Haken devised an algorithm that tested for "reduction obstacles" (see figure 4.17), together with a rule of thumb known as the "m-and-n rule" for configurations without obstacles: let n be the ring size of the configuration, and m the number of vertices inside the ring (in Shimamoto's "horseshoe," figure 4.16, for instance, $n = 14$ and $m = 8$). For given n, the "likelihood of reducibility" goes up as m goes up, and if m is greater

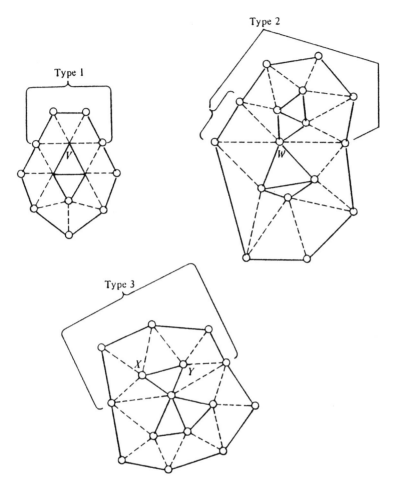

Figure 4.17
Examples of the three Heesch reduction obstacles, shown as their dual graphs.
From K. Appel and W. Haken, "The Four-Color Problem," in *Mathematics Today,*
ed. L.A. Stern (New York: Springer, 1978), 153–180, at p. 167.

than $(3n/2) - 6$ then the configuration "is almost certainly reducible."[92] The "horseshoe," for example, does not pass this test.

The test for reduction obstacles, and the *m*-and-*n* rule, meant that only those configurations that were likely to be reducible needed to be submitted to a time-consuming full reducibility analysis. Appel and Haken's work on reducibility was also eased by the recruitment of a University of Illinois computer science graduate student, John Koch. Koch had just discovered that the problem on which he had been working for his Ph.D. thesis had been solved by someone else, so he was happy to take on a new topic.[93] Koch did not use the high-level programming languages used by Dürre, but he wrote an extremely efficient program, in IBM 360 assembly language, for testing the reducibility of configurations of ring size 11. Appel modified it for size-12, size-13, and size-14 rings.[94]

Although D-reducibility could be checked exhaustively, C-reducibility could not, since with large configurations it was not feasible to try out every possible reducer. So Appel and Haken placed pragmatic limits on their efforts to prove C-reducibility, choosing only reducers without interior vertices,[95] and imposing a thirty-minute time limit on the most powerful computer available to them. With the assistance of the D-reducibility and C-reducibility programs, checking the reducibility of an individual configuration was not generally an overwhelming task, although it remained a demanding one: the analysis of a single configuration could still absorb hours of computer time. For configurations of ring size less than eleven, Appel and Haken relied on tables in a preprint of an article by Frank Allaire and Edward Swart;[96] they also turned directly for help with one particularly intractable larger configuration to Frank Allaire, and Allaire's analysis yielded a reducer that could be used to prove the configuration to be C-reducible.[97]

With reducibility checking appearing relatively straightforward, if still very onerous, Appel and Haken were able to devote most of their creative effort to refining Heesch's method of finding unavoidable sets of configurations, "all of whose members were likely to be reducible."

We used a computer to develop the techniques that produced such unavoidable sets of likely to be reducible configurations and, in the process, learned enough to be able to carry out a final routine that produced an unavoidable set of reducible configurations by hand. In the construction of our unavoidable set we constantly made minor modifications in the construction routine to avoid difficulties caused by likely to be reducible configurations we could not prove reducible by computer.[98]

It was a complex process of human-computer interaction, where Appel, at least, began to think of the computer as an active partner, albeit one that "thought" in ways quite different from a human mathematician:

Initially, when we got outputs, they would be something that was quite predictable. . . . At a certain point, after a couple of years, we started getting things that weren't so obvious—I mean, things that would take us half a day to verify. And I thought of this as almost . . . something in artificial intelligence. . . . The computer was, to the best of my feeling about the subject, not thinking like a mathematician. . . . The computer was using . . . these bits of knowledge it had in every conceivable way, and any mathematician would say, "No, no, no, you have got to organize yourself, you have got to do it that way," but the computer wasn't doing that. And it was much more successful, because it was thinking *not* like a mathematician.[99]

Even Appel's skills as what Haken calls an "amateur politician"[100] (Appel was an alderman of the Urbana City Council) were brought into play to remove what could have been the intractable obstacle of getting access to over 1,000 hours of computer central processing unit time. The University of Illinois, one of the historic homes of computer science in the United States, was well-endowed with powerful machines, but, even so, the time that Appel and Haken needed vastly exceeded their routine allocation, so they entered a domain in which what mattered was how persuasively one could argue for extra time. It helped that Appel "had friends throughout the computer establishment."[101]

What might have been particularly tricky was the access gained to the most powerful computer used by Appel and Haken, the IBM 370–168 that had just been installed at the University of Illinois Administrative Data Processing Unit. The university administrators "were reluctant, of course, to allow the scientists to use the computer for the reason that then one might get into the administration's file and raise one's own salary, or do anything." Appel discovered, however, that the new computer was not being heavily used by the administration, and so he was able to get permission to use some of the computer's spare time. "It was definitely the political skills of Ken [Appel]" that made possible getting the computer time they needed, concludes Haken.[102]

Appel and Haken knew they could not afford too leisurely an approach. Allaire, Heesch, Stromquist, and Swart were all working hard on the problem. Any one of them could have reached a solution before Appel and Haken did; they were probably no more than a year away.[103] Appel and Haken's task was of great complexity over and above the time-consuming

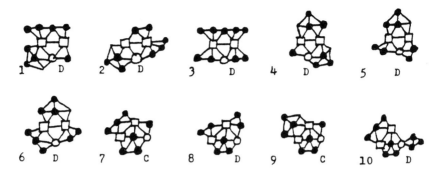

Figure 4.18
Ten members of Appel and Haken's unavoidable set of 1,936 reducible configurations. These are represented as the dual graph of the corresponding map, and only the subgraph inside the ring is shown. The degrees of vertices are indicated by symbols introduced by Heesch. A solid circle indicates a degree-5 vertex, an unmarked vertex is degree-6, a hollow circle indicates a degree-7 vertex, and a square a degree-8 vertex. The letters C and D indicate that the configuration is, respectively, C-reducible or D-reducible. From K. Appel, W. Haken, and J. Koch, "Every Planar Map Is Four Colorable. Part II: Reducibility," *Illinois Journal of Mathematics* 21 (1977): 491–567, at p. 565.

computer analysis. The construction of the unavoidable set involved the application, by hand not computer, of 487 discharging rules. Nor was it enough to check the reducibility of every individual configuration in the set. They also had to deal with the possibility that a configuration "might be immersed" in a larger graph "in such a way as to make untrue some of the hypotheses of independence which are basic to C- and D-reducibility." Complications arose from the fact that some configurations "wrap around and meet themselves."[104]

Eventually, Appel and Haken's immense effort was successful. In June 1976 they completed their construction of an unavoidable set of 1,936 reducible configurations, later reduced to 1,482, and then to 1,405, by the elimination of redundancies and simplification of the argument (see figure 4.18 for part of this set).

The four-color theorem was proved. We had used 1,200 hours of time on 3 different computers. The final discharging procedure differed from our first approximation by some 500 modifications resulting from the discovery of critical neighborhoods. The development of the procedure required the hand analysis of some 10,000 neighborhoods of vertices of positive charge and the machine analysis of more than 2,000 configurations. A considerable part of this material, including the reduction of 1,482 configurations, was used in the final proof.

Although the discharging procedure (without the reductions) can be checked by hand in a couple of months, it would be virtually impossible to verify the reduction computations in this way.[105]

Appel and Haken chose to submit the result of all this work to their "local" journal, the *Illinois Journal of Mathematics*. Their paper was nearly 140 pages long and came in two parts. The first, by Appel and Haken, described the overall proof strategy and detailed the humanly conducted discharging procedure used to construct the unavoidable set of configurations; the second, by Appel, Haken, and Koch, listed the unavoidable set and described the computer programs used to check that every member of it was reducible.[106] The journal also published, as a back-cover insert, over 400 microfiche pages of further diagrams and of detailed verification of lemmas used in the main text.[107]

According to Haken, they chose the *Illinois Journal,* not because they felt it would be easy to get publication there, but because they wished to ensure expert refereeing. In Haken's view, the leading European specialist on the four-color problem, aside from Heesch, was Jean Mayer, a remarkable figure in that he was a professor of literature (at the Université Paul Valéry, Montpellier) rather than a professional mathematician. Mayer had succeeded in raising the Birkhoff number (the lower bound on the number of countries in a five-chromatic map) to 96.[108] Appel had arranged to spend a sabbatical with Mayer:

We wanted to have [the paper] reviewed by the best possible experts. And so we arranged with the editor [that] the referee for the unavoidability, that should be Jean Mayer, because he was the best man in the world on that at that time, and Ken was spending his sabbatical there, . . . and was present to answer any questions. . . . And so the other one, the best man for the computer programs was Frank Allaire. He had programs at that time even better than Heesch's, and much better than ours. He was the referee for the computer . . . for the reducibility.[109]

Close contact between referees and the authors of a paper being refereed might appear unusual to scientists in other disciplines, but may not necessarily be so in mathematics. For example, Andrew Wiles was in intensive contact, via electronic mail and fax, with the referees of his celebrated work on the proof of Fermat's last theorem, as those referees sought to build up their understanding of his proof.[110]

Allaire carefully compared the results of Appel, Haken, and Koch's reducibility programs with his own. He checked not only whether the two programs agreed in whether they classed a configuration as

D-reducible but also carefully examined the configurations that were C-reducible but not D-reducible. For example he counted the number of "bad colorings," after application of the D-algorithm, in configurations that are not D-reducible ("bad colorings" are colorings of the ring that cannot be extended to the vertices inside the ring).[111] In all the cases Allaire checked he found exact agreement, "so that convinced him that if our program had a bug, then there could not have been 400 agreements versus 0 disagreements."[112]

A year later this comparison exercise was also done with a list of 2,669 reducible configurations produced by Dürre, Heesch, and their colleague Friedrich Miehe.[113] Two disagreements in numbers of "bad colorings" were found, causing Appel and Haken some alarm. When Heesch reran his computations, however, the results were found to agree with Appel and Haken's, the original discrepancy probably being the result of a clerical error.[114] Not every configuration in Appel and Haken's unavoidable set appeared on Allaire's or Heesch's lists (over 500 did not),[115] but the fact that the different programs agreed when applied to the same configurations was clearly most reassuring.

It is interesting to note the extent to which Appel and Haken's work was a collective effort. As well as the assistance provided by Koch, Allaire, and all those especially Heesch whose work they had built upon, Appel and Haken even recruited their families to the huge and tedious hand checking tasks that were necessary. It was essential, for example, to check that each configuration had been entered correctly into the reducibility checking programs so that the configuration analyzed was the one that had been intended. The hand proof of unavoidability was particularly demanding, said Haken:

We needed . . . 450 pages. . . . It took us four-and-a-half months of very . . . exhausting work. I've never been so overstressed . . . mentally so exhausted. It was Ken Appel, my daughter Dorothea, and I. We worked the way that one of us wrote a section, and then the second one was reading it over, checking it for mistakes, and bringing the errors to the attention of the one who wrote it, and then the third person read it a third time.

Armin Haken and Laurel, Peter, and Andrew Appel also helped in this work: particularly important was the contribution of Appel's daughter, Laurel. This collective checking effort was crucial in persuading Haken that their proof was sound enough to "go public":

She [Laurel Appel] found, I think, 800 mistakes, which is not many on 700 pages. And 650 she could correct herself. There was just . . . a wrong number, or so.

And then 50 remained, and that was in early July '76. And so, over the 4th of July weekend, Ken . . . re-computed those 50 configurations which really had been missing . . . and only 12 of them did not work. And then I worked on those for one day, and I found that they could be replaced . . . by something like 20 others, and 2 of them did not work, and then again a day, . . . So I said, "Then, here somebody has worked one month full-time and found 800 mistakes. And then we have needed only five days to repair all that. This looks so stable—it is this incredible stability.[116]

Reactions

Appel and Haken's proof met with a wide range of responses, "from a furious reaction to greatest enthusiasm . . . it couldn't be more extreme."[117] The University of Illinois Mathematics Department adopted the triumphant postmark "FOUR COLORS SUFFICE" (see figure 4.19). Graph theorist W. T. Tutte was even moved to poetry:

Wolfgang Haken
Smote the Kraken
One! Two! Three! Four!
Quoth he "The monster is no more."[118]

Support from Tutte, a leader of graph theory and editor-in-chief of the prestigious *Journal of Combinatorial Theory*, "was the first big step in our credibility problem," says Appel.[119] Tutte had previously distanced himself publicly from the reformulated Kempe strategy being used by Heesch, Haken, and others; in Appel's words:

one would have expected that when the newspaper people came to talk with him [about the Appel-Haken solution], it would be natural to say, "Well, it may or may not be true." But instead what he said was, "If they say they've done it, I have no doubt that they've done it." And when people heard Tutte say, "This probably works," a lot of them, unless they really were close to the area and

Figure 4.19
Postmark celebrating the proof of the four-color theorem, courtesy of Professor Wolfgang Haken.

looking at things closely, said, "Tutte is a man of sufficient prestige. If he's willing to say this, I'll believe it."[120]

"The newspaper people" became interested quickly. A faculty member on the Urbana-Champaign campus, Tony Ortoni, was a "stringer" for the London *Times,* and it reported Appel and Haken's solution of the four-color problem on July 23, 1976. A storm of publicity, almost without precedent in pure mathematics, ensued, as newspapers worldwide reported both the breakthrough and the means by which it had been achieved. Appel and Haken "may well have ushered in a new era of computer computation on the frontiers of higher mathematics," wrote *Time* magazine.[121]

As we have seen, however, many mathematicians were less than enthusiastic about the dependence of Appel and Haken's proof on computer analysis. Age appeared to play some role in determining responses to use of the computer. Armin Haken, then a graduate student at the University of California at Berkeley, gave a talk there describing the proof: "at the end of his talk the audience split into two groups, roughly at age forty. The people over forty could not be convinced that a proof by computer could be correct, and the people under forty could not be convinced that a proof that took 700 pages of hand calculations could be correct."[122] Wolfgang Haken sometimes met with sharp hostility. He recalled one mathematician trying to prevent him meeting any of the graduate students in his department:

Since the problem had been taken care of by a totally inappropriate means, no first-rate mathematician would now work any more on it, because he would not be the first one to do it, and therefore a decent proof might be delayed indefinitely. It would certainly require a first-rate mathematician to find a good, satisfactory proof, and that was not possible. So we had done something very, very bad, and things like that should not be committed again, and he had to protect the innocent souls of his students against us.[123]

Ian Stewart, Professor of Mathematics at the University of Warwick, complained that the Appel-Haken proof:

doesn't give a satisfactory explanation *why* the theorem is true. This is partly because the proof is so long that it is hard to grasp (including the computer calculations, impossible!), but mostly because it is so apparently structureless. The answer appears as a kind of monstrous coincidence. Why is there an unavoidable set of reducible configurations? The best answer at the present time is: there just is. The proof: here it is, see for yourself. The mathematician's search for hidden structure, his pattern-binding [sic] urge, is frustrated.[124]

A symptom of this unease among mathematicians was the currency of rumors that there was a serious "bug" in the programs used by Appel and Haken. These rumors were sufficiently persistent in the early 1980s to cause the editor of *The Mathematical Intelligencer* to invite Appel and Haken to set the matter straight,[125] but they could still be heard in 1993–1994 when the interviews upon which this chapter is based were conducted. These rumors are "urban legends":[126] no such bug has been discovered. The 600 pages of material (the *Illinois Journal of Mathematics* articles and microfiche pages containing further diagrams and checks of lemmas) that constituted the Appel-Haken proof certainly contained typographical and copying errors,[127] but no error has been found in the computerized reducibility analysis. People such as Allaire or Swart, who would have had most to gain from the existence of such an error, because it might have permitted them to have constructed the first correct proof of the four-color conjecture, found none.

Allaire, Swart, and Frank Bernhart, who had all worked on computerized reducibility proofs, were present at the 1976 Toronto meeting where Haken described the proof. Many in the audience were "uncomfortable," as Swart put it, with Appel and Haken's use of the computer: "I did notice a lot of people asking those of us who had worked with the computer reducibility . . . What did we think? Did we think he [Haken] had really done it? And I can only tell you that we were unanimous in our view that he'd done it. Unanimous."[128] What sociologist of science Harry Collins would call "the core set,"[129] those mathematicians attempting the same task by similar methods, were convinced of the correctness of Appel and Haken's computerized reducibility analysis. "I do believe that the configurations in [Appel and Haken's] list are in fact reducible," wrote Allaire. "[T]hose of us who have worked on reducibility testing are happy about Haken, Appel, and Koch's reducibility results," wrote Swart, because they were able "to a large extent" to check them using "different programs on different computers."[130]

Such worries as were evinced by this "core set" focused instead on the highly complex proof of unavoidability. Appel and Haken had begun by using discharging procedures implemented on a computer but then shifted to hand analysis. Swart commented: "I would go so far as to say that any lack of reliability of the present proofs of the 4CT [four-color theorem] resides less in the use of a computer for the reducibility testing and more in the fact that a computer was not used to create the unavoidable set of configurations arising from the discharging procedure."[131]

Allaire put it more bluntly: "I cannot express any confidence in their [Appel and Haken's] discharging scheme."[132]

These doubts were partially confirmed by the one significant error in the Appel-Haken proof that has been discovered. It was found by a master's student in Electrical Engineering at the Technische Hochschule Aachen, Ulrich Schmidt. The four-color problem was of interest in electrical engineering because there are analogies with the process of checking the design of computer chips. For his 1982 *Diplom* thesis, Schmidt checked around 40 percent of the Appel-Haken unavoidability proof and he found an error. It was, however, one that Appel and Haken were able to correct by modifying the discharging procedure.[133] A more comprehensive check in 1985 of the unavoidability proof, by H. Enomoto and S. Saeki of the University of Tokyo, found only one further, less serious, error.[134]

Differences in attitude to the trustworthiness of computer analysis could be perceived even among Appel, Haken, and Koch. While the computer scientist Koch was deeply commited to the computer analysis, Haken was more skeptical:

Haken . . . didn't do any [assembly-language] programming at all.[135] . . . He was, and still is . . . a strait-laced German professor . . . who doesn't trust computers. So he was our internal check on the whole process. . . . In other words, if we had computer-generated results we were very careful to look at them and check them out before showing them to him, because, you know, if one of them came with an error in it he was likely not to trust anything from the computer from then on. . . . So that was a good kind of balance, because when you get into . . . any of these programs . . . you are so close to it that sometimes you don't see what is right there in front of you. So he was a completely non-computerized check on the whole thing throughout the process.[136]

Not everyone within computer science, however, was happy with the Appel-Haken solution. Those specializing in applying formal, deductive proof to programs tended to believe that the Appel-Haken proof was unsatisfactory because the programs on which it relied had not themselves been subject to formal verification.[137] The community of verification specialists (the main focus in this book) is alert to the possibility of apparently correct programs concealing subtle bugs that do not become evident in program testing, and so, as seen in chapter 2, its members are unwilling to vest too much trust in programs that have not been subject to formal verification. One of the leaders of that community, David Gries, obtained a copy of the main reducibility program from Appel and Haken, and he inspected it, hoping to find a bug: to have found one would have been a dramatic demonstration of the need for formal verification. The program did not conform to Gries's views of what a well-structured program should look like: it was "a very horribly twisted program because they wanted it to be efficient," that is, to take the minimum amount of computer time to run. The only error Gries could find, however, was "the wrong way around": it was, according to Gries, "a safe mistake," one that meant that a configuration that was reducible might not be listed as such.[138]

The possibility of a bug in a reducibility program did not greatly trouble Appel and Haken. They gained confidence from the fact that reducibility can be checked by independently written programs, written in different languages and run on different machines. Furthermore, they believe that the very "inelegance" of their proof gives it a certain robustness compared to proofs, of other theorems, that consist of a more elegant, but more fragile, chain of reasoning. They do not claim to have found the only, or the best, proof of the four-color theorem, but only one proof among many possible:

In a purely mathematical and ingenious proof like [Andrew Wiles's proof of] Fermat's last theorem . . . something relatively simple may have been overlooked, and that may destroy everything. . . . Our thing is much more primitive, and no great ingenious ideas, only technical things. But . . . the number of possible unavoidable sets is just very large, and we need only one of them. And if there is a mistake . . . a technical mistake in that one, we can give another . . . unavoidable set of reducible configurations. . . . It is impossible that one bug in a program or one error in the work done by hand destroys it.[139]

Appel and Haken wrote: "there are thousands of different proofs of the theorem, and any particular proof is only selected by a series of choices among the many proofs extant. Thus, an understanding of the principles involved in the proof makes the reader somewhat less concerned about the horrendous bookkeeping necessary to give all details in a particular proof and even may relieve the anxiety about the possibility that some particular computer proof of the reducibility of a configuration is incorrect."[140] Appel said that the density of reducible configurations reminded him of "being in a moderately thick forest":

You know very well that if you shoot a gun in any direction it's eventually going to hit a tree. But you are by a very complicated method proving this. I mean, intuitively it's obvious that yes, there is a tree there no matter where you look. But yet you haven't got enough of a description of a forest to formally prove there is a tree there, and the thing you always worry about is [if] there is one little direction where you just shoot it and there is no tree, and it goes out of the forest entirely. . . . I just think of that—being in the forest and shooting a gun.[141]

A second proof of the four-color theorem, using the same overall approach, but a different discharging procedure, a different unavoidable set of reducible configurations, and more powerful proofs of reducibility, was announced and described by Frank Allaire in 1977, although, to my knowledge, the full detail has not been published.[142] A third proof was constructed in 1993 by Neil Robertson and Daniel P. Sanders of Ohio State University, Paul Seymour of Princeton and Robin Thomas of the Georgia Institute of Technology. "[T]he proof by Appel and Haken," they wrote, "has not been fully accepted. There has remained a certain amount of doubt about its validity." Appel and Haken's use of a computer "may be a necessary evil," but the complication of the hand proof was "more disturbing, particularly since the 4CT [four-color theorem] has a history of incorrect 'proofs.' So in 1993, mainly for our own peace of mind, we resolved to convince ourselves somehow that the 4CT really was true." They computerized their discharging procedure (which is based upon a method developed by Jean Mayer) as well as their reducibility proofs and succeeded in constructing a significantly smaller unavoidable set (of 633 configurations) than Appel and Haken's. The resultant proof is simpler than Appel and Haken's, but it still depends on computer analysis, and Robertson and his colleagues also have encountered the reaction that "nobody likes very much a proof that uses a computer."[143]

Enter the Philosophers

Appel and Haken's proof was of interest not just to mathematicians but also to philosophers of mathematics. Just as the responses of mathematicians differed, so too did those of philosophers. Much of the resultant debate was sparked by an article by philosopher Thomas Tymoczko, who argued that: "if we accept the 4CT [four-color theorem] as a theorem, we are committed to changing the sense of 'theorem,' or, more to the point, to changing the sense of the underlying concept of 'proof.' " Unlike traditional proofs, the proof of the four-color theorem was not "surveyable," wrote Tymoczko: it could no longer be understood and checked in its entirety by human being. So a "wedge has been driven between the two explanations of proof in terms of surveyability and formalizability. . . . [A] new technique has been developed for establishing mathematical truths." Tymoczko concluded that either one had to admit "a new method (computer experiment) of establishing mathematical results in addition to proofs" or the concept of proof had to be modified "to include computer-assisted proofs." [144] It was the latter possibility that Tymoczko embraced.

This expanded notion of proof was, in Tymoczko's view, part of a necessary move to a "more realistic philosophy of mathematics that allows for fallibility and empirical elements."[145] Tymoczko was echoing, in sophisticated form, the conclusion of an earlier discussion, by computer scientist Elsie Cerutti and mathematician P. J. Davis, of the impact of the automation of proof. Their position was one that "is rarely discussed in works on the philosophy of mathematics and which is very unpopular—that a mathematical proof has much in common with a physical experiment; that its validity is not absolute, but rests upon the same foundation of repeated experimentation."[146]

In response to Tymoczko, other philosophers defended existing, "orthodox" philosophy of mathematics against an empiricist, fallibilist viewpoint and denied that there was any need for a changed notion of "proof." Proofs existed independently of the human capacity to survey them, argued Paul Teller:

Surveyability is needed, not because without it a proof is in any sense not a proof . . . but because without surveyability we seem not to be able to verify that a proof is correct. So surveyability is not part of what it is to be a proof. . . . It is a characteristic which some proofs have. . . . The fact that mathematicians have extended their powers of surveying proofs by relying on computers . . . does not show that a new concept of proof is at hand, nor that knowledge in mathematics is more like knowledge in the natural sciences than might be thought on other grounds.

Teller believed that underlying Tymoczko's argument was the view "that mathematics is an essentially human activity." One could imagine, however, said Teller, organisms similar to human beings that do something like human mathematics; other organisms, more dissimilar; and eventually "objects that look more like computers than people." Where on that "slippery slope" could one draw a boundary between doing mathematics and doing "something else"? The slippery-slope argument might even suggest, said Teller, that "mathematics is *not* an essentially human activity."[147]

Like Teller, Stuart Shanker disagreed with Tymoczko's conclusion that the meaning of "proof" should be changed. Unlike Teller, however, Shanker concluded that a correct understanding of "proof" implied that the Appel-Haken solution was not a proof. Shanker drew upon the authority of Wittgenstein to contest "the general consensus rapidly emerging . . . that the growing role of computer proofs in pure mathematics is forcing us to reconsider and 'liberalise' our concept of proof." In Shanker's reading of him, Wittgenstein's view was "that proofs are grammatical constructions which establish the rules for applying mathematical concepts and hence must be surveyable." If that was what "proof" was, and Shanker clearly believed that it was, then an unsurveyable computer-assisted analysis could not be a proof:

> it is because the "algorithm" which the computer mechanically "calculates" is not humanly surveyable . . . that we must deny that their [Appel and Haken's] argument constitutes a mathematical proof (a point which turns on the logical grammar of the concepts calculation, proof and mechanical symbol-manipulation). . . . Quite simply, the problem with the Appel-Haken "four-colour theorem" is that it cannot be understood as the result of applying grammatical conventions.

Shanker had no wish to "cast doubt on the validity of the Appel-Haken solution," but he argued that "the basic nature of their solution is experimental, and hence, that it makes no sense to speak, as Tymoczko supposes, of Appel and Haken 'proving' the 'four-colour theorem,' let alone of their 'proof' forcing us to modify our understanding of the concepts of *proof* and *theorem*."[148]

After the Fall

Explicit debate over whether Appel and Haken's solution was a proof, whether they had indeed defiled the mathematicians' Eden, and whether they had changed the meaning of "proof," gradually petered out, although even in 1991 Daniel I. A. Cohen of the City University of New York could write that "[a]dmitting the computer shenanigans of Appel and Haken to the ranks of mathematics would only leave us intellectually unfulfilled."[149] Rather than the debate being resolved, or any clear-cut consensus emerging, published discussion simply ended as interest moved on to other topics. Computers continued to be used in mathematical proofs with increasing frequency, but none of this subsequent work involved problems as famous as the four-color conjecture, so comment was relatively limited.

Within pure mathematics, perhaps the best-known computerized demonstration, after Appel and Haken's, was the 1988 demonstration by Clement Lam, L. H. Thiel, and S. Swiercz that there are no finite projective planes of order ten.[150] Their demonstration involved examination of 10^{14} cases, using several thousand hours of time on a supercomputer even faster than the Control Data 6600, a Cray-1A at the Institute for Defense Analysis at Princeton. With this huge amount of computation, Lam and his colleagues had to consider not just possible software bugs but also the chance of random hardware faults, like the changing of one or more bits (binary digits) by cosmic radiation. The Cray-1A, like most other computers, automatically detected and corrected one-bit faults, and detected two-bit faults, but infrequent combinations of faults might not be detected; the machine was believed to be subject to such undetected faults "at the rate of about one per one thousand hours of computing." Lam and his colleagues believed that a discrepancy they found was indeed caused by just such an undetected hardware fault. They argued that the way in which their overall result was constructed made the probability that it was affected by hardware faults "infinitesimal." They did not claim, however, claim that their analysis constituted "proof": "one should not consider these results as a 'proof,' in the traditional sense," they wrote. "They are experimental results."[151]

The fundamental issue raised by the Appel and Haken solution, the nature of mathematical proof, however, did not vanish from view. As computer graphics developed in the 1980s and 1990s, visual display became an ever more important expository tool, and some mathematicians began to suspect that computerized graphical demonstration was replacing traditional proof, at least in the teaching of mathematics. With intense, fruitful interchange between theoretical physics and areas of mathematics such as geometry and topology—especially in the theory of "superstrings"—there were even signs that arguments based upon the physical interpretation of mathematical structures, long banished as unacceptable forms of mathematical proof, were reemerging.[152] Journalist John Horgan drew on these developments to write in a 1993 *Scientific American* article of "The Death of Proof." He suggested that both computerized proofs and increasingly complex human proofs might force mathematicians to accept that "their assertions are, at best, only provisionally true."[153] Responding, in an article entitled "The Immortality of Proof," mathematician Steven G. Krantz told the members of the American Mathematical Society:

. . . the ideas presented there are dangerous—dangerous to you, to me, and to our profession. . . . The wolves are in our midst, and it is time for us to decide what we believe and what we value. . . . It may or may not be true that in ten or fifteen years we will have abandoned proofs and will be letting computers tell us what is probably true. But in ten or fifteen years it will be too late to decide what we want. We have to decide today.[154]

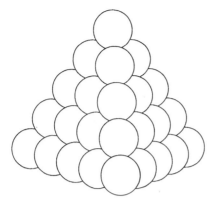

Figure 4.20
Spheres arranged in a face-centered cubic packing (courtesy Tom Hales).

In the summer of 1998 the issue of computer proof, once again, was thrown into the spotlight when mathematician Thomas Hales of the University of Michigan announced a computer-assisted proof of the Kepler conjecture, that there is no tighter way of packing identical spheres in infinite space than the "face-centered cubic" packing, in which infinite triangular "plates" of spheres are placed one on top of the other in the way a grocer might stack oranges in a pile (see figure 4.20). In 1900 David Hilbert included the conjecture, at that point some three centuries old, in his famous list of unsolved mathematical problems, but it continued to resist solution for most of the twentieth century. For example, a 1991 claimed proof by Wu-Yi Hsiang of the Department of Mathematics, University of California at Berkeley, appears not to have been accepted. There is no great difficulty in comparing the density of the face-centered cubic with any *particular* alternative: the difficulty is showing that no conceivable alternative is tighter. The programs and data files comprising Hales's complex claimed proof occupy over 3 gigabytes of memory space. It will be of considerable interest to track the reaction to this proof (unlike Lam a decade earlier, Hales regards his computerized analysis as proof) and compare it to that which greeted Appel and Haken two decades earlier.[155]

A Changing Ecosystem?

It is interesting to compare the case of the four-color proof with that of Euler's theorem discussed by Lakatos. There, concepts "grew," the meaning of "polyhedron," "face," and "edge" changed, and gradually a stable, universally accepted, proof emerged, which can now be given in a deceptively simple paragraph or two in textbooks of graph theory. This proof is no longer even remotely controversial. In the case of the four-color conjecture, however, the meaning of "map," "country," "border," and "coloring," were essentially unchanged from Cayley's statement of the conjecture in 1878. The Appel and Haken proof, however, remained controversial, not so much in its details (despite the doubts about their discharging procedure expressed by the relevant "core set") but in its general form, in its dependence upon computer analysis. Thus while the meaning of the "lower-level" concepts involved in the four-color theorem could not successfully be changed (no one, for example, tried to save Kempe's proof by restricting the meaning of "maps" to maps in which no country had more than four neighbors), the meaning of the "higher-level" concept of proof remained in a significant sense open.

For some, like Paul Halmos and Daniel I. A. Cohen, to put one's trust in the results of computer analysis was to violate the essence of mathematics as an activity in which human, personal understanding is central. To others, such as the "core set" working on computerized reducibility proofs, using a computer was no different in principle from using pencil and paper, which is universally accepted in mathematics. As Swart put it:

. . . there is precious little of substance in the world of mathematics that can be done [in your head] without some assistance from pencil and paper. And for the most part I regard computer-assisted proof as just an extension of pencil and paper. I don't think there is some great divide which says that ok, you are allowed to use pencil and paper but you are not allowed to use a computer because that changes the character of the proof. . . . I find such an argument strange.[156]

Those who find the assistance of the computer natural typically see it as more reliable than the human mathematician. John Slaney, a specialist in automated theorem proving, admitted in 1994 that: "Taking the working out of 124 cases on trust because of the behaviour of a machine is unlike doing so because your graduate students claim to have checked them." He went on, though, to point out that "on the score of reliability computers have it over graduate students by a wide margin." He proposed the checking of automated proofs by independently written proof-checking programs (see chapter 8), but accepted that not everyone would agree that a mechanically generated, mechanically checked, derivation is actually a proof. "[T]he Luddites, like the poor, are always with us," he commented:

> ... those who object to computational results on ideological or mystical grounds, as not having received the breath of life from a warm and cuddly graph theorist in contrast to an emotionless workstation, will continue to object to computer verification of the results. Well, they will have to shop in a different store.[157]

It would be premature to talk of the emergence of an entire realm of pure mathematics that depends upon computerized "proof," and therefore acceptable to its practitioners but not to those who adhered to traditional "human" versions of proof. To date, for example, not much has appear to depend upon the four-color conjecture. It was not like the Shimura-Taniyama-Weil conjecture, unifying the mathematics of elliptic curves and modular forms, the partial proof of which was the fundamental achievement of Andrew Wiles's work on Fermat's last theorem, and which was the basis of a large number of mathematical results that would fall if the conjecture were not true.[158] For two decades after 1976, the four-color theorem appeared, in contrast, as Stewart had put it, just a "monstrous coincidence": of interest because of its fame but not because its proof led anywhere mathematically. The new proof by Robertson and his colleagues, however, may augur a change. They devoted the considerable amount of effort it took to construct their proof, not because they expected much credit for the proof in itself (they did not), but because they had reduced the proof of another theorem (the five-color case of Hadwiger's conjecture) to the four-color conjecture.[159]

Their goal was to be sure of the proof of the latter so that they could use it as a lemma in their proof of this further theorem (this conventional, noncomputerized proof was judged significant enough to win Robertson, Seymour, and Thomas the Fulkerson Prize in 1994) and then make progress on related open problems in graph theory. If they succeed, a substantial body of new results in graph theory may come to depend upon the four-color conjecture. Whether these results are, or are not, taken to be part of the corpus of mathematical knowledge will then depend upon whether the conjecture is accepted as a theorem, and thus upon whether computerized analysis is acceptable as mathematical proof.

Ten years after the Appel-Haken solution, mathematician Lynn Arthur Steen wrote: "The intruder [the computer] has changed the ecosystem of mathematics, profoundly and permanently."[160] By 1993 only three of a sample of fourteen mathematicians, arbitrarily chosen from three

British university mathematics departments as a supplementary part of this research, were not using computers as part of their mathematical work. But only two were using computers to conduct proofs. Krantz appears to represent a considerable body of mathematical opinion when he said that while he excluded Appel and Haken's work from his strictures against "inconclusive numerical/graphical models," he "would be much happier if there were a written proof that I could comprehend in my usual fashion."[161]

To those who hold this preference, using a computer to conduct a proof is still, at best, "a necessary evil," as the authors of the new computerized proof of the four-color theorem put it.[162] However pervasive the acceptance among mathematicians of the use of the computer in calculation and in the exploration of complicated mathematical structures, as well as its use for more mundane tasks such as electronic mail and typesetting, its use in proof is still not fully accepted. The areas where "proof" is predominantly computer proof, and where computer proofs are positively welcomed indeed more highly valued than human proofs, have, therefore, to date remained mainly outside of pure mathematics. By far the most important of those areas is in the formal verification of computer systems, and this is the main theme of the next four chapters. To begin, chapter 5 considers the most influential community to embrace computer proof and to support it financially: the national security community.

5

Covert Channels

London, England, May 12, 1994. Though it was still springtime, the night was hot. The police officers, who had spilled from half a dozen cars, flashed warrant cards and rushed up the stairs of the north London house, were sweating but perhaps from excitement as well. They were on the trail of a perpetrator of one of the worst computer security breaches ever suffered by the U.S. military, at its premier command-and-control research facility on Griffiss Air Force Base outside Rome, New York.

The previous month, a systems' administrator at Rome had noticed the presence of an unauthorized computer file, and her alertness enabled the laboratory belatedly to discover it was under electronic attack. Undetected, two computer hackers had been in control of Rome's computer network for around three days, getting access to sensitive files. Masquerading as a legitimate user of Rome's system, they also found their way into the computer systems at other U.S. government sites and at defense contractors such as the Lockheed Missile and Space Company.

The Rome laboratory brought in U.S. Air Force computer security specialists, who were able to regain control of Rome's systems and to restrict the activities of the hackers to a deliberately isolated network that acted as an "electronic fishbowl." They retraced the intricate pathways through cyberspace that the hackers had used: the connections led back through commercial sites in the United States to telephone switching systems in Bogotá, Colombia, and in Chile, and eventually to London. The Air Force feared the involvement of a hostile intelligence service with the possible intent of installing malicious programs, "which could be activated years later, possibly jeopardizing a weapons system's ability to perform safely and as intended, and even threatening the lives of the soldiers or pilots operating the system."

The scene that met the English police officers, following the Air Force's tip-off to Scotland Yard, however, was more mundane than that suggested by these agitated fears. The hacker who, at his trial, was said to have "caused enormous consternation to the American authorities" was a sixteen-year-old schoolboy using a £750 computer. "Oh, shit," he thought, as the police entered his attic bedroom. It was "surreal," his mother was later to recall, her son's baking-hot room full of police officers ripping up the floorboards, while she—"very English"—made them coffee, "asking them how many sugars they wanted."[1]

The Rome intrusion was no worse than an expensive embarrassment for the Air Force. The sheltered schoolboy had, in the words of his lawyer, become "immersed in the game and it was one way of making friends, friends he never met, whose real names he never knew. He meant no harm, made no material gain and the last thing he was thinking of was subverting the western alliance."[2] His alleged collaborator was a young programmer who was later to join a "team of reformed hackers" offering its services for a fee to firms that wished to test the security of their information systems. He too was cleared of malicious intent by the British courts.[3] Yet the fevered imaginings of what might have been— if the hackers had indeed been working for a hostile power; if the Rome Laboratory had been involved in military operations, and not just in research and development; if America had been at war—resonated with a Washington, D.C., becoming obsessed with the notion of "cyberwar."

"The electron," CIA Director John Deutch told a U.S. Senate committee, "is the ultimate precision guided weapon." The Defense Information Systems Agency estimated in 1996 that defense computer systems had been subject to a quarter of a million hacker attacks the previous year; it found its own efforts to use the Internet to gain illicit access to military systems were successful two times out of three, and only 4 percent of the successful attacks were discovered. Nor was the vulnerability of United States and its allies restricted to their military systems.

Asked in 1995 to think of ways in which the information infrastructure of the Western alliance could be attacked, a panel of national security and industry representatives had no difficulty in imagining dire possibilities:

an adversary attacks computer systems throughout the United States and allied countries, causing accidents, crashing systems, blocking communications, and inciting panic. For example, in the scenario, automatic tellers at two of Georgia's largest banks are attacked. The attacks create confusion and panic when the automatic tellers wrongfully add and debit thousands of dollars from customers' accounts. A freight train is misrouted when a logic bomb [a program designed to cause damage when triggered] is inserted into a railroad computer system, causing a major accident involving a high speed passenger train in Maryland. Meanwhile, telephone service is sabotaged in Washington, a major airplane crash is caused in Great Britain; and Cairo, Egypt loses all power service. An all-out attack is launched on computers at most military installations, slowing down, disconnecting, or crashing the systems. Weapons systems designed to pinpoint enemy tanks and troop formations begin to malfunction due to electronic infections.

In other circles, thoughts began to turn to the offensive use of "cyberwar" by the United States: for example, to ways of disabling enemy systems by introducing computer viruses into them. Skeptical voices commented that the best way to destroy a computer system was to bomb it, but they were at least temporarily sidelined.[4]

Time-Sharing and Computer Security

The upsurge of interest in the 1990s in "cyberwar" was a reexpression of an issue that went back thirty years. Computer security began to be seen as distinct from other security concerns with the advent in the 1960s of "time-sharing" computer systems. These made it possible for several people to interact, seemingly simultaneously, with the same computer system via terminals that could be in a separate room or separate building. In earlier "batch-operated" computer systems, different users' programs were executed one after the other. Users could not interact with the computer system while their programs were being run. Having sent or carried their coding forms, punched cards, or reels of paper tape to their organization's computer center, all that users could do was to wait to pick up their program's output.[5]

Batch systems had potential security problems—for example, the output of a previous program would normally still be in peripheral storage, such as on magnetic tape or on discs, when a new one was being run—but these issues elicited little comment or concern. Time-sharing, however, was different both technically and socially. Programs or data "belonging" to different users would be present simultaneously in the computer's main memory, not just in peripheral storage. Users could interact with their programs as they were being run, and they could do so while sitting at their separate terminals, invisible to each other and to a system's operators. The activities, and even the identities, of users were potentially problematic.

Time-sharing greatly increased the efficiency of computer installations. Most importantly, users could "debug" programs interactively instead of having to wait for several hours to see if a program had run successfully. Time-sharing also raised the issue, however, of how to prevent different users and different programs from interfering with each other. Most obviously, the computer's main memory had to be divided among different users' programs to prevent one program overwriting a memory location being used by another. Ideally, though, these memory bounds had to be flexible, for otherwise portions of memory might remain unused by programs with modest memory demands, while other users were unnecessarily constrained. The twin demand for efficient use of resources and for keeping different programs from interfering with each other rendered the design and development of system software for time-sharing systems a difficult and crucial task.

Much of the early development of time-sharing in the late 1950s and early 1960s took place at the Massachusetts Institute of Technology. By 1963 MIT's Multiple Access Computer (MAC) could be used by up to twenty-four people at once via teletypewriter terminals linked to the central computer by telephone lines.[6] In a university environment, security was not a dominant issue. Programs certainly had to be prevented from writing to (in other words, modifying the contents of) portions of memory being used by other programs. Stopping different users, however, from retrieving the contents of memory space being used by others, in other words reading others' data, was not in practice a major concern.[7] Furthermore, freedom to grant permission to read or to modify files was entirely at users' discretion (unlike in the military, where the basic rules of security are mandatory) and controls over access to the overall system were typically relaxed.

For example, access to a typical early university time-sharing system, Edinburgh Multiple-Access System (EMAS), was controlled even as late as the end of the 1980s by each user's four-letter password, which could be a meaningful English word, and which users were under no compulsion ever to change. Each of these features of the password would be regarded with scorn by computer security specialists. For example, passwords that are meaningful words—especially meaningful words of a short, set length—are vulnerable to "dictionary attack," in which a machine-readable dictionary is used to generate and to try possible passwords.

The quite different priorities of national defense, however, were present from the beginning of time-sharing. Much of the interest at MIT in time-sharing grew out of earlier experience developing the interactive air defenses that eventually became the continent-wide Semiautomatic Ground Environment (SAGE) System described in chapter 2. The Department of Defense's Advanced Research Projects Agency, sponsor of much computer science research in the United States, funded Project MAC and other early time-sharing work, notably at the RAND Corporation's spin-off company, the System Development Corporation (which was responsible for programming SAGE).[8] The armed services could not be expected to take the relaxed attitude to security that was possible at universities. By the second half of the 1960s, important actors in the U.S. defense sector had realized that time-sharing computer systems posed security issues that went beyond the traditional concerns for secure communications, for protection against physical intrusion, and for the vetting of key personnel.

Computer security issues first came into clear focus in 1967, with an authoritative statement of them by Bernard Peters of the National Security Agency (NSA) at the Spring Joint Computer Conference. NSA is responsible for decoding the communications of actual or potential foes of the United States and for protecting the security of U.S. government classified communications. Far larger than the better-known CIA, NSA grew to employ some 50,000 people inside the barbed-wire fence surrounding its thousand-acre headquarters at Fort Meade, Maryland, as well as many more in its worldwide network of listening posts. It probably has been the world's largest customer for ultrapowerful computers (by the early 1980s, Fort Meade's computers occupied eleven acres of underground floor space) and is said to employ more mathematics Ph.Ds. than any other organization worldwide.[9]

Peters's speech was unusual, in that his affiliation to NSA was openly stated at a time when the agency's existence was not usually acknowledged: computer-industry insiders used to joke that the initials stood for "No Such Agency." NSA officers did not usually disclose their affiliation in public, and academics receiving research grants from NSA were not permitted to reveal that the agency was supporting their work. Instead, they would be provided with a "cover story": a different agency whose support could be acknowledged when, after obligatory vetting by NSA, their papers were submitted for publication.[10]

The special session of the 1967 conference was opened by one of the senior figures in U.S. computer science, Willis Ware. Ware had taken part in the celebrated digital computer project inspired by John von Neumann at the Institute for Advanced Study,[11] and he had gone on to become a member of the RAND Corporation's Computer Science Department and, later, its head. Ware, Peters, and some of Ware's RAND colleagues had been discussing computer security for some time (Ware joined the NSA's Scientific Advisory Board in 1964 and became its chair in January 1967)[12] and RAND had done some penetration studies (experiments in circumventing computer security controls) of early time-sharing systems on behalf of the government.[13]

In his talk to the conference, Ware tied the new security problem firmly to time-sharing: "With the advent of computer systems which share the resources of the configuration among several users or several problems, there is the risk that information from one user (or computer program) will be coupled to another user (or program)." He identified possible threats using what was to become a famous, often copied, illustration (see figure 5.1).[14]

Ware then turned the floor over to the NSA's Peters, who spelled out the question that was to dominate research and development in computer security for much of the following twenty years, to the extent that it became known as the "classical computer security problem": how to embody security in the system software of a "large multi-programmed system with remote terminals."[15] NSA's judgment was that no adequate solution to this problem was available, either in the university time-sharing systems or in the commercial products that were beginning to appear (in October 1967, for example, IBM released its Time Sharing System, TSS, for the System/360 Model 67).[16]

Peters emphasized that from a military security point of view it was necessary to do more than prevent one user's program inadvertently overwriting a memory location being used by another. Programs—and by extension human users—"must be considered to be hostile," said Peters. "Memory protect must be sufficient so that any reference, read or write, outside of the area assigned to a given user program must be detected and stopped. There are several forms of memory protect on the market which guard against out-of-bounds write, thus protecting program integrity, but they do not guard against illegal read. Read protect is as important as write protect, from a security standpoint, if classified material is involved."[17]

Peters did little more than to sketch how it might be possible to design system software to prevent illegal "reads" as well as illegal "writes." Nevertheless, his talk outlined three issues that were to become of great importance as the field of computer security developed. First was the key role in security played by the operating system or "monitor," which "acts as

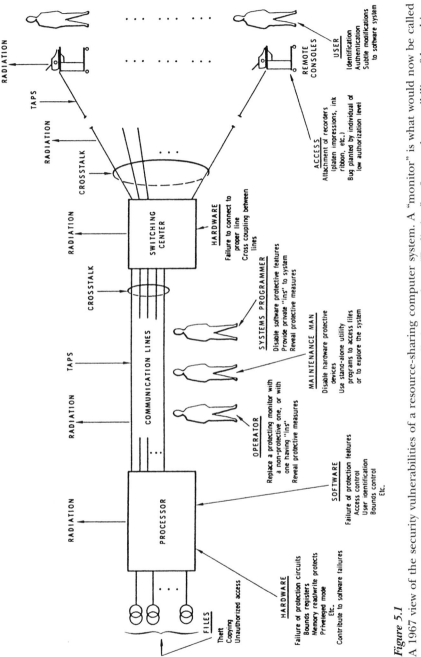

Figure 5.1

A 1967 view of the security vulnerabilities of a resource-sharing computer system. A "monitor" is what would now be called an operating system, and a "private in" would now be called a trapdoor. "Radiation" refers to the possibility of breaching security by analysis of electromagnetic emissions from a system. From Willis H. Ware, "Security and Privacy in Computer Systems," in *AFIPS Conference Proceedings, Volume 30: 1967 Spring Joint Computer Conference* (Washington, D.C.: Thompson Books, 1967), 279–282, at p. 280.

the overall guard to the system. It provides protection against the operators and the users at the remote terminals." Second, Peters raised the issue of certification, emphasizing that a monitor must be "approved by appropriate authority." In the military this would be a security officer, or senior management in business. "Who can tell who is in charge in a University?" he added dryly. The need for authoritative approval implied that it was necessary "to adequately demonstrate the security capability to the governing authority."

To facilitate this, suggested Peters (raising a third issue that was a harbinger of later developments), the monitor "must be carefully designed to limit the amount of critical coding [programming]." Critical security functions (in particular, the software handling the "interrupts" that transferred control between user programs and the monitor) should be implemented in relatively small amounts of code: "When an interrupt occurs . . . [t]he monitor must, as soon as reasonable, adjust the memory bounds to provide limits on even the monitor's own coding. This requires that the coding which receives interrupts be certified as error free for *all* possible inputs and timing. . . . By keeping the amount of coding that can reference any part of core without restriction to a few well-tested units, confidence in the monitor can be established."[18]

During 1967 increasing numbers of the new time-sharing systems were procured for U.S. government installations. Concerns about their security began to grow, in particular after a large defense contractor proposed selling to commercial users time on an IBM mainframe computer employed in a classified aircraft project, and the Department of Defense realized it had no policy to cover such a situation.[19] In response to these concerns, the Defense Science Board set up a task force in October 1967 to address the security of "multi-access, resource-sharing computer systems." The task force was chaired by RAND's Willis Ware with representation from the NSA, CIA, Department of Defense, defense contractors, and academia. It produced its classified report (originally drafted by Ware, but extensively rewritten by Thomas Chittenden of NSA) in February 1970.

The task force focused particularly on how to design a secure operating system or "supervisor." It proposed that the system maintain a "catalog" of "flags" to indicate the security status of users, terminals, and the files within which information was stored in computer memory. The system of flags would be modeled upon the existing system for classifying written documents. Users, terminals, files, particular jobs (computing tasks), input, and output would be classed into a vertical hierarchy of "top secret," "secret," "confidential," and "unclassified," according to their clearances and security statuses. Provision was also included for horizontal compartmentalization, such as the special category of clearance (Q-clearance) required for access to information about nuclear weapons.[20]

The Ware task force's proposed access-control rules were common-sense extensions of those that applied to documents. Fundamental was the rule that can be summarized as no read up: for example, a user with a "secret" clearance, using an appropriate terminal, would (unless barred by horizontal compartmentalization) be permitted access to files bearing the flags "secret," "confidential," and "unclassified," but not access to files bearing the "top secret" flag (see figure 5.2). The no read up rule appeared extremely simple, but by 1970 it was already clear to the task force that implementing it securely was a difficult task. Complications arose from the fact that computing was a dynamic process: a

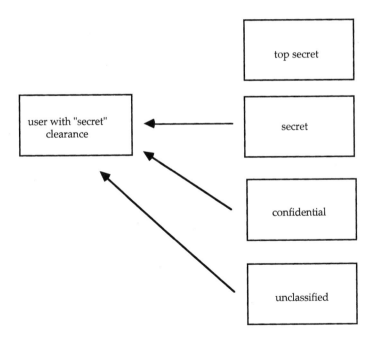

Figure 5.2
An example of no read up. A user with "secret" clearance can read "secret," "confidential," and "unclassified" files, but not "top secret" files.

figure for the range or the effectiveness of a weapon might, for example, be more sensitive than the individual pieces of data from which it was calculated.

More generally, "as a job unfolds, [its] security flag may have to be modified automatically by the system to reflect the security flags of files of information or files of other programs that are used." The task force also noted that "operating systems are very large, complex structures, and thus it is impossible to exhaustively test for every conceivable set of conditions that might arise," so it was necessary to separate the design of the supervisor into distinct modules, each of which "must be fully described with flowcharts to assist in its security analysis."[21]

The Ware task force's proposals appear not to have produced any immediate response. Less than two years later, in February 1972, a further study was commissioned by Major Roger Schell of the Electronic Systems Division of the U.S. Air Force. In Schell's view, "the Ware panel put together an assessment that says, 'You've got all these problems.' They offer almost nothing by way of solutions. And what the Air Force was interested in was 'How do we provide solutions?' "[22] Leading the new study was James P. Anderson, a computer consultant who headed his own company based in Fort Washington, Pennsylvania. The tone of the Anderson panel's report, completed in October 1972, was more urgent and more alarmist than that of its predecessor.

Its argument was that no existing system could securely be operated in a multilevel mode (that is, accessible to users with different levels of security clearance), and the Air Force was losing $100 million a year through the resulting inefficiencies. Whenever "tiger teams" had attempted to circumvent the security controls of existing systems they had succeeded. (As Ware now puts it, the operating systems of the 1960s were "Swiss cheese in terms of security loopholes."[23]) It was difficult, expensive, and probably futile to try to patch the vulnerabilities that made this possible. Nor, in the view of the Anderson panel, were computer science or the computer industry producing solutions. "[T]here is virtually nothing now being done that is applicable to the problem of secure computing in the USAF," and if the Air Force itself did nothing, "The situation will become even more acute in the future as potential enemies recognize the attractiveness of Air Force data systems as intelligence targets, and perceive how little effort is needed to subvert them."[24]

The Anderson panel proposed an $8 million research and development program to address these problems. Among the intended foci of

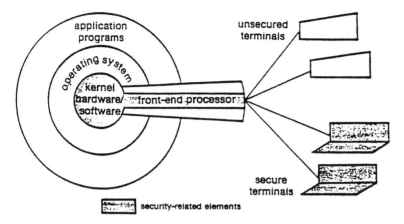

Figure 5.3
Security kernel (schematic). From Roger R. Schell, "Computer Security: The Achilles' Heel of the Electronic Air Force?" *Air University Review* 30(2) (January–February 1979): 16–33, at p. 29.

work was what Schell called a "security kernel." It involved a shift in design philosophy. Instead of adding security controls to a full, existing operating system, security functions were to be isolated into a kernel, which was essentially a primitive operating system interacting directly with the computer's hardware. All security-relevant requests by non-kernel programs (for example, requests for access to data files) would have to invoke the kernel's subroutines, and the kernel would accept only requests that did not compromise security. The analogy that naturally comes to mind is of concentric shells (see figure 5.3). A kernel "represents a distinct internal security perimeter. In particular, that portion of the system responsible for maintaining internal security is reduced from essentially the entire computer to principally the kernel."[25]

If security functions were implemented properly in the kernel (the term was sometimes taken to include security-relevant hardware as well as software),[26] then the design of the rest of the operating system was not critical from the point of view of security. The functions of a kernel were many fewer than those of a full operating system, so the hope was that the former could be kept "simple" and "formal."[27] Although later kernels were to become significantly more complex, a demonstration security kernel commissioned by the Air Force Electronic Systems Division consisted of only some twenty subroutines, totaling around 1,000 instructions. The kernel was developed for the Digital Equipment Corporation PDP-11/45 by the MITRE Corporation, an offshoot of MIT's Lincoln Laboratory that was originally set up to take over the latter's responsibilities for the SAGE system.[28]

Embodying "security" in a kernel had social as well as technical advantages. A persistent worry in the development of secure systems was the risk that they might be compromised from the start. A hostile agent who was part of the development team might, for example, deliberately build in a "trap door" (a surreptitious entry point) that allowed security controls to be circumvented. It was far easier to guard against this in the development of a kernel than in that of a whole system: "protecting the kernel . . . involves far fewer people and a much more controlled environment . . . thus, in contrast to contemporary systems, the kernel makes it tractable to protect against subversion."[29]

The Digital Equipment Corporation's VAX security kernel, discussed below, exemplified what a "controlled environment" meant:

The CPU [Central Processing Unit] and console of the development machine were kept inside a lab that only members of the VAX Security Kernel development group could enter. Within that lab, the development machine was protected by a *cage*, which consists of another room with a locked door. Physical access to both the lab and to the cage within the lab was controlled by a key-card security system. . . . [O]ur development machine was not connected to Digital's internal computer network, so as to minimize the external threat to our development environment and our project.[30]

Modeling Security

To design a security kernel successfully, however, one had to have a clear notion of what "security" was. To the Electronics Systems Division's Roger Schell, ad hoc "penetrate and patch" approaches were grossly inadequate. The fact that a system survived "tiger team" efforts to circumvent its security controls might mean only that the team had not been skilled enough or imaginative enough. Indeed, in practice the situation was worse than that: serious tiger team efforts appeared always to succeed, even after expensive "patching" of the vulnerabilities discovered by earlier penetration experiments.

For Schell, this implied "the impossibility of arriving at anything that you would classify as a secure system by informal means. I saw . . . instances of systems where people had put . . . millions of dollars into making them secure, and to no real avail." What was needed was a mathematical model of security that would raise "the kernel design and evaluation process above a mere game of wits with an attacker. . . . A dramatic effect is that the kernel facilitates objective evaluation of internal security. The evaluator need not examine the nearly endless number of possible penetration attempts; he need only verify that the mathematical model is correctly implemented by the kernel."[31]

The Ware panel had provided a "formal specification of the decision rules" involved in "determining whether an individual with a particular clearance and need-to-know can have access to a quantum of classified information in a given physical environment."[32] Its model (largely restricted to formalizing the no read up rule) was never applied practically. The first application of a mathematical model of multilevel military security to a real system was ADEPT-50, developed in the late 1960s by Clark Weissman and colleagues at the RAND offshoot, the System Development Corporation, with support from the Advanced Research Projects Agency. ADEPT-50 was an operating system designed to improve the security of a standard commercial computer (the IBM System/360 model 50). It embodied an algorithm that reclassified the security status of files dynamically, analyzing the security profile of a job and classifying the files created by the job according to the job's security "high-water mark," which was analogous to "the bath tub ring that marks the highest water level attained."[33]

Schell and the Air Force Electronic Systems Division were not satisfied with either the high-water mark model or the Ware panel's approach. The Anderson panel indeed explicitly criticized the latter for possibly having "a negative effect due to its specification of necessary, but not sufficient, criteria" of security.[34] The tighter definition the panel sought emerged from research funded by the Electronic Systems Division between 1972 and 1976 at Case Western Reserve University in Cleveland, Ohio (where K. G. Walter and colleagues developed a security model similar to, if less elaborate than, that developed by Bell and LaPadula),[35] and at the MITRE Corporation, where David Elliott Bell and Leonard J. LaPadula produced the paradigmatic mathematical approach to "security" that came to bear their names. They—especially LaPadula—were influenced by the "general system theory" then current. In 1968, for example, Ludwig von Bertalanffy issued a celebrated call for a systems approach, identifying "a change in basic categories of thought of which the complexities of modern technology are only one . . . manifestation. . . . [W]e are forced to deal with complexities, with 'wholes' or 'systems', in all fields of knowledge."[36]

Bell and LaPadula drew upon general system theorists M. D. Mesarović, D. Macko, and Y. Takahara of Case Western, who defined a "system" as a mapping between two mathematical sets, one representing inputs and the other outputs.[37] The way Bell and LaPadula applied this notion to model a computer system was dauntingly abstract in its most general formulation, but as far as security properties were concerned the key issue was access by "subjects" (not just human users, but also their "surrogates," processes and programs in execution) to "objects" such as data files. Bell and LaPadula realized that the rules of access had to go beyond the no read up rule (or "simple security property" as they called it) governing access by human readers to documents. In particular, Bell and LaPadula argued that it was vital to have an explicit mechanism to prevent "high classification material [being] added to a low classification file without appropriate changes being made to the security classification lists."[38]

In document-based systems, human users were implicitly trusted not to "write down" in this way, but the broadening of the notion of "subject" to include computer processes and programs raised a new issue: the risk that a hostile agent might insinuate a "Trojan horse" into a trusted system. Introduced by Daniel Edwards, an NSA representative on the Anderson panel,[39] the term referred to a program that, in addition to performing its overt function, surreptitiously violated security controls, for example by writing classified data to an unclassified file (see figure 5.4). Continually checking each and every piece of software used on a

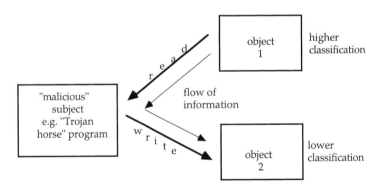

Figure 5.4
Why the *-property is needed. Based on figure in D. E. Bell and L. J. LaPadula, "Secure Computer System: Unified Exposition and Multics Interpretation" (Bedford, Mass.: Air Force Systems Command, Electronic Systems Division, March 1976, ESD-TR-75–306), p. 17.

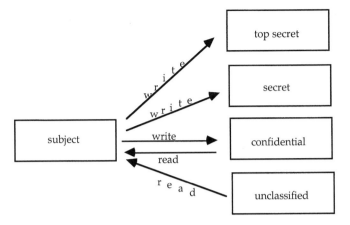

Figure 5.5
An example of no write down. A subject with "read" access to confidential objects has "write" access to confidential, secret, and top secret objects, but does not have "write" access to unclassified objects.

secure system to ensure that it was not a Trojan horse would be a daunting task, but Trojan horses could be defeated, Bell and LaPadula concluded, if systems satisfied not just the simple security property but also what they called the "*-property" (pronounced "star property"), which required that a subject can simultaneously have "observe" access to one object and "alter" access to another only if the classification level of the second object was greater than or equal to that of the first.[40] If the "simple security property" was no read up, the *-property was no write down (see figure 5.5).

As well as showing the need for the *-property, Bell and LaPadula formulated what they called the "basic security theorem." Later to become the object of controversy (see below), the theorem, in their view, greatly simplified the mathematics of security by showing that security was mathematically inductive. If a system begins in a secure state, and if changes of state satisfy the simple security property and *-property, then the system would remain secure.[41] Bell and LaPadula wrote: "The importance of this result should not be underestimated. Other problems of seemingly comparable difficulty are not of an inductive nature. . . . The result, therefore that security (as defined in the model) is inductive establishes the relative simplicity of maintaining security: the minimum check that the proposed new state is 'secure' is both necessary and sufficient for full maintenance of security."[42]

That was an optimistic conclusion—albeit immediately qualified by some important provisos concerning, inter alia, "trusted subjects" and "covert channels" (see below)[43]—and an influential one. In 1979, for example, Roger Schell (by then promoted to Lieutenant Colonel) spelled out for an Air Force audience what he believed to be the significance of the "foundation of mathematical completeness" provided by the Bell-LaPadula and similar modeling efforts: "Security theorems have been proved showing that (since the kernel precisely follows the model) the kernel will not permit a compromise, regardless of what program uses it or how it is used. That is, the kernel design is penetration-proof—in particular to all those clever attacks that the kernel designers never contemplated."[44]

Security and Proof

But how was an evaluator to verify that an actual kernel or system was a correct implementation of a mathematical model of "security"? Here, the history of computer security became intertwined with the more general developments discussed in chapters 2 and 3. As noted in chapter 2, in the late 1960s there was rapidly growing interest in showing that programs were correct implementations of their specifications, not just by testing them empirically (as the NSA's Peters had implied in 1967),[45] but by the application of mathematical proof. By 1972, "program proof" or "formal verification" was a focus of much research effort, and the notion was particularly attractive to those concerned with military security, because it, together with a formal model of what "security" was, appeared to promise certainty that systems were without security flaws.

Without proof, even the most determined efforts to make systems secure were often seen as producing ambiguous results. For example, "[t]he ease of defeating" the security controls of the System Development Corporation's ADEPT-50 operating system was "a matter of some debate."[46] The Anderson panel wrote in 1972 that: "because the reference validation mechanism [that is, the mechanism that allows or disallows security-relevant requests by user programs] is the security mechanism in the system, it must be possible to ascertain that it works correctly in all cases and is always invoked. If this cannot be achieved, then there is no way to know that the reference validation takes place correctly in all cases, and therefore there is no basis for certifying a system as secure."[47]

The strength of the perceived need to verify security, together with the ample resources available to National Security Agency and other defense organizations, made computer security by far the most important source of support for research and development work on formal specification and program proof. That support turned the theoretical developments of the 1960s in these areas, especially those of Floyd and Hoare (see chapter 2), into verification systems that, though still research tools, could be applied not just to "toy" programs but to prototypes of real-world kernels, secure operating systems, and communications processors. For example, the first automated program verifier was that reported in James King's 1969 Ph.D. thesis (King's system is described in chapter 2). The following year, Donald I. Good, a student of University of Wisconsin verification pioneer Ralph London, described a second automated verification system. Unlike King's automatic verifier, Good's system was designed to support human-computer interaction in proof construction: it "was largely a sophisticated bookkeeping system for accepting and keeping track of manual proofs," said Good.[48]

In the early 1970s Good and his fellow formal verificationists had "been dinking around with [verifying] 20-, 30-, maybe 40-line programs if we were really tough." That was, of course, far short of what was needed for computer security, and NSA offered for competitive tender a contract to "see how far you can get [in] scaling this up to about 1,000 lines. And . . . while you're doing that, focus on [verifying] communication systems." Good, who had moved in 1970 to the University of Texas at Austin, won the contract, and in 1974 he began development of what he called the Gypsy Verification Environment, containing a programming and specification language (based on the PASCAL programming language), an editor, a compiler, a verification condition generator (which produced the predicate-logic formulae that have to be proved in order to show that a program satisfied its specification), and an interactive, automated theorem prover. For the prover, Good adapted a system developed by his Austin colleague Woody Bledsoe (see chapter 3) and Peter Bruell. The Gypsy prover, wrote Good in 1983, "is really more like a proof checker than a proof constructor. It provides a list of sound deductive manipulations that a user can apply interactively to the current subgoal. The user directs the prover by telling it what manipulations to perform until the formula is reduced to TRUE."[49]

From January 1977 to December 1981, Good and his colleagues applied their new system to a practical verification task: the specification, design, and verification of an Encrypted Packet Interface, a message protection unit designed to sit between a host computer and the ARPAnet (the Advanced Research Projects Agency's pioneering computer network, the construction of which was a crucial step in the development of the Internet).[50] The interface consisted "of 4211 lines of executable Gypsy which is distributed over two PDP 11/03 computers," and Good's team used their verification system to prove that those lines of program were a correct implementation of the interface's specification. "All of the 2600 verification conditions were constructed automatically, and 88 percent of these were proved fully automatically. The remaining 12 percent were proved with the interactive theorem prover. Only two unproved lemmas were assumed in these proofs." Although neither the Encrypted Packet Interface, nor a simpler Message Flow Modulator designed for the U.S. Navy, was deployed in the field, both were developed to the stage of successfully working prototypes.[51]

Another group prominent in the early application of formal verification to security was the nonprofit corporation, SRI International, an offshoot of Stanford University (its original name was Stanford Research Institute). SRI was located in the area just south of San Francisco that was rapidly becoming "Silicon Valley." Among members of the SRI group were Peter Neumann, who had previously worked on the development of Multics, which was the first important operating system developed with a strong emphasis on security and which was, indirectly, the progenitor of the pervasive Unix operating system; Robert S. Boyer, who with J Strother Moore (at the nearby Xerox Palo Alto Research Center) had created the Boyer-Moore theorem prover, which was used in the automation of proofs in the early SRI work; Richard J. Feiertag, who developed an influential tool for analyzing information flow between the variables in a system specification;[52] and Karl N. Levitt and Lawrence Robinson, who played a crucial role in the development of SRI's overall approach, called Hierarchical Development Methodology (HDM).[53]

Perhaps SRI's most significant computer security project was the Provably Secure Operating System (PSOS), begun in 1973.[54] As its name suggests, PSOS was an entire operating system, not a security kernel. Although Feiertag and Neumann also worked on a Kernelized Secure Operating System (KSOS), the SRI team believed that the advantages of kernels had to be weighed against disadvantages, such as the inflexibility arising from the fact that a kernel was specific to a particular security model.[55] The SRI team began its work on PSOS with a loosely defined system and gradually moved to a complete specification of the design, which was decomposed into a hierarchy of different modules at different levels. The full formal specification of PSOS was 400 pages long.[56]

Considerable work was devoted to proving that PSOS as defined by that specification could be used to implement the Bell-LaPadula model, together with a loosely analogous model covering the integrity of data. Some attempts were also made to show that the detailed specification was, in its turn, correctly implemented in PSOS's code (in other words, in its program text). These efforts to prove PSOS secure, however, turned out to be demanding. The 1980 report on the project, by then seven years old, was careful not to exaggerate what had been done: "PSOS," said the report, "might be considered an acronym for a 'Potentially Secure Operating System,' in that PSOS has been carefully designed in such a way that it might someday have both its design and its implementation subjected to rigorous proof."[57]

Slow progress with verification of security was not an experience unique to SRI and was encountered even when a kernel, rather than operating system, was the target. At the University of California at Los Angeles (UCLA), considerable effort was expended in the late 1970s to verify the correctness of a kernel designed to allow the Unix operating system, then growing rapidly in popularity, to be run securely on the widely used Digital Equipment Corporation PDP-11 minicomputer. The approach taken was different from that of SRI, with less attention to work on specifications and more on verification "of the lowest level assembly code." Again, considerable difficulties were encountered. The work was never completed, although "the verification of 35 to 40 percent of the kernel led developers to claim that, given sufficient resources, verification of the entire kernel was feasible."[58]

With the SRI and UCLA research projects meeting with problems, it is not surprising that severe difficulties struck the most ambitious 1970s' effort to apply formal verification to a system designed not as a prototype but for actual deployment. Autodin (Automatic Digital Network) II was a plan to build a secure military computer network using the sophisticated packet-switching[59] approach developed for ARPAnet. The first version of Autodin had been much simpler, without packet-switching, while the ARPAnet itself was not secure. Two industry teams competed for the contract to bring together security and packet-switching in Autodin II: one team, involving ARPAnet prime contractors Bolt, Beranek, and Newman, proposed in essence simply adding encryption to a network akin to the existing ARPAnet; the other team, led by Western Union, and including Ford Aerospace and the System Development Corporation, proposed a system involving a security kernel and formal verification. The latter team was awarded the contract late in 1976.

The request for proposals, however, was drawn up "without adequately defining 'kernel' or the requirements for formal specification and verification. There were many problems in its development, including a court fight over the definition of 'formal specification,' "[60] and a contradiction was found in its formal top-level specification.[61] These problems contributed to difficulties in achieving security certification and, although this was eventually gained, the system was by then two and a half years behind schedule and plagued with worries about its expense and its survivability in the face of attack. In 1982 it was canceled in favor of a revived version of the original, less ambitious, cryptographic alternative.[62]

Trusted Subjects and Covert Channels

The difficulties of PSOS, UCLA "data secure Unix," and Autodin II indicated that it was a demanding task formally to verify that a real operating system (or even a real kernel) conformed to a mathematical model of "security." One reason for the problems was that formal verification was a new field, in which many of those involved were still feeling their way and the automated tools to assist them were still immature. Another reason was that applying security models such as the Bell-LaPadula model to real systems was more difficult than it first appeared. As Bell put it, "simple rules . . . need to be refined to accommodate reality better." The MITRE effort, referred to above, to apply the Bell-LaPadula model to a prototype security kernel led to the realization that the *-property was "overly simple."[63] There was in practice a need for "trusted subjects," which could be relied upon never to "mix information of different security levels" and could therefore be allowed to operate without the *-property being imposed upon them.[64]

Consider, for example, the subject (print spooler or print driver) that controls printing in a multilevel secure system. Unless completely separate print control paths are provided for all security classes, the print spooler must be permitted to violate the *-property. If it is to read, say, top secret information and to write it to the queue for an appropriate printer, the spooler must be a subject with top secret status. The *-property would then prevent it from writing secret, confidential, or unclassified data to queues with these lower classification levels. So it must be trusted to perform "writes" in violation of the *-property without mixing information of different security levels.[65] The need for "trusted subjects" of this kind increased the formal verification task.

It was not enough to verify that the simple security property and *-property had been implemented correctly in a security kernel. It was also necessary to prove that the nonkernel trusted subjects in a system— such as programs to backup and retrieve files, connections with networks, and input-output spoolers[66]—were indeed trustworthy: that they would not violate security, even if "attacked" by a hostile agent. The "trusted computing base"[67] that had to be subject to formal verification, therefore, had to include the trusted subjects as well as the mechanisms enforcing the simple security property and *-property.

The second practical complication in applying security models was "covert channels," a term introduced into the open literature in a 1973 paper by Butler Lampson of the Xerox Palo Alto Research Center. Lampson was not directly considering military security: his description of what he called the "confinement problem" talked about a customer using a computer service who wished to ensure that data could not be read or modified without permission.[68] The phenomena Lampson was referring to, however, were already known to defense-sector computer security practitioners,[69] and those theorizing about the latter field, such as Bell and LaPadula,[70] quickly realized that here was an issue they had to tackle. "Covert channel" is a slippery term with no entirely stable meaning. The notion is parasitic on the enterprise of producing mathematical models of security: covert channels are all those means of transferring information that are not encompassed by a formal security model, especially by the Bell-LaPadula model. In any real, physical computer system there is potentially a variety of mechanisms by which a subject with a high security clearance (a subject which could be a Trojan horse program) could pass information to an uncleared, or less highly cleared, subject without violating the simple security property or the *-property.

A typical covert channel in a time-sharing system involves a high-security subject being able to "signal" to a low-security subject by periodically denying the latter access to some shared computing resource. For example, suppose a subject with read access to top secret files and an uncleared subject both have access to the same unclassified file. Because of the *-property, the top secret subject cannot modify the file's contents, but it can read the file; the uncleared subject can both read it and write to it. The software of a time-sharing operating system will usually contain an interlock mechanism to prevent a file being modified by one program while being read by another, so the top secret subject can "signal" to the uncleared subject simply by reading the file, because the uncleared subject's requests to write to the file will be rejected while the top secret subject is reading it. The interlock is not intended as a repository of information (so it would not usually be treated as a Bell-LaPadula "object"), but it can be used for that purpose, with the secret user conveying information, one binary digit at a time, by either reading the file or by refraining from doing so. This example would be referred to by computer security specialists as a "storage channel," because the interlock is being used covertly to store information.[71]

A second type of covert channel is what is called a "timing channel," in which the high-security subject signals to the low-security subject by affecting the amount of time it takes the latter to detect a change in some system attribute or to receive access to some system resource. Nearly all computer systems, for example, contain an electronic "clock," which all user programs can read. Suppose (for reasons of simplicity) that only two user programs are present. The higher security program could signal to the lower security program by occupying the system's central processing unit up until a particular clock time. The lower security program could then infer that clock time by recording when it was able to begin execution, and so clock time could be used to transfer information.[72]

Any actual multiuser system will usually have more than two users, so a timing channel is likely to be "noisy," and sophisticated information-theory techniques may be needed to exploit it in practice. Furthermore, both storage channels and timing channels will typically have small bandwidths: that is, they can be used to transmit information only slowly. The secure systems development efforts of the 1970s, however, found that it was infeasible completely to remove all possible covert channels. In a time-sharing system, computing resources had to be shared, and efforts to block the resultant covert channels by preventing direct, unmediated, access by subjects to these resources caused unacceptable deterioration of system performance: secure systems were already much slower than their insecure counterparts.[73] The best that could be done in practice, concluded the authors of one influential project (to develop a security kernel for IBM's widely used System/370 computers), was to reduce covert channels to "acceptable bandwidths."[74]

The Computer Security Evaluation Center

The difficulties of formal verification, the need for trusted subjects, and the practical infeasibility of entirely eliminating covert channels all indicated by the end of the 1970s the technical complexity of computer security. Some of its social complexities were also beginning to emerge by then. The most pressing issue in the United States was who should have organizational responsibility for ensuring the security of the design of military computer systems. The obvious answer was the National Security Agency. Although the NSA was powerful and well-funded, however, there were tensions between its entrenched culture and what many perceived as the requirements of the new field.

The key relevant facet of the NSA's culture was its approach to what NSA insiders called "COMSEC," communications security. The obverse of NSA's more celebrated role of breaking other nations' codes, the goal of COMSEC was to preserve the communications security of the United States. Practitioners of COMSEC were steeped in a culture of secrecy and of government dominance of industry. In effect, NSA's experts decided what technologies were needed to protect U.S. government and military communications, provided industry with detailed instructions as to what it was to produce, and insisted that firms comply with stringent security classification. The emphasis on extreme secrecy flowed from the centrality of cryptography to COMSEC: traditional codes were immediately vulnerable if their keys were known,[75] and even knowledge of general design features of encryption devices could be of great use to an enemy. The COMSEC tradition in the United States stretched back to World War I.[76] The success of Allied COMSEC in World War II, and the successful breaking of the Axis codes, gave the activity considerable status within the inner circles of government and in the intelligence community.

COMPUSEC, as computer security is known within NSA, was much more recent than COMSEC, much less prestigious, and much less well entrenched in NSA's hierarchy. Its attitude to secrecy was different. Academics—with their need to publish—were far more important in the emergence of COMPUSEC than they had been in that of COMSEC. Furthermore, COMSEC typically sought probabilistic security: codes with an extremely low probability of being broken. In contrast, at least until the practical infeasibility of entirely eliminating covert channels was accepted, COMPUSEC's goal was deterministic security (systems that *could* not be penetrated) and deductive, proof-based, certainty of that security. If that goal was achieved, was the secrecy that had to surround COMSEC necessary for COMPUSEC?

In the words of NSA officer George F. Jelen: "if a system could be *proven* to be impenetrable, then there would appear to be nothing

gained from secrecy." Jelen also suggested that the different circumstances of the two fields' birth left their mark:

Most of the significant early development of COMSEC devices took place during
an era when government was generally trusted. That of COMPUSEC did not.
When COMSEC device technology was maturing, the environment was that of
a country unified by war against a common, foreign enemy. The current [1985]
political environment surrounding the government's efforts in computer security is set against the backdrop of Watergate. . . . The 'high politics' factor, then,
is that in the minds of many people today, the enemy most to be feared is the
government itself.[77]

More immediately troublesome for computer security practitioners,
however, was what Jelen called "low politics," in other words "bureaucratic battles over turf."[78] Despite the speech by Peters discussed here,
NSA did not move decisively and openly into the new field of computer
security, preferring to operate as it always had done: behind the scenes
and anonymously. NSA's secrecy and hesitancy left computer security in
an organizational vacuum. An obvious alternative to NSA was the Department of Defense's Advanced Research Projects Agency (ARPA), with its
considerable experience of supporting research and development in
computing, most famously the construction of the ARPAnet.[79] ARPA was
suspected by many in the military, however, of insufficient focus on real
defense needs.

The Anderson panel noted pointedly that ARPA-funded projects "appear to be focusing on one or more interesting (to the principal investi-
gator) research problems, but do not evidence a comprehensive or
cohesive approach to solve the USAF [U.S. Air Force] Computer Security
Problem."[80] The organizational vacuum was filled in the early 1970s by
Major Roger Schell and his colleagues at the Air Force's Electronic Systems Division. They gave currency to the idea of a security kernel, created the Anderson panel, supported the modeling work of Bell,
LaPadula, and others, and by the mid-1970s they had made significant
progress toward practical implementation of these ideas. They were less
successful, however, in keeping the support of their Air Force superiors,
who were not convinced that the service should be devoting its own resources to a generic Department of Defense problem. Without wholehearted, top-level Air Force backing, congressional support in turn
became problematic. The upshot was a sudden cutoff in funding in 1976,
which created a "hiatus from which the [Department of Defense] has
had difficulty recovering."[81]

Central to the efforts at recovery was Stephen T. Walker who was hired by the Advanced Research Projects Agency in 1974 to head its computer security work. In early 1978 he moved on to the Office of the Secretary of Defense, where he became the single most influential public figure in U.S. computer security.[82] Although Walker had come to ARPA from behind NSA's real and metaphorical barbed-wire fences, he was influenced profoundly by ARPA's more open style. He came to believe that computer security could not successfully follow the COMSEC tradition of government direction and tight security. Instead, he favored the ARPA approach of using government research and development funding (such as the Department of Defense's Computer Security Initiative headed by Walker and launched in 1978) to encourage academic and industrial activity in computer security, while not directing that activity too closely nor shrouding it in secrecy. Walker began to see computer security as a governmentwide issue, not just a military problem, and he wanted "to get industry involved in figuring out how to build trusted systems," bringing in government only to evaluate how successful firms had been in this effort.[83]

The natural candidate for the role of evaluating putatively secure computer systems was NSA, but Walker's experience of the agency led him to conclude that its COMSEC culture did not fit the vision of computer security he was developing. He briefly and unsuccessfully floated a plan for a Program Management Office for computer security, located within NSA but organizationally autonomous.[84] He soon broadened his horizons, however, to propose a federal (not just Department of Defense) Computer Security Center. Such a center, he said:

> needed to be able to sit down and talk with industry and convince industry to do things, as opposed to the typical NSA communications security model, which was, "I'll write you a contract, I will clear all your people, I will tell you exactly what to do, and you'll do it only my way." I [Walker] had had extensive discussions in the '79–'80 timeframe with folks at NSA, trying to argue that this needed to be done as an open activity, where you tried to convince people, as opposed to telling them. . . . [W]e wanted to get industry to do this as part of their normal product, which they'd make available to anyone, not as a special-purpose product just for the Defense Department."[85]

Walker hoped that funding for his proposed center would come from the Department of Commerce as well as the Department of Defense and he envisaged its potential home as the National Bureau of Standards, a civilian organization (part of the Department of Commerce) that had, among its other roles, responsibility for advising federal agencies on computer procurement.[86]

Early in 1980 Walker began circulating his proposal around Washington, D.C. The threat that computer security might move outside its ambit galvanized NSA. Walker realized that the agency was unhappy and he sought a meeting with its director, Vice Admiral Bobby R. Inman, to explain his ideas. He finally got to meet Inman in August 1980. Years afterward, the meeting, in what Walker remembered as Admiral Inman's impressively huge office at Fort Meade, remained vivid in his mind. Inman listened quietly as Walker spoke until he came to his proposal to involve the Department of Commerce and site the center in the National Bureau of Standards. Then Inman erupted, rolling forward in his chair, pounding his fist upon his desk: "I will never let that happen. I will go to the President to keep that from happening!" To Walker's surprise ("I was sitting there thinking, *How can I get out that door?*"), Inman's tone then became conciliatory. He asked Walker what had become of his earlier proposal for a computer security center situated within NSA and indicated that he would be willing to support that idea. He even agreed with Walker when the latter insisted "that this should not be done in the same way COMSEC is done." Inman asked Walker to set the bureaucratic procedures in motion by writing to him about a computer security center.[87]

Unknown to Walker, his dramatic meeting with Inman was following a partially prearranged script. Hearing of Walker's campaign, Inman had several months previously asked Walker's boss, Assistant Secretary of Defense Gerald P. Dinneen, to meet with him privately, and the two men had between them "hammered out" the agreement that apparently emerged from Walker's meeting with Inman.[88] It was Walker, though, who was responsible for the crucial—albeit, as we shall see, temporary— separation of the computer security center from the NSA COMSEC organization.[89] In the final days of President Carter's administration, Walker worked furiously to flesh out, and to gather further support for, what came to be called first the Department of Defense Computer Security Evaluation Center and then (from 1984) the National Computer Security Center. In the words of the 1982 directive that officially established the center, it was to be "a separate and unique entity within the NSA," whose prime tasks were to "[e]stablish and maintain technical standards and criteria for the evaluation of trusted computer systems," evaluate actual systems against those criteria, and "conduct and sponsor" computer security research and development.[90]

The Orange Book

From the late 1970s onward, attention began to focus on the criteria that should be used to evaluate trusted computer systems. By then there was little doubt that some form of mathematical proof would be demanded for systems in the highest assurance category. But what form of proof was still an open question. Thus, when Grace Nibaldi of the MITRE Corporation sketched out in 1979 a suggestion for a hierarchy of security classes for operating systems, the three highest levels were distinguished largely by different requirements for proof. Level four required mathematical proof that a detailed specification of the system was a correct implementation of "a security model." Level five extended this formal verification to the source code (program text) of the implemented system. Level six extended the analysis (though not necessarily the formal proof) to the object code generated from that source code by the compiler. Proof ought eventually to extend even to the hardware itself, wrote Nibaldi: "Axiomatization of the underlying hardware base, and formal verification of the security-relevant hardware mechanisms, are also required. It is recognized, however, that these requirements are beyond the anticipated state-of-the-art of verification in the 1980s."[91]

During the early 1980s, doubts began to appear not just about hardware verification but also about the verification requirements of Nibaldi's levels five and six. The essential problem was the practical difficulty of verifying programs of the size required for a security kernel. As Stephen Walker put it in 1980: "Our success in achieving the widespread availability of trusted systems is more dependent upon progress in the verification field than in any other single activity. It is for this reason that I have made support of verification technology the single primary technology development activity in the Computer Security Initiative."[92] Despite the research funds flowing from the initiative, NSA, and ARPA, however, progress in program verification remained slow. Automated program verification systems were far from automatic: many hours of work by highly skilled human beings were needed to guide these systems to a proof of even a simple real-world program.

The Encrypted Packet Interface stood out among the early security verification projects in that it was brought to a successful conclusion; Good and his coworkers were skilled specialists, yet they could each produce no more than an average of two to six lines of verified program per working day.[93] In the early 1980s there were probably fewer than 200 such specialists in the United States. Furthermore, though the interface was a substantial program (over 4,000 lines long), it was still considerably smaller than the security kernels being considered in the early 1980s.

When the Department of Defense *Trusted Computer System Evaluation Criteria* was issued in 1985 (a final draft was circulated in 1983), code verification was not demanded, therefore, even for the highest evaluation category. Universally known (because of the color of its covers) as the "orange book," the *Criteria* provided for four ascending divisions, some with subcategories. Division D consisted of systems that provided minimal or no protection. Division C systems had audit capabilities and were judged capable of supporting the maintenance of "need to know," or discretionary, security among users all with the same level of clearance, but were not certified as usable in an environment in which users had different levels of security clearance.

Division B systems, however, were judged suitable for this "multilevel" use. The trusted computer base of a division B system preserved "the integrity of sensitivity [i.e., classification] labels and uses them to enforce a set of mandatory access control rules." B2 systems had to be "based on a clearly defined and documented formal security policy model," and in B3 systems there also had to be "a convincing argument" that the specification of the trusted computer base was consistent with the security model. A1 certification (the highest) required use of an automated verification system endorsed by the National Computer Security Center to show, using both "formal and informal techniques," that the system specification was consistent with the security model.[94]

Even for A1 orange book systems, therefore, proof meant "design proof" (demonstration that the detailed specification of a system correctly implemented a formal security model) rather than "code proof" (demonstration that the actual programs making up the system were correct implementations of the specification). In the early 1980s it had been expected that a higher, A2 subdivision, incorporating code proof, would eventually be added but the addition was never made. To some, the restriction of the meaning of "proof" to "design proof" was unjustifiable. Automated theorem-proving specialists Robert S. Boyer and J Strother Moore (who had by then left SRI) wrote in 1985:

a program whose design has been verified is unworthy of trust until the running program has been shown to implement the design. Especially to be distrusted are those software products constructed by two unrelated teams: those who write the code, and those who simultaneously and independently write the formal specifications which are then checked for security. Alas, several such projects are currently funded by the U.S. Government. This travesty of mathematical proof has been defended with the claim that at least it gives the government better documentation. The Department of Defense has published official standards authorizing this nonsense."[95]

To others, such as SRI's Peter Neumann, "design proof" was a perfectly sensible strategy:

the attitude of having to prove everything from the hardware, or from the ions, all the way up into the application, is untenable . . . By the time you have finished it, the system is no longer what it was when you proved it, because the system tends to be a moving target. . . . By the time you get a system evaluated against those criteria, the vendor has already moved on to three or four versions later. And so the idea that one can thoroughly prove a system from stem to stern, and from bottom to top, is unreal. So the question is, where does the biggest pay-off come? . . . [W]e [SRI] took the attitude that the code proofs were absolutely irrelevant if the specifications were wrong, and that the immediate pay-off would come from showing that the design was no good. Rather than trying to prove things are correct, you are really trying to find the flaws. So the interesting challenge becomes to model the properties of the system that you're trying to achieve, at whatever layer of abstraction you're dealing with, and to try to prove, say, that the specifications are consistent with those properties.[96]

Even with "proof" restricted to design proof, meeting the demands of the orange book's A1 category was expensive and difficult. The specialized skills required for formal proof, and the sheer time it took, meant that the tendency to dissociation between design verification and system construction, identified by Boyer and Moore, was indeed present in early efforts at A1.[97] Among systems used for security verification were Good's Gypsy, the System Development Corporation's Formal Development Methodology (FDM), SRI's Hierarchical Development Methodology (HDM), and the Boyer-Moore theorem prover. Although the first two of these were the first systems on the Computer Security Center's Endorsed Tools List, all four systems had begun as research prototypes, and they still had significant practical limitations.

For example, Gypsy, the Boyer-Moore prover, and SPECIAL (the HDM specification language) were all used in the verification in the first half of the 1980s of the first system to achieve A1 rating, Honeywell's Secure Communications Processor (SCOMP). "The amount of effort required to verify the SCOMP system was very large. The tools were often very slow, difficult to use, and unable to completely process a complex specification. There were many areas where tedious hand analysis had to be used."[98] Donald Good, designer of Gypsy, comments that his verification system went "from a research instrument essentially through a little bit of a hardening phase into the hands of the contractors without ever really going through a real development stage. It was a system that was put together by about 30 different graduate students and it was creaky and moaned and groaned. The poor contractors!"[99]

The skilled researchers that might have helped the development of systems like Gypsy from "research instruments" to industrial tools were in short supply, and their energy was in part absorbed in meeting the Computer Security Evaluation Center's demand that endorsed tools be converted to run on the security-oriented time-sharing Multics operating system, which was employed by the center but not widely used elsewhere. Endorsed tools, furthermore, became subject to export controls, restricting not merely their distribution but also publications about them.

Stephen Walker began to believe that his vision of the development of computer security was being undermined by the reimposition of NSA's secretive, directive approach:

they made everybody port everything to Multics at the same time that the world was going to stand-alone machines. . . . They burned up everybody's energy on the conversions to Multics, and then they restricted who could see them or use them. So without actually advancing the technology at all, they basically submerged it. . . . I remember complaining rather bitterly to management at NSA that, "Don't let your people get a hold of some of these technologies, because they'll kill them." I have this image of giant oak trees . . . and then these vines start growing up round them. . . . [S]ome of these technologies, that are very important, are being killed by the very guys that ought to be trying to promote them.[100]

Despite these problems, computer security practitioners painfully learned to overcome the difficulties of formal verification. The System Development Corporation, for example, had found considerable difficulty in its early work using its FDM verification system on security-critical projects such as Autodin II. As a participant described it:

The field of formal notations and mathematical formalism was new and most programmers unaware of its properties. . . . The formal specs were treated like code, not math, and impossible for them to comprehend, let alone prove. [The] "throwing it (formal specs) over the wall" method failed. Next we tried doing it ourselves with skilled mathematicians . . . that was not a success . . . because of . . . "dissociation" of teams. The [specification] and [code] were in a race to finish, and code won. As is typical in large programming jobs, the code deviated from the DTLS [detailed top level specification] and the DTLS was not updated. In the end, the FTLS [formal top level specification] was being developed from the code, a terrible form of "reverse engineering."

With time, experience, and refinement of FDM, however, the System Development Corporation eventually began to overcome the difficulties that beset its early work.

This was evidenced by the corporation's BLACKER program, a set of cryptographic devices designed to ensure that low-clearance users of the Defense Data Network could not read high-security traffic on the network. Development of BLACKER began in 1984, and it received A1 rating in 1991, "after 5 years of very detailed . . . evaluation" by the National Computer Security Center. Classes were held to educate the programmers involved in the formal notation being used, while "the formal team was trained on the programming tools and methods. . . . To integrate the teams further, the formal team was required to do quality control on all the specs and design documentation, and later the unit code. Many hours of 'burned eyeballs' were spent by the formal team reading DTLS [detailed top level specification] and code and uncovering problems early."[101] This painful work kept the design proof from becoming disconnected from the actual coding, although the former still required considerable skill: "There is a delicate balance between the level of detail in the spec, the number of invariants, and the difficulty in achieving proofs. Achieving that balance is still an art. We have on average written/proven specs about three times before the balance is achieved."[102]

Proofs and Refutations in Security Modeling

As the practical difficulties of formal verification were gradually overcome, the effort's environment—intellectual, technical, and political—began to shift. Although all three aspects of the shift were intertwined, the most striking intellectual change was the decline in the dominance of the Bell-LaPadula model of "security," a decline evidenced both by criticism and by the emergence of different models.

The most prominent critic of the Bell-LaPadula model was John McLean. After studying mathematics, computer science, and philosophy, McLean taught at the University of North Carolina at Chapel Hill and researched philosophy of science and logic before joining the U.S. Naval Research Laboratory in 1980, where he became head of its formal methods group and, later, director of its Center for High Assurance Computer Systems. The prestigious laboratory was the only organization in the United States with a standing in communications and network security in any way comparable to that of NSA. For example, in the early 1990s, the laboratory became a cryptographic certification recommendation authority, the one and only such authority outside of NSA. It pioneered a solution to the narrowband secure voice problem (the problem of encoding human speech so that it can be transmitted securely at low data rates), and it developed the Navy Key Distribution System, the first system to distribute cryptographic keys electronically rather than on unencrypted paper tape.[103]

At the Naval Research Laboratory, McLean and his colleagues Carl Landwehr and Constance Heitmeyer developed what they called the Military Message System Model. Less abstract than the Bell-LaPadula model, their model described the security requirements for the specific application—military messages—suggested by its title. NSA insisted that they prove, for their model, the equivalent of Bell and LaPadula's basic security theorem, which was regarded, for example by Schell, as justifying confidence in the security of systems. McLean and his colleagues did as they were requested. In the effort to prove a basic security theorem for the Military Message System Model, however, McLean came to the conclusion that the theorem was essentially empty. "Stripped of all formalism," he wrote, "the theorem states that if a system starts in a secure state and if all its transitions are such that at each state any old access that violates security under the new state's clearance functions is withdrawn and no new access is introduced that violates security, then the system will remain secure. But this is so obvious that it is of virtually no help."[104]

Time spent proving such a theorem was "wasted," concluded McLean, because it provided no grounds for justifying claims of the security of actual systems. As McLean started to tell others of his growing doubts, he was challenged by Marvin Schaefer of the National Computer Security Center to prove a basic security theorem for a system incorporating, not the *-property, but the "†-property," which permitted subjects freely to transfer information from higher to lower security levels. McLean was able to do so, even though a model incorporating the †-property "is not secure since it allows secret information to be copied into unclassified files, e.g., the *Washington Post*."[105]

McLean was asked to give a talk on his critique of the basic security theorem at Carnegie Mellon University. Preparing this talk, he tried to formulate a theorem about the Bell-LaPadula model that would justify the claim that systems built according to the model were secure. Instead of finding and proving such a theorem, however, McLean found a counterexample, a system that appeared to him to conform to the model yet patently to be insecure.[106] On June 22, 1986, he sent a brief message to the Computer Security Forum, an electronic discussion group on Dockmaster, the National Computer Security Center's Multics system that provided remote access, via the ARPAnet, to the endorsed tools. In the message, McLean described his counterexample, a hypothetical "System Z," which responded to any access request by downgrading the security level "of every subject and object in the system . . . to the lowest possible level."[107]

McLean argued that System Z was allowed by the Bell-LaPadula model. Starting from a secure state, it produced only secure states (in the Bell-LaPadula sense): in its state after the comprehensive downgrading of security levels neither the simple security property nor the *-property could be violated, and nothing in the axioms of the Bell-LaPadula model appeared to forbid the downgrading. Yet, intuitively, System Z was not secure: "any subject can access any object." If System Z conformed to the Bell-LaPadula model, surely the model itself must be flawed fundamentally? As McLean was later to put it, polemically: "The Bell-LaPadula model was a monumental piece of work, but it has lived in an overly sheltered environment which has permitted it to survive beyond its rightful time. Like a pampered offspring, it has endured, not because it is fit, but because it has been protected from harm."[108]

McLean's claimed counterexample triggered strikingly varied responses. Some rejected System Z as an irrelevance, while others welcomed it; some argued that the Bell-LaPadula model had implicit features that ruled out System Z, while others suggested System Z was not as plainly insecure as it seemed. Leonard LaPadula replied on Dockmaster the day after McLean's original message, conceding that it might be possible to prove that System Z's access rules conformed to the Bell-LaPadula model. "But, so what?" he asked. "The system Z has stupid rules of operation, so that no one is likely to want to implement such a system." David Bell agreed, arguing that: "Models don't really allow or forbid. The model can represent system Z IF someone thinks it is worth representing," but it was not worth representing: it was "a bad example"; its rules were "bizarre." On later reflection, however, Bell was to argue that there were real, sensible, secure systems in which Z's comprehensive downgrading of security levels was implemented, and that there was an error in McLean's judgment that the rule was patently insecure. It might, for example, be a good idea to give "forward observers" in battlefield situations the capacity, if they were about to be captured by the enemy, to overwrite and then regrade as "unclassified" all the files in any system they carried with them. A model such as that developed by Bell and LaPadula was "an abstraction within which to investigate a problem of interest," said Bell, not an attempt to capture what "security" might subjectively be taken to mean. The latter was, in any case, variable: while McLean might believe that System Z was insecure, Bell argued that the forward-observer system showed that under some circumstances its comprehensive downgrading mechanism would be regarded as desirable.[109]

LaPadula's MITRE colleague, Jonathan Millen, took a different tack, attacking McLean's premise that System Z conformed to the Bell-LaPadula model. Implicit in the latter, said Millen, was an "informal axiom": the "tranquility principle," that "the classification of active objects will not be changed during normal operation." LaPadula, too, commented that when he and Bell had produced their model, they had implicit restrictions in mind. These restrictions were embodied in the Multics interpretation they gave their model, and they had assumed that other interpretations would also embody them. Such rules "are definitely part of the model itself," said the Computer Security Forum's convenor, Ted Lee. Don Good, on the other hand, leapt to McLean's defense. That System Z was "dismissed as a 'stupid' and 'bizarre' system" was "the price of asking fundamental questions about sacred cows!" Instead, Good argued, System Z should be seen as demonstrating the inadequacy of the Bell-LaPadula model and of the viewpoint, fundamental to the orange book, that "a system is secure if and only if it produces a sequence of secure states."[110]

The variety of responses to System Z is reminiscent of the different styles of reaction to counterexamples to Euler's theorem, as analyzed by Imre Lakatos (see chapter 4). The dismissal of System Z as "bizarre" is what Lakatos calls "monster-barring"; reinterpreting System Z as what security might in some circumstances demand is "monster-adjustment"; citing an informal axiom that excludes it is "exception-barring."[111] The promotion of the apparent counterexample against the theorem, with its implication of the need for radical change in security theory, is Lakatos's "dialectical" method: "Foundations of Computer Security: We Need Some," was how Don Good titled his contribution to the debate.[112]

David Bloor has argued that different styles of response in mathematics to counterexamples may depend upon different patterns of social relations: the strength of the social boundary between insiders and outsiders ("group," in the terminology of the anthropologist Mary Douglas), and the strength of internal social differentiation ("grid," in Douglas's terms). "Monster-barring," suggested Bloor, will be found in high-group, low-grid situations; "monster-adjustment" and "exception-barring" in high-group, high-grid situations; and the "dialectical" method in low-group, low-grid situations.[113] Unfortunately, the data to check the applicability of this schema properly are not available here, but it is worth noting that it appeared to McLean that the authority of the National Security Agency (which is certainly high group, with a strong insider/outsider divide) stood behind the Bell-LaPadula model. Although the latter's development was originally supported by the Air Force, rather than by NSA, it had come to underpin much of the work of the National Computer Security Center: Roger Schell, for example, who had been the original sponsor of the Bell-LaPadula work, had become prominent in the center and Bell also worked there.

Although the orange book stopped short of explicitly demanding use of the Bell-LaPadula model, its approach and terminology drew on it heavily. In McLean's opinion, this made it difficult for those dependent upon NSA funding to be critical of the Bell-LaPadula model. His criticism of the latter (and of the later modeling work at Odyssey Research Associates, discussed below) was possible, he believed, only because his research was funded not by NSA but by the Office of Naval Research. "Certain individuals at NSA were extremely upset with me at the time for criticizing NSA-funded work," he said, "and the only reason I was able to pursue my research was because I was about the only player in the game who was not surviving on NSA funds."[114]

The barriers of security classification make it impossible to trace internal debates within NSA about security modeling. In the research institutes and firms working on computer security, however, which can probably be characterized as both lower group and lower grid than NSA, even if they were dependent for funding on the latter, something akin to Lakatos's "dialectical" method does indeed appear to have prevailed. A series of challenges to the hegemony of the Bell-LaPadula model emerged. The most influential early alternative was a model developed at SRI in the early 1980s by Joseph Goguen and José Meseguer. Bell and LaPadula had given rules that, they believed, preserved "security," but had not attempted to say more directly what the latter was. Goguen and Meseguer, however, offered a definition. Security was "noninterference": "one group of users, using a certain set of commands, is noninterfering with another group of users if what the first group does with those commands has no effect on what the second group of users can see."[115] Noninterference subsumed the Bell-LaPadula *-property, since it clearly prohibited the first, higher-clearance, group writing to files that the second group could read, and covert storage channels (which had to be analyzed separately in the Bell-LaPadula approach) were addressed by the noninterference model; the two models differed in other respects as well.[116]

Further development of notions of "security" took place as those involved started to grapple with the difficulties involved in the move (discussed below) from a focus on a time-sharing computer to one on networks linking computers. That latter concern, for example, lay behind David Sutherland of Odyssey Research Associates offering another, subtly different, notion of what "security" was. (Odyssey was a consulting firm established in 1982 in Ithaca, New York, by Richard Platek, a Cornell University mathematical logician whose research had, for example, been drawn on by Dana Scott in his work on the λ-calculus discussed in chapter 8.[117] Platek was inspired by the presidency of Ronald Reagan to leave academic life and take a direct part in the Cold War: "I thought that under his leadership the country could win the Cold War."[118]) In Sutherland's "nondeducibility" model, "security" was defined as the incapacity of users to deduce the actions of other users with higher security status. This notion was similar to "noninterference," but less strict than the latter and arguably "closer in spirit to the informal notion that security means 'nondisclosure of information.'" Crucially, Sutherland believed it to be more suited to a network interpretation.[119]

Noninterference was seen by many as too rigid, overlimiting of the functions of systems. For example, noninterference prohibits systems in which low-level users can read encrypted high-level messages, because high-level inputs affect what those low-level users can see, even though because of the encryption the low-level users cannot tell what the high-level inputs are.[120] Nondeducibility, on the other hand, was seen by John McLean as being "too weak." The key issue was whether a system was deterministic: whether, when in a given state and presented with a given input, it could enter only one new state.[121] Nondeducibility might be a satisfactory model of security for a deterministic system, concluded Daryl McCullough also of Odyssey, but many actual systems had to be thought of as having nondeterministic aspects, especially when they consisted of different computers configured in a network.

In nondeterministic systems, argued McCullough, nondeducibility permitted violation even of the basic no read up rule. A plausible nondeterministic system, for example, might fill in the spaces between messages with strings of random digits to prevent enemies being able to analyze the flow of traffic on the system. Nondeducibility would then be preserved even if a low-level user could read unencrypted high-security messages. If such a user read the message, "We attack at dawn," he or she could not, strictly, deduce anything, since the digits corresponding to such a message might in principle have been produced randomly, even though forms of reasoning less strict than pure deduction would enable such a user to conclude with high practical confidence that he or she had read a genuine message.[122]

McCullough also found counterexamples to the "obvious" conclusion that computers that were individually secure (in either a nondeducibility or a noninterference sense) would, when "hooked-up" (connected together) form a secure network. As part of a project funded by the Air Force's Rome Laboratory, he sought to prove this result, which was one of the premises of the then emerging Department of Defense guidelines on network security. He wrote, "The routine task turned into a frustrating one, and after much wasted effort, we came to the conclusion that the theorem was false! Secure components connected securely did not guarantee a secure system." One counterexample constructed by McCullough consisted of two systems, each of which received and sent high-security messages and three low-security messages: *stop_count, odd,* and *even* (see figure 5.6). In the case of A, *stop_count* was an output followed by either *odd* or *even,* according to the total number of high-security messages system A had either received or sent. B was similar, except that *stop_count* was an input, not an output. Imagine an enemy who wants to discover whether a high-security message has been received (in some circumstances, such as when an attack is imminent, that knowledge might be useful militarily even if the content of the message cannot be read). The enemy cannot tell, by observing the low-security behavior of either system individually, whether a high-security message has been received: the output *odd* might mean only that a high-security message had been sent; the output *even* might mean no messages received, or every incoming message balanced by an outgoing one.[123]

Consider, however, the enemy observing the two systems linked together as in the lower half of figure 5.6: all high-level outputs from A, and the *stop_count* output, become inputs to B; and all high-level outputs from B become inputs to A. Now, argued McCullough, the joint system was no longer secure. Since all outgoing messages from either component A or component B become inputs to the other, "the fact that A says *odd* while B says *even* (or vice-versa) means that there has been at least one high-level input from outside." McCullough's counterexample was artificial and open to the same accusations of lack of realism that were directed at System Z, but, in McCullough's view, it underlined the need for a notion of "security" that was composable, in other words in

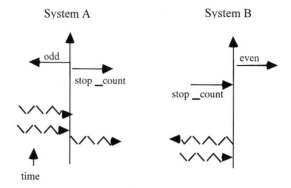

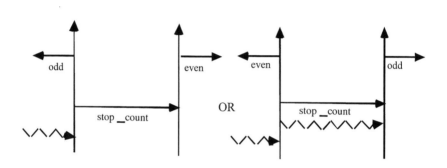

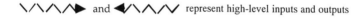

\/\/\▶ and ◀/\/\/ represent high-level inputs and outputs

Figure 5.6
An example of individually secure systems that are insecure when connected
together. Based on figure in Daryl McCullough, "Noninterference and the Composability of Security Properties," in *Proceedings of the 1988 IEEE Symposium on
Security and Privacy,* 177–186, at p. 182. ©1988 IEEE

which secure components securely connected together were guaranteed to produce a secure system. McCullough defined a "hook-up" or "restrictiveness" model of security that subsumed noninterference and nondeducibility and made composability a theorem.[124]

To McLean, however, "restrictiveness" was "very nonintuitive." It imposed limitations on system design that were not necessary for security, and programs that functionally satisfied restrictive specifications might not themselves be restrictive. Furthermore, restrictiveness did not address the probabilistic behavior of systems. In the course of developing a general theory of the preservation of security properties when components are hooked-up into systems, McLean proposed a variety of security properties and examined their composability under several different types of hook-up. Among those security properties was "separability," a property which, McLean argued, was simpler than restrictiveness. He and Jim Gray, a member of his section at the Naval Research Laboratory during this time, also developed "probabilistic" models of security for nondeterministic systems.[125]

The Fragmentation of Computer Security

These processes of "proofs and refutations" indeed involved dialectical development of the notion of security. But did they solve the practical problem of building secure systems? McLean's criticism of the Bell-LaPadula model was unfair, contended McCullough: the model was intended not as a "theory of security," more as "a way of organizing information about the security of a system," and practical system designers clearly found it useful in that role. In contrast, McCullough's and others' attempts to define security were "in some sense 'toy' models, created so as to be simple enough to succumb to mathematical analysis. In any real computer system, some aspects of . . . security may be analyzed using noninterference or deducibility security, but other aspects will be beyond such analysis."[126] No single definitive model of "security" had emerged from the Lakatosian dialectic. Even if one restricted "security" to its primary military meaning of "confidentiality," commented the author of a 1997 textbook of secure computing, one had to conclude that researchers did not yet "fully understand" it.[127]

Furthermore, the intellectual development of notions of "security" was accompanied by growing difficulties of the practical activity that surrounded it. Many of these difficulties arose from the growing move to computer networks. The classical computer-security problem was to embody security in a time-sharing operating system. By the end of the 1980s, however, the time-sharing mainframe was beginning to appear an outdated technology. Networking brought with it new challenges, and it crossed the divide between COMPUSEC and COMSEC, a divide that had been institutionalized by the setting up of the National Computer Security Center as an entity separate from NSA's COMSEC functions.

The BLACKER system, the formal verification of which was discussed earlier, underlined the blurring. In its network role, it bridged the fields of COMPUSEC and COMSEC. Its security model, however, was the traditional COMPUSEC Bell-LaPadula model, and design proof against a formal security model was not carried out for its COMSEC functions:

> Since BLACKER is to be COMSEC and COMPUSEC secure, we initially considered a security policy that captured both requirements. We had no examples of formal specification of COMSEC design reduced to practice, and BLACKER is a product development program, not an R&D vehicle for advancing the state of the art. It was concluded that COMSEC and COMPUSEC [specification] was more than A1 certification required, and beyond the state of the art.

Applying the Bell-LaPadula model to a network is not straightforward: it is, for example, not always clear which entities should be considered "subjects" and which "objects." In the development of BLACKER, "there were many unusual situations that arose . . . that required going back to first security principles to arrive at a solution." The different cultures of COMSEC and COMPUSEC caused problems: "It was decided from inception to keep the bulk of the staff and the formal specifications at the lowest possible security level, to encourage peer review. That is an underpinning of COMPUSEC, but not, however, of COMSEC."[128]

As the divide between COMPUSEC and COMSEC blurred, the separation of the National Computer Security Center from the rest of NSA was eroded. Almost as soon as it was set up, the center began to lose its hard won autonomy. A 1985 reorganization merged NSA's COMSEC and COMPUSEC functions, and in 1990 the National Computer Security Center's "research and evaluation functions were integrated with the NSA's communications security functions."[129] Walker, furthermore, had hoped that the computer industry, rather than government, would play the central role in the development of high-assurance, high-security systems. This aspect of his vision also did not come to pass. There was a long gap between the first A1 product, SCOMP, achieving its rating in

1985 and any further system doing so: the next two, BLACKER and the Boeing Secure Local Area Network, were graded A1 only in 1991. The period 1991–1997 saw only one more product, the Gemini Trusted Network Processor, graded A1. By 1997, SCOMP was no longer being sold in an A1 version, and BLACKER had always been restricted to government agencies, so the National Computer Security Center's *Evaluated Product List* for that year contained only two A1 products.[130] Other projects aiming at commercially available A1 systems did not come to fruition.

A sharp illustration of the difficulties faced by A1 projects was the security kernel developed by the Digital Equipment Corporation (DEC) for its widely used VAX minicomputers (see figure 5.7). Despite some dissociation between the formal proof work and code writing ("We never really achieved what I would call ideal coupling between the formal specification/verification process and the system development process,"[131] and the formal top level specification was never completed), those involved were confident that the VAX security kernel was "capable of receiving an A1 rating," and it "underwent a highly successful external field test." Nevertheless, DEC never brought it to market. The project team believed that there were enough potential users, but Steven Lipner, then of DEC, believed otherwise: "The project was abandoned because there was not a sufficient market and Digital (I in particular as the responsible group manager) determined that canceling the project was a better business decision than shipping the product and living with an unprofitable offering." Restrictions on the export of A1 systems, even to America's allies, were part of the reason why DEC decided that the market for the VAX security kernel would be insufficient. More fundamentally, however, the world of computing changed radically between the project's start and its completion.[132]

The kernel was conceived in 1981, and a research prototype was operating by 1984, but it was late 1989 before full external field testing began. By then, its intended "hardware base was late in its life cycle and thus slow and costly compared to the newest VAX offerings." To shorten development time, "Ethernet" facilities to support networked use were not included, an absence that attracted critical comment from potential users. Above all, though, in Lipner's words, "we were prepared to offer an A1 timesharing system in a world that had largely moved to workstations." DEC had plans to tackle all these matters, "but doing the requisite development would have cost money that we could not convince ourselves the market would ever repay us."[133]

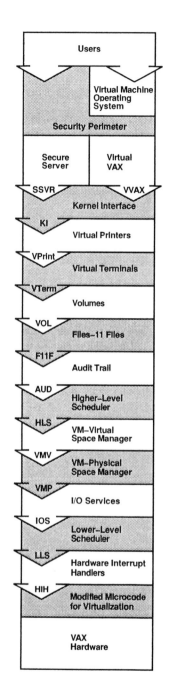

Figure 5.7
VAX security kernel layers. From Paul A. Karger, Mary Ellen Zurko, Douglas W. Bonin, Andrew H. Mason, and Clifford E. Kahn, "A Retrospective on the VAX VMM Security Kernel," *IEEE Transactions on Software Engineering* 17 (1991): 1147–1165, at p. 1154. ©1991 IEEE.

These problems were not specific to DEC. The original version of SCOMP, for example, achieved only few sales: "under 30. It never broke even." When SCOMP's developers, Honeywell, decided to rework the system for a newer, more sophisticated hardware platform, the company's marketing staff investigated how much "additional market is opened up by having an A1 system versus a B3 system." They came back with the answer: "At best, you are maybe looking at 5%." So the decision was taken not "to do any more formal work" and to aim only for the lower rating.[134]

By the early 1990s there was a widespread perception that the computer security market "has not worked well."[135] There was a vicious circle in which the demands of developing a demonstrably secure system, and of having it evaluated by the National Computer Security Center (a process that could take several years), led to products that were expensive and, by the time they were on the market, outdated by comparison with analogous technology that had been developed without high assurance of security in mind. System procurers were therefore tempted to go for the cheaper, more up-to-date, less high assurance, possibly less secure, alternative: "The government was saying all along that they needed this type of [high assurance, high-security] system, yet the market was never really as large as people expected. . . . You would get . . . Requests for Proposals that would imply strong security requirements, and then they would be waived, watered down. . . . Things never really materialized like people expected."[136] A small market in turn increased unit costs, and so the vicious circle continued. Export controls further intensified the problem, however understandable they were from the point of view of national security: as well as the desire not to make U.S. systems available for detailed scrutiny, there was also the worry that "[a]dversaries' uses of computer security technologies can hamper U.S. intelligence gathering."[137]

It was therefore seen by many to be imperative to increase the size of the market for secure systems. There were two obvious routes to this. One was to make the market more international. The orange book had considerable influence on America's NATO partners, with Canada, Germany, the Netherlands, France, and Britain all setting up their own organizations akin to the National Computer Security Center and writing their own analogues to the orange book. But overseas, especially in Britain, the orange book was perceived as embodying a serious flaw.

The orange book's classes were hierarchical in two senses: security functionality and assurance. A division B system, for example, was intended to have more sophisticated security functions than a division C system, *and* greater assurance of the correct implementation of those functions. This "bundling" of security and assurance in the orange book was a quite deliberate decision. The goal was to provide a simple system of categories that "the average marketing guy, the average program manager" could understand, said Walker. "You are giving him a shorthand for something, that if it meets this level, I can use it here. If I need something better than that, I need something higher. . . . People understand. They don't understand what goes into a B2, but they know what to do with it. And that's very, very valuable."[138]

The problem with bundling functionality and assurance, however, was that it ruled out systems that had simple functions but high assurance of the correctness of the implementation of those functions. Despite the emphasis on simplicity in the notion of a security kernel, kernels aiming at A1 status were typically quite large. The SCOMP security kernel, for example, consisted of approximately 10,000 lines of PASCAL code, and the trusted software outside the kernel consisted of approximately 10,000 lines of the C programming language.[139] The VAX security kernel consisted of almost 50,000 executable statements; even its formal top level specification would, if it had been completed, have been over 12,000 lines long.[140] Overseas observers concluded that part of the reason for the difficulty of conducting even design proof was the sheer complexity of the systems to which it was being applied. So they sought to separate assurance and functionality, thus providing for the possibility of applying formal verification to simple systems. The development of international standards forced a decision between the orange book "bundled" approach and the European "unbundled" one. The international Common Criteria that emerged from this effort largely reflected the European approach, although there was provision for "bundled" protection profiles.[141]

The other way of extending the computer security market was to include in it sectors that were nonmilitary but had computer security concerns: other departments of government, and the commercial sector, especially banking. This, for example, was part of the rationale for the Reagan administration's September 1984 National Security Decision Directive which elevated the Department of Defense Computer Security Center to the status of National Computer Security Center. The attempt to integrate military, nonmilitary governmental, and commercial security, however, was at best only partially successful. Proponents of civil liberties opposed the extension of NSA's role, and congressional reaction forced the abandonment of the more controversial aspects of the move.[142] Most of civil government and industry did not see itself as facing the same "high level threat" as the defense sector faced, and so did not perceive the same need for high-assurance, formally verified systems to meet it. In addition, the meaning of "security" for the banking and financial services sector, which did have strong security concerns, was subtly different from its meaning in the defense sector.

The primary defense meaning of "security" was confidentiality: prevention of unauthorized disclosure of data. Banks and financial institutions, on the other hand, were more interested in security in the sense of integrity: prevention of unauthorized alteration of data.[143] For a bank, keeping the details of customers' accounts confidential is a less pressing concern than stopping fraudulent transactions. Although integrity was clearly of importance in military systems and had been modeled in the early 1970s' MITRE work,[144] it was never as prominent a concern as confidentiality. Furthermore, other sectors did not have the military's elaborate system of multilevel clearances and security classifications, so the A and B divisions of the orange book, designed to satisfy the needs of a military environment, were largely irrelevant to the requirements of other sectors. What they saw themselves as needing were systems of the type of the orange book's division C and the relatively low levels of assurance that went with division C were not a major concern.

In the late 1970s and early 1980s, the path to achieving computer security had appeared clear. A dominant problem had been identified: designing a multilevel secure, time-sharing operating system. The route to a solution—a security kernel—was widely, if not universally, agreed. There was a single dominant model of "security": the Bell-LaPadula model. There was widespread acceptance that mechanized proof should be applied to demonstrate correspondence to that model, and it was anticipated that, while "proof" might initially mean design proof, code proof would follow. Formal verification—on the face of it, an academic, even an esoteric, approach—had secured the endorsement of powerful, practically minded organizations such as the National Security Agency. The United States played the unquestioned leading role in matters of computer security, and within the United States there was at least outline agreement as to the appropriate nature and role of an organization to certify the security of actual systems.

A decade later, that consensus had fragmented. As computing moved beyond the traditional multiuser mainframe, the classical computer security problem had largely been superseded by a host of diverse problems, many having to do with the integration of computer and communications security in networks, and there was no clear unitary route to the solution of these. The Bell-LaPadula model was no longer dominant, but none of the plethora of alternatives to it played anything approaching the paradigmatic role it had. Formal verification of trusted systems did not progress "downward" from specifications deeper into systems, as had been anticipated at the start of the 1980s. Instead, "proof" remained frozen as "design verification," and even the latter was no more common in practice in the 1990s than it had been in the 1980s. The United States was no longer as dominant as it had been, and the workings of its computer security evaluation system had been criticized sharply.[145]

In the interim the Cold War had ended, and the Soviet Union had collapsed. The subsequent cuts in defense budgets threw a harsh light on the costs of developing high-security, high-assurance systems designed specifically for defense needs, and the search was on for cheaper "commercial off the shelf" solutions. Yet the fragmentation of computer security was not the result of the end of the Cold War alone. The field was torn by internal tensions, in particular the vicious circle of prolonged development and evaluation processes, high costs, and limited sales that could be seen, even in the 1980s, undermining the high-assurance end of the market.

These conflicts meant that even though there was sharply increased interest in military computer security in the latter half of the 1990s (as noted at the start of this chapter), and the rise of electronic commerce brought another set of security needs to the fore, there was no sign of the fragmentation of computer security being reversed. Defense support for formal verification, and for formal methods in computer science more generally, declined sharply. Key proponents of formal methods within the National Security Agency retired, and other agencies did not step in to replace the loss of funding to the field. One important U.S. formal verification firm, Computational Logic, Inc., described in chapter 7, closed down in 1997, while others shed staff. Odyssey was taken over. Although concerns for computer security had, for almost three decades, been the chief practical support for formal verification in the United States, they ceased to be so at precisely the point in time when those concerns were dramatically resurgent.

6

Social Processes and Category Mistakes

In Garmisch's autumn sunshine, Edsger W. Dijkstra had felt programming's Middle Ages ending. The rationality of the Enlightenment, together with the rigor and the elegance of mathematics, were going to transform programming into a science. Instead of programs being thrown together by ad hoc hacking, they would carefully be constructed in such a way that there was a formal, deductive proof that they were correct implementations of their specifications. No longer would the programmer have to rely merely upon empirical testing of programs, with its inevitable weakness that it could not demonstrate the absence of bugs. In 1977, though, it appeared to Dijkstra that the Middle Ages, apparently vanquished at Garmisch in 1968, were not yet dead.

Two young computer scientists, Richard A. DeMillo, of the Georgia Institute of Technology, and Richard J. Lipton of Yale University, together with Alan J. Perlis, one of the leaders of American computer science, had attacked the very basis of the effort to mathematicize computer science, or so it appeared to Dijkstra. Proofs of mathematical theorems and "proofs" of computer programs were quite different entities, they argued. They knew well that what they were claiming was "shocking." In anything like its current form, program verification, the effort to apply deductive proof to computer programs, was "bound to fail in its primary purpose: to dramatically increase one's confidence in the correct functioning of a particular piece of software."[1]

To Dijkstra the paper by DeMillo, Lipton, and Perlis was "a political pamphlet from the Middle Ages." It was "very ugly." It was "pre-scientific in the sense that even the shallowest analogy is accepted as justification," wrote Dijkstra. "[T]heir text is slippery . . . written in sometimes very poor English . . . and their arguments are rambling. Supposing that they had something sensible to say we can only regret that they have buried it under so much insinuating verbiage." The authors "confirm the impression of [being] anti-intellectualistic reactionaries." To others, however, DeMillo, Lipton, and Perlis's paper, eventually published in the flagship journal of American computer science, the *Communications of the Association for Computing Machinery* (ACM), was "Marvelous, marvelous, marvelous!" "It was time somebody said it—and loud and clear—the formal approach to software verification does not work now and probably never will work in the real programming world." One practitioner and manager admitted that he usually found the *Communications* "to be arcane, difficult to follow, and above all, of no practical use." In contrast, he wrote, the paper by DeMillo, Lipton, and Perlis was "the first article in *Communications* that I have enjoyed since I joined ACM." Another reader wrote to the editor of the *Communications:* "Thank you for publishing it, and thanks to the authors for their wisdom, fairness, style, rigor, and wit. Such an article makes me delight in being an ACM member, and, indeed, in being a member of the human race."[2]

Programs and Theorems

On the face of it, DeMillo and Lipton were unlikely figures to lead an attack on formal verification. Both were deeply versed in the mathematical aspects of computer science. DeMillo graduated in 1969 with a degree in mathematics from St. Thomas, a liberal arts college in Minnesota. No computer science was taught there, but the college did own one old computer, a Control Data Corporation 160-A. While an undergraduate, DeMillo earned money by programming the machine for the college and for local industry, first employing assembly language and then using a FORTRAN compiler he had written.

After graduating, DeMillo moved into a world quite different from his liberal arts college with its old computer. He worked for four months on a summer assistantship program at the nuclear weapons laboratory at Los Alamos, which had one of the world's most advanced computer centers. The laboratory had previously relied primarily on IBM computers, but in the 1960s it introduced the new Control Data 6600 and 7600 supercomputers. DeMillo was assigned to help a group of physicists transform a FORTRAN program that he remembers as being ten million lines long into a form suitable for the new machines. The program was "this huge incomprehensible thing," recalled DeMillo:

. . . as an undergraduate I was programming on a very small computer for very small applications, and then in the space of just a couple of weeks there was this huge discontinuity where all of a sudden I was confronted with this ten million line program. . . . [N]othing I had learned—no mathematical concept, no programming concept—was sufficient to deal with . . . this size and complexity.

DeMillo "knew that people were thinking about various ways of applying mathematical logic . . . to handling intellectually large, complex things like computer programs." Previously, he had felt logic to be "sort of a barren activity." Hands-on experience of the "huge, complex, important codes" that the Los Alamos laboratory used to design nuclear weapons changed his attitude. He began to read graduate texts on logic, and discovered the early literature on formal verification discussed in chapter 2.[3]

When DeMillo began his graduate work at the Georgia Institute of Technology in the autumn of 1969, he came under the influence of the charismatic Lucio Chiaraviglio, a student of the famous logical positivist, Rudolf Carnap. Logical positivism was an austere philosophy. It allowed as cognitively meaningful only those statements that are mathematical or logical tautologies or that can be confirmed by empirical evidence, and it thus effectively banished from philosophy much of the traditional content of areas such as metaphysics and ethics. Chiaraviglio "is a very powerful personality," said DeMillo, "so I was drawn to him kind of on a personal level, but I was also sort of sucked up into the logical positivism view of the world." DeMillo and his fellow students in Chiaraviglio's "Seminar on the Unification of Mathematics for Information Science" immersed themselves in the literature of the 1930s and 1940s on the foundations of mathematics, reading the crucial original papers by authors such as Gödel, Kleene, Rosser, Church, and Post. The goal of Chiaraviglio's seminar was to find "logical foundations of programming [that] would somehow mirror what happened to the logical foundations of mathematics."[4]

DeMillo wrote his thesis on how an algebraic approach to logic can give a formal mathematical interpretation, a formal "semantics" as it is called, to programming languages.[5] In his last summer as a graduate student, he returned to Los Alamos to work in a group that was designing a high-level programming language, Madcap, that permitted subscripts and superscripts to be used as they are in ordinary mathematics (in most programming languages one cannot use characters above or below the line). After receiving his Ph.D. in 1972, DeMillo went on to develop a formal semantics for Madcap, and to work on the general problem of providing semantics for high-level programming languages to support proofs of the correctness of programs. That interest brought DeMillo an invitation in the summer of 1974 to the U.S. Army research laboratory in Fort Monmouth, New Jersey.

There, for the first time, he met Richard Lipton. Like DeMillo, Lipton was a computer scientist with strong interests in logic and in mathematics. Indeed, Lipton almost chose to major at graduate school in mathematics, but instead received his Ph.D. degree from the department of computer science at Carnegie Mellon University in 1973, where his Ph.D. adviser was one of the emerging leaders of software engineering, David Parnas. Lipton's thesis was on the mathematical foundations of a key topic in the design of operating systems: the "synchronization primitive" used to handle communication between different processes in a multiuser computer system. Interest in the topic within theoretical computer science had largely been created by the work of Edsger W. Dijkstra who would no doubt have approved of the succinct and elegant use of mathematics in Lipton's thesis. DeMillo and Lipton found that they had many common interests in areas of mathematics relevant to computer science such as combinatorial problems and graph theory (see chapter 4), and they often spent their summers together, first at Fort Monmouth and later at the Mathematics Research Center at the University of Wisconsin.[6]

In the autumn of 1974 DeMillo was invited to give a seminar at Yale University, where Lipton was an assistant professor. The seminar was eventually to change the course of DeMillo's intellectual life. He talked about his research in verifying programs written in very high-level languages. One of his examples was a "topological sorting" algorithm originally presented in Donald Knuth's classic compendium of algorithms, *The Art of Computer Programming.* DeMillo wrote a ten-line program in Madcap to implement the algorithm, and then he spent a number of weeks constructing a proof of the correctness of this implementation, using the formal semantics of Madcap that he had developed. "I was very proud of it [the proof]," recalled DeMillo, "because it was very hard to do. It was a sort of symbol-manipulation feat. . . . The verification-oriented semantics had to deal with postconditions and preconditions, and funny operators to take care of updating sets, and things."[7]

As DeMillo worked his way through this proof before his audience at Yale, covering blackboard after blackboard, he noticed Alan Perlis, Yale's most prominent computer scientist, listening carefully. Perlis, who received his Ph.D. in mathematics from MIT in 1950, was a specialist in programming languages and a senior figure in computer science: from 1962 to 1964, for example, he had served as president of the ACM.[8] He was not convinced that proof-based approaches to software were either necessary or practicable. At the 1969 Rome conference, described in chapter 2, Perlis questioned whether Dijkstra's methods could be taught to traditional programmers, and argued against Dijkstra and Hoare that, with proper choice of test cases, what was in effect exhaustive testing was feasible.[9]

When DeMillo finished presenting his proof, Perlis raised his hand and asked politely but pointedly, "Why does it take 20 pages to prove a program that is obviously correct?" As the room cleared at the end of the seminar, DeMillo, Lipton, and Perlis stayed behind, locked in conversation. Gradually, DeMillo came to understand what Perlis had meant: "that the program was its own proof. That is, you could argue only from the mathematics of what the program was manipulating to the correctness of the program without going through this long symbolic [detour]." It was, recalls DeMillo, "an idea . . . that just had never occurred to me before."[10]

Lipton had never been as immersed in formal verification as DeMillo had been. He was heavily involved in research on computer security, however, and, as seen in chapter 5, formal verification was increasingly influential in that field in the 1970s. Lipton recalled attending a summer-long workshop at the RAND Corporation on computer security:

One of the experts in the area came in and explained that he had a certain statement, that he was going to prove, that was going to capture [what] data security [meant] for his operating system. And I looked at it [the statement] for a little while, and then I said to him, "Well, I could prove it for you now." And he said, "I don't understand. You know, we are going to work a year on this, I mean, how could you prove it this afternoon?" . . . After a while . . . half an hour, I convinced him it was a tautology. It was a statement about set theory that was always true. . . . It was true about any system, including his. So if he ever proved it . . . it didn't capture anything.[11]

As they worked together, DeMillo and Lipton talked not just about technicalities but about the deep issues that interested them both. Although both were computer scientists, they saw themselves as, at root, mathematicians: "By training and inclination I was fundamentally a mathematician," said DeMillo. "Lipton was fundamentally a mathematician. We had both read mathematical biographies. We had both read recreational . . . mathematics." At one point, probably in 1974,[12] DeMillo and Lipton were sharing a car journey from New Jersey to New Haven, Connecticut. Their conversation turned to the question: "What's a proof?" They considered the standard logician's definition: a series of formulae that are either axioms or derived from axioms by formal rules of inference. They rejected that answer as a "caricature" of what a proof is. Then, DeMillo recalled, Lipton offered the insight that was to become central to their paper: "That proofs are nothing more or less than what mathematicians do. It doesn't make any sense to explain what mathematics is and what mathematicians do. It doesn't make sense to talk about proofs in terms other than what they appear to be."[13]

As Lipton and DeMillo drew Perlis into their conversations, the idea of a joint paper emerged. Perlis originally had in mind a mathematical article about the computational infeasibility of formal proofs of the correctness of programs. It was clear to Lipton and to DeMillo, however, that "there was going to be no such mathematical paper, that what we were talking about was going to lead to some kind of essay about why the concept of 'proof' that was being offered as appropriate for mathematical proofs of properties of programs was not the appropriate concept. . . . What was being borrowed . . . was [an] inappropriate view of proof."[14]

DeMillo wrote the first draft of their paper longhand in one sitting, and as they passed it between them the argument elaborated. Eventually, DeMillo, Lipton, and Perlis submitted their paper to the fourth ACM Symposium on *Principles of Programming Languages* held in January 1977. Their paper was scheduled as the first presentation after lunch on the second day of the conference, traditionally the point at which attendance was at its peak. Perlis's health was beginning to fail (he battled courageously against multiple sclerosis for many years until his death in 1990) and he could not attend. DeMillo and Lipton flipped a coin to decide who was to present the paper: "I lost," recalled DeMillo, "I presented the paper." DeMillo remembered being warned that "these assistant professors [DeMillo and Lipton] would be torn apart by the lions of the field," in front of the audience of 500 people. As he talked, DeMillo recalled seeing one leading verificationist, Ralph London, pacing up and down in the back of the room. But the crushing rebuke that was feared never came, and indeed the debate was not nearly as acrimonious as DeMillo expected: "That came later."[15]

The paper DeMillo presented in 1977 began by distinguishing two views of proof, and he and his coauthors considered the distinction so important that in the paper's written version they indicated it typographically.[16] One view of proof was the "sort of valid, step-by-step, syntactically checkable deduction as may be carried out within a consistent, formal, logical calculus." The other view was "the common notion of informal proof used in everyday mathematics." "We have been conditioned," wrote DeMillo, Lipton, and Perlis, to confuse the two sorts of proof:

Let us call this viewpoint *monolithic*. The monolithic view is [that] mathematics proceeds from axioms (or postulates or hypotheses) to theorems by steps, each of which is easily justifiable from its predecessors by a fixed allowable rule of transformation.

"[M]athematics is (and must be) highly nonmonolithic," they wrote. An ordinary mathematical proof was not a chain of formal logic, but an argument to be heard and to be read by other mathematicians:

. . . mathematicians talk to each other. They give symposium and colloquium talks which attempt to convince doubting (sometimes hostile) audiences of their arguments, they burst into each others' offices with news of insights for current research, and they scribble on napkins in university cafeterias and expensive restaurants. All for the sake of convincing other mathematicians.[17]

If a theorem is of interest, other proofs are typically offered. Important theorems are used as lemmas (intermediate steps) in larger proofs, sometimes in other areas of mathematics. "[T]he successful transferral of information between distinct branches of mathematics . . . increases confidence in theorems," wrote DeMillo, Lipton, and Perlis.[18] They cited, as an example, the celebrated proofs of the independence of the axiom of choice[19] and of the continuum hypothesis[20] from the other axioms of set theory. The Stanford University mathematician Paul Cohen had used a novel mathematical technique, called "forcing," to demonstrate their independence.[21] Cohen was not by background a logician, and his original proof "was so radical that it was believed (i.e., understood) by very few logicians," claimed DeMillo, Lipton, and Perlis. The logicians Dana Scott, Robert Solovay, and J. Barkley Rosser, however, gave an alternative account of Cohen's key notion of "forcing," and Abraham Robinson and others "connected forcing arguments with more familiar ideas in logic, generalized the concept and found the generalization to be immensely useful. When Cohen announced his results to the National Academy of Sciences in 1964, very few logicians believed his 'proofs.' By 1976 forcing arguments are routinely studied by graduate students in logic and are used as standard tools."[22]

In summary, wrote DeMillo, Lipton, and Perlis, "mathematical theorems get believed because they are"

1. read

2. refereed, published and reviewed

3. discussed

4. internalized and paraphrased

5. generalized

6. used, and

7. connected with other theorems.

This "*social* mechanism" was central to proof in mathematics but could not play the same role, DeMillo, Lipton, and Perlis argued, in software verification. As they put it, using italics to indicate the formal, logical, rather than informal, mathematical, notion of proof:

What program *provers* have failed to recognize is that the *proofs* will be unbelievable, not because the theorems that are being *proved* are deep, but rather because the social mechanisms that we have discussed here simply will not apply to the kinds of theorems that they are *proving*. The theorems are neither simple nor basic, and the *proofs* of even very simple programs run into dozens of printed pages. Thus, the incentive for a community to access and assimilate the "proof" of an individual piece of software is no longer present; *proofs* simply will not be read, refereed, discussed in meetings or over dinner, generalized, or used. They are too specialized for any of those activities. The sad fact is that the kind of mathematics that goes on in *proofs* of correctness is not very good.

The construction of automated theorem provers would not help. Even if an entirely automatic system could be built and worked with reasonable reliability, it would not solve the credibility problem. "[I]magine," wrote DeMillo, Lipton, and Perlis, "the reaction of a programmer who inserts his 300-line input-output package and returns several hours later to find the message 'VERIFIED,' followed by a 20,000 line proof."[23]

DeMillo and Lipton believed themselves to be countering "what we thought was the orthodoxy that had sway in computer science. It's difficult to imagine now, but the amount of influence that formal verification had in computing at the time [the 1970s] was enormous. It was *the* only way to understand programs; it was *the* only way to understand the foundations of programming." They were not afraid to oppose this orthodoxy in a variety of ways. They published a paper that could be read as a defense of the **go to** instruction (the subject of Dijkstra's famous attack described in chapter 2), arguing that "there are natural **goto** programs which can *only* be simulated by structured programs that are either very large or very slow."[24] They contributed to the emerging literature on program testing, in particular developing a systematic approach to testing, "mutation testing,"[25] which could be used to counter claims that testing was necessarily ad hoc and inconclusive. Mutation testing was a development independent of (and later than)[26] their critique of program verification, but they could point to it when critics asserted that they were being entirely negative in their critique.

As a community of researchers working on program testing began to develop in the 1970s, some of its members clearly believed they needed to argue against the formal verificationist "orthodoxy." Andrew Tanenbaum of the Free University, Amsterdam, for example, wrote a 1976 article "In Defense of Program Testing or Correctness Proofs Considered Harmful," that anticipated much of the argument (discussed below) later made by James Fetzer.[27] In that climate DeMillo and Lipton's attack on formal verification and their research on program testing "got bound terribly closely together," as DeMillo put it.

The impact of their critique of program verification, particularly the severity of the hostility it provoked, shocked DeMillo and Lipton: "I really thought that we were a couple of assistant professors who were just having a ball," recalled DeMillo. Lipton had the protection of Perlis, Yale's senior computer scientist, but DeMillo, who had returned to the Georgia Institute of Technology, had no equivalent protector. The fact that he had written a controversial paper that had angered "powerful people" was used as an argument against giving him tenure (although he did in fact get tenure in 1978).[28]

As their position became public, DeMillo, Lipton, and Perlis were frequently invited to take part in debates about it. Some of these debates were quite heated: at one, members of the audience started yelling. One of what DeMillo called the few "real dialogues that took place" was held at the Xerox Palo Alto Research Center in August 1977, where Lipton and Perlis debated with two of the leading figures in software engineering, Susan Gerhart and Jim Horning. The latter's notes for the debate survive. He suggested that "it would be a serious mistake for Xerox to be seduced by superficially plausible, but fundamentally misleading, arguments into ignoring an important area of research." DeMillo, Lipton, and Perlis were attacking a "caricature of program verification," said Horning. Verification "raises our confidence in programs" not because "we have some mystical belief in the absolute reliability of the verification process," but because of experience that verification found errors even in "tested" programs. Mathematics did involve "creative" processes as well as "computational" ones that could be mechanized, but the bulk of the mathematics of program verification was of the latter kind, not the former. Furthermore, there was more to even creative mathematics than just a social process:

The seven steps [refereeing, discussion, etc.] that it is asserted [by DeMillo, Lipton, and Perlis] lead to belief in theorems by mathematicians are also applied in other disciplines (e.g., sociology, English literature) where there is less general agreement and confidence in the results. Surely the reason mathematics has more credibility is that disputes can generally be resolved by very formal methods, rather than by appeal to authority, or intuition, or whatever.[29]

In Rosser's Office

The opposition they met did not diminish DeMillo, Lipton, and Perlis's confidence that they were right. In 1977 DeMillo spent one of his summer visits to the University of Wisconsin in the office of the famous mathematical logician, J. Barkley Rosser, who had been one of the young DeMillo's heroes: "His original papers, which I thought were incredibly cool as a graduate student, . . . had barely an English word in them, and they were almost purely symbolic." Talking to Rosser, and reading documents such as the marginalia Rosser had added to his original handwritten notes on Gödel's Princeton lectures on undecidability, DeMillo realized that the abstraction of Rosser's papers was but the tip of a much more complex iceberg. The marginalia were essentially informal and through them, together with his conversations with Rosser, DeMillo believed he caught a glimpse of the 1930s' Princeton in which much of modern mathematical logic was forged. The final published papers by Gödel and his contemporaries might be highly abstract, but their way of doing mathematics and mathematical logic was very much a social process. "If you believe the notes [Rosser's marginalia], . . . these guys . . . would walk round the halls at Princeton questioning Church's thesis, 'Is everything calculable? No, can't be right, can't be right!' They would go off and try to scribble counterexamples. So they were going through the Lakatosian *Proofs and Refutations* [see chapter 4] idea on their own." It was, for example, in conversation with Rosser that Alonzo Church appears to have begun to formulate the far-reaching conjecture that became the Church-Turing thesis (see chapter 8).[30]

In 1979 DeMillo, Lipton, and Perlis's "Social Processes and Proofs of Theorems and Programs" received its definitive publication in the *Communications of the ACM*. The argument was essentially unchanged from the earlier version, but the editor-in-chief of the *Communications,* Peter Denning, believed that the prose of the original was turgid, and a Yale University secretary who was also an author helped DeMillo, Lipton, and Perlis make the paper more readable. The result was a powerful piece of polemical writing.

DeMillo, Lipton, and Perlis started by identifying what they believed to be the key weakness of program verification: that, to increase confidence in the correctness of a program, "the device that verifiers use . . . is a long chain of formal, deductive logic." Although mathematicians "*could* in theory" use the same device to increase confidence in theorems, "in fact they don't. What they use is a proof, a very different animal. . . . [I]n the end, it is a social process that determines whether mathematicians feel confident about a theorem—and we believe that, because no comparable social process can take place among program verifiers, program verification is bound to fail." Although "[o]utsiders see mathematics as a cold, formal, logical, mechanical, monolithic process of sheer intellection," DeMillo, Lipton, and Perlis argued that it was not: "insofar as it is successful, mathematics is a social, informal, intuitive, organic, human process, a community project." A mathematical proof "is a message," and "[t]he proof by itself is nothing; only when it has been subjected to the social processes of the mathematical community does it become believable."

These same mechanisms doom the so-called proofs of software, the long formal verifications that correspond, not to the working mathematical proof, but to the imaginary logical structure that the mathematician conjures up to describe his feeling of belief. Verifications are not messages; a person who ran out into the hall to communicate his latest verification would rapidly find himself a social pariah. Verifications cannot really be read; a reader can flay himself through one of the shorter ones by dint of heroic effort, but that's not reading. Being unreadable and—literally—unspeakable, verifications cannot be internalized, transformed, generalized, used, connected to other disciplines, and eventually incorporated into a community consciousness. They cannot acquire credibility gradually, as a mathematical theorem does; one either believes them blindly, as a pure act of faith, or not at all.[31]

As seen earlier in this chapter, many readers of the *Communications* appear to have greeted DeMillo, Lipton, and Perlis's paper enthusiastically. DeMillo believed that he and his coauthors had become "probably for reasons . . . unrelated to what we said," spokespersons for computer industry practitioners who believed that academicians were "trying to force something down [their] throats that [they] don't think is going to work. . . . Rightly or wrongly we were painted as spokesmen for that point of view, so practitioners would say, 'Damn it, we are glad someone finally said it.' "[32] Only two of the letters published in the *Communications* took serious issue with their paper. W. D. Maurer, a verification specialist at George Washington University, drew an analogy between mechanized, formal verification and the process of compiling a program written in a higher-level language (that is to say, transforming a program into instructions in machine language):

> Originally, this was done by hand; people wrote out programs in sequences of steps specified informally in English and then proceeded to translate these into machine languages. Then compilers came along, and started to do this job automatically. At first people were against this. . . . Compilers did what had previously been a fascinating human job in a machine-like, humorless manner. (They also produced overly long object code, in much the same way that a [mechanized] verifier produces overly long proofs.) Nobody is ever going to read the object code produced by a compiler, either; one simply trusts the compiler and goes about one's business. What we hope for in verifiers is that we will at least be able to trust them to show program correctness.[33]

Leslie Lamport of SRI (whose work will be discussed in chapter 7) challenged the core of DeMillo, Lipton, and Perlis's view of mathematical proof, writing that he was "one of those 'classicists' who believe that a theorem either can or cannot be derived from a set of axioms. I don't believe that the correctness of a theorem is to be decided by a general election." Prior to the development of program verification, argued Lamport, computer scientists were "in the position of geometers before Euclid." They could only draw some diagrams and check if the theorems they were interested in were true for those diagrams: "But the work of Floyd and others [see chapter 2] has given us another way. . . . After Euclid, a theorem could no longer be accepted solely on the basis of evidence provided by drawing pictures. After Floyd, a program should no longer be accepted solely on the basis of how it works on a few test cases."[34]

After responding so combatively to the earlier version of their paper, Edsger W. Dijkstra did not comment on the version published in the *Communications.* Many years later, however, Dijkstra visited Purdue University where DeMillo then taught and a debate between them was organized. In the 1970s there had been a degree of common ground between Dijkstra's position and that of DeMillo, Lipton, and Perlis. He agreed with them that "communication between mathematicians is an essential ingredient of our mathematical culture," and that "long formal proofs are unconvincing." What he disagreed with was that "proofs of program correctness" had to be noncommunicable and long.[35] By 1993, when Dijkstra debated with DeMillo, the gap between them had widened, even though Dijkstra's cordial personal manner and gentlemanly behavior masked that as effectively as his acid pen had masked the earlier measure of agreement. The implicit common ground—that computer scientists should emulate mathematicians—had vanished. Mathematicians indeed did not practice the Leibnizian, formal ideal of proof, just as DeMillo, Lipton, and Perlis had claimed, but that was the defensive reaction of what Dijkstra dismissed as a "guild."[36]

Computer scientists, Dijkstra had come to believe, could surpass, rather than defer to, mathematicians' notions of rigor. Debating with DeMillo, Dijkstra spoke strongly in favor of formality: the formality to be gained by purging mathematics of informal, pictorial, and psychological aspects. For example, graph theory (see chapter 4) was, he argued, "an incredible mess." It was full of "silly pictures" and "[t]o use pictures in graph theory is absolutely horrendous. They are incredibly overspecific," since "the only thing you can draw is a special graph. You can't draw a general graph." Dijkstra admitted that when he did formal proofs in geometry, he did refer to a "picture," but only "because Euclid's axioms are insufficient." "[T]he reason that you need the pictures," said Dijkstra, "is not for visual flavor or intuition or God knows what, it's just because Euclid's axioms are no good." Mathematics, Dijkstra asserted, "has nothing to do with psychology, thank the Lord!"[37]

DeMillo responded that there was an interplay between the visual and the symbolic aspects of mathematics, and he cited in support of this Lakatos's *Proofs and Refutations* (see chapter 4), provoking sharp disagreement:

Dijkstra: Did you dislike that book also very much?
DeMillo: No, I loved the book.
Dijkstra: Oh, I hated it.
DeMillo: I loved the book.[38]

In the 1970s, Dijkstra had come close to suggesting that there was something inherently defective in mechanized proofs:

To the idea that proofs are so boring that we cannot rely upon them unless they are checked mechanically I have nearly philosophical objections, for I consider mathematical proofs as a reflection of my understanding and "understanding" is something we cannot delegate, either to another person or to a machine.[39]

By 1993, however, he was no longer concerned with "understanding" or with what he believed to be the peripheral, psychological, issue of "how we are humanly wired. When I consider proofs . . . I don't try to understand, I just try to keep the rules as homogeneous [and] as simple as possible." He still shared DeMillo's lack of enthusiasm for the mechanization of proof but now for hedonistic reasons: "I'm afraid I'm not interested in mechanization. Why delegate to a machine what is so much fun to do yourself?"[40]

The effects upon program verification of the critique by DeMillo, Lipton, and Perlis are hard to ascertain. The essence of their critique was memorable: fifteen years later, those interviewed for this book had no difficulty in recalling it. The terminology of "social processes" entered the vocabulary of the field. Direct debate eventually ended: as DeMillo put it, "it was basically a firestorm that took five years to die down to any reasonable [level]." He believed that "the end result was to sort of remove the patina of orthodoxy [from formal verification]. It is now one of the fields that one does research in, that is no longer *the* field; it is no longer *the* approach to doing software engineering." Although they had had no intention of affecting the funding for formal verification research, it "was cut dramatically," recalled DeMillo, who was close to some of the agencies, especially in the U.S. military, which had been supporting the work.[41]

His former debating opponent, Susan Gerhart, agreed: "It makes the people in the funding agencies skittish to be funding in an area which is controversial." That contributed, she suggests, to the growing identification in the United States of formal methods with computer security (see chapter 5). Government bodies responsible for computer security, especially the National Security Agency, were self-confident enough and autonomous enough to continue their funding of formal methods. But in other agencies, even in the defense sector, the sense that program verification was controversial made it harder for its sympathizers to achieve the consensus necessary for large-scale funding.[42]

A Philosopher's Critique

Fears about funding contributed to the even greater heat generated a decade later in the second major controversy over program verification, sparked this time by a 1988 article in the *Communications of the ACM* by James H. Fetzer.[43] DeMillo, Lipton, and Perlis had all been computer scientists, albeit with a strong identification with mathematics. Fetzer was by inclination and by training a philosopher. He entered Princeton University as an undergraduate in 1958. After his first semester, he knew that he wanted to major in philosophy. Particularly inspiring was a course he took in his junior year from the philosopher of history, Burleigh Taylor Wilkins:

I remember when he [Wilkins] came into the room . . . he just slammed his books down on the desk, and he said, "Well, what do you think?" The guy . . . I had been waiting for all my life was suddenly asking me what I thought! Then, I'll tell you, from then on, man, philosophy was just absolutely sensational. I mean here was a guy who cared about what we thought, and goddamn it, I had thoughts, and I was prepared to present them and defend them.[44]

Fetzer graduated magna cum laude in 1962, winning Princeton's Dickinson Prize for the best senior thesis in the areas of logic and theory of knowledge. Fetzer's parents had not been wealthy enough to pay Princeton's high fees, and he had been supported by a U.S. Navy scholarship that required him to serve as a commissioned officer on graduation, so he spent the years 1962–1966 in the Marine Corps. After leaving the corps, he returned to graduate work in philosophy, gaining a Ph.D. from Indiana University in 1970. A tenure-track position at the University of Kentucky followed, but despite a growing list of publications and a distinguished teaching award (mainly for his success in teaching the traditionally difficult area of logic), he was denied tenure. Fetzer believed that senior faculty had been offended by his outspoken and disrespectful manner: "when we would be at faculty meetings, I was still wearing my combat boots from the Marine Corps, . . . and I'd put my boots up on the table, and act like I was one of the faculty. . . . I wasn't showing the proper level of deference."[45]

For almost a decade Fetzer survived on a succession of one- or two-year visiting posts. "Things were petering out," he recalled. "I was very concerned . . . because I had not found that permanent job I was looking for." The turning point in his career came in the summer of 1986 when Fetzer received a telephone call from a friend, Chuck Dunlop, who was about to enter a program in computer science and artificial intelligence at the Wright State University in Dayton, Ohio. The program was designed to convert people with Ph.D.s in philosophy or linguistics into computer scientists. Fetzer had never owned nor used a computer. The closest he had come to computing was when he had been engaged as a consultant by a former student of his who had gone on to work for IBM on artificial intelligence, and who had thought that it might be possible to make use of the "probabilistic causal calculus" that Fetzer and fellow philosopher Donald E. Nute had developed. The $200 per hour that IBM had paid him, and the parlous state of his career in philosophy, enticed Fetzer to gamble and enrol in the new course: "We sold our home and we used our equity to get us through that year."[46]

Despite the formidable technicality of his philosophical work, Fetzer found that he was "terrible at programming. Everybody thought I was going to be wonderful at programming. Well, I was terrible at programming." In retrospect, he even believes he suffered from "machine anxiety." He bought a personal computer, but couldn't bring himself to unpack it: "I left that damn machine in the box for months." Dunlop kept telling him that he was going to love it: "Of course, he was right, it just took me forever to get round to it."[47] The gamble appeared to be turning into a disaster. One of the courses Fetzer was taking, however, involved a general introduction to the idea of a programming language. The course textbook contained an annotated bibliography, and Fetzer's professor, Al Sanders, suggested to the students that they use it to find topics for their term papers. "I went poring through that bibliography to see if I could find anything that would interest me," recalled Fetzer, "something that appeared to have philosophical content." He found, in his textbook's bibliography, a reference to DeMillo, Lipton, and Perlis's "Social Processes and Proofs of Theorems and Programs." As soon as Fetzer read the paper, he knew he had struck gold: "There were just a host of inadequately understood philosophical issues here." Encouraged by Sanders, who had himself gained a Ph.D. in philosophy before turning to computer science, Fetzer wrote his term paper on DeMillo, Lipton, and Perlis's argument. When he got it back from Sanders, the latter had written on it, "fascinating, fascinating!"[48]

Unaware of the prestige of the journal, Fetzer decided to send his term paper to the *Communications of the ACM,* simply because that was where the article by DeMillo, Lipton, and Perlis had appeared. The original title of Fetzer's draft made reference to "Social Processes," so the executive editor of the *Communications* assigned it to the editor of the latter's social aspects department, Rob Kling. (That it was handled by Kling, a specialist on the social aspects of computing, rather than by John Rushby, the editor of the "dependable computing" department and a verification specialist, was a subtext in later criticism of the *Communications.*) Kling and the referees put Fetzer through four rounds of revision before finally recommending acceptance.[49]

Fetzer believed that DeMillo, Lipton, and Perlis had reached the right conclusion—that program verification could not succeed—for quite the wrong reason. The fallacy in their reasoning, Fetzer believed, was that "[s]ocial processing . . . is neither necessary nor sufficient for a proof to be valid." Whether or not a chain of argument constitutes a proof is completely independent from whether it is believed to be a proof, "just as what makes a sentence true is [that] what it asserts to be the case is the case, not merely that it is believed." A proof, said Fetzer, "strictly speaking, is a (not necessarily long) chain of formal logic," a sequence of formulae in which each formula "is either given (as an axiom or as an assumption) or else derived from preceding members of that sequence (by relying upon the members of a specified set of rules of inference)." "Complete proofs," in this sense, had to be distinguished from mere "proof sketches." Although there might be uncertainty about the validity of proof sketches, complete formal proofs offered certainty, at least so long as one was operating within the realm of logic and of pure mathematics, in which the only assumptions made were simply consequences of the definitions of the concepts being reasoned about. In this realm—the realm of what philosophers call a priori knowledge—theorems for which there were complete, formal proofs "cannot be false," said Fetzer. The use of automated theorem provers to validate such proofs raised for Fetzer (unlike for DeMillo, Lipton, and Perlis) "no special difficulties": computers could process strings of symbols without understanding their meaning, and a formal proof was simply a string of symbols manipulated according to fixed, mechanical, syntactic rules.[50]

Fetzer was certainly not seeking to defend program verification, however, for he believed that the notion contained a philosophical error of a quite different kind. It confused the realm of a priori knowledge (pure mathematics and formal logic) with the realm of a posteriori knowledge (applied mathematics or physics, for example) where statements were, at best, only "relatively verifiable" because they involved assertions about the real, empirical world that could never be proved absolutely in the way that a theorem in pure mathematics could. A computer program, Fetzer insisted, was not just a mathematical algorithm, implemented by some abstract machine: it was a causal entity designed to change the state of some real, physical, "target machine." Although the properties of algorithms implemented on abstract machines could be established by formal, deductive reasoning, the properties of programs as causal entities running on real, physical machines could not be established purely deductively. "[O]ur knowledge of the behavior of causal systems must always be 'imperfect,'" said Fetzer: it must be "experimental and tentative (like physics) rather than demonstrative and certain (like mathematics)." From the axioms of the theory of the natural numbers one could prove, absolutely and deductively, that $2 + 2 = 4$. But that did not imply that two units of alcohol added to two units of water must yield four units of mixture, nor, as he put it elsewhere, that two lumps of plutonium added to two lumps of plutonium would necessarily produce four lumps of plutonium. Two plus two necessarily equaled four only in the abstract realm of pure mathematics, of a priori knowledge. It need not remain true if used in the realm of a posteriori, empirical knowledge "for the purpose of describing the causal behavior of physical things like alcohol and water."[51]

According to Fetzer, "the very idea" of program verification was, therefore, what philosophers call a "category mistake": the notion of "program" referred to the realm of empirical, a posteriori knowledge; the notion of "verification" referred to the realm of a priori knowledge. "Program verification" was, literally, a form of nonsense. Formal, deductive verification could not establish the properties of programs as causal entities running on real, physical machines. This conclusion followed, Fetzer argued, not from any mere contingency such as the absence of "social processes" in program verification, but "emanates from the very nature of these objects of inquiry [programs and deductive reasoning] themselves. The fact that one or more persons of saintly disposition might sacrifice themselves to the tedium of eternal verification of tens of millions of lines of code for the benefit of the human race is beside the point. The limitations involved here are not merely practical: *they are rooted in the very character of causal systems themselves.*" Where human lives were at risk, in situations such as air traffic control or President Reagan's "Star Wars" strategic defense initiative, the category mistake at the heart of the idea of program verification was positively dangerous: "There is little to be gained and much to be lost through fruitless efforts to guarantee the reliability of programs when no guarantees are to be had."[52]

Fetzer's attack infuriated the verification community. Electronic mail systems, which were rudimentary around the time of the DeMillo, Lipton, and Perlis controversy, were universal in Western computer science by 1989 and helped make possible a collective, rather than just an individual, response. Ten leading figures in software engineering launched a fierce joint attack both on Fetzer's article and on the editorial process at the *Communications of the ACM:* "by publishing the ill-informed, irresponsible and dangerous article by Fetzer," they wrote, "the editors of *Communications* have abrogated their responsibility, to both the ACM membership and to the public at large, to engage in serious enquiry into techniques that may justify the practice of computer science as a socially responsible engineering endeavor."[53]

Others were equally scathing. Lawrence Paulson, Avra Cohn, and Michael Gordon of the University of Cambridge (all developers and/or users of automated theorem provers) commented that "Fetzer has condemned a subject of which he knows nothing." William R. Bevier, Michael K. Smith, and William D. Young, of the verificational specialists Computational Logic, Inc., wrote that Fetzer's article "though presented as ostensibly careful philosophical analysis, distorts the practice and goals of program verification." No "intellectually honest application" of verification could result in a claim of "absolute certainty." That was not its aim: "the goal . . . is to make it possible to make highly accurate predictions about the behavior of programs running on computers."[54]

Correspondence on Fetzer's article continued in the *Communications* for a year. Fetzer reveled in what others might have found deeply stressful: responding to sharp attacks in the leading journal of a discipline that was not his, with tight publication deadlines to meet. He had never shrunk from controversy nor hid his opinions. Even at graduate school his sketch of his intended critique of a fellow student's paper was sufficient to cause her not to give her intended presentation and to drop out of the program. "In philosophy courses, we go after each other regularly," said Fetzer. He knew that his reputation as a philosopher was "absolutely on the line: if I was not able to rebut these criticisms and disarm them, then I was in a serious way." But he had "dismantled arguments from some of the most prominent philosophers in the world, and I sure was not going to be intimidated by these people." It was, he recalled, "probably the most exhilarating intellectual experience of my life."[55]

In a very real sense, Fetzer believed that his discipline, philosophy, stood behind him. By the time his paper appeared, he had finally obtained a permanent position as professor of philosophy at the University of Minnesota, Duluth. Although he had not used the terminology of a priori and a posteriori knowledge in his critique, he felt that the fact that his position was grounded in this well-established philosophical distinction stood him in good stead:

I never put in the language "*a priori*," because that was too much philosophical technical terminology. But you can be damned sure in my own mind it was so clear to me, I mean, how obvious it was. I knew my position was absolutely, absolutely theoretically impeccable. . . . [T]hat really gave me the confidence to withstand this huge assault, psychologically. If I had not known that I was on impeccable ground I might have been overwhelmed by all this.

Indeed, he believed that it was largely biographical accident that led him to be the person to make his case against program verification: "I have no doubt that other competent philosophers, had they been in the position of confronting this problem, would have said things similar to what I said."[56]

The fiercest of Fetzer's replies to his critics was to the collective response by the ten leaders of software engineering: the "Gang of Ten," as Fetzer called them. Formal verification, they had pointed out, was not restricted to the verification of programs in high-level languages, but had also been applied "to compilers, operating systems, and computer hardware." That was beside the point, replied Fetzer:

The compilers, operating systems and computer hardware they have in mind, no doubt, are physical entities, i.e., complex causal systems whose properties in principle cannot be ascertained independently of experience. Hence, there is a crucial ambiguity in their use of the phrase "formal verification methods," by which might be meant those of *absolute* or those of *relative* verification.

The difference, of course, is critical, since the methods of absolute verification are conclusive but cannot be applied to causal systems, while those of relative verification can be applied to causal systems but are not conclusive.

The letter from the "Gang of Ten" embodied a "pathetic quality of thought," said Fetzer:

If the intellectual deficiencies of the position they represent are appalling, the unwarranted abuse to which they subject the editors of this magazine [*Communications of the ACM*] is both vicious and vindictive. . . . In its inexcusable intolerance and insufferable self-righteousness, this letter exemplifies the attitudes and behavior ordinarily expected from religious zealots and ideological fanatics.[57]

Peter J. Denning, editor-in-chief of the *Communications,* stepped in to defend the decision to print Fetzer's article. He too attacked the "Gang of Ten," albeit in more measured terms than Fetzer's:

I am dismayed by the *ad hominem* attacks sprinkled through the letter [from Fetzer's ten critics], which detract from the thoughtful criticisms and worthwhile suggestions for more discussion. The ACM does not condone such attacks. I am publishing their letter in full as an opportunity to remind all readers of our stand.[58]

Though sympathizing with Fetzer's critics, and with computer science rather than with philosophy, Leslie Lamport (author of the sharpest reply in the *Communications* to DeMillo, Lipton, and Perlis) had refused to sign the collective "Gang of Ten" response to Fetzer: he had drafted an alternative letter that they rejected. He believed that the critics had mishandled their case, and he wrote to them that: "Fetzer made mince meat of you, and Denning ground the remains into the dust. You failed to realize that philosophers, not having any objective foundation to their work, can achieve success only by becoming masters of rhetoric."[59]

In reality, though, beneath the fierce rhetoric employed by both sides in the debate lay a surprising degree of substantive agreement. Paulson, Cohn, and Gordon, for example, summarized Fetzer's argument as follows: "a computer system involves physical components that can behave unpredictably, so no deductive argument can guarantee that the system will work perfectly." That was an argument that "[p]ractically everyone" would accept as "obvious," they said; indeed, prompted by the VIPER verification discussed in chapter 7, Cohn had already written a paper of her own making precisely that point. Systems could fail for physical reasons, such as "wear and tear," as well as for logical reasons, such as design faults. This did not mean, however, that formal specification and verification were useless, argued Cohn and her colleagues. These techniques had, at least, the potential to "locate logical faults at the design stage— before they can cause harm." Similarly, Bevier, Smith, and Young of Computational Logic, Inc., accepted that there was always a gap between even the most detailed mathematical model and physical reality: "formalism does not account for such contingencies as Luddite antiverificationists with hammers smashing the [logic] gates to bits." They believed, however, that the formal modeling of hardware could render "the semantic gap" small enough "to render Fetzer's objections inconsequential."[60] Their firm's efforts to do so are discussed in chapter 7.

The British computer scientists John Dobson and Brian Randell were invited by Peter Denning, editor of the *Communications,* to comment on the controversy. What had occurred, they wrote, was a clash between "public image" and "private reality." They accepted the core of Fetzer's argument, in their words that "the hypothesis 'This program will execute correctly' is one that can never be proven, only falsified." Formal program verification could never guarantee that the execution of a program on a real, physical machine will produce the desired result. Clearly, the proponents of program verification felt they knew that and believed that Fetzer was, as another correspondent in the *Communications* put it, "belaboring [a] rather obvious fact." But, concluded Dobson and Randell, formal verificationists had only themselves to blame if others took them as thinking that the proofs they produced proved more than they really did. Even if verificationists were not consciously and deliberately encouraging an inflated view of the assurance that "proof" could confer, they were guilty of not alerting others to the danger:

. . . there is a well-known class of philosophical pothole which comes from ignoring the dictum "To understand what a proof has proved, study the proof." Some fall into this pothole through ignorance or oversight. Some make a living out of falling into it and encouraging others to do so. Some, though they may not fall into it themselves, are aware of it but signally fail to put any fences or warning notices around it. Of these, all, it seems to us, are culpable; but the last maybe more so.[61]

In the debate following Fetzer's paper, few were concerned to defend DeMillo, Lipton, and Perlis's position against his critique of it. The only correspondent in *Communications* to do so was Aaron Watters, a computer scientist at the University of Pennsylvania. He believed that while Fetzer's alternative argument against the idea of program verification was correct, it was "of very little interest." Fetzer's dismissal of DeMillo, Lipton, and Perlis's argument was "facile." Watters wrote that he had "arrived at college" believing "that mathematics was, fundamentally, the study of the manipulation of strings of symbols," a belief that may have come from a science text for lay readers: "Later, although my math classes were fascinating and well taught, I was haunted by the knowledge that my instructors were cheating. Where was the step-by-step shuffling of symbols leading from the premise to the conclusion? Why did they use so many unnecessary words and examples?"[62]

Gradually, through personal contact with mathematicians, Watters "discovered that my original notion was wrong." The true heart of mathematics was not formality and both the program verificationists and Fetzer were wrong to believe that it was:

Mathematics is not about the manipulation of strings [of symbols]; mathematics is about ideas. . . . Mathematical rigor is achieved by a combination of discussion, examples, counterexamples, diagrams, and the use of notation, when it helps people understand. Exactly how rigor is achieved is fundamentally mysterious in general, but in a particular case, the establishment of rigor is normally undeniable and exhilarating.[63]

Chapter 8 turns to questions that arise in the mechanization of the formal, syntactic notion of proof that Watters was originally seduced by and then rejected. First, though, it is necessary to see how the issues raised by DeMillo, Lipton, and Perlis, and by Fetzer played out, not at the level of abstract debate, but in the actual practice of program and hardware verification. That is the topic of chapter 7.

7

Clocks and Chips

It was an unlikely beginning for an episode that was to damage one of the world's largest corporations. Thomas Nicely is a mathematician at Lynchburg College, set beneath Virginia's Blue Ridge mountains. He specializes in number theory, and in 1994 he was working on the calculation that number theorists call Brun's sum. The problem was spelled out in 1919 by the Norwegian mathematician Viggo Brun, but it harkened back to an issue that the ancient Greeks would have recognized: the distribution of the prime numbers. As numbers get larger, fewer of them tend to be prime, but every now and then two successive odd numbers are both prime, like 3 and 5, 11 and 13, 59 and 61, and 10,007 and 10,009. Like the prime numbers themselves, twin primes do not appear to follow an exact, predictable pattern. Nevertheless, Brun showed that even though there may be infinitely many twin primes, the series formed by adding their reciprocals, $(1/3 + 1/5) + (1/5 + 1/7) + (1/11 + 1/13) + (1/17 + 1/19) + \ldots$, converges.[1]

Despite all the advances in number theory in the twentieth century, Brun's sum remained of interest. Whether or not there are infinitely many twin primes is still unknown. With neither analytical methods nor calculation providing an exact value for the sum of their reciprocals—the series converges to its limit with what Nicely calls "agonizing slowness"—mathematicians such as Nicely turned to the power of modern computing to improve existing answers.[2] Adapting the ancient Greek sieve of Eratosthenes,[3] Nicely had written a program to work through the natural numbers, checking for primes, identifying twin primes, calculating their reciprocals, and summing. Although the numbers he was working with became huge, Nicely had no need for a supercomputer: by 1994 personal computers using Intel's 80486 microprocessor, or its new Pentium™ chip, had the requisite speed and power. Nicely's colleagues allowed him to distribute the massive computational task over several computers by using their machines at night and on weekends. Beginning with five 80486 machines, he added a Pentium computer in March 1994.[4]

Nonspecialists often imagine that arithmetic performed on a computer will be exact, but Nicely knew perfectly well that he was entering an imprecise domain. He was working with integers larger than could be represented directly on the machines he was using and doing arithmetic with them: he thus had to use floating-point arithmetic[5] in which rounding error has always to be borne in mind. Nicely knew that programs and even the compilers that transformed them into machine language could have bugs, and that cosmic rays and other factors could cause errors in computer memories. So he worked carefully, cross-checking the results calculated using Intel's on-chip floating-point arithmetic against those obtained using software specially designed for high-precision integer arithmetic. Gradually he identified the effects of program and compiler bugs and by September 10, 1994, he had a "version of the code produced with all known sources of error eliminated."[6]

Nicely then restarted the entire computation, using the new Pentium machine and his wife's 486DX-33. It was quickly clear, however, that the two computers were producing different answers. A computerized comparison of the two sets of calculations revealed that the discrepancy lay deep in the calculation of Brun's sum with the twin primes 824,633,702,441 and 824,633,702,443. There was a discrepancy in the calculations of the reciprocal of the former. The division error was tiny—it arose only after the ninth significant digit—but it mattered to a very precise calculation such as Nicely was attempting. Nicely spent several days "looking for the culprit; compiler error, system bug, etc. By 19 October 1994 I was all but certain the error was within the floating point hardware unit of the Pentium C[entral] P[rocessing] U[nit] itself." Nicely told Intel Customer Support but received no immediate response. On October 30, 1994, he sent an electronic mail message to some other number-crunching users of the Pentium. Forwarded and reforwarded, the message reached Terje Mathisen, a computer scientist working for the Norwegian oil and energy company, Norsk Hydro. On November 3, Mathisen sent a message to the Internet news group, comp.sys.intel, describing the problem, and on November 7 the story was picked up by one of computing's many specialist newspapers, the *EE Times.*[7]

A German computer consultant, Andreas Kaiser, set his Pentium calculating the reciprocals of twenty-five billion random integers, and found twenty-three further instances of the error. Kaiser's list allowed Tim Coe, an engineer at Vitesse Semiconductor Corporation, who had himself designed floating-point arithmetic units, to guess that the problem lay in a specific mistake in Intel's implementation of a fast floating-point division procedure called the SRT algorithm after its inventors, D. Sweeney of IBM, J. E. Robertson of the University of Illinois, and T. D. Tocher of Imperial College London. Having correctly inferred the underlying fault, Coe was able to construct a more serious instance of the error than Nicely or Kaiser had. The division 4195835/3145727 should have the answer 1·33382044 . . . ; on the Pentium, the answer was 1·33373906. . . .[8]

Coe's simple example helped the story go beyond the Internet's "hard-core techies"; by the end of November 1994 it had reached the *New York Times* and television news. Nicely was "besieged by inquiries and visits" from journalists. Intel had not originally been overly concerned. It had detected the bug in-house before Nicely had, analyzed it, and decided that the trigger—a particular pattern of binary digits in the denominator of a division—occurred so infrequently (once in nine billion random divisions) that it would be of no concern to most Pentium users: a typical user might encounter it only once in 27,000 years, and it could at worst affect only the fourth decimal digit in a division. Intel planned to correct the design fault in the next set of the masks used to fabricate Pentium chips, but it did not intend to do anything about the majority of the chips—over one million—that had already been produced and were being sold. There had been more serious problems with Intel's earlier microprocessors, the 80386 and 80486, Intel president Andrew Grove reminded comp.sys.intel: "After almost 25 years in the microprocessor business, I have come to the conclusion that no microprocessor is ever perfect; they just come closer to perfection with each stepping [new, corrected, set of masks]." Anyone whose use of the floating-point divide instruction was intensive enough to merit a replacement chip could ask Intel for one, though the user, not Intel, would be responsible for labor costs.[9]

Grove was certainly correct that design faults in microprocessors were not unusual, and it was indeed true that for most personal computer users the Pentium divide bug was of no greater consequence than the other, often arcane, faults enumerated in table 7.1, almost no other one of which had occasioned public comment. Intel's response, however, was insufficient to halt a growing frenzy. The most damaging blow came on December 12, 1994, when IBM announced it had stopped shipping

Table 7.1
Reported Design Faults in 80 × 86 Microprocessors

Microprocessors	Number of Reported Design Faults	
386 A1 step	28	
386 B0 step	12	
386 B1 step	15	
386 D0 step	3	
386 "some versions"	19	
386 "all versions"	1	
Total for 386 family		78
486 "early versions"	6	
486 "some versions"	8	
486 A-B4 steps	3	
486 A-C0 steps	2	
486 "all versions"	2	
Total for 486 family		21
Pentium 60- and 66-MHz	21	
Pentium 75-, 90-, and 100-MHz	42	
Total for Pentium (to February 1995)		56

Microprocessors prior to the 386 are not included, and data for 386 and 486 are not comparable with those for Pentium, since the latter contain all errata known to Intel by February 1995, while the former are based on published reports alone. Totals for Pentium do not add up because seven errata were common both to 60-MHz/66-MHz processors and to 75-, 90-, and 100-MHz processors. Known bugs usually will have been corrected in later versions of the microprocessor in question. Figures for 386 and 486 are taken from Olin Sibert, Phillip A. Porras, and Robert Lindell, "The Intel 80 × 86 Processor Architecture," paper read to the IEEE Computer Society Symposium on Research in Security and Privacy, Oakland, Calif., May 1995. Figures for Pentium are my calculations based upon Intel Corporation, "Pentium Processor Specification Update" (Santa Clara, Calif.: Intel, 1995). "Pentium" is a trademark of the Intel Corporation.

personal computers containing chips with the bug. Intel's share price fell. A week later the corporation capitulated, offering free replacements to any customer not just to heavy number crunchers. The corporation set aside $475 million, half to cover costs of replacements, half representing the value of stocks of the chip that had to be discarded.[10]

SIFT

At one level, the Pentium divide bug was simply a tale of how clumsy handling allowed a limited problem to become a public-relations disaster. The episode also revealed how public expectations of perfection from technology can backfire, wrong-footing insiders like Grove who have learned to anticipate and to tolerate imperfection. It was, furthermore, a story of how the Internet makes it possible for geographically dispersed people with an esoteric concern quickly to coalesce into a force to be reckoned with: that was the role of the news group, comp.sys. intel. At yet another level, however, the divide bug is the most dramatic demonstration to date of why the verification of software may not be enough, if design faults can lurk also in computer hardware. That was the controversial conclusion drawn from the most ambitious of the early software verification projects, Software Implemented Fault Tolerance (SIFT) by two of the key participants in the project, Robert S. Boyer and J Strother Moore.

SIFT was the first major effort to apply formal verification to a system in which safety rather than security was the prime concern. SIFT was an experimental fault-tolerant flight control system developed by SRI International, whose research on computer security was discussed in chapter 5. SRI had worked on the development of fault-tolerant systems—systems that will continue to function correctly despite the presence of faults—since 1961, but SIFT moved SRI and the field of fault-tolerant computing onto new terrain.

The "oil shock" of 1973 (when the cost of oil shot up following the Israeli-Arab war and concerted price-raising by the oil-exporting countries) focused attention on the use of high technology to make aircraft more fuel-efficient. Achieving the latter, it was argued, might involve a move away from traditional designs to aircraft that were aerodynamically unstable and that would require continuous computer control. Such a control system would, of course, have to be ultradependable, but the steady increase in the number of components in microchips meant that the physical size of computers was shrinking fast, and it began to be conceivable to build in fault tolerance not by replicating individual components (the predominant earlier approach) but by creating a system consisting of several separate computers and reconfiguring the system to cope with faults in one or more of them. That approach was the one taken in SIFT.[11]

SIFT's sponsor was the National Aeronautics and Space Administration (NASA) which had responsibility not just for spaceflight—the key traditional domain of fault-tolerant computing[12]—but also for encouraging new technology for civil aviation. NASA's Langley Research Center supported two major projects in fault-tolerant computing in the 1970s. In the first, the Draper Laboratory in Cambridge, Mass. (formerly the MIT Instrumentation Laboratory and the main U.S. developers of missile and space guidance systems) built a system of separate processor and memory modules.[13] SRI worked on the other project, SIFT. The term "software implemented" in the project's title conveyed its central concept, the key original advocate of which was John Wensley of SRI: to use standard, commercially available computers as the components and to perform the tasks of identifying and isolating faults entirely by software.[14]

The SIFT system consisted of between five and eight computers, and tasks critical to safety were performed on a subset of either three or five of them (see figure 7.1). The different computers were physically isolated, each possessing its own power supply and memory, and, crucially, each having its own clock. (A computer's clock is an electronic metronome that issues electrical pulses separated by very short periods of time—around a microsecond in the computers used for SIFT—to ensure synchronized operation of the computer's components.) As a task was performed, the results of performing it on each of the subset of SIFT's computers were broadcast to the others through interconnections ("buses," as they are called) and a storage unit. "Voter" software running on each processor compared the different results.

"Global executive" software—itself replicated on each processor—received error reports from the voting software and reconfigured the SIFT system to exclude processors diagnosed as faulty (see figure 7.2) by removing them from the pool of processors to which tasks were assigned (see figure 7.3). If each fault was confined to one processor, and if the time between faults was sufficiently long to permit their detection and the exclusion of the faulty processor from the pool, an N-processor SIFT system could still work correctly after N-2 failures, a significant improve-

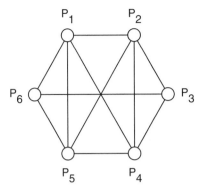

Figure 7.1
The interconnection of processors in SIFT. Based on figure in Janet E. Brunelle
and Dave E. Eckhardt, Jr. "Fault-Tolerant Software: Experiment with the SIFT
Operating System," American Institute of Aeronautics and Astronautics, *Fifth
Computers in Aerospace Conference*, 355–360, at p. 355. The figure shows a six-
processor version of SIFT and is highly schematic, excluding many features of
the actual SIFT system.

ment on less flexible designs. For example, a six-processor system employing rigid majority voting could be relied upon to survive only two
faults (with three faults, the good and bad processors could deadlock).
A six-processor SIFT system, in contrast, could tolerate up to four faults
by successively excluding the faulty processors from the pool, although
certain types of error state might no longer be detectable after three
faults.[15]

Although SIFT was experimental, it was intended to demonstrate the
feasibility of high reliability in computerized flight control. In civil aviation by the late 1970s "highly reliable" had a specific, extremely demanding interpretation: that the probability of failure should be less
than one in a billion (10^{-9}) per hour in a ten-hour flight.[16] (This figure
was roughly that demanded of the safety-critical mechanical and elec-
tro-mechanical systems in state-of-the-art civil airliners.) With such a
stringent requirement, the SRI team argued that program testing was
insufficient: "When failure rates are extremely small, it is impossible to
determine their values by testing. Therefore, testing cannot be used to
demonstrate that SIFT meets its reliability requirements. It is necessary
to *prove* the reliability of SIFT by mathematical methods."[17] SIFT,
therefore, became a test-bed not just for fault-tolerance but for formal
verification.

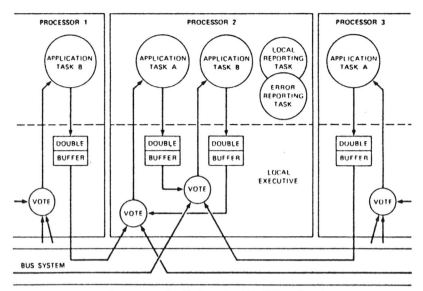

Arrangement of application tasks within SIFT configuration.

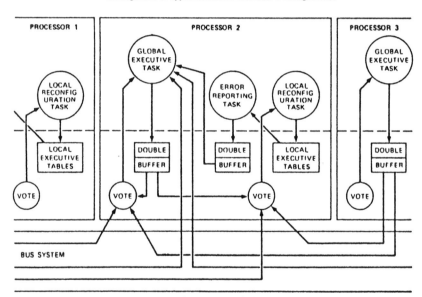

Arrangement of executive within SIFT configuration.

Figure 7.2

Arrangement of application and executive tasks in SIFT. From John H. Wensley, Leslie Lamport, Jack Goldberg, Milton W. Green, Karl N. Levitt, P. M. Melliar-Smith, Robert E. Shostak, and Charles B. Weinstock, "SIFT: Design and Analysis of a Fault-Tolerant Computer for Aircraft Control," *Proceedings of the IEEE* 66 (1978): 1240–1255, at p. 1248. ©1978 IEEE. The "application tasks" are the computing needed for flight control. The "executive tasks" control the execution of the application tasks and perform the error detection, voting, and reconfiguring needed to keep the SIFT system in a safe state.

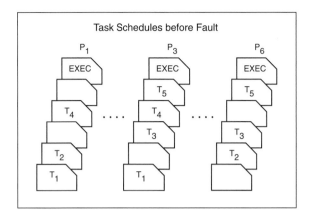

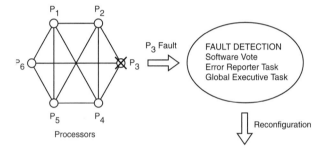

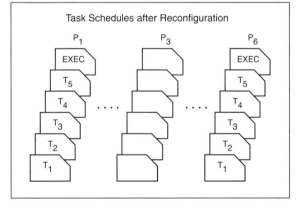

Figure 7.3
Reconfiguring SIFT to exclude a processor deemed faulty. Based on figure in
Brunelle and Eckhardt, "Fault-Tolerant Software," p. 355. "Exec" indicates executive tasks (see figure 7.2) and $T_1, \ldots, T_5$ are application tasks. If processor P_3
is deemed faulty, its tasks are allocated to other processors in such a way that
majority voting remains feasible.

Byzantine Clocks

Key to SIFT was the problem of time. Any distributed system involving multiple clocks faces the issue of how to ensure their time-keeping is consistent. Nineteenth-century railway systems, for example, confronted that problem, and historian Peter Galison suggests that Albert Einstein's reflections on their efforts to solve it may have in part inspired his famous undermining, in the theory of relativity, of the ideas of absolute space and absolute time.[18] Leslie Lamport of SRI had been fascinated for many years by time and by its treatment in Einsteinian physics: indeed, he had been inspired to return to graduate school at MIT, after earlier dropping out from Brandeis University, because "What really inspired me was a desire to understand time."[19] Just as Einstein concluded that a centralized solution to clock coordination—a "master clock" controlling all other clocks[20]—was inadequate theoretically, so the SIFT team knew it was undesirable practically. Having a single master clock would defeat the goal of fault tolerance, since a single fault in the master clock could cause failure of the entire system. Equally, though, it was vital that the times shown by SIFT's different clocks did not drift too far apart. Its separate computers processed data that varied with time and compared the results of that processing. If their clocks were not synchronized to within around 50 microseconds, SIFT's "voting" mechanism would no longer work as intended.[21]

A breakdown of synchronization, for example, would mean that the sensor readings that formed the input to the computations being done by the different processors could differ substantially because those readings were being taken at different points in time. Comparison between the output of these computations would then be misleading, and the voting and fault-isolation measures intended to promote safety might then cause catastrophe. Test-flights of a differently designed digital flight control system, fitted to an experimental version of the F-16 fighter, showed what could go wrong. In one flight, fluctuation in sensor readings and lack of synchronization of the three control subsystems caused each of the subsystems to declare the others to have failed. More than one subsystem failing simultaneously had not been anticipated, so control was not switched to the backup, analog system and "the aircraft was flown home on a single digital channel." Even though there had been no hardware fault, "all protective redundancy had been lost."[22]

Prior to SIFT, distributed systems had typically used a simple synchronization algorithm, which, in the case of a three-processor system, required each processor to observe all three clocks and reset its clock to the median or middle value. Using this algorithm, it appeared clear that two good clocks would always "outvote" a single faulty one. Charles Weinstock of SRI described the reasoning that had led others to believe that this algorithm would always permit masking of a single faulty clock: "with a single faulty clock, the median clock is either a good clock . . . or else it is a value between two good clocks, in which case synchronizing to that value is acceptable."[23] The SRI team, however, in particular Robert Shostak, Michael Melliar-Smith, and Marshall Pease, had realized that this reasoning was incorrect.[24]

Synchronization to the median could be defeated by a particular type of fault that Lamport, who joined the SRI group in 1977, christened "Byzantine": it was most easily thought of by imagining the components of a distributed system, such as clocks, as actively malicious and treacherous. Suppose that a system contains three computers, A, B, and C, each with its own clock, and that the single faulty clock (C's) is, so to speak, two-faced: that is, suppose it sends different messages to the others. Assume that although A's and B's clocks are both "good," A's is somewhat faster than B's (as real, physical artifacts, even good clocks will not stay in exact synchronization). C reports its clock's reading to A as being ahead of A's clock, so A calculates that its own clock's value is the median and does not change it. C reports its clock's value to B as being behind B's clock, so B also sees its own clock's value as the median and does not change it. As a result, the difference between A's and B's clocks gradually grows larger. Eventual catastrophic failure of the system becomes possible.[25]

In consequence Shostak and Pease discovered that four clocks, not three as one might at first assume, are required always to handle a single faulty clock (and $3N + 1$ clocks are required to mask N simultaneous faults).[26] Lamport's "interactive convergence algorithm," implemented in SIFT, showed how clock consistency could be maintained. Each processor finds the apparent skew between its clock and those of the other processors. Skews greater than a threshold value are set to zero, the skew of a processor's own clock is assumed to be zero, and the arithmetic mean of the resultant skews, the so-called "egocentric mean," is used to correct the processor's own clock. In a 1985 paper in the *Journal of the ACM,* Lamport and Melliar-Smith offered a mathematical proof that this algorithm allowed the masking of faulty, malicious clocks.[27,28] A sketch of this proof can be found in note 28 of this chapter.

The hidden complexity even of the apparently elementary matter of clock synchronization reveals just how complex and how demanding a project SIFT was. The system design had to accommodate not merely the possibility of malicious clocks but the whole range of "Byzantine" behavior (such as malicious messages from a processor's voting software, containing false error reports). A detailed specification "of what it means for the SIFT software to be correct is too complicated to be humanly comprehensible," wrote the SRI team.[29] Accordingly, they employed in the SIFT verification the same hierarchical approach used in the SRI security work described in chapter 5. As Michael Melliar-Smith and Richard Schwartz wrote, "The intent of formal specification and verification is to increase one's confidence that a system will function correctly. As such, the specification and proof of system conformance must be believable. The problem of specification credibility in the proof of SIFT is addressed through the use of hierarchical design specification and verification. This approach allows incremental introduction and verification of design aspects, making a step-by-step connection between the high-level, abstract view of the system to the detailed control and data structures employed in the implementation."[30]

The SRI team derived a hierarchy of specifications, from an input/output specification designed to capture the system's overall intended behavior, down to a specification for the Pascal program to be written for the Bendix BDX930 avionics computers to be used in the prototype (see figure 7.4). The top-level input/output specification "contains only 8 axioms and is intended to be understandable by an informed aircraft flight control engineer,"[31] while the lower-level specifications would not be comprehensible to a nonspecialist. In the input/output specification, the SIFT system was modeled as a single, sequential computer. As the hierarchy of specifications is descended, more and more detail is added. The overall goal of the proof was to show that each property derivable from the input-output specification is also derivable from the replication specification; each property derivable from the replication specification is also derivable from the activity specification; and so on as far down the hierarchy as feasible. One would then have shown that the lowest level of the hierarchy reached was a correct implementation of the overall, input-output, specification. The latter could not itself be proved correct: "That the axioms of the [top-level input/output] specification

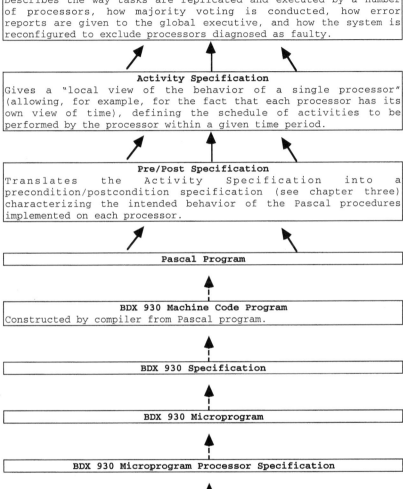

Input-Output Specification
A statement of the overall goal: that the output of any of a given set of tasks, computed on a SIFT system in a safe state, will be the correct mathematical function of the inputs to the task, and will be computed within the appropriate time-period.

Replication Specification
Describes the way tasks are replicated and executed by a number of processors, how majority voting is conducted, how error reports are given to the global executive, and how the system is reconfigured to exclude processors diagnosed as faulty.

Activity Specification
Gives a "local view of the behavior of a single processor" (allowing, for example, for the fact that each processor has its own view of time), defining the schedule of activities to be performed by the processor within a given time period.

Pre/Post Specification
Translates the Activity Specification into a precondition/postcondition specification (see chapter three) characterizing the intended behavior of the Pascal procedures implemented on each processor.

Pascal Program

BDX 930 Machine Code Program
Constructed by compiler from Pascal program.

BDX 930 Specification

BDX 930 Microprogram

BDX 930 Microprogram Processor Specification

BDX 930 Logic Design

Figure 7.4
The SIFT Hierarchy. Based on P. Michael Melliar-Smith and Richard L. Schwartz, "Formal Specification and Mechanical Verification of SIFT: A Fault-Tolerant Flight Control System," *IEEE Transactions on Computers* C-13 (1982): 616–630 at p. 621. ©1982 IEEE. Solid arrows indicate where the proof effort was most intensive.

characterize 'correct' system operation remains a subjective judgement," wrote Melliar-Smith and Schwartz.[32]

Initially, the SRI team wrote formal specifications and performed proofs without mechanical assistance, but they quickly found that to be less than satisfactory: "Our early experience in formulating formal 'paper' specifications and giving informal mathematical arguments of correctness was fraught with specification ambiguity and oversights in the informal correctness proofs." Accordingly, the SRI team turned to the use of automated theorem provers, originally the one developed by team members Robert S. Boyer and J Strother Moore, and later a different theorem prover building primarily on the work of another team member, Robert Shostak (these provers are described in chapter 8). The formal analysis and verification effort uncovered not just the flaw in the "obvious" conclusion that a three-clock voting system would always survive a single fault but also three errors in the original design of SIFT, one of which, for example, could have led to transient error states (which are common in real-time systems) accumulating dangerously. Furthermore, the SIFT team hoped that formal verification would do more than find design faults. If it could be used to show that no design faults remained, then attention could focus on physical faults in hardware. The latter could be studied empirically, and data on them combined probabilistically, to show that a demonstrably ultrareliable fault-tolerant system could be produced using components of only modest individual reliability.[33]

Success in the formal verification of a system as complicated as SIFT would have been a triumph for the field. For example, it would have deflected the effects of DeMillo, Lipton, and Perlis's celebrated critique (see chapter 6). DeMillo recalls being told often that SIFT was going to be a "counterexample" to his argument.[34] Yet what "success" meant in the context of SIFT was problematic. In the later words of SRI: "The purpose of the 'Performance Proving' project, under which SIFT design verification efforts were performed, was to advance the state of the art in verification, rather than to prove SIFT."[35] Measured against the former goal, the project was unquestionably a success. But many were also expecting the project to achieve the latter goal—formally to verify at least the prototype of a real-world system—and progress toward this was much more chequered.

Compared to other forms of research, it was unattractive said Lamport: "when somebody was hired [by SRI], the first thing that they were likely to do was [to] be put on the verification of SIFT, and the first thing they tried to do was get off there."[36] The SIFT verification work was begun using the Boyer-Moore theorem prover, but Boyer and Moore left SRI before the SIFT project was completed and others there found their prover hard to use. Its austere formal logic, described in chapter 8, appeared to them unnatural; and automated as it was, the Boyer-Moore prover still could not prove significant theorems without human guidance which had to take the indirect form of proposing appropriate lemmas (intermediate steps) for the system to prove. As SRI put it, however: "The normal user does not have the detailed understanding of the internal structure of the prover and its heuristics needed to provide this assistance." In consequence, the theorem prover used for SIFT code proofs was "abruptly" changed to a new system drawing on Shostak's work. The switch meant that crucial elements of the intended verification were started only toward the end of the project, "too late" in SRI's later judgment.[37]

The difficulties caused by the switch of theorem prover were compounded by the fact that SRI won its NASA contract for SIFT's formal verification only after work to design SIFT itself was well under way. Although SRI had committed itself to perform only "design proof" on SIFT (that is, to work only at the top four levels of figure 7.4), "it was our objective to carry out a verification of running code."[38] The prototype version of SIFT that SRI delivered to NASA, however, had problematic features from the point of view of program verification. Some of this delivered system was written not in a high-level programming language but in assembly language, and SRI "never made much progress" on its verification (see below). Other parts of the system were written in PASCAL, which was a modern, well-structured, high-level language, but the PASCAL compiler used in the system had been modified to permit "hooks into the hardware" to increase efficiency.[39] Most notably, a particular global variable was always allocated to a specific location in the processor's memory—something a generic PASCAL compiler would not do—and a value assigned to that variable would be sent to the other processors within a given amount of time.[40]

Such features were hard to formalize and were seen at SRI as the consequence of the use of hardware that would be superseded: "because those computers we were using were so antiquated, had so little memory, the code had to be packed. . . . [N]obody in their right mind . . . wanting a reliable system . . . would stint on memory. . . . [A]ny reasonable production . . . system . . . would use unpacked PASCAL code, and so what was verified was the unpacked PASCAL code."[41] For the verification effort, therefore, a "cleaned up version" of the Pascal code was produced. In consequence, "[t]he code we did consider for verification was close to the Pascal portion of the delivered SIFT system, and handled most of the features that were addressed in the design verification, but was not the running executive [as delivered to NASA]." Furthermore, the short time remaining after the switch in theorem prover meant that "[t]he Pascal code sections verified were only those required to support the incomplete design proof. . . . In particular, the global executive, reconfiguration, interactive consistency, and clock synchronization were not verified."[42]

The issue of whether the limitations of what had been done were adequately represented in publications describing the effort was to haunt the SIFT verification. The NASA project officer responsible for it, Ricky W. Butler, had little previous experience with formal verification,[43] but his superior, Billy Dove, knew that the approach was controversial: De-Millo, Lipton, and Perlis's critique of it, discussed in chapter 6, was still fresh. Dove commissioned a peer review of the SIFT verification effort. DeMillo was engaged as the review's local arrangements' coordinator and Lipton was also on the panel. Formal verification was represented by Donald I. Good (of the University of Texas at Austin), Richard Platek (founder of the security specialists, Odyssey Research Associates), Friedrich von Henke (then at Stanford University), Edmund Clarke (Carnegie Mellon University), and Bret Hartman (Department of Defense Computer Security Center). Others involved had less clear sympathies (for example, leading software engineer Susan Gerhart, and automated theorem-proving pioneer Donald Loveland), but they brought to bear an impressive body of experience. At Don Good's suggestion, J Strother Moore, who had been part of the SIFT project, but had left SRI two years before the July 1983 peer review, was added to the panel because of his "first-hand knowledge."[44]

What might have been expected was that the issues dividing the formal verificationists from DeMillo and Lipton would be thrashed out by a group that represented the cream of American computer science, with reference not to abstract issues but to a specific proof. Events, however, were to take a quite different turn. This was presaged about a month into the planning of the peer review when DeMillo was on his way from Georgia to the west coast of America. His secretary started to track him across the country with a series of phone calls, telling him that someone whom he will identify only as "one of the principals in the verification community" was trying to get hold of him. When they finally spoke,

DeMillo was taken aback to hear not a defense of SIFT's achievements, but an attack on how the project had been reported.[45]

The phone call set the tone for the peer review. SRI sent Melliar-Smith, Shostak, and Schwartz, who arrived confident that their design-proof achievements had successfully turned around a verification effort that had been in the doldrums and unafraid of potential criticism from DeMillo and Lipton. Instead of collegial discussion, however, they encountered a detailed grilling, more akin to an adversarial Senate hearing than to computer science's generally relaxed meetings. The grilling focused on the relationship between what had actually been done in the SIFT verification, up to that point, and various published descriptions of the effort. The questioning went beyond the design proof aspects on which Melliar-Smith, Schwartz, and Shostak had worked to include other aspects, notably code proof. The tension in the room rose as the questioning became more hostile: by the end of the meeting one of the panel members had to leave the room, physically ill, as a result of the emotional atmosphere.[46]

A draft of the panel's report, containing sharp criticism of the reporting of the SIFT project, leaked out. The outcome of the peer review, the draft concluded, "is probably unsatisfactory for all concerned." Although its remit had been to assess "the role of formal methods in the validation of fault-tolerant computer systems with emphasis on the work done by SRI," the panel "spent a great deal of its time trying to ascertain what had been accomplished by the contractor rather than assessing the importance of the accomplishments relative to the issues. Frustration reigned; acrimony flourished."[47] The final version of the report was more measured but still contained pointed criticism of the reporting of the project: "The incompleteness of the SIFT verification exercise caused concern at the peer review. Many panel members who expected (from the literature) a more extensive proof were disillusioned."[48]

Those involved in the SIFT verification effort believed, and still believe, that much of the criticism was unfair. Richard Schwartz conceded that some of the descriptions of the effort at the system-wide level "were claims that were too grand." He pointed out, however, that some members of the peer review panel were committed to an approach to verification as "code-level proof-of-correctness," an approach that differed from SRI's higher-level "design proof" approach.[49] From the other side, J Strother Moore, a critic of the reporting of the SIFT verification, now conceded that, "if you read their papers carefully enough you might understand what they were really claiming." At the time, though, he worried about the fact that what verification had been applied to was not the actual running prototype of SIFT. If this prototype, an apparently verified system, exhibited failures, that would reflect badly on the whole fledgling enterprise of formal verification. Furthermore, if sponsors gained an inflated idea of what had been proved in the SIFT effort, they might then not provide the research funds necessary to advance the field, "because it looks like you're proposing to do research [on] problems that have already been solved." The SIFT verification effort was "incredibly ambitious," he said. The fact that there were limitations on what was done "is not at all a reflection of the quality of the people or how much work they put into it, but a reflection of how far away the state of the art was from what was needed to do that project."[50]

The SIFT verification peer review was a traumatic experience and striking in that the primary criticism of claims of proof came from within the formal verification community, rather than from outside it. Dramatic though it was, however, the peer review episode should not blind one to the significance of the SIFT work. The project encouraged and helped support two of the important automated provers discussed in chapter 8. The elegant architecture and sophisticated algorithms developed for SIFT were of continuing importance in the field of fault-tolerant computing. Although SIFT was originally a research prototype, John Wensley, leader of the original design effort, turned it into a successful product that has been used widely in the nuclear industry, in oil and gas production, and in other safety-critical fields.[51] From the viewpoint of this book, however, SIFT's most important role was as a spur driving formal verification deeper into systems.

A Bit Pattern Flickers

Two of those involved in the SIFT verification, Robert S. Boyer and J Strother Moore, left the project convinced that "proof" had to be driven downward—from abstract models into the code of programs and the compiler, and eventually even into hardware design itself. Only if that were achieved would the full promise of system verification bear fruit. When, seven years after leaving SRI, they believed they had reached their goal, it was, to them, "the first major demonstration of system verification."[52] "I'm Pythagorean to the core," said Boyer, "Pythagoras taught that mathematics was the secret to the universe." Boyer's dream—not a hope for his lifetime, he admitted—is that mathematical modeling of the laws of nature and of the features of technology will permit the scope of deductive reasoning to be far greater than it currently is. "If you have a nuclear power plant, you want to prove that it's not going to melt down. . . . One fantasizes, one dreams that one could come up with a mathematical characterization . . . and prove a giant theorem that says 'no melt-down.' In my opinion, it is the historical destiny of the human race to achieve this mathematical structure. . . . This is a religious view of mine."[53]

It was a dream that was a long time coming into focus. Boyer was something of a prodigy, whose schoolboy reading had included Descartes and Leibniz. When he entered the University of Texas at Austin in 1964, he immediately started taking third-year mathematics courses. Graduating after only three years of study, Boyer went on to complete his Ph.D. on resolution theorem proving supervised by Woody Bledsoe, whose work was discussed in chapter 3.[54]

J Strother Moore (J is his first name, not an initial) was also an early developer, one whose skills were most strikingly apparent in programming. As a high school student in Texas, he learned to program at a National Science Foundation summer school in 1964. In the mid-1960s computers were still large and expensive, and Moore did not have access to one on which to practice his newly acquired skills. So, during his last two years in high school, he "wrote a lot of paper computer programs. I kind of kept in touch with it, even though I could never run my programs." In 1966 he went to MIT to study mathematics. To supplement his scholarship he took up a part-time job as a "gopher" in the famous laser research group at MIT. He was, he admitted, little use at returning from the stores with the right "widget," nor at wiring up switches. He saw, however, "all those graduate students scratching their heads over their FORTRAN programs." Suddenly, he had found his role. By the end of the spring semester of his freshman year he was programming for the laser research group, and by the start of his sophomore year he was put in charge of the laboratory's computing budget, with the responsibility of ensuring that it was carefully rationed over the year and that everyone could get their programs run.[55]

The first run for which Moore was responsible was an unforgettable lesson in the consequences of bugs in computer programs. A mistake in the program caused the machine in MIT's computation center to enter an endless loop, printing for a whole night on a single page of paper. The horrified Moore discovered the next morning that in one night he had spent almost the entire annual programming budget allowed by MIT to the laser group. In retrospect, that was no worse than an excruciating embarrassment, but Moore soon learned about programs in which mistakes could cost human lives.

In the summer of 1968, between his sophomore and junior years, Moore helped to debug the Apollo onboard computer software that was shortly to guide the mission to the moon. He found two bugs, one of which would have been fatal if it had been triggered in real life. To help the debugging, he used the computer simulation of the Apollo mission described in chapter 2. The simulator fascinated him: "it was possible to have a real world embedded in a computer . . . I began to think of the computer as sort of the host for a world, and you could build anything inside it." When he returned to MIT, he continued to study mathematics, but his academic focus shifted to artificial intelligence. He took courses from the director of the MIT Artificial Intelligence Laboratory, Marvin Minsky, and changed advisers to Minsky's colleague Seymour Papert.[56]

Boyer and Moore were brought together by a time they each spent in the early 1970s in the artificial intelligence community at the University of Edinburgh: their creation in this period of the Boyer-Moore theorem prover is discussed in chapter 8. When they returned to the United States, it was to California's Silicon Valley. Boyer went to work for SRI in Menlo Park and Moore to the nearby Xerox Palo Alto Research Center, but he too soon joined SRI. There, funded in part by the SIFT project, they continued to develop their theorem prover and worked upon a variety of aspects of the SIFT proof, most consequentially upon a small but crucial part of the system called the "dispatcher." Buried away in section 17 of the SRI report submitted to the SIFT peer review is a five-page discussion by Boyer and Moore of why the proof work on the dispatcher had to fail. This apparently esoteric appendix contained the heart of their emerging view of system verification.[57]

Clocks and time are crucial to a concurrent system such as SIFT. Computing tasks have to be executed within real-time constraints. They may have to be run for a certain amount of time, suspended following an "interrupt" from the processor's clock, saved, and reactivated at some later point in time. In the dispatcher, brute force considerations of real time had to intrude into the more abstract, high-level, PASCAL software. There was no way to use PASCAL to handle the notions of a clock interrupt, or of executing a subroutine for a specific period of time and later resuming its execution. So the dispatcher (shown in figure 7.5) was written not in PASCAL but in the assembly language of the Bendix 930, the computer used as SIFT's processors.

```
CINT    PUSHF   15              save the flags
        PUSHM   1,13            Save registers
        PUSHM   0,0             and the resume address
        LOAD    0,ACLK          indicate a clock tick
SCHG    TRA     1,15            save the current stack pointer
        LDM   / 15,15,STACK     point at the "exec" stack
        PUSHM   0,1             set function code and resume stack
        JSS*    ASCHE           call the scheduler which is a pascal function
        TRA     15,12           that returns the new tasks r15 value.
        POPM    0,0             restore the resume PC to R0
        POPM    1,13            restore some registers.
        POPF    15              and the flags
        CONT    ES              allow interrupts
        RET     0               and go resume this routine
```

Figure 7.5
The SIFT dispatcher program. From Robert S. Boyer and J Strother Moore, "On Why It Is Impossible to Prove that the BDX930 Dispatcher Implements a Time-Sharing System," in K. N. Levitt et al., *Investigation, Development, and Evaluation of Performance Proving for Fault-Tolerant Computers* (Hampton, Virginia: NASA Langley Research Center, August 1993, NASA Contractor Report 166008), 475–482, at p. 475.

What the dispatcher and the associated, PASCAL-programmed scheduler had to do was to cause the system to behave as if application programs were running continuously: that is, it had to be possible in the higher-level verification work to ignore clock interrupts, suspensions, and reactivations. As Boyer and Moore wrote, "the dispatcher and scheduler apparently implement a time-sharing system in which each user task is running on a 'virtual' BDX930. We set out to try to prove that the 14 lines of code [in figure 7.5] correctly implemented those virtual BDX930s."[58] The task drove them down from the verification of programs in high-level languages such as PASCAL or LISP (one of the earliest uses of the Boyer-Moore prover was to prove theorems about LISP functions)[59] toward the hardware of the BDX930. Indeed, for them the task of verifying the 14 lines of assembly language began to appear like a prototype of how the entire SIFT verification might have to be carried out. Because of the "hooks into the hardware" that had been used in progamming SIFT, there was a sense in which verifying properties of the PASCAL code was, in their view, misleading. If one substituted a generic PASCAL compiler for the modified compiler actually used on SIFT, "the code would cease to function, despite the fact that the theorems proved would all still hold," said Moore:

Boyer and I took the view that the programming language in which SIFT was written was not really Pascal, as that is understood at the abstract level. Instead, we thought of SIFT as being programmed in Bendix 930 machine code (where things like memory locations and time are modeled). The expression of the code in a syntax similar to Pascal was a convenient fiction. In essence, the programmers were using that syntax as a macro expansion language to produce Bendix 930 machine code *and they clearly had in mind the machine code they were producing.* To prove SIFT correct one would need a model of the machine code, complete with timing measures.[60]

In Boyer and Moore's emerging view, program verification, as it was practiced in the 1970s, had almost a theological quality in its abstraction from the machines on which programs ran. Dominant approaches, they suggested, implicitly assumed that it was a "god" rather than a physical machine, "that actually steps through one's programs."[61] Boyer and Moore concluded that, to verify SIFT, it was necessary to construct a mathematical model of what BDX930 machine code instructions did. They sought to encode in the logic used in their theorem prover a function that described the changes in the state of the BDX930 effected by each instruction. The formula for the function covered thirty pages, even though it was described not in the most primitive terms possible but in terms of functions such as 8-bit (binary digit) addition.[62] The formula was so large that it could not be processed by their theorem prover.

Improvements to the prover eventually permitted the formula to be entered into it, but, wrote Boyer and Moore, "[w]e still anticipate great difficulty proving anything about the function because of its large size." The problems that eventually stopped them went beyond these practical difficulties of automated proving. They found it impossible to provide entirely unambiguous specifications, valid for all cases including "pathological" ones, of what the BDX930 instructions were intended to do. Time was again a key problem. It was difficult to be sure how long instructions would take to execute, but clock interrupts occurred at fixed, real-time intervals. For this reason, wrote Boyer and Moore, they "abandoned the idea of trying to model precisely the clock interrupt mechanism." Their overall conclusion was a deeply pessimistic one: "an attempt to verify the few lines of machine code in SIFT lead to the requirement that we have formal specifications for several huge objects which have never yet been adequately formalized."[63] The most daunting of these objects was the BDX930 computer itself. Clearly, a mathematical model of an entire computer was a daunting task; in practice, it was an impossible one for a machine such as the BDX930 that had not been designed with formal verification in mind. The extension of proof down toward hardware would require hardware to be redesigned with proof in mind.

In 1981 Boyer and Moore left SRI to take up posts in the Department of Computer Science at the University of Texas at Austin where they began to collaborate with program verification pioneer Don Good, whose work was discussed in chapter 5. Good had earlier come to the same conclusion as Boyer and Moore: that hardware verification, as well as program verification, would eventually be necessary. The statement, "A proof of [program] correctness guarantees that a program will run correctly every time it is executed," was not necessarily true, Good warned in a paper written in 1974, long before Fetzer made the same point. The other software needed for a program to run, such as the compiler, could malfunction, as could the system hardware. Good, Boyer, and Moore, however, did not draw Fetzer's conclusion that program verification should be abandoned as a category mistake. Instead, they concluded as Good put it in 1974 that there would be an "eventual need for a completely proved computing system."[64]

Providing such a system became the central goal of Computational Logic, Inc., the firm set up in Austin in 1983 by Good, Boyer, and Moore, along with colleagues Michael Smith and Richard Cohen. The University of Texas allowed its employees to do consultancy work for one day a week, and the firm's five founders began to put half of their consultancy earnings into it. By 1987 the new company had sufficient capital, and sufficient credibility with research sponsors, to begin to operate in a self-supporting way with its own offices, computers, and staff.[65]

At Austin, Boyer and Moore had joined a computer science department becoming prominent in formal methods: in 1984, for example, Edsger W. Dijkstra joined the faculty. Boyer and Moore began to gather around them a group of graduate students who used their prover to perform a series of increasingly impressive proofs. This group's frequent face-to-face interaction in Boyer and Moore's graduate course, in their weekly logic seminar, and in other activities was key. Using their prover was hard, and few people were able to pick up the requisite skill without personal contact with the prover's designers: "Almost all of the successful users of [the prover] have in fact also taken a course from us . . . on proving theorems in our logic."[66] Their graduate students helped Boyer and Moore to continue toward the goal that they had begun to set themselves in the SIFT project: driving "proof" down toward hardware. The task that proved so daunting for the SIFT component computer, providing a formal specification of the changes in state induced by an instruction, was performed, for example, with some success for a widely used commercial microprocessor, the Motorola 68020: Boyer's student, Yuan

Yu, constructed a formal specification of four-fifths of its "user mode" instructions.[67] Formal specification and verification of computer hardware design, however, were likely never to be more than partially successful if performed only in retrospect on a machine designed without verification in mind. To realize Good's, Boyer's, and Moore's dream, Computational Logic, Inc. decided it had to develop its own formally specified and verified hardware platform. The effort to do so was led by Warren A. Hunt, Jr. Hunt "triple majored" in electrical engineering, computer science, and mathematical sciences at Rice University before moving for his graduate work to the University of Texas at Austin. He interspersed his studies with periods spent working in digital systems design for firms such as Texas Instruments. He was thus experienced in conventional hardware design before he began a series of microprocessor designs intended for formal verification: the FM8501, FM8502, and FM9001.[68]

Hunt's goal was to use Boyer-Moore logic, the formal system implemented in the prover, to describe both the intended behavior of a piece of hardware and its actual design, and then to use the prover to show that the two mathematical models were consistent, in other words that the detailed design was a correct implementation of the formal specification. The FM8501, for example, was modeled essentially at the level of the logic gates that were the basis of its capacity to perform arithmetical and logical processing.[69] A total of 991 lines of text were required to express the theorem that captured the "correctness" of the FM8501, that is to say, the correspondence between its gate-level description and its specification.[70]

Although the gate-level model was detailed, Hunt was well aware that it was not a physical actuality: "Since the theory used to represent digital hardware is not quantum mechanics or some finer model, there is a gap between my lowest level objects and the physical world of hardware."[71] Indeed, neither the FM8501 nor its successor, the 8502, was built. The mathematical model that was used was considered by Hunt "too weak to be believable from an engineering viewpoint."[72] As the work proceeded, however, Hunt and his colleague Bishop C. Brock (who joined Computational Logic, Inc. in 1988) made the model of hardware more expressive: by the early 1990s their hardware description language, formalized in Boyer-Moore logic, could support the inspection of circuits for "physical" matters not captured by simple logical models, such as "fanout violations," in which the output of a logic gate is connected to the inputs of so many others that it physically cannot "drive" them.

Even then, though, their language could not model some features of commercial microprocessors because, for example, it made the assumption that "every state-holding device . . . update[s] its internal state simultaneously." They continued to emphasize that their hardware description language was "a model of physical reality," which "should be inspected by digital design engineers to determine whether [it] corresponds with physical reality."[73] Nevertheless, their format could be translated by a short program into the Network Description Language used by microchip fabricators LSI Logic, Inc. to control the machines used to make the "masks" needed to fabricate microchips. Brock knew this language well (he had worked on a simulator for it) and he and Hunt were confident of the correctness of the translation. By October 1991 actual FM9001 chips had been manufactured.[74]

Computational Logic, Inc. did not intend to sell the FM9001 as a product for others to use.[75] Rather, it was the foundation of what the firm came to call the "CLInc stack," the goal of which was to demonstrate full system verification in Good, Boyer, and Moore's sense. J Strother Moore introduced a 1989 special issue of the *Journal of Automated Reasoning* devoted to the CLInc stack: "In the fall of 1988, a bit [binary digit] pattern flickered across the screen of a workstation in Austin, Texas. This particular pattern had a property that no previous bit pattern had ever had: it had been proved by computer to implement a high-level language program."[76]

The base of the stack was a microprocessor, or, to be more precise, a mathematical model of a microprocessor (in 1989 the CLInc stack was based on the FM8502, which was a design, not an actual chip; only later was the base shifted to the physically implemented FM9001). On that base, CLInc "assembled a series of successively more 'abstract' (farther from the hardware level) system components, each . . . implemented on its predecessor, and each implementation . . . formally specified and mechanically verified. The system we have constructed contains a microprocessor, a machine code, an assembly language [Piton], and a simple high-level programming language [Micro-Gypsy], together with the compiler, assembler and linker necessary to connect them."[77]

This hierarchy of proofs (in which lower layers were proved to be correct implementations of the more abstract layers above them) may on the surface appear reminiscent of the SIFT proof strategy, and there is indeed a sense in which the CLInc stack is a descendant of the earlier, troubled verification effort. But the differences outweigh the similarities. The chain of proof in the CLInc stack stretched downward toward "hardware" (conceptual hardware with the FM8502; later, real hardware with the FM9001) that was designed from the start with verification in mind. Piton and Micro-Gypsy, similarly, were constructed specifically to facilitate verification. This very specificity, however, meant that the CLInc stack remained a research tool, not adopted outside of CLInc. Nevertheless, it is of considerable interest in exemplifying one point of view on what "proof" should mean in the context of computer systems.

Introducing the CLInc stack, Moore was careful to say what was and what was not being claimed: "In a verified system one can make the following startling claim: if the [logic] gates behave as formally modeled, then the system behaves as specified. Of course, two almost philosophical questions remain: Does the formal model at the gate level accurately reflect reality? Does the formal specification at the high level accurately reflect the requirements? These questions are nontrivial. But note that they do not require consideration of any software."[78] The gap between formal verification and physical reality, pointed to by James Fetzer (see chapter 6), had not disappeared. To a philosopher, it might yawn as wide as it ever had. But Computational Logic, Inc. believed it had narrowed the gap significantly.

As William Bevier, Michael Smith, and William Young of CLInc put it in their contribution to the Fetzer controversy: "To deny any relation between, say, a physical AND gate and the corresponding boolean function is to deny that there can be any useful mathematical model for physical reality. This is tantamount to asserting the impossibility of physical science."[79] Nor did Moore see the narrowing of the gap between model and reality achieved with the CLInc stack as the limit. "[R]ight now we model gates at the logical level," he said, but he can imagine (though he does not currently advocate) "modeling gates at the physical level and introducing a little formal quantum mechanics." Proof, in other words, can be driven downward even deeper into systems, even if (in Moore's current opinion) the greatest practical gains will come from driving it upward from circuits to systems.[80]

VIPER

The distinctive approach to computer system verification developed by Boyer, Moore, and Computational Logic, Inc. contained an implicit— and sometimes explicit—critique of other approaches. It was clearly at odds with the design-proof approach to the verification of trusted systems taken at SRI and embodied in the orange book (see chapter 5). An equally significant clash came with the development of a British hardware verification project, Verifiable Integrated Processor for Enhanced Reliability (VIPER)[81] which was developed at the U.K. Ministry of Defence's Royal Signals and Radar Establishment (RSRE), Britain's leading research and development laboratory in military electronics. The aim of the VIPER project, like that of CLInc's FM8501 series, was to develop a microprocessor whose detailed, logic-gate-level design could be proved to be a correct implementation of a top-level specification of its intended behavior.

The VIPER team sought to construct the proof of correspondence between top-level specification and gate-level design in the form of a chain of mathematical reasoning connecting four levels of decreasing abstraction (see figure 7.6). Most abstract was the top-level specification itself, which laid down the changes that should result from each of the limited set of instructions provided for use by VIPER's programmers. Below that was the "major-state machine," still an abstract description, but one that contained more details on the steps gone through in executing an instruction. Next came the "block model," which was more concrete and consisted of a diagram (of a kind familiar to designers of integrated circuits) of the major components of VIPER, together with

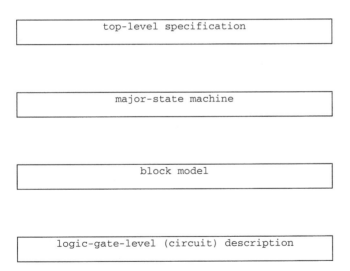

Figure 7.6
VIPER: four levels of mathematical model. Details of the implementation increase as one proceeds down the levels.

a specification of the intended behavior of each component. The gate-level description, the bottom-most layer of mathematical model, was sufficiently detailed that it could be translated into an input to the automated equipment used by the electronics firms, Ferranti and Marconi, to construct the "masks" used to fabricate VIPER chips.[82]

The RSRE team used a mathematical formalism specifically designed for hardware verification: LCF_LSM, a variant of Robin Milner's LCF, which is described in chapter 8. The top-level specification, major state machine, and the units in the block model were all described in LCF_LSM. The units in the block model were also described in the RSRE-developed hardware language ELLA which was used for the logic-gate level model. (ELLA could be transformed automatically into the input formats for the computer-aided design systems used to construct the masks needed to fabricate chips.) The RSRE team constructed, by hand, a proof of the correspondence between the LCF_LSM expressions of the top-level specification and the major state machine.

The team also used a "method of proof called 'intelligent exhaustive simulation'" to demonstrate, for each block in the block model, that "for all combinations of inputs for a particular block, the block specification and circuit [gate-level] implementation deliver the same results." Exhaustive simulation, like exhaustive testing, is generally seen as infeasible because of the sheer number of cases that need to be explored (2^N cases for a circuit with N binary inputs). In intelligent exhaustion, however, inputs to a block that its specification implied were "irrelevant under some sets of conditions" to its output were labeled "DONTCARE." (ELLA supports a logic in which values in addition to TRUE and FALSE are permissible.) If a mistake had been made in the implementation of the block, and an input that should be irrelevant had an effect on its output, a further value, "DONTKNOW," was produced, indicating the mistake. Intelligent exhaustion radically cut the number of cases that needed to be checked. For example, the VIPER instruction decoder block had eighteen inputs. Conventional exhaustive testing would require 2^{18} or 262,144, tests "to prove correspondence between specification and implementation," but by using intelligent exhaustion "an equivalent level of proof has been achieved using just 995 tests." In consequence, it was possible to translate a contractor's circuit description into an ELLA gate-level description and check the latter's correspondence to the block model in as little as two hours.[83]

RSRE's approach demonstrated its value by revealing several design mistakes.[84] Completing the chain of proof from top-level specification down to logic-gate-level description, however, turned out to be hard. By the end of 1986 the team at RSRE had completed, to their satisfaction, the proofs connecting top-level specification to major state machine and block model to gate-level description, but this left a gap between major-state machine and block model. The RSRE team decided that this part of the chain of proof required mechanized help. The team decided to check the correspondence between block model and major state machine by simulation but also awarded a contract to the Cambridge University Computer Laboratory to perform formal, mechanized proof. At Cambridge, Avra Cohn used the Higher-Order Logic (HOL) automated theorem prover, which is described in chapter 8, to do so. First, using HOL, she repeated the original RSRE hand-proof of correspondence between the top-level specification and the major state machine.[85] Cohn then turned her attention to the block model.

Cohn judged that it was more straightforward to attempt to prove correspondence between the high-level specification and the block model directly, rather than via the intermediary of the major state machine. After a person-year of effort, however, and proof work amounting to seven million computer-generated primitive inference steps, Cohn had still not completed the full proof, and she found the research interest of what she was doing to be dwindling. For example, in the case of addition with overflow (a result larger than the maximum expressible in VIPER's arithmetic), Cohn wrote that "[o]ne can convince oneself that the two sums [as specified by the top-level and block models] are equivalent, but . . . the infrastructure to do this formally in HOL is at present rather limited."[86] Inspecting what she had done, the RSRE team concluded that "[t]he final HOL proof . . . is complete apart from 12 theorems," all relating to overflow or the "twos complement" arithmetic used on VIPER. These theorems, they reported, had all been proved "by hand."[87]

Did all the proof, analysis, simulation, and testing of VIPER—the extent and limitations of which the RSRE team were careful to describe in their publications on the chip[88]—amount to a proof of the correctness of its design? The then director of RSRE appeared in no doubt that it did. In a foreword to a 1987 marketing brochure produced by Charter Technologies, Ltd. (a small firm based in Worcester, England, which licensed aspects of the VIPER technology from the Ministry of Defence), he wrote that "VIPER is the first commercially available microprocessor with a proven correct design." Charter's brochure went on to make what appears at first sight to be an equivalent statement, but, as the Fetzer dispute has shown, is actually a significantly stronger one: "VIPER is the first commercially available microprocessor with both a formal specification and a proof that the chip conforms to it."[89] Press reports in Britain were glowing. The *New Scientist* called VIPER "The mathematically perfect chip," with "a design that has been proved mathematically to be correct." It was "failsafe," said *Electronics Weekly*. It had been "mathematically proved to be free of design faults," said the *Engineer*.[90]

The VIPER team, however, knew that the chain of mathematical argument it had constructed was not a proof that the microprocessor as a physical artifact conformed to the formal specification. The bottom of the chain of mathematical arguments was still a mathematical model of the microprocessor, not its actual silicon. For this reason the team sought independent physical implementations of VIPER, implementations that could (in the 1A version of the chip) be run in parallel, checking one another. At Cambridge, Cohn went to some lengths in her 1989 report on the partial verification of the VIPER block model to make sure that the difference between a mathematical model and the microprocessor itself was clear.

"When we hear that a chip such as Viper has been 'verified,' it is essential to understand exactly what is meant," she wrote: "Ideally, one would like to prove that the chip correctly implemented its intended behaviour in all circumstances; we could then claim that the chip's behaviour was predictable and correct." She argued, however, that "neither an actual *device* nor an *intention* are objects to which logical reasoning can be applied. The intended behaviour rests in the minds of the architects and is not itself accessible. . . . At the same time, a material device can only be observed and measured, not verified. . . . In short, verification involves two or more *models* of a device, where the models bear an uncheckable and possibly imperfect relation both to the intended design and to the actual device." If these limitations of the assurance conveyed by formal verification were not understood—if verification was taken as implying "the impossibility of design failure in safety-critical applications"—such false confidence "could have catastrophic results."[91]

All those most centrally involved were thus in agreement on the limitations of the assurance that could be conveyed by proof. Where disagreement broke out was over whether the chain of mathematical reasoning constructed at RSRE and at Cambridge constituted a proof. To Cohn, "verification" meant "complete, formal proof in an explicit and well-understood logic." Intelligent exhaustion, in her view, did not constitute formal proof, and so, she wrote: "no formal proofs of Viper (to the author's knowledge) have thus far been obtained at or near the gate level."[92] That was also the conclusion reached when Computational Logic, Inc. was commissioned by NASA to review the VIPER verification work.

The assessment was done by the firm's hardware specialists Bishop Brock and Warren Hunt. "There are different degrees of rigor possible when applying formal methods to hardware design," wrote Brock and Hunt in their January 1990 report: "hand-written specifications, hand proofs, mechanically recorded specifications, and mechanical proofs." Brock and Hunt allowed only the last of these as "formal proof," as the diagram from their report reproduced in figure 7.7 suggests. They were critical of what they regarded as unverified translations between different formalisms and counted only the Cambridge HOL work as formal proof. Like Cohn, Brock and Hunt did not regard intelligent exhaustion as constituting formal proof because, in their view, there was not an adequate demonstration "that the input patterns used for IE [intelligent exhaustion] provided complete coverage of every possible case." Although they praised "the efforts of the groups at RSRE and Cambridge who took on a formidable verification task," they did not accept that what had been done, up until 1989, constituted mathematical proof that VIPER's detailed design was a correct implementation of its specification. "VIPER has been verified in the traditional hardware engineering sense, i.e., extensively simulated and informally checked," they concluded, but "VIPER has not been formally verified."[93]

The report by Brock and Hunt was injected into an increasingly difficult situation in England. Charter Technologies, Ltd., which had licensed aspects of the VIPER technology from the U.K. Ministry of Defence, was finding that the market for these was much smaller than had been hoped and the firm was losing money on its investment. The combination of a disappointing market and differing judgments on whether the chain of mathematical arguments constituted "proof" prompted Charter to begin, early in 1991, a law suit against the Secretary of State for Defence. The suit is unique in that, as far as is known, it was the first litigation to hinge upon what mathematical proof consists in: Charter alleged, among other things, that the claim of proof was a misrepresentation, and sought damages for it.[94] (In 1987 at the start of the research on which this book is based, colleagues and I, informed by the sociology-of-knowledge conviction that proof is not the absolute matter it is ordinarily taken to be, predicted just such a law suit.[95]) With the Ministry of Defence vigorously contesting Charter's allegations, however, the lawsuit never came to court because Charter became bankrupt before there was

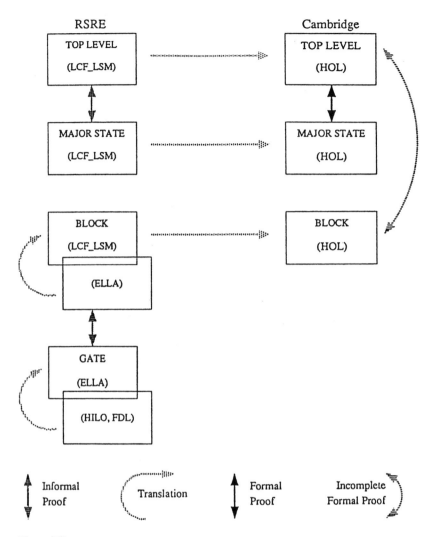

Figure 7.7

Brock and Hunt's evaluation of the chain of mathematical arguments connecting VIPER's top-level specification to its gate-level description. From Bishop Brock and Warren A. Hunt, Jr., "Report on the Formal Specification and Partial Verification of the VIPER Microprocessor" (Austin, Texas: Computational Logic, Inc., January 15, 1990, Technical Report 46), p. 3. HILO and FDL are the design languages used by the manufacturers of the physical VIPER chips.

a hearing. When that happened, its suit lapsed and Martyn Thomas, head of the software house Praxis and a leading figure in the British computing community, mounted a defense of the VIPER proof. "We must beware of having the term 'proof' restricted to one, extremely formal, approach to verification," wrote Thomas. "If proof can only mean axiomatic verification with theorem provers, most of mathematics is unproven and unprovable. The 'social' processes of proof are good enough for engineers in other disciplines, good enough for mathematicians, and good enough for me. . . . If we reserve the word 'proof' for the activities of the followers of Hilbert [see chapter 8], we waste a useful word, and we are in danger of overselling the results of their activities!"[96]

Considerable further work verifying VIPER's design was done after the litigation ended.[97] What is most interesting about the controversy, however, is that it revealed a variety of meanings of "proof." John Kershaw of the RSRE team was driven to an explicitly relativistic conclusion. " 'Proof,' " he wrote, "is a typical Humpty Dumpty word, which means precisely what you want it to mean. . . . In practice proof seems to mean 'an argument that most practitioners in the field accept as valid,' no more and no less."[98]

The dominant notion of proof in the hardware verification efforts described so far in this chapter was that of Cohn, Brock, and Hunt: formal proof, a chain of applications of inference rules, leading from axioms to a theorem, performed by an automated theorem prover. That was what Cohn had tried to provide; its incomplete provision in the VIPER verification as it stood at the end of the 1980s was the core of Brock and Hunt's criticism; Thomas's belief that it was an overnarrow notion of proof was the basis of his defense. By the time the VIPER controversy ended, however, an alternative approach to hardware verification was beginning to develop. It was one that was much less demanding of user skills than the automated provers used by Cohn, Brock, and Hunt, and (spurred in part by the consequences of the Pentium divide bug) it achieved a degree of acceptance by the computer hardware industry that had so far eluded theorem provers.

Model Checking

The alternative approach was called "model checking." Key to its development was a 1981 paper by Edmund M. Clarke and E. Allen Emerson (both then at Harvard University). In their approach, the specification for a system is expressed in temporal logic, a formal logic for reasoning about states of affairs that change with time, and the system itself is modeled as a graph of transitions between a finite set of states. Clarke and Emerson provided an algorithm—"a model checker"—that determined whether the graph representing the system was what logicians call a "model" for the temporal logic formula expressing the specification: in other words, whether the graph was an interpretation of the logic in which the formula was true.[99] In the years that followed, a large number of ramifications and variants of the model-checking approach emerged.[100]

Model checking offered two potential advantages compared to theorem proving. First, model checking was algorithmic: it could be implemented in such a way that the human user "pushes a button and waits,"[101] rather than having to undertake the skilled task of guiding a theorem prover like the Boyer-Moore system or HOL. Second, if the design does *not* satisfy the specification, the model checker will "give a counterexample execution that shows why the formula is not satisfied," and the explicit counterexample is invaluable in "debugging" a complex design.[102]

The main immediate obstacle faced by model checking was computational complexity: the checking algorithm could easily become infeasibly time-consuming even for simple designs. During the 1980s, however, key improvements were made to methods of expressing and handling propositional formulae, so increasing considerably the practical scope of model checkers. The most important of these was the ordered binary decision diagram representation of Boolean functions developed in the early 1980s by Randal E. Bryant of Carnegie Mellon University (see figure 7.8).

Although the basic notation of the binary decision diagram long preceded Bryant's work, he showed how placing "restrictions on the ordering of decision variables in the vertices" permitted canonical representations of Boolean functions and algorithms for manipulating them that were remarkably efficient. The diagram in figure 7.8, for example, represents a propositional logic function of six variables: its truth table representation (see chapter 3) would require a table with 2^6 or 64 rows. The question of efficiency was key. Many problems in hardware verification can be reduced to investigating whether a Boolean expression representing a specification is equivalent to an expression representing a design, but the problem of determining if Boolean expressions are inequivalent is NP-complete (see chapter 3). Ordered binary decision diagrams, however, exploited the structure of specifications and of designs to keep the size of diagrams limited and the equivalence check computationally feasible. In the worst case, the method is computation-

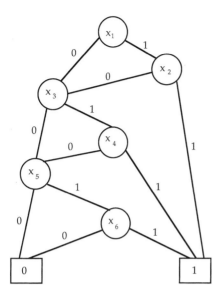

Figure 7.8
Ordered binary decision diagram representation of the Boolean function $x_1 \cdot x_2 + x_3 \cdot x_4 + x_5 \cdot x_6$. Based upon figure in Randal E. Bryant, "Graph-Based Algorithms for Boolean Function Manipulation," *IEEE Transactions on Computers* C-35 (1986): 677–691, at p. 681. ©1988 IEEE. · and + are operations in Boolean algebra corresponding to the propositional logic connectives ∧ ("and") and ∨ ("or"). So the diagram represents the propositional logic function $(x_1 \wedge x_2) \vee (x_3 \wedge x_4) \vee (x_5 \wedge x_6)$, with 0 representing "false" and 1 representing "true."

ally as bad as the method of truth tables (see chapter 3), so to use it "on anything other than small problems (e.g., functions of 16 variables or more), a user must have an intuition about why certain functions have large function graphs, and how the choice of input ordering may affect this size." With a good choice, the method can "achieve a high degree of efficiency."[103]

Model checking and ordered binary decision diagram methods[104] were already starting to be adopted in hardware design in the early 1990s. The 1994 Pentium division bug debacle accelerated that process. In Intel, for example, model checking had moved by the end of 1996 "from what was considered a year ago an experimental and unproven technology to a mainstream activity."[105] To date, model checkers have been used in industry predominantly as sophisticated debuggers rather than as verifiers: in other words, they have been used to find design mistakes (in the form of counterexamples showing that a design is not a model of the logical formula expressing its specification) rather than to certify the absence of mistakes. Nothing intrinsically limits them to the role of debugger, however, and Edmund Clarke comments that: "It is really too early to say how model checking will be used."[106]

Even with all the conceptual and technical developments in recent years, the computational complexity of model checking means that complicated designs are unlikely to be amenable to straightforward checking. Several options nevertheless remain. Designs can be modeled in simplified ways so that model checking remains tractable,[107] though if strong claims of "proof" are based on the results of simplifications, those responsible for them clearly need to be able to justify the adequacy of their abstractions. In the early 1990s Clarke's student David Long devised a methodology for simplifying models that is "conservative": one that will produce counterexamples if they exist, though it may also produce "false negatives," apparent counterexamples to correct designs.[108] Another of Clarke's students, Kenneth McMillan (who moved to the Berkeley Laboratories of the hardware design firm, Cadence), developed a hybrid methodology that uses a simple theorem prover to generate "subgoals" that can be model checked.[109]

Indeed, the growing industrial uptake of model checking was followed in some places, notably at Intel's main competitor, Advanced Micro Devices, Inc. (AMD), by adoption of theorem proving. AMD and Computational Logic, Inc. collaborated in the mechanized formal verification (using ACL2, the late-1990s version of the Boyer-Moore prover discussed in chapter 8) of the floating-point division algorithm implemented in the $AMD5_K86^{™}$ microprocessor, its equivalent of Intel's Pentium.[110] David Rusinoff continued the use of the theorem prover within AMD in further formal verification work on the implementation of floating-point arithmetic on the $AMD5_K86^{™}$ and later AMDK7 processors, finding several bugs in the intended designs for the latter.[111] Computational Logic, Inc.'s Bishop Brock provided similar formal support for the designers of another microprocessor, Motorola's Complex Arithmetic Processor.[112]

The use of theorem proving remained much more demanding of human skill than model checking, but the down-turn in other sources of support for formal verification (evidenced by the closure of Computational Logic, Inc., in 1997) had the paradoxical benefit of making skilled personnel available. Boyer and Moore's Pythagorean project of driving proof down into hardware was beginning to come to fruition, not just in research but in industrial practice, albeit not in a manner that could have been anticipated when the project emerged from their work on SIFT.

Yet even the driving of proof down into hardware designs does not exhaust the issues potentially raised by the formal verification of computer systems. The simplifications necessary to subject complex designs to model checking are a possible source of future dispute, and the use of automated theorem provers prompts a further question raised during the VIPER dispute by RSRE's Kershaw, who noted that such provers were themselves computer programs. Was there not a risk that "[a] design may be pronounced 'correct by construction' by a faulty software tool?"[113] Ought a putative proof not be checked by an independent proof-checking program? Indeed, if one was to apply the formal, mechanical notion of proof entirely stringently, might not the software of the automated theorem prover itself have to be verified formally? By that criterion, even the verifications constructed by Boyer, Moore, and their colleagues would fail to count as "proof" because they, like the other developers of automated theorem provers, had not verified the correctness of their prover's implementation. The formal, mechanized notion of proof thus prompted a modern version of Juvenal's ancient question, *quis custodiet ipsos custodes,* who will guard the guards themselves? That and other questions raised by mechanized proof are the subject of the next chapter.

8

Logics, Machines, and Trust

The Remonstrant Church, Haarlem, Holland, April 1898. For some a confirmation ceremony, in which candidate members of the church reply to standard questions, might have been an occasion for routine piety. Not so for this young man, just turned seventeen but already an undergraduate at the University of Amsterdam, who read out his *Profession of Faith* to the congregation. His reply to the question, "What is the foundation of my faith in God?", was conventional enough: "Belief in God is a direct, spontaneous sensation in me." This student went on, however, that his belief must be taken "in a somewhat unusual sense, mainly because my belief is founded on a philosophy which recognizes only myself and my God as the sole living beings." Other human beings, other egos, might exist "but these are not real, they are part of my images and therefore of me."

For this young student, "the only truth to me is my own ego of this moment." God, he said, has "given me the ambition to make my life, i.e., my images, as beautiful as possible." That, too, might have been heard as unobjectionable, but the comments that followed were blunt. "I am struck," said this student, by the world's "loathsomeness." His desire to make his life as beautiful as possible by removing this loathsomeness could hardly be called "love-of-my-neighbour," he admitted, "for I don't care two-pence for most people. . . . The human spectres around me are the ugliest part of my world of images." If those thoughts appeared to the congregation to be at variance with New Testament doctrine, this student made clear that he had no respect for "church domination and dogma," saying that he considered "religious forms to be good for the stupid masses, to be kept in reverent ignorance under the thumb of a power-thirsty church."[1]

This young student, Luitzen Egbertus Jan Brouwer, was to become the greatest iconoclast of twentieth-century mathematics. A burst of extraordinarily productive research in topology brought Brouwer an international reputation and in 1912 a chair in mathematics at Amsterdam University. In the long run, however, Brouwer's technical contributions were overshadowed by his work on the foundations of mathematics. He vehemently rejected any reduction of mathematics to logic, such as that proposed by Alfred North Whitehead and Bertrand Russell, and he also distanced himself decisively from the growing tendency to see mathematics as a formal process of deriving deductions from essentially arbitrary axioms. Mathematics was not a mere formal game, argued Brouwer, but deeply rooted in the human mind.

The "old form of intuitionism," developed by the philosopher Immanuel Kant, "in which time and space are taken to be forms of conception inherent in human reason," had to be abandoned, Brouwer admitted. The nineteenth-century development of non-Euclidian geometry made the spatial aspect of Kant's intuitionism untenable by showing that "the phenomena usually described in the language of elementary [Euclidian] geometry may be described with equal exactness . . . in the language of non-euclidian geometry." Instead, Brouwer sought to rebuild intuitionism by focusing on conceptions of time. "[T]he falling apart of moments of life into qualitatively different parts" was a "fundamental phenomenon of the human intellect" that gave rise to the idea of the ordered sequence of the natural numbers $(0, 1, 2, 3, . . .)$. The formalists might believe that mathematics was the manipulation of symbols; Brouwer held that it could not be divorced from its roots in the mind. "The question where mathematical exactness does exist, is answered differently by the two sides; the intutionist says: in the human intellect, the formalist says: on paper."[2]

What was most disturbing to Brouwer's contemporaries, such as the leading formalist mathematician David Hilbert, was not Brouwer's general philosophical views but the conclusions he drew for mathematical practice. The clearest single focus of Brouwer's attack was a central feature of classical logic, the law of the excluded middle: $p \lor \neg p$ ("p or not-p"). Consider, for example, a simple application of excluded middle to real numbers, the numerical equivalent of points on a continuous line: that given two real numbers, x and y, then either $x = y$ or $x \neq y$. For a follower of Brouwer, what is troublesome about this application of excluded middle is that one may have no way of determining whether x and y are equal or not.[3]

Real numbers do not in general have finite representations in decimal arithmetic or in arithmetic with other bases. Suppose, for example, that one calculates the values of x and y in ordinary decimal arithmetic

(2.71828 . . . , for instance). It might be that no matter how extended one makes this calculation, it is not possible to show a difference between the digits in the representations of x and y (and so one cannot show that $x \neq y$) while being unable to prove that $x = y$. The intuitionist is uneasy about appeal to "p or not-p" in contexts in which we may not be able to determine which alternative holds. Brouwer's attack on excluded middle was part of his wider dissent from contemporary logicism (exemplified above all by Russell and Whitehead) and formalism (exemplified by Hilbert). Both were misleading and impoverished philosophies of mathematics. As Brouwer put it, "the basic intuition of mathematics, living in a human mind" was "indispensable." If one neglected "the idea of the mathematical system under construction" and used the law of excluded middle, in the formalist fashion, "to operate in the corresponding linguistic structure," one was moving into unjustifiably risky terrain.[4]

Brouwer's attack on the use of the law of the excluded middle threatened significant parts of mathematical practice, most importantly nonconstructive existence proofs: those that proved the existence of a mathematical entity, not by showing how the entity could be constructed, but by showing that its nonexistence would imply a contradiction. By the early twentieth century, nonconstructive existence proofs were commonplace, but to Brouwer and those influenced by him, they were dubious and should be avoided. "Brouwer—das ist die Revolution!" wrote the German mathematician Hermann Weyl.[5]

It was not, however, a revolution that many welcomed. To Hilbert, as to many others, to bar mathematicians from using the law of the excluded middle was like denying "the telescope to the astronomer or to the boxer the use of his fists." Without it, only "wretched remnants" of modern mathematics would remain, said Hilbert. "I am most astonished by the fact that even in mathematical circles the power of suggestion of a single man, however full of temperament and inventiveness, is capable of having the most improbable and eccentric effects." It was "the task of science," said Hilbert, "to liberate us from arbitrariness, sentiment, and habit and to protect us from the subjectivism that . . . finds its culmination in intuitionism."[6]

Brouwer's intuitionist philosophy of mathematics was an aspect of his more general mystical, solipsistic,[7] and pessimistic worldview. His 1905 *Leven, Kunst en Mystiek* [Life, Art, and Mysticism] argued that "Originally man lived in isolation." In that situation, there was no "sorrow, hate, fear or lust"; however, "man was not content, he began to search for power over others and for certainty about the future." The "Intellect" was "the symbol of man's fall." Brouwer poured scorn on the use of language:

"People . . . try and train themselves and their offspring in some form of communication by means of crude sounds, laboriously and helplessly, for never has anyone been able to communicate his soul by means of language." Nor did he hope for improvement. "[F]oolishness and injustice are essential in human society"; were they removed, society "simply would not exist." Self-reflection was the only true guide: "The free see their fellow-men as hallucinations."[8]

Only men, not women, were capable of the solipsistic freedom Brouwer recommended: as Walter P. van Stigt put it, "woman to [Brouwer] epitomizes the human condition in all its 'social' aspects." At the time of writing *Leven, Kunst en Mystiek,* Brouwer was being supported financially by his wife, a pharmacist. This did not stop him from writing that: "The usurpation of any work by women will automatically and inexorably debase that work and make it ignoble." The admission of women to university was, to Brouwer, an "alarming" feature of modernity. "To the old Germanic tribes tilling the land was regarded as ignoble work and therefore done by women. When all productive labour has been made dull and ignoble by socialism it will be done exclusively by women."[9]

Given his views, it is not entirely surprising that although he was Dutch, Brouwer was attracted to German nationalism and that, at least to a limited extent, the attraction was mutual. German mathematicians suffered partial exclusion from international bodies after World War I. Brouwer vigorously opposed this, and he campaigned to stop German mathematicians from taking part in the 1928 International Congress of Mathematicians held in Bologna because he, along with some German mathematicians, believed "that the Germans were tolerated only as second-rate participants."[10] The German mathematician Ludwig Bieberbach, a formalist prior to World War I, embraced intuitionism as after 1918 he drifted toward National Socialism and, famously, into the politically charged activity of trying to distinguish a specifically "German" mathematical style. Brouwer did not follow Bieberbach that far, and charges of collaboration laid against Brouwer after the German occupation of the Netherlands appear to have been unfair. He was a "reactionary romantic," but not a Nazi.[11] Nevertheless, the fate of Brouwer's intuitionism, especially after 1918, reveals the connections that can exist between philosophies of mathematics and wider cultural, even political, concerns.

Constructing a Theorem Prover

The ties between scientific theories and their cultural and political context, however, are contingent rather than necessary matters.[12] The connections in Brouwer's thought and in the 1920s' and 1930s' German context among mathematical intuitionism, cultural pessimism, solipsistic individualism, and nationalism dissolved as others took up the intuitionist cause and did so in different contexts. Intuitionism gradually became *constructivism* (note that this usage of the term is different from ideas of "social construction"). Mathematical reasoning, the constructivists argued, must remain within the bounds of entities that could, at least in principle, be constructed. In the words of the constructivist mathematician Errett Bishop:

Mathematics belongs to man, not to God. We are not interested in properties of the positive integers that have not descriptive meaning for finite man. When a man proves a positive integer to exist, he should show how to find it. If God has mathematics of his own that needs to be done, let him do it himself. . . . A set is not an entity which has an ideal existence. . . . To define a set we prescribe, at least implicitly, what we (the constructing intelligence) must do in order to construct an element of the set, and what we must do to show that two elements of the set are equal.[13]

The mathematician who was Brouwer's most direct disciple, Arend Heyting, departed in significant ways from his teacher. While Brouwer had been at best ambivalent (and sometimes downright hostile) to logic, Heyting developed an intuitionist logic. Brouwer supported the publication of Heyting's work but also made clear to him that he viewed it as "an interesting but irrelevant and sterile exercise."[14] Heyting's logic was just as formal as its classical competitors, but it did not include the law of the excluded middle. "$p \vee \neg p$ [p or not-p] demands a general method to solve every problem," wrote Heyting, "or more explicitly, a general method which for any proposition $\wp$ yields by specialization either a proof of $\wp$ or a proof of $\neg \wp$. As we do not possess such a method of construction, we have no right to assert the principle."[15]

The development of intuitionist or constructivist formal logic connects Brouwer's philosophy of mathematics to the technological world of automated theorem provers. In general—but with a key exception to be discussed—theorem provers perform formal proofs, sequences of deductions in which each step is the application of mechanical, syntactic, rules of logical inference. The existence of alternative logics (for example, incorporating or refusing the law of the excluded middle) creates a choice for the developers of provers which logic shall they use? Other issues must also be confronted by the developers of provers.

What kind of proofs will a prover be able to produce? How quickly? How much human guidance will be needed to produce those proof and guidance of what kind? In the background, too, lurks another set of questions. How can a theorem prover be known to be trustworthy? It is itself a computer program. As such, it is potentially subject to the problems of software development examined in chapter 2: it may have bugs in it. Does that matter? If so, what should be done? What is the best overall structure, the best "architecture," for a prover when reducing risk of unsoundness? Ought the output of a theorem prover be checked by a different proof-checking program? Ought one to seek formally to verify the prover itself? Can the human user of a prover be assumed to be trustworthy?

In earlier chapters, the theorem provers used to verify computer systems have been treated as "black boxes": the "automatic" provers examined in chapter 3 are generally not regarded as powerful enough for verification. It is now time to open the black box and examine the internal design of the interactive provers used in verification, seeing how their designers treat the above issues in practice. The Boyer-Moore prover will be examined, as will the systems that replaced it at SRI, and HOL (used in the VIPER proof work); the last of these will be placed in context by discussing Robin Milner's Logic for Computable Functions (LCF), the system from which HOL is descended. Another LCF-style system, Nuprl, which is of particular interest will also be examined because it implements not a classical but a constructive logic.

A Little Trick

Let us begin with the system that has appeared most often in this book, the Boyer-Moore prover. The collaboration between Robert S. Boyer and J Strother Moore began in 1971 at the University of Edinburgh's Metamathematics Unit, which was part of a research community in artificial intelligence that ranged from resolution theorem proving to the construction of robots. Debilitating tensions existed between the leaders of the Edinburgh community's different subgroups, and the reduced funding for artificial intelligence after the 1973 Lighthill Report (see chapter 3) was to scatter its members. For the two young Texans, however, "[t]he time and place seemed to be embued with quiet inspiration."[16]

Fired with enthusiasm for artificial intelligence, Moore began graduate work at Edinburgh in 1970 with one of the field's British pioneers, Donald Michie, on the natural language understanding required for children's stories. He also sought a part-time job programming and ended up helping logician Robert Kowalski program a resolution theorem prover. Boyer arrived the following year to continue work he had begun under the supervision of Woody Bledsoe on automated proving.

Boyer and Moore shared an office and became fast friends. Moore taught Boyer POP2, the programming language then popular in Edinburgh artificial intelligence, and he showed Boyer the theorem prover that he had written for Kowalski. Boyer taught Moore an alternative way of viewing resolution theorem proving, based upon the LISP programming language developed by John McCarthy.[17]

The collaboration with Boyer shifted Moore's interests away from children's stories and eventually away from mainstream artificial intelligence. Resolution provers, Boyer and Moore realized, had a major limitation. There was no straightforward way to use them to perform proof by mathematical induction. Suppose, to take the simplest form of induction, one wants to show that a formula $P(n)$ is true for all the natural numbers, n (that is, for 0, 1, 2, . . .). The principle of mathematical induction permits one to show this by proving, first, that $P(0)$ is true and, second, that if $P(k)$ is true for an arbitrary natural number k, then $P(k + 1)$ is true. It is a pervasive form of mathematical reasoning, but to state the principle of induction is to say something about all predicates, and as such, it goes beyond the first-order[18] logic of resolution provers; it can be expressed in first-order terms only indirectly.

Boyer and Moore came to believe that the Edinburgh theorem provers, based as they were in first-order logic, could prove theorems only "about elementary things. . . . What we didn't have was induction." The limitation mattered because, like others in the early 1970s, Boyer and Moore were becoming interested in program verification. Proof by induction, they believed, was central to verification, and not just in its elementary form of induction over the natural numbers. Drawing upon the work of John McCarthy, Boyer and Moore's Edinburgh colleague, Rod Burstall, had shown in 1969 that induction over the structure of a programming language was a powerful technique for constructing proofs about programs.[19] LISP, for example, was a list-processing language, and one could prove theorems about lists by induction by, first, showing that the theorem holds for the empty list and, second, showing that if it holds for an arbitrary list, it also holds for that list with one new element added. For months, Boyer and Moore proved theorems by induction on the blackboard in their office, examining the principles and procedures involved. "Then, one day [we] sat down to actually code up what we were doing," recalled Moore, "and basically we have been doing the same thing ever since."[20] The Boyer-Moore theorem prover was being born.

The Boyer-Moore prover, in a sense, was a crystallization of the biographies of its authors and it was to evolve with them. For the two young enthusiasts for artificial intelligence, developing a theorem prover was initially an exercise in that emerging subject. "In the early days," said Boyer, the prover "was totally, exclusively, religiously automatic."[21] By 1973, when Moore gave the first comprehensive description of their prover in his Edinburgh Ph.D. thesis, several other automated systems for program verification were already in existence or in development (including Milner's LCF, described below). Nearly all such systems, Moore wrote, "were designed to provide mechanical aid to a human verifier. . . . Their automatic theorem proving capabilities are purposely limited or nonexistent." For those committed to artificial intelligence, however, a program that merely provided "bookkeeping services" to a human prover was an uninspiring goal: Boyer and Moore hoped as well to automate what Moore called the "creative" aspects of proof.[22]

Their commitment to artificial intelligence also provided them with insulation against the early 1970s' pessimism about the limitations of automated provers, a pessimism that derived in part from work in complexity theory: since the complexity of theorem proving did not stop human provers, Boyer and Moore believed that it should be no a priori barrier to machines. Inheritors of a tradition that stretched back, via Boyer's supervisor Bledsoe to Simon and Newell, Boyer and Moore began by studying how they, as human beings, did proof by induction. From this they sought to construct heuristics that would help guide a machine intelligently and thus circumvent the combinatorial explosion that defeated indiscriminate searches for proof.

"[O]ur research is really more artificial intelligence than logic," wrote Boyer and Moore in 1979.[23] But Boyer had been interested in logic even as a high school student and, as shown in chapter 3, Edinburgh had the reputation of being the heart of artificial intelligence's "Logicland." About the subject's stereotyped dichotomy, Boyer and Moore were "neats" not "scruffies." For all his and his supervisor Bledsoe's commitment to artificial intelligence, Boyer had chosen to do his dissertation work on resolution "rather than some woolly AI [artificial intelligence] system."[24] In constructing their prover, Boyer and Moore drew not just upon the heuristics used by human mathematicians but also upon mathematical logic and the foundations of mathematics. The single most important resource they found there dated back to 1919 and to the Norwegian mathematical logician Thoralf Skolem's reflections upon Whitehead and Russell's *Principia Mathematica*.

Much of the elaborate logical apparatus of the *Principia* had been developed to circumvent paradoxes such as the one that Russell himself had constructed: the self-contradictory notion of the class of all classes that are not members of themselves. Whitehead and Russell sought to avoid the paradox by constructing a hierarchy of "types" in which a "class of classes" for example, is an entity of higher type than a class and in which entities of mixed type are prohibited. Skolem made a simpler, more radical suggestion: in effect, to do away with the notion of mathematical existence and thus, for example, with the existential quantifier ($\exists$, "there exists"). "What does it mean for a set to exist if it can perhaps never be defined?" asked Skolem. "It seems clear that this existence can be only a manner of speaking, which can lead only to purely formal propositions—perhaps made up of very beautiful *words*—about objects *called* sets. But most mathematicians want mathematics to deal, ultimately, with performable computing operations and not to consist of formal propositions about objects called this or that." Instead, Skolem argued, the foundations of at least elementary arithmetic could be "established by means of the recursive mode of thought, without the use of apparent variables ranging over infinite domains."[25]

In 1919 Skolem did not know of Brouwer's work and the system he developed, which became known as primitive recursive arithmetic, differs philosophically and technically from Brouwer's intuitionism. Nevertheless, it had a strong constructivist flavor, and the main English developer of primitive recursive arithmetic, R. L. Goodstein of the University of Leicester, published his work in a series edited by Brouwer, Heyting, and E. W. Beth.[26] For example, Goodstein defined the "operations":

(1) replacing x by $x + 1$,

(2) replacing x by 0,

and constructed the numerals by applying operation (1) repeatedly and then applying operation (2).[27]

Skolem's work was published in English translation in 1967,[28] and a colleague of Boyer's and Moore's in the Edinburgh theorem-proving group, Alan Bundy, had been one of Goodstein's students. The single most important step in the development of the Boyer-Moore prover was its authors' decision that Skolem and Goodstein's primitive recursive arithmetic was a suitable foundation for a theorem prover using induction. Primitive recursive arithmetic prohibited explicit use of the ordinary predicate logic quantifiers $\forall$ ("for all") and $\exists$ ("there exists"), so the mathematical entities on which the Boyer-Moore prover operated had to be defined by recursive functions: a function f over the natural numbers, for example, can be defined recursively by defining the value of $f(0)$ and giving a means of computing the value of $f(k + 1)$ from that of $f(k)$.

Insistence on recursive definition has the crucial effect of "forcing the user to hint implicitly how to prove conjectures" by mathematical induction.[29] Key to the Boyer-Moore theorem prover is its consequent "little trick of sometimes guessing an induction to do," said Boyer.[30] But from little tricks big things can flow because without the help of the "hint" provided by the definition of recursive functions, an automated prover can easily be defeated by the huge variety of inductions that could be tried. A human mathematician may readily be able to "see" the form of induction required to prove a theorem, but there is no simple, algorithmic way always to identify an appropriate induction step or form of induction, and in forms of induction other than over the natural numbers it may not even be obvious over which mathematical structure to induct.

Hence the importance of the heuristic built into the Boyer-Moore prover from its earliest days: if seeking to prove a property of a function f, "induct upon the structures on which f recurses."[31] Called upon when simpler proof procedures such as rewriting failed and guided by the way they failed, the induction heuristic gave the version of the Boyer-Moore prover they had constructed by the time they left Edinburgh in 1974 the capacity to prove, entirely automatically, simple theorems such as that the LISP function APPEND, which concatenates lists, is associative.[32]

Forcing all definitions to take the form of recursive functions did more than begin to provide a heuristic for performing proofs by induction. "[T]here are two different objectives that people in AI [artificial intelligence] can have," said Boyer: "one is to do really exploratory work in the hard problems of just trying to investigate how people think. And the other objective is to produce a theorem prover that can be trusted." From their Edinburgh days on, Boyer and Moore were committed to the second objective. Others in artificial intelligence might go for humanlike proving power, at the expense of the checks essential to soundness, such as checking that the input provided by the user consisted of well-formed formulae.[33] In contrast, Boyer and Moore "always kept soundness as a number-one priority." In pure research in artificial intelligence, soundness might not matter too much, and "scruffies" might be justified in not giving it top priority, but it was vital if theorem provers were going to verify real-world programs. Particularly troubling to Boyer and to Moore was what they saw as other verificationists' habit of introducing "ad hoc axioms" to facilitate their proofs, axioms sometimes necessitated by the fact that they were using resolution provers that could not do inductive proofs.

"[T]his offended Bob [Boyer] and me [Moore] a great deal, because it seemed to undermine the whole program of trying to mechanically verify something, because all you were doing was by hand making up a bunch of facts and mechanically showing that your program's correctness depends on these facts. . . . [I]t was just like translating the program into another collection of theorems that were unproved."[34] Above all there was a risk that adding axioms might render a formal system inconsistent,[35] and its mechanical implementation could then churn out worthless proofs of any formula whatsoever. In contrast, Boyer and Moore's insistence on the use of recursive functions meant that axioms could be added only in a form that could be subject to a correctness test (of the well-foundedness[36] of the definitions of new recursive functions) that prevented the inadvertent introduction of inconsistencies.

Over the years, as Boyer and Moore moved from Edinburgh, first to California (and to the work at SRI International on SIFT described in chapter 7) and then to Austin, Texas, their theorem prover changed. Gradually, artificial intelligence became less salient in their work and the verification first of software and then of hardware more salient. In 1978, when they were both in the Computer Science Laboratory of SRI, Boyer and Moore wrote: "The motivation behind our work comes from computer programming itself. Suppose it were practical to reason, mechanically and with mathematical certainty, about computer programs. . . . Then there would follow a tremendous improvement in the reliability of computer programs and a subsequent reduction of the overall cost of producing and maintaining programs."[37]

Although artificial intelligence was not altogether abandoned, the new emphasis meant that there was no longer a need for the prover to be "religiously" automatic and, as Moore had put it in 1973, free of "any taint of user supplied information."[38] For example, in the early 1980s Boyer and Moore added a "hint facility" that allowed the user to guide the system's search for a proof directly. Other changes were also made. Although the early versions of the prover incorporated no decision procedures, one for the decidable fragment of number theory called "linear arithmetic" was added in the early 1980s. (A decision procedure is an algorithm that determines, in a finite number of steps, whether or not a formula in a given mathematical domain is a theorem; it usually does so in a way quite different from how a human being might try to find a proof. As shown in chapter 3, Simon and Newell, with their commitment to "human-like" artificial intelligence, eschewed decision procedures.) The underlying logic was elaborated (for example, "bounded" quantification, ranging over finite sequences, was defined within the logic) and gradually the heuristics used were made more sophisticated and more powerful. The prover grew in size. Written in Common LISP, its source code was by 1988 "more than 900,000 bytes long."[39]

Despite all these elaborations, the Boyer-Moore theorem prover did not become easy to use. One had to learn the distinctive formal logic embodied in it and submit oneself to the discipline of Boyer and Moore's consistency-preserving definition principle. More fundamentally, one had to understand how the prover went about searching for proofs. Even after the addition of the "hints" facility, the user still guided the prover primarily indirectly, by suggesting lemmas (intermediate steps toward the proof of the desired theorem) for it to try to prove. That meant that in a proof of any depth the human user had to have a good idea of how the proof was to proceed; and the user's planned proof, the lemmas he or she suggested, had to be consistent with the internal workings of the prover. If it was not, then he or she was destined for a prolonged, frustrating, fruitless effort. As Boyer put it:

When you are proving theorems with our theorem prover you type in conjectures. And if the conjectures are of a certain form and you are extremely lucky, then the theorem prover will say that they are true. But, more likely than not, it will start printing out all kinds of messages about what it's trying to do and so forth, and after using the thing for a number of years you can decipher these messages and say "Aha! what the problem is, is that the theorem prover does not know about the following intermediate lemma," so you go off and you say: "first try to prove such-and-such," so it goes off and tries to prove such-and-such, and if you are extremely lucky it will prove that lemma, then it will prove the theorem that you wanted in the first place. More than likely you will have to do this process hundreds of times.[40]

The Boyer-Moore system's indirect, lemma-driven, control could be "like pushing a piece of string."[41] In the hands of a skilled user, however, the prover was a powerful tool. The single most impressive use of it was the mechanized proof by a graduate student in Boyer and Moore's group, Natarajan Shankar, of Gödel's first incompleteness theorem.[42] Chapter 7 demonstrated how the Boyer-Moore prover was used in the proof of the CLInc Stack and in hardware verification, and it was also used to perform many other proofs: for example, by Boyer and Moore of properties of the famous public key encryption algorithm developed by Rivest, Shamir, and Adleman; and by logician Kenneth Kunen of the Paris-Harrington theorem, the first incompleteness with a "natural" mathematical content to be found in elementary number theory.[43]

Theorem Provers and Decision Procedures

A significant part of the development of the Boyer-Moore prover took place at SRI International, when the research and development institute was working on the security projects discussed in chapter 5 and on SIFT (chapter 7). The departure from the SIFT project of Boyer and Moore created an opportunity for others in the institute to try out, in a major verification effort, a different approach to theorem proving. Key to that alternative approach was Robert Shostak, who joined SRI in 1974 when the prospects for automated proving looked bleak. The "optimism" and "excitement" over resolution had collapsed: it was as if one had climbed over a hill, he said, "only to discover the next peak before you," and resolution appeared to offer little hope of scaling that peak.[44]

While Boyer and Moore had thought the way forward lay in artificial intelligence, Shostak's approach was to concentrate on "more specialized theorem provers that might be more successful in their own limited domains" and in particular on decision procedures. That the latter existed only for limited domains and thus were "never going to explore all of the universe" of mathematics did not disturb Shostak unduly. At SRI he quickly learned that the mathematics involved in verification work like the security projects and SIFT was, as he put it, "wide" (intricate, complicated, and tedious) rather than conceptually "deep." Efficient decision procedures for the mathematical domains encountered in system verification might enormously ease the practical task, even if those decision procedures were not by any stretch of the imagination the automated mathematician of which artificial intelligence dreamed. That the decision procedure be efficient, however, was crucial: it was all too easy for a procedure to be of little practical use because its computational complexity was too great. Shostak quickly acquired an impressive grasp of the tricky theoretical and programming issues involved, an expertise displayed in an important series of papers on decision procedures from 1977 onward.[45]

Shostak's pragmatic vision of a theorem prover that would encompass only limited mathematical domains but that would be highly automated and easy to use was attractive to his colleagues in the SIFT project, Richard Schwartz and Michael Melliar-Smith. For them "the predictability of machine aid," and the capacity to control a prover directly, were gains for which it was worth jettisoning the Boyer-Moore prover's capacity for the occasional, heuristic-driven, "burst of inspiration."[46] The difficulties of the SIFT verification effort (described in chapter 7) provided an immediate need. In as little as a couple of months,[47] Shostak, Schwartz, and Melliar-Smith combined Shostak's work on decision procedures with Schwartz's and Melliar-Smith's on formal specification languages, creating a verification system they called Simple Theorem Prover or Shostak Theorem Prover (STP).[48]

The design of STP involved a distinctive partition of responsibility between the human user and the machine. The user was to be in direct control of the process of proof, not just giving a proof its overall structure by presenting lemmas to the machine (as in the Boyer-Moore prover) but directing it in detail by choosing appropriate substitutions. This detailed human control allowed machine inference to take the form of decision procedures (heuristic search was not needed) while still making it possible to have enough expressive power in STP's formal system to handle the practical demands of verification work. Direct user control and use of ordinary predicate logic, in the opinion of the SRI team, permitted human-machine interaction that was more "natural" than was possible, for example, with Boyer and Moore's insistence on recursive functions. Above all, though, the underlying decision procedures were fast enough, at least when applied to the kinds of formulae encountered in verification work such as SIFT, that users genuinely could work interactively with the machine rather than submitting theorems to it and then having to wait for lengthy periods while it searched for a proof.[49] Richard Schwartz describes how he, Shostak, and Melliar-Smith used STP. "[K]nowing the expressive limits" of STP, they would formulate a sequence of lemmas "that were both believable by us and decidable by the prover." That they had to supply the prover not just with the lemmas but also with appropriate substitution instances was not troublesome, in Schwartz's experience at least. It was, he said, "a light task to perform and constituted only a small portion of our specification and proof exercise."[50]

Like the Boyer-Moore prover, STP evolved. During the 1970s SRI had developed a verification system called Hierarchical Development Methodology (HDM) that was used in its security work described in chapter 5. When the National Computer Security Center was created, it provided funding to transform HDM and other verification systems used in security work so that they could be run on the center's system, Dockmaster, which used the Multics security-oriented operating system. The SRI team decided not simply to port HDM to Dockmaster but to change it radically, developing a new formal specification language and replacing HDM's primitive proof support with an improved version of STP. The work started just as the British computer scientist John Rushby joined SRI at the end of February 1983: "[Michael] Melliar-Smith and [Richard] Schwartz spent a couple of weeks designing the specification language in Michael's garden . . . while Rob [Shostak] worked on the theorem prover," and Rushby developed a "security analyzer" for the examination of information flow. The development of the new system, EHDM (Enhanced HDM), cost far more than the National Computer Security Center contract allowed. The center was told at a meeting with the SRI team that there was a "cost growth" of about $1 million, recalled Rushby, "and they'd have to pay up or EHDM would never be finished."[51]

Fresh from the relatively staid world of British computer science, Rushby was "too naive at that time to appreciate the theater of the situation." The center "paid up": indeed it continued to fund EHDM generously. The SRI team, however, began to split up. Shostak and Schwartz left: they had started to work on a personal computer database management system they called Paradox, and the company they founded to commercialize it made them millionaires. "[T]here were a lot of good ideas in [EHDM], some of them . . . really good," said Rushby. "But the implementation was a real crock because it was cobbled together from various bits and pieces and various people quit the project." By the end of the 1980s, however, further funding from the National Computer Security Center and new team members sorted out the problems. Natarajan Shankar, who joined SRI from the Boyer-Moore group, "got the prover back in shape and Sam [Owre] rebuilt most of the rest of the system."[52]

In 1990 the SRI verification group, by then led by Rushby, began the development of PVS, initially thought of as a prototype for a new, third generation prover. The acronym stood for Prototype Verification System, or as irreverent in-house usage had it, People's Verification System (there was widespread dissatisfaction with the restrictions involved in developing "government verification systems" for the orange book).[53] The prototype, however, became a full-blown prover. In its development, a host of detailed improvements were made (such as the integration of Shostak's decision procedures with a mechanism for transforming expressions according to appropriate "rewrite" rules), but the underlying design philosophy remained little changed. As Melliar-Smith and

Rushby had put it in 1985: "Rather than build an intelligent (or 'expert') system, we have attempted to construct a system to provide support for an intelligent and expert user. We believe that our users have a comprehensive understanding of the reasons why their theorems are true, and of how to construct their proofs; the computer is excellent at reasoning in decidable domains and at recording what has been done."[54]

Decision procedures rather than heuristics remained central, and great attention was paid to their speed and efficiency: in PVS, for example, the new method of ordered binary decision diagrams (see chapter 7) was used to handle propositional logic formulae.[55] "[Y]ou have to have decision procedures," said Rushby. "[T]he people who think you don't simply don't know what it's like to prove big theorems."[56] The result of all this development work was an impressively capable system used not just at SRI but widely adopted elsewhere.

Among the proofs to which the SRI provers were applied was a mechanical reproof of Lamport's clock convergence algorithm (see chapter 7). Rushby and Friedrich von Henke (leader of the EHDM team at SRI) took on this proof to complete part of SRI's work on SIFT for NASA. "By chance, it was uniquely well-suited to EHDM," said Rushby: "it requires heavy arithmetic." He and von Henke found that Lamport's and Melliar-Smith's manual proof, published in the *Journal of the Association for Computing Machinery*, was "flawed." Some of the mistakes were simply typographic errors, but the main induction required a "strict inequality" when only "an approximation" had been proved. It was, Rushby and von Henke observed, a refutation of the view that the "social process" of ordinary mathematics was the ultimate arbiter of proof. That process had not uncovered the flaws in the refereed journal proof: mechanized proof, using an automated theorem prover, had. "Contrary to parodies erected by some of the detractors to formal verification," they wrote, such a prover "does not act as an oracle that certifies bewildering arguments for inscrutable reasons but as an implacable skeptic that insists on all assumptions being stated and all claims justified." Furthermore, at least something of a social process could be applied to a mechanical proof: Rushby and von Henke's proof of the clock convergence algorithm was checked "lemma by lemma" by William D. Young of Computational Logic, Inc., using a different prover, the Boyer-Moore system. Though neither the names of DeMillo, Lipton, and Perlis, nor that of Fetzer (see chapter 6), were mentioned, Rushby and von Henke saw their proof as a powerful counter to their claims.[57]

Language for the Prosthetic Limb

The next family of systems considered here, like the SRI provers, is under more direct user control than the Boyer-Moore system but is constructed in an entirely different way. The key figure in its development was the British computer scientist Robin Milner. As an undergraduate at Cambridge University, Milner studied both mathematics and philosophy, and like Dijkstra he took (in his case in 1956) the short course that Cambridge offered in how to program its early computer, the EDSAC. Unlike Dijkstra, however, Milner found the experience "rather oppressive. . . . [I]t didn't make me think computers were wonderful things . . . [t]he computer programs that we came up with were . . . poorly related to the way one thinks. . . . It seemed that computing was disjoint from thinking." Nevertheless, Milner learned that he could program.

After graduating from Cambridge, Milner briefly became a school teacher and then in 1960 a programmer for the British electronics and computer firm, Ferranti, Ltd. A position at what was to become London's City University followed in 1963, but in 1968 Milner took the risk of leaving this teaching post for a research fellowship at Swansea University. Gradually, he began to focus his initial dissatisfaction with computing into a research program in which the "study of formal language for controlling this prosthetic limb which is the computer is just completely fundamental." From the mid-1960s on, Milner came into contact with the emerging discipline of computer science, meeting people such as his future Edinburgh colleague Rod Burstall, Christopher Strachey (leader of Oxford University's Programming Research Group and a scion of the famous Bloomsbury group of intellectuals and literary figures), and a key collaborator of Strachey's, Peter Landin.[58]

Theoretical computer science in Britain in the 1960s was an exciting but still a haphazard world. (Burstall, for example, had met Landin because, while looking for a logic text in a London bookshop, he had asked a man whether the shop had a copy. The man, Mervyn Pragnell, told him, "I'm not a shop assistant," and "stalked away," only to return to invite Burstall to join an informal seminar which included Landin.)[59] As shown in chapter 2, by the latter half of the 1960s there was growing interest within computer science in applying proof to computer programs. At Swansea, Milner wrote a resolution-based automatic prover and sought to use it in program verification. It was not an encouraging experience: like others at this time, Milner found that the power of resolution provers was limited, and he was struck by what he called the "ultimate uselessness" of entirely automatic proving. He also began to suspect that the ordinary first-order predicate logic of resolution provers was not the best basis for formal reasoning about programs.

After leaving Cambridge, Milner had taught himself mathematical logic, and in 1969 he traveled regularly from Swansea to Oxford University to listen to talks by the mathematical logician Dana Scott. Scott was in transition between a joint appointment in the Departments of Philosophy and Mathematics at Stanford University and a similar post at Princeton. He, Landin, and Strachey had all come to the conclusion that the best foundation for a semantics of programming languages was a formal system called the λ-calculus. (Strachey was introduced to the λ-calculus by Oxford mathematician Roger Penrose, mentioned in chapter 3 as a critic of artificial intelligence.)[60]

The λ-calculus had been developed in the early 1930s by the Princeton logician, Alonzo Church. Although the dominant tendency in much of the twentieth century was to seek foundations of mathematics in the theory of sets, in the λ-calculus the notion of "function" occupied center stage. The Greek letter lambda (λ), which gives the calculus its name, indicates "abstraction," which can be thought of as making it possible to conceive formally of a function independently of the mathematical entities to which it applies. Thus the expression

$$\lambda x. f(x)$$

is just the function f. So, for example, $\lambda x.x^2$ is the "square" function.[61] As Church put it, in the λ-calculus:

> we regard the operation or rule of correspondence, which constitutes the function, as being first given, and the range of arguments then determined as consisting of the things to which the operation is applicable. This is a departure from the point of view usual in mathematics, but it is a departure which is natural in passing from consideration of functions in a special domain to the consideration of function in general.[62]

The λ-calculus was a powerful formalism that quickly led to deep results. Gradually, Church and his students Stephen C. Kleene and J. Barkley Rosser came to realize that more and more functions could be defined with the calculus. In conversation with Rosser late in 1933, Church speculated that all "effectively calculable functions from positive integers to positive integers" can be defined in the λ-calculus ("effectively calculable" functions are those that can be calculated by an algorithm). In 1936 the British mathematician Alan Turing gave another definition of "effectively calculable function" as a function computable on a Turing machine—a simple, hypothetical computer—and he proved that computability in that sense was equivalent to definability in the λ-calculus. Gradually, a range of other notions of "effectively calculable" were shown to be equivalent to Turing-computability and to λ-definability, and support built for what came to be called the Church-Turing thesis, that what one intuitively means by "algorithm" is captured by these equivalent formulations.[63]

Given this connection between the λ-calculus and computability, it is not surprising that the former was attractive to several people within computer science. John McCarthy, for example, drew on the λ-calculus in developing his widely used LISP programming language. As, in the 1960s, attention moved toward the formal semantics of programming languages, the λ-calculus, which offered a precise formalism within which to conceive of a program as a function composed of simpler functions representing its constituent parts, was a natural place to turn. In Oxford in the autumn of 1969, Scott and Strachey worked furiously on the use of the λ-calculus to provide a semantics for programming languages. Crucially, Scott found "the first known 'mathematically' defined model" for the λ-calculus. "That term was one of feverish activity for me," recalled Scott, "indeed, for several days, I felt as though I had some kind of real brain fever."[64] Milner was caught up in the excitement, and his growing belief that ordinary predicate logic was "not the right logic" for formal semantics or for program verification turned into the conviction that the λ-calculus was a good basis for these.

In early 1971 Milner moved from Swansea to John McCarthy's artificial intelligence laboratory in the hills above Stanford University. There, with help from computer scientists Richard Weyhrauch and Malcolm Newey, Milner constructed a program verification system quite different from the resolution prover he had built at Swansea. It was based upon a version of the λ-calculus; it was interactive, rather than automatic; and the user built proofs "backward" from the theorem to be proved. Working backward was not a novel idea: that was, for example, how Simon, Shaw, and Newell's Logic Theory Machine had searched for proofs. The Logic Theory Machine, however, had been an entirely automatic system, and in the 1950s computers were not designed to allow users to interact with programs as they ran. By 1971, however, time-sharing machines permitting direct human-computer interaction were commonplace at centers of computer science such as Stanford.

"[T]he way that I thought of it," said Milner, "was that you have some assumptions at the top of the [computer terminal] screen, and you have a goal [theorem] at the bottom of the screen. You have a blank hole on your screen, and you're trying to fill the gap." By 1972 Milner had implemented an automated prover—Logic for Computable Functions (LCF)—for the version of the λ-calculus that he had adopted. His system had a facility for the creation of subgoals, a mechanism for the automatic simplification of formulae, and a means of storing theorems so that the user could build up a "library" of theorems over several sessions of work.[65]

Use of the λ-calculus helped close the gap between "computer programs" and "thinking" that had frustrated Milner when learning to program EDSAC in 1956. Nevertheless, constructing proofs using Stanford LCF was scarcely a joy: the user had to type in large numbers of often highly repetitive commands. In 1972, however, Milner visited the University of Edinburgh for one of the series of workshops on "machine intelligence" organized by the artificial intelligence group there. Milner and his wife wanted to return to Britain so that their children could grow up there; Edinburgh University was seeking to build up its new Department of Computer Science and was looking for a lecturer. Those were still informal days: "within about 24 hours I had applied for [the lectureship] and been offered it and accepted it." At Edinburgh, Milner set to work to turn the user's painstaking interaction with Stanford LCF "into itself a sophisticated linguistic activity." He began to build up a group around him: Newey (who moved with him from Stanford), Lockwood Morris, Chris Wadsworth, Michael Gordon (who was one of Rod Burstall's students), and Milner's own student, Avra Cohn, seen in chapter 7. From the work of the group emerged a "metalanguage" (ML) which the user of LCF could use to write proof procedures.[66]

ML gradually became a full-blown programming language in its own right, one of the "functional" programming languages that became popular in the 1980s.[67] ML also introduced a subtly different way of thinking about automated theorem proving, in particular about how to ensure that a putative proof was indeed correct. The compiler for ML, like that for many other programming languages, "type checks" the programs submitted to it. (In programming, one often deals with different kinds of data structures, such as numbers, arrays, and lists. Each kind of data structure can be assigned a "type," and type checking can detect some forms of errors, such as attempts to add an array and a number.)

The technical heart of ML was a type-checking algorithm (based upon the unification algorithm used by Alan Robinson in resolution) developed by Milner and implemented by him within Edinburgh LCF by 1976. Milner constructed a conventional hand proof (not a mechanical proof) that if the algorithm accepted a program, then that program was "well typed," and that if a program was well-typed, it "could not suffer a run-time type error."[68] Among ML's types was and is the type <u>thm</u> ("theorem"). Objects of type <u>thm</u> could be constructed in Edinburgh LCF only by applying the inference rules of the version of the λ-calculus it embodies (called PPLambda, or Polymorphic Predicate λ-calculus) to existing objects of type <u>thm</u>, which may include user-defined axioms. Rules of logical inference are thus seen in ML as functions from theorems to theorems. Milner's type-checking algorithm then guarantees that anything of type <u>thm</u> is either an axiom or has been formed by applying rules of inference to axioms, so that a proposition denoted by a term of type <u>thm</u> is indeed a theorem (that is, can be derived from the axioms by application of the rules of inference). The dependability of inference, therefore, rests not upon the entirety of the implementation of LCF but on those program segments that encode axioms, the rules of inference of the logic, and Milner's type-checking algorithm. Although those segments amount to over a thousand lines of program, that is many fewer than an entire automated theorem prover.

The type-checking "firewall" around inference in LCF is highly prized by proponents of this style of theorem proving. Milner's original motivation for the introduction of ML, however, was initially at least equally to ease proof construction. Formal proof would be hopelessly tedious if the user had to instruct the machine to perform each and every primitive inference; as seen in chapter 7, "real world" proofs such as those conducted by Avra Cohn can involve millions of inferences. Stanford LCF already permitted a degree of automation of this process, and Edinburgh LCF and ML allowed the user to encode "recipes"[69] for constructing proofs. These recipes include "tactics"—ways of reducing the goal, a desired theorem, to "a list of subgoals such that if every subgoal holds then the goal holds also"[70]—and higher-level "tacticals," which combine tactics.

HOL

In the Boyer-Moore prover, their logic is "hard wired" into the system. In contrast, in LCF rules of logical inference are encoded in a separate program segment and are, therefore, relatively easy to change. Milner is a pluralist about logic: "there is a logic for each task," he said, rather than one true or best logic.[71] Others could adopt LCF and ML and apply them differently, embodying different logics in them, while still being able to reuse large chunks of program, such as ML compilers and type-checking code.

Perhaps the most influential system derived from LCF has been Higher Order Logic (HOL) developed by Michael J. C. Gordon, a member of Milner's team who had worked on Edinburgh LCF's parser (a parser is a program that determines how statements are structured). After graduating in mathematics from Cambridge University in 1970, Gordon came to Edinburgh to work in artificial intelligence, but he moved sideways to do his Ph.D. in programming language semantics and then to help build LCF. As he had no formal training in computer science, he began to read textbooks in his new field, including one written by Andrew S. Tanenbaum (whose defense of program testing was referred to in chapter 6). As an illustration, Tanenbaum described a simple minicomputer in great detail.[72]

Reading the description, Gordon thought "Aha, that's something that I could formally model using LCF." He needed funding, so he applied to the Science Research Council for an advanced fellowship to study hardware verification which, he pointed out, had been neglected in comparison to program verification. The Research Council was won over; Gordon got his fellowship, and onto LCF he "kind of welded on" what he called Logic for Sequential Machines (LSM), which was designed to prove that hardware designs were correct implementations of their specifications. With LCF_LSM Gordon verified, among other simple hardware designs, that of a computer similar to Tanenbaum's.[73]

Though LCF_LSM was "manipulatively quite effective," Gordon realized that "[i]t was a bit ad hoc." When he moved to Cambridge University as a lecturer in 1981, Gordon acquired a research assistant, Ben Moszkowski, who was an enthusiast for temporal logic (see chapter 7). Moszkowski kept criticizing LCF_LSM's ad hoc formalism, saying "that temporal logic was much better." Though Gordon "didn't buy his [Moszkowski's] entire story," he "saw his point. Working in a general logic gave you much better flexibility than working in some ad hoc thing." Gordon agonized over whether he should adopt the formalism of the mathematical theory of sets, because it appeared "like the lingua franca of mathematics." The Cambridge University logicians he consulted, however, told him that set theory had become "very unfashionable" and that "intuitive reasoning was actually better formalized in higher-order logic."[74] Gordon also realized that LCF could relatively readily be adapted to implement higher-order logic, while a theorem prover for set theory was a much more daunting task. The combination of this "engineering pressure" and the "feeling that I was doing something which was sort of theoretically kosher" led Gordon to build a theorem prover for higher-order logic. Gordon was also aware of the argument by Keith Hanna of the University of Kent, seen in chapter 3 as a critic of Lenat's AM, that higher-order logic was well suited for hardware verification.[75]

In his HOL automated prover, Gordon chose to implement a rich, expressive, classical higher-order logic: the "simple theory of types," put forward by Alonzo Church in 1940.[76] Gordon modified Church's axiomatization to ease its implementation in LCF and constructed HOL "on top of" a new version of LCF constructed at Cambridge University by Larry Paulson. For example, "LCF has a substitution rule," said Gordon. "If you give it a list of pairs of variables and terms, and then you give it a subject and it'll substitute each term. So multiple parallel substitution was a primitive in LCF. . . . Robin Milner had written this code and optimized it, so it was very fast, and I decided I would use that code in my systems, so that meant I had to have . . . parallel substitution as a primitive, whereas if you look up in a standard book on simple type theory, you'd have a different primitive."[77]

HOL had the same basic theorem-proving architecture as Edinburgh LCF: ML's type-checking mechanism ensured that objects of type <u>thm</u> could be constructed only from other objects of type <u>thm</u> by application of HOL's inference rules. Gordon's system, however, quickly became more widely adopted than its parent. HOL embodied a powerful logic that placed few constraints on the user. It used the ordinary symbolism of predicate logic and, though the user had also to understand the λ-calculus, knowledge of the latter was widespread in theoretical computer science by the late 1980s. By comparison with the Boyer-Moore prover, HOL was not highly automated, but the obverse of that drawback was that HOL was under direct user control via its LCF-style tactics, so the user could straightforwardly tell the system what to do rather than try to lead it down the right path by suggesting appropriate lemmas. The combination of a relatively familiar logic with direct user control meant that HOL could be learned reasonably quickly. A week's training was enough to get users with the right background started, though Avra Cohn, who used it in the VIPER proof, said that a year is needed to become fully skilled. By 1991 HOL had around fifty users. Most had learned either by being trained at Cambridge or through personal contact with someone who had trained there, but around ten had learned on their own how to use the system.[78]

Initially, much of the use of HOL was for the original purpose for which Gordon developed it: hardware verification. Unlike LCF_LSM, however, HOL was not tailored specifically to that application. It could also be used for software verification or for the kind of "design proof" that was done in security-critical computing. In Britain HOL began to enter the latter world. In the latter half of the 1980s, British regulators, based in the Communications-Electronics Security Group attached to the famous Government Communications Headquarters (GCHQ) near Cheltenham, began to follow their American counterparts in demanding high assurance of security through mathematical proof that the design of a secure system correctly implemented a formal model of what "security" was.[79]

Among suppliers attempting to meet U.K. regulatory demands for secure systems was the Secure Systems High Assurance Team of the British computer firm International Computers, Ltd. (ICL). The provers mandated for use under the orange book in the United States were not available to them because of export restrictions, so when in the late 1980s the ICL team reviewed candidates for use as a theorem prover for secure systems, they focused on HOL and the Boyer-Moore prover. The security-critical and safety-critical computing communities in Britain had begun to adopt the Z notation (a version of the mathematical theory of sets) for writing specifications. The ICL team knew that being able to work with Z specifications would be a considerable practical advantage, and this (together with the directness of user control) inclined them toward the adoption of HOL: Z specifications were more easily handled by the luxurious expressiveness of higher-order logic than by the spartan Boyer-Moore logic. They applied a modified version of HOL to the verification of the first system to meet the new U.K. level 1 assurance requirement (roughly equivalent to the orange book's A1): the one way regulator, a relatively simple system that, in essence, allows sensitive information to flow inward to a system but not outward from it. Starting in 1990 the ICL team also reimplemented HOL more radically to turn it from an "academic research" tool into a more highly automated industrial one, which they christened ProofPower.[80]

A Constructive Alternative

Much of HOL's attractiveness came from its rich logic. That very richness, however, would give a constructivist occasion to pause. Like all the systems discussed so far, HOL embodied the law of the excluded middle, the focus of Brouwer's attack on conventional mathematics. It also incorporated David Hilbert's ε-operator, introduced in the 1920s by Hilbert and his student Wilhelm Ackermann in the hope of using it to prove the consistency of arithmetic and analysis. The ε-operator denotes some unspecified member of a set. Thus, for example, the term ε*n. n* < 10 "denotes some unspecified number less than 10." Gordon admitted that in its less straightforward usages "the ε-operator looks rather suspicious," and including it "builds in" to HOL the axiom of choice. This had been the subject of considerable controversy earlier in the twentieth century. To some, the axiom was less than self-evident when applied to arbitrarily large families of sets (say a family containing as many sets as there are real numbers), but mathematicians could not find a way of deriving it from the other axioms of set theory.[81]

The way in which the inference rules of a logic occupied only a discrete part of LCF, though, made for flexibility. Those who distrusted the richness of a classical, higher-order logic, such as that implemented in HOL, could develop LCF in a different way. Had he lived to see it, Brouwer might have been scandalized at the idea of implementing intuitionism on a machine, but that is the enterprise of the final system to be discussed here. As the discipline of formal logic developed and grew in the 1950s and 1960s, logicians eager to display their skills moved beyond the boundaries of classical logic, and constructive logic became an increasingly central research topic, for example, in the influential work of the Swedish logician Per Martin-Löf.[82] Constructivism, indeed, began to appear attractive for a reason that was in a sense the very opposite of the roots of Brouwer's embrace of it.

Like Brouwer, modern constructivists demand that one should show how to construct mathematical objects rather than use excluded middle to prove their existence by showing that their nonexistence implies a contradiction. Unlike Brouwer, however, some modern constructivists see this as preparing the ground for the mechanization of mathematics. If one's logic forced one to show how to construct an object, one had moved a considerable way toward being able to turn a proof that an object exists into a computer program to generate it. This made constructivism more attractive to computer scientists than it had been to mathematicians, to whom, despite the work of Heyting and Bishop, constructivism had appeared an oddity: "[S]omehow one imbibed from the atmosphere, 'This is not the way to succeed as a mathematician.' Only a few strange people, like mathematical logicians, bothered about such questions, and one did not see any of them winning Fields Medals," mathematics' highest honor.[83]

As constructivism gained adherents within computer science, it was only to be expected that efforts would be made to produce a theorem prover embodying constructive logic. One of the most sustained efforts in this direction was led by Robert L. Constable who emerged from the heartlands of modern symbolic logic. He was a mathematics undergraduate at Princeton University where his junior and senior theses were supervised by Alonzo Church, developer of the λ-calculus, and he then moved to the University of Wisconsin for a Ph.D. supervised by Church's student Stephen Kleene, who was deeply interested in intuitionism.[84] Although Constable shared neither Brouwer's solipsism nor his politics, like Brouwer he came to worry that modern mathematics was being built on dubious foundations. "[E]ven when I was an undergraduate I became sceptical about set theory," he said.[85]

His notebooks from his student days reveal his concerns. "[T]he entities of a Platonic world," the 21-year-old Constable wrote, "have the disadvantage that we as human beings can never calculate with one of them or examine one of them as a whole. It just isn't possible to get human hands on some of these things." What he called "finite constructability" had already started to appeal to him as a means of giving "an orderly account" of the foundations of mathematics. Such an account would replace "the static, cold, rigid forms" of Platonism with a view of mathematics as "a special 'linguistic activity' of [intelligent] systems," and communication, "either with itself or others," was taken to be the fundamental activity of intelligence.[86]

As Constable learned more set theory, his distrust of it as a foundation of mathematics deepened. "[I]t seemed to me that we were losing all intuition in the work we were doing in set theory. It was just technique. . . . [Y]ou had no sense of what the meaning of this stuff was." Did the inaccessible cardinals defined by set theorist Georg Cantor, which expressed different forms of infinity, actually exist? Was Cantor's continuum hypothesis[87] true? After mathematician Paul Cohen showed in 1963–1964 that the axiom of choice and the continuum hypothesis were independent from—not provable or disprovable on the basis of—the other axioms of set theory (see chapter 6), "I was absolutely convinced that set theory was on the wrong track," said Constable. It provided "no insight into what was really true." For Constable, "mathematics has meaning, and it's not just a formal game. And what I saw happening in set theory looked to me more and more like a formal game."[88]

At Wisconsin, Constable took a minor in computer science along with his work in mathematical logic. He was attracted by the work of John McCarthy and by McCarthy's LISP programming language, based as it was in the λ-calculus developed by Constable's undergraduate advisor,

Church. Constable also started studying the emerging field of complexity theory, with its attempt systematically to characterize the computational hardness of different problems. He tried to speak about complexity theory in the Wisconsin logic seminar but found that his fellow logicians "didn't want to hear about that, so I went over to computer science and talked about it." He got to know the complexity theorist Juris Hartmanis, who was in the computer science department at Cornell University, and that link, together with the beauty of Cornell's upstate New York location, led Constable to accept a position in computer science there in 1968.[89]

To begin with Constable worked at Cornell on complexity theory. A couple of years after he joined the department, however, computer scientist Richard Waldinger came to give a talk about program synthesis, the idea that instead of writing first a specification, then a program, and finally proving the two to be in correspondence, one should be able to transform certain kinds of mathematical arguments into programs. It was an attractive notion: the "correctness" of a program might then be guaranteed by how it was constructed rather than having laboriously to be verified. But Waldinger was using classical logic and, in consequence Constable decided, he was having to impose "a number of extra conditions on a proof that would allow you to find a program in it." As Kleene's student, Constable was well acquainted with constructivism, and he believed that the key issue was not to use excluded middle. If one forswore that and produced a constructive proof, no other restriction was necessary, concluded Constable: from the proof, one could extract a program. Unlike classical logic, in which the availability of excluded middle meant that "not all classical existence proofs can be translated into programs," constructive logic could form a more suitable basis for what in 1971 Constable called an "automatic program writer."[90]

Two goals drove Constable's work. The first was to automate program writing by finding a way of turning "constructive" proofs into programs. "How is the solution to a mathematical problem presented?" asked Constable and his Ph.D. student Joseph L. Bates in 1985. "It is often in the form of a *proof* . . . [which] displays the result of the problem-solving process in such a way that the difficult steps are explained and exposed to public scrutiny." Too often however, the solution to problems in programming were presented "*raw*, without explanation," or, at best, with hastily produced, imprecise documentation. "This is especially bad because a good explanation may be more important than the program, especially if the program must later be modified or if it becomes critical to know its correctness." The PRL system (Proof Refinement Logics; PRL is pronounced "pearl") that Constable, Bates, and their Cornell team produced was intended to support this process.[91]

Second, however, was Constable's even more ambitious goal of creating a new, formalized mathematics. "It has always been my dream that we create a new subject," formalized mathematics, said Constable. His work in theorem proving "can be seen as a tool for creating a new kind of mathematics. The HOL community is generating reams of new materials, showing what volume is possible. We are trying to show what high quality is possible—material better than any textbook, for clarity as well as reliability." Constable is not imputing carelessness to HOL's users: he is making a constructivist comment on HOL's rich, classical logic and on its "lack of proof objects [textual traces of proofs] that are readable."[92]

Constable's twin dreams needed mechanized implementations. Constable was a frequent visitor to Edinburgh and got to know Milner well. While on a sabbatical visit there in 1982, Constable came to realize not just that Edinburgh LCF provided a convenient way to implement the logic of PRL, but that Milner's idea of controlling machine proofs via "tactics" might help make those machine proofs (whose notorious unsurveyability was castigated by DeMillo, Lipton, and Perlis) more high-level and hence more readable. After all, if one's goal was mathematics "better than any textbook, for clarity as well as reliability," one would fail immediately if a reader had to pore over page after page of computer printout comprehensible only to the aficionados of the theorem prover.

Constable realized that Milner's "tactics" might make it possible to capture the notions used in ordinary, informal mathematical proof. His aim was to combine the clarity of this kind of proof with the dependability of the machine and so flesh out his long-standing constructivist conviction that mathematics is best founded on "computational intuition ..., which I think is sounder than set-theoretical intuition." Intuitionism had always sought to base mathematics "in some of the fundamental intuitions that the human mind uses in its information processing," said Constable, but the mechanization of that processing offered a new opportunity to root mathematics "in terms of communications and information processing, rather than in terms of any kind of Platonic world."[93]

By 1983 PRL had been transformed into the LCF-style Nuprl (pronounced "new pearl") that Constable hoped would produce "gems of theorems that are rock-solid like diamonds." Nuprl performs its formal proofs in a constructive version of type theory, which draws upon the work of Per Martin-Löf and N.G. de Bruijn (the latter's AUTOMATH system was referred to in chapter 3). The metalanguage used to instruct Nuprl to construct its proofs was a version of ML, modified from the Edinburgh LCF system to suit Nuprl.[94] Nuprl's constructive type theory includes (in its late-1990s' formulation) seventy-five inference rules. The large number, said Constable, is for reasons of computational efficiency and pedagogic clarity. The rule set could be reduced to twelve, he argued, but that would, for example, slow the performance of proofs in arithmetic. He does note, however, that it makes it possible for the supporters of HOL, which has only eight primitive inference rules, to "give them grief" over Nuprl's extensive rule set, and Randy Pollack, developer of LEGO, another constructive theorem prover, similarly criticizes the complexity of Nuprl's inference rules. To believe a mechanized proof, said Pollack, "we must be able to read and understand the formal system we are checking; this is an essential part of bridging the gap between a formal property and our informal belief." Nuprl's complicated logic, he argued, is unsatisfactory in this respect.[95]

Nuprl, however, has been applied successfully to a variety of important problems, for example in the investigation of Girard's paradox (a paradox in the λ-calculus) and to give a new, constructive proof of a result called Higman's lemma, used in a part of graph theory that plays a significant role in the study of complexity. Nuprl has also been employed in practical computer-system verifications. In the late 1990s, for example, it was being used heavily in a project funded by the Advanced Research Projects Agency to improve the reliability of distributed group communications systems used in banking, air traffic control, and military command and control.[96]

Logics

So far this chapter has examined the development of a number of particularly influential automated theorem provers. Let us now step back from these developments and consider some of the choices that those involved had to make. The most obvious issue is the choice of a formal system to implement. A key decision is between a classical and a constructive logic. Although constructivism has been quite a minority stance in mathematics, within computer science it is a serious and respected alternative. Temporal logic, too, is effectively mainstream in computer science, as seen in the discussion of model checking in chapter 7. Even more esoteric choices, however, are available.

For example, in the 1980s a group of researchers at the Australian National University set out to automate relevance logic. This insists that the premises of a deduction be relevant to (share some content with) its conclusion. For the proponents of relevance logic, the elementary theorem of classical logic that a contradiction implies any proposition whatsoever is a paradox to be avoided. Automated relevance logics were not intended for mainstream mathematical reasoning nor for system verification: the main hoped for application was database management. Suppose that my university's staff database contains two contradictory pieces of information: for example, that Professor Bloor both is and is not a member of the sociology department. Applying classical logic one could then deduce any proposition whatsoever: that my salary is £1,000,000, or that the moon is made of green cheese. Relevance logic would prevent either of those inferences from being made.[97]

Among those involved in mechanized proving, there are variable attitudes to the plethora of available formal logics. At one extreme is the position of Alan Robinson, whose work on resolution was discussed in chapter 3. He noted that he has "always been a little quick to make adverse judgments about what I like to call 'wacko logics,' especially in Australia." (Australia has been a prime site of work on the automation of nonclassical logics.) "I conduct my affairs," he said, "as though I believe . . . that there is only one logic. All the rest is variation in what you're reasoning about, not in how you're reasoning. . . . [Logic] is immutable."[98] Another key figure with distinct preferences between formal logics is Robert Constable, although in his case constructive logic is taken to be superior to classical logic. Thus, he contrasts constructive systems such as his Nuprl with the classical HOL, which not only incorporates excluded middle and has a Hilbert ε-operator but also implements an impredicative[99] type theory. For those reasons, "I think it's much dicier," said Constable.[100]

Dominant opinion on choices between logics, however, can be characterized as eclectic and pragmatic. Often the task of a logic is seen as being to model the operations of a machine. Since machines vary, those who see logics in this light, as modeling tools, can scarcely be expected to believe that there is one true logic and all else is error. Asked in 1994 why computer scientists appeared to need a multiplicity of logics when mathematicians appeared to get by with one (classical logic), Robin Milner replied that if mathematicians modeled machines they too would be forced to turn to nonclassical logics.[101] Furthermore, developments within logic itself may have led to a softening of what, earlier in the twentieth century, were sometimes bitter disputes over matters like excluded middle. Relative consistency and translation results enhance the possibility for "peaceful coexistence," as it were.[102]

If logics are viewed eclectically and pragmatically, and if results in one formal system can sometimes (though certainly not always) be translated into another, then the decision as to which logic to incorporate in an automated theorem prover could even begin to be seen as in part "a marketing decision," as logician turned computer scientist Michael Fourman puts it, describing the decision to transform a constructivist theorem prover into a classical one. The law of the excluded middle was added largely because the engineers who used the prover wanted it.[103]

Trusting the Machine?

The choice of a formal system within which to perform proof is only one of the decisions confronting the designer of an automated theorem prover. Another set of issues arises because a theorem prover is itself a computer program, indeed typically quite a complex program. As such, can it be trusted? The developers and intensive users of mechanized provers appear nearly all to have experienced bugs in provers. Robin Milner, for example, recalled changing the implementation of the mechanism of substituting one term for another that runs underneath ML, with the goal of making it more efficient. "I switched it, no problem. It works faster." A year later, he found that LCF had an inconsistency—it could be used to prove that "true was equal to false"—and he realized that the inconsistency was caused by the "improvement" he had made.

Inadvertently, Milner had permitted "variable capture," a common form of theorem-proving error, in which a variable that ought to have been free becomes bound as a result of renaming. (In the λ-calculus expression $\lambda x.(y + x)$, for example, y is a "free variable" and x a "bound variable.") Milner removed the cause of the error and the revised algorithm "lived on" in early versions of HOL. It was "corrected," said Milner. "But what do we mean by that?" There was no realistic prospect of formally verifying its correctness: "it would be very hard to formalize the proof of that algorithm, because it was swinging pointers. It was doing replacements, and doing imperative programming—quite dirty stuff. . . . You need dirty stuff to get the efficiency."[104]

There is nothing particularly surprising about bugs in theorem provers, said Robert Constable. Although variable capture is a result of a mistake in implementing a process central to theorem proving, other typical design faults are common to complex programs of any sort. Mistakes "occur at the interfaces between modules," said Constable; for example, when the person responsible for one module has not completely understood the work of the person responsible for another. "They come in when you change something, and there's some ramification that you haven't foreseen." Interviewed in 1994, he and his team were in the process of "shaking down" version 4 of Nuprl. "I would say every four or five months a problem crops up. And so far none of these problems have led to an inconsistency, but they were surprising. We thought, 'Oh my God, I didn't know we were able to do *this*.' "[105]

In 1984–1985 the question of the soundness of the automated systems used in formal verification was directly addressed in a study funded by U.S. National Computer Security Center. The study was led by Richard A. Kemmerer, a verification specialist at the University of California at Santa Barbara. Four verification systems were examined: the System Development Corporation's FDM and Don Good's Gypsy, which were the two systems then being used in orange book A1 secure-systems verification; SRI's Enhanced HDM (described earlier in this chapter); and a system called Affirm developed by General Electric. As well as Kemmerer and another independent member, the Canadian verification specialist Dan Craigen, the team included a key figure in the development of each of the systems—Deborah Cooper (FDM), Good (Gypsy), Karl Levitt (Enhanced HDM), and David Musser (Affirm)—so each system could be examined by developers of its competitors. The full report of the *Verification Assessment Study* is subject to the U.S. arms export legislation because of the role of these systems in the verification of computer security, but an unrestricted summary makes a central finding clear: all the systems studied had "some areas of unsoundness."[106] None had "a rigorous mathematical basis," wrote Craigen. "This makes any claims to formality or rigour . . . suspect."[107]

How serious a matter is the possibility of bugs or other sources of unsoundness in the design of a theorem prover? To Alan Robinson it was indicative of a vicious regress undermining the entire current approach to verification. "You've got to prove the theorem-proving program correct. You're in a regression, aren't you? And that's what people don't seem to realize when they get into verification. They have a hairy great thing they're in doubt about, so they produce another hairy great thing which is the proof that this one's ok. Now what about this one which you've just used . . . ? I say that serves them jolly well right. They shouldn't be doing it that way." Those involved in computer system verification should be doing what Robinson called "real proofs, which are scannable, intelligible, . . . , surveyable things that a human can use as a 'conviction producer.' There is no other way."[108]

Naturally, the central figures discussed in this chapter do not accept that the enterprise of producing formal, mechanized proofs about computer programs or hardware designs is flawed, or that its notion of proof is inadequate. "[T]oo much scepticism will lead us into an ultimately barren regress in any field of knowledge," wrote HOL user John Harrison.[109] Kemmerer said that the "soundness issues" raised in the report of the group he chaired "were overblown," in part because those involved in the study "were all competing for the same money."[110] The potential unsoundnesses were real enough, but their significance was exaggerated. At worst they might be pitfalls for inexperienced users: "These problem areas usually can be avoided or finessed by an expert user."[111] More generally, a significant current of opinion in the community examined here believes that the unsoundness, potential or actual, of automated theorem provers is not the main issue. The reality of the experience of interactive theorem proving is of great effort to get a prover, which is "an implacable skeptic," to accept as a proof a chain of reasoning that the human user already believes.[112]

A mechanized prover failing to prove a theorem one knows to be correct is a common experience; a prover proving a result one knows to be false is rarer; a prover producing a proof one at first believes and then finds to be faulty is rare indeed. Indeed, in this study only one instance of a theorem-proving unsoundness leading to a fallacious, publicly claimed, "proof" was discovered. In May 1995 the Université d'Orléans theorem-proving specialist Siva Anantharam announced that the Robbins conjecture in Boolean algebra had been proved using a theorem prover called REVEAL. By the end of August he retracted the announcement: the claimed proof had an error caused by a bug in REVEAL.[113]

If, however, one is not satisfied with the pragmatic judgment that the risk of a theorem-proving bug having serious consequences is small, what measures can be taken to improve the trustworthiness of automated proving? Suppose someone claims to have produced a machine-checked proof of a theorem, how is one to believe it, asked Randy Pollack. One cannot plausibly read such a proof in detail, as one might read a proof in a mathematics journal. The best approach, said Pollack, is to check the putative proof by running it through an independently-written proof-checking program for the formal system in question. A proof-checking program could be much simpler than a full automated theorem prover (checking that a sequence of formulae is constructed according to the inference rules of a formal system is an easier task than finding an appropriate sequence of formulae in the first place). Although a mechanized proof cannot plausibly be read and understood in detail, a proof checker can be, argued Pollack:

> my favoured technique for believing the correctness of a simple proof checker is to read and understand the program in the light of your knowledge of the logic being checked and the semantics of the metalanguage in which the checker is written. . . . If the logic is simple enough, and the metalanguage has a simple enough semantics, then the sum total of what you are required to read and understand is neither longer nor more difficult to understand than a conventional [non-mechanized] proof, and belief in the putative derivation is attained through your personal level of understanding.

The trust necessary is no longer trust in a complex program written by someone else but in a simple program, perhaps written by oneself, or "publicly available from a library of checkers that are refereed by experts."[114]

Pollack's is the most extensive discussion of an idea others have found attractive. Independent mechanical proof checking was, for example, advocated by the U.K. Ministry of Defence in its 1991 procurement standard governing safety-critical software in defence equipment, Interim Defence Standard 00-55.[115] By the end of the 1990s, however, a separate proof-checker had been constructed for only one of the systems discussed in this chapter: Wai Wong, a Cambridge University colleague of Mike Gordon, had built various prototypes of a HOL proof checker.[116] (There is also a proof checker for the Argonne system, Otter, which William McCune was able to use to check his proof of the Robbins conjecture, described in chapter 3.) Constable's team, for example, had an outline design for a checker for Nuprl but had not found a sponsor for its development.[117]

In part, the paucity of separate proof checkers (especially of genuinely independent ones written by those with no stake in the system whose proofs are being checked) reflects the belief that theorem-proving bugs are a small risk compared, for example, to inadequacies in the specification of the system being verified. In John Rushby's words, "the resources expended on such 'second opinions' would probably be better expended on independent scrutiny of the assumptions and modeling employed, which are rather more likely to be faulty than mechanically checked proofs."[118] In part, though, it also reflects the fact that most of the systems discussed here perform proofs rather than produce proofs.

That is, they do not produce records (electronic or printed) of the chains of elementary inferences that lead from axioms to a theorem.

"Proofs evaporate," as Bob Boyer put it, describing the operations of the Boyer-Moore prover. The "proof object"—the record of all the applications of elementary rules of inference—has been too large to be stored in the memory of the type of workstation on which automated theorem provers are run. What the Boyer-Moore prover produces, if the user requires it to, is what Boyer called a "commentary," which "is accurate, is invaluable, and nevertheless . . . is far from complete." From it, one cannot reconstruct the full proof object: "Just to give you one example, the output will often say that a certain lemma was used, but it doesn't tell you how that lemma was instantiated in its use. And so it's undecidable, you know, what instantiation was used. So the commentary is nothing but commentary, and the proof that is found is simply not recorded. It's not there to be checked."[119]

This evaporation of proof, until recently, was found in all the systems discussed in this chapter except Nuprl. HOL has been modified to produce a full proof object, and resolution provers of the type discussed in chapter 3 can also do this. Although the proofs produced by a fully automatic prover of the latter type are typically much shorter than the proofs performed by the interactive provers discussed in this chapter, even there what looks on the surface like an individual step may have had many substitutions of "equals" for "equals" performed without being incorporated in the proof object. Reliance upon an evaporating proof may appear strange, but Boyer pointed out that, seen from the viewpoint of computation, it can seem natural.

When used to perform arithmetic, a calculator or computer goes through its programmed steps and produces an answer: it does not produce a record of how that answer was generated. If the user said, "'Well, where's the proof?' then the programmers would look at you oddly and they'd say, 'Well, what do you mean? We added the numbers up.'" In that sense, Boyer saw the impermanence of the proof object as natural. Interviewed in 1994, Moore was uncertain whether the production of a full proof object in any usable form was feasible, even with the powerful machines then available. In principle, the Boyer-Moore prover certainly "could produce a formal proof object," but, he asked, "is it in fact so large that I can't actually process it with a machine that I have today?" Indeed, Moore argued that independent proof checking is a far bigger technical challenge than it might on the surface appear. Suppose, he speculated, his and Boyer's prover were being used in such a central role that a sponsor saw a need for "absolute assurance that every proof is really a proof" and was prepared to support Moore's work for the rest of his life if such certainty could be provided. "Then, what I would do is sit down to instrument [the Boyer-Moore prover] to create formal proofs, and then I'd write a simple proof checker and get the community to agree that that was a proof checker. That would be my first attack. Whether that attack would be successful because of these engineering reasons [such as the size of the full formal proof object], I don't know."[120]

Without such an effort, the Boyer-Moore prover (like the other systems discussed here) "doesn't produce a formal proof, it just does a computation that Boyer and I [Moore] believe established to our satisfaction that a formal proof . . . exists. And so right now there isn't any avoiding that leap of faith that Boyer and Moore did their job."[121] The "leap of faith" is perhaps not a huge one—only one person has "ever found an unsoundness in a released version" of the Boyer-Moore prover—but its necessity troubled the Pythagorean Boyer and Moore. They found they were frequently asked, "Have you verified the verifier?" and came to regard it as being practically as well as intellectually important to have an answer. "Perhaps surprisingly, this metamathematical question is often asked by engineers—for example, project monitors in NASA and the FAA [Federal Aviation Administration]—and not merely by academics."[122]

One way of deflecting that question would be to develop independent proof checking, but Moore has instead sought to answer it directly by applying verification to the prover itself. In the late 1980s he began to construct a new version of the Boyer-Moore prover, called ACL2 (A Computational Logic for Applicative Common Lisp) which was released in 1995. Nearly all of ACL2 is programmed within a subset of LISP that Boyer and Moore axiomatized to make it "an executable mathematical logic." Although Moore, Matt Kaufmann, and their colleagues included some new features in ALC2, its basic structure remains similar to earlier versions of the Boyer-Moore prover. A key point of rewriting the prover, however, "as a set of recursive functions in its own logic" was the apparently paradoxical goal of asking "the theorem prover to prove itself."[123]

At the time of writing, Moore's effort to use ACL2 to prove itself correctly implemented is unfinished. Indeed, given the complication of the program he is seeking to verify, there is a case for regarding it as the most ambitious verification effort yet undertaken. It is important to note, however, that Boyer and Moore see the obstacles to that effort as practical rather than philosophical. Moore is *not* seeking to use ACL2 to prove the consistency of the formal system that it embodies: that effort, he knows, is rendered hopeless by Gödel's incompleteness theorems. Instead, what is being proved, are "theorems about the [implementation of the] system using the system." Boyer and Moore, however, would hope to go beyond verification of the correctness of ACL2's software implementation. Ideally, they would like to see it running on a computer system whose hardware design had also been subject to proof. "[T]he dream Boyer and I've had . . . since almost the beginning," said Moore, "is that the theorem prover be verified mechanically and that it run on a machine that's been verified mechanically."[124]

Architectures

To some, like Rushby, the possibility of theorem-proving bugs is not an important practical matter; to others, it justifies (and may eventually necessitate) independent proof checking or even self-verification of the verifier. The proponents of one set of systems, those derived from Milner's LCF, however, believe that this issue is differential in its impact. What is most distinctive about LCF, and its derivatives such as HOL and Nuprl, is their use of the type thm and ML's type-checking mechanism to protect the soundness of inferences. The supporters of these systems regard this as a better overall structure, a superior "architecture," by comparison with that of systems such as the Boyer-Moore or SRI provers.

Instead of the code (program text) critical to the soundness of inference being widely distributed through the system, in an LCF-style system the critical program segments are concentrated in ML's type-checking mechanism and in the way the rules of inference of the logic are implemented in the definition of type thm. As of 1994 the type-checking module, together with the related signature-matching module, of a typical ML compiler comprised around 1300 lines of source code, while there were 222 lines in the HOL thm module.[125] This simple architecture is more conducive to theorem-proving soundness than more complex designs, say the proponents of LCF-style provers.[126]

That an LCF-style architecture gives greater assurance of soundness is a contested judgment. Boyer sees the attraction of what he calls LCF's "secure cordon" architecture. But he has also "tried to do a little bit of empirical investigation on this matter." The "right question," he believed, is "how much code does one have to trust to believe the reports?

. . . I say, let's count every line of code, which, if an enemy were allowed to edit it *ad lib*, could result in the proof of ƒ [false]." If you ask that question, said Boyer, the answers for systems as varied as HOL, the Boyer-Moore prover, and Argonne's Otter are surprisingly similar. Randy Pollack, however, defends what he calls the "accepted wisdom" of the superior trustworthiness of an LCF-style implementation of a logic with only a small number of inference rules. LCF-style provers such as HOL do "contain much less critical code" than the Boyer-Moore prover. Furthermore, the latter's code is complex. To "trust" the Boyer-Moore prover, said Pollack, "you have to trust code for complicated and optimized algorithms for unification and rewriting, while the critical code in [an] LCF-style [prover] just checks that each step in a putative proof follows some syntactic rule. Furthermore, code in an LCF-style prover is (should be) written in a principled, strongly typed and formally specified language, like SML [Standard ML], while the Boyer-Moore prover [is] written in LISP, a language favored for tricky hacking."[127]

Selling Your Soul to the Devil

Closely related to the question of theorem-proving architectures is the issue of the use in automated provers of unverified decision procedures. These are algorithms, implemented as subprograms within an automated prover, that determine in a finite number of steps whether or not formulae in limited mathematical domains such as Presburger arithmetic are theorems. They do so not by producing a formal proof, but by performing a computation, often quite a complex computation, that determines whether a formula is a theorem. The consequences for proof of their use are controversial, but positions in the resultant spectrum of opinion are subtly different from those on general issues of the trustworthiness of mechanized proof.

Again, Rushby occupies the pragmatic end of the spectrum. Decision procedures, he noted, "are big tricky pieces of code, and essentially they have linear programming inside them. And at present it's somewhat unfeasible . . . to formally specify and verify . . . the guts of the decision procedure." He does not believe that this matters very much: "if you're looking for an unsoundness in a verification, would the decision procedures of the theorem prover be the most likely source? I believe they wouldn't be." Not only are deficient specifications *the* dominant risk, but mistakes in the implementation of decision procedures are not high in the spectrum of theorem-proving risks: "variable capture" (discussed above) is a much more likely source of error.[128] Although the position of Boyer and Moore on overall questions of trust in machine proof is quite different from Rushby's, on the specific matter of decision procedures their views are similar. By the stringent standard they envisage—that a properly trustworthy theorem prover should be verified and ideally should run on a machine with a verified design—unverified decision procedures of course fail, but to no greater extent than other components of current theorem provers. As Moore pointed out, for many years he and Boyer had no "correctness proofs for the whole system," and they did not in practice worry more about their decision procedures than other, equally unverified, parts of the system.[129]

The other end of the spectrum of opinion about decision procedures is thus occupied not by Boyer and Moore but by Milner and the developers of LCF-style systems. What troubles them is that unverified decision procedures, outputting only the judgment "true" or "false," escape the discipline of ML's type checker and the "firewall" it builds around type thm. Using an unverified decision procedure, said Milner, is "like selling your soul to the Devil—you get this enormous power, but what have you lost? You've lost proof, in some sense."[130] Constable and his team have sought to prove the correctness of the implementation of decision procedures, believing that if they could succeed they could tap into a substantial market of those who wanted the decision procedure's power without its diabolical risk. As of 1997, however, they had not succeeded in verifying the kind of decision procedures that are used in practice within theorem provers—they are "nasty" (that is, written in ways that are hard to verify) "because they have to run fast," said Constable—but were working actively on the problem.[131]

Mike Gordon has sought a different way of avoiding the weakening of proof by decision procedures. Instead of seeking to verify decision procedures, he has tried to implement them in such a way that they have "to perform a proof behind the scenes," in precisely the same way as an entire LCF-type system like HOL has to perform a proof. There is a cost in performance—"to decide the sort of arithmetical formulas that come up [in verification] takes us two or three seconds versus a fraction of a second in something like [SRI's] PVS"—but Gordon, unlike Rushby, believes the trade-off is worth it and traces the difference between them to differences in the contexts within which they work. Rushby, said Gordon, is "very much concerned with effectiveness in the interaction with the machine, and getting large proofs done," whereas in Gordon's university environment the latter is not such a crucial concern.[132]

A Demon Incarnate

Which logic to use to perform proof and how to trust the machine are two of the overarching questions raised by the mechanization of proof. A third issue, explicit in one context only, is that of human trustworthiness, specifically of malice. To be certain of a proof, noted the philosopher Ludwig Wittgenstein, one needed to know "[t]hat no demon can have deceived us by making a sign disappear without our noticing, or by adding one, etc."[133] Wittgenstein's demon was merely a philosophical device, but the developers of automated theorem provers have sometimes had to consider the possibility of a demon incarnate: a deliberately deceptive human user.

For example, despite the sophisticated technical firewall around HOL's type thm, it is easy to get it, or most other LCF-style provers, to perform an utterly fallacious "proof." The HOL function **mk_thm** allows the user to have the system treat as a theorem any formula the user chooses to assert. Using **mk_thm,** the user can introduce an inconsistency, for example, so that any formula then becomes provable. Together with the analogous function **new_axiom** (which adds an axiom to the formal system within which one is working), **mk_thm** shifts responsibility from the technical system to the human user.[134] In the academic world within which HOL was born, the question of user responsibility is a question of competence. A naive or careless user might abuse **mk_thm,** but a trusted member of the theorem-proving community is in practice relied upon not to use it to short-cut the process of proof. Although the Boyer-Moore system attempts technically to prevent a user introducing an inconsistency, Moore trusts others, not subject to this discipline, not to do so: "I implicitly trust people like Mike Gordon, Bob Constable, [Natarajan] Shankar, John Rushby. Those people value soundness as much as I do."[135]

Systems like HOL and the Boyer-Moore prover, however, originating as they did in universities, gradually came into contact with a world in which human trustworthiness is not just a matter of competence. For Mike Gordon contact with this new world came as a surprise. In the late 1980s leading figures in the National Security Agency began to believe that European work in formal methods was ahead of that in the United States, a situation that their critics, such as Steven T. Walker, blamed on their own oversecretiveness.[136] They began to seek contact with leaders of that European work such as Gordon. For example, invitation-only meetings were held in Halifax, Nova Scotia, in 1989 and in Drymen,

Scotland, in 1991 bringing together officials from the National Security Agency and similar bodies with academic and industrial practitioners of formal methods. (I was present at some of the Drymen meeting, invited to give a talk on the first results of the research reported in this book.)

Gordon was surprised at the issues raised by NSA officials:

> they asked me questions which suggested that there would be people around wanting to tinker maliciously with the system, and what had I done to stop that? Of course, I had never really . . . you know, I worried a bit about accidents [inadvertent unsoundnesses], but I hadn't assumed that my graduate students would actually want to corrupt the system. Then I noticed that in some companies that I consulted for, they lock up their designs overnight. . . . So there's a whole world that HOL doesn't live in.[137]

It was a world within which distrust, of necessity, was institutionalized; a world within which, for example, interviewees said (though never documented in print) that the National Security Agency maintained its own chip fabrication facility behind its security fence so that insecurities could not be introduced into microchips as they move from design to fabrication. It was a world within which Wittgenstein's demon might be incarnate as the agent of a hostile power.

In a world of necessary distrust, HOL's **mk_thm** was judged too dangerous. In the late 1980s the security-oriented High Assurance Team at International Computers, Ltd. modified HOL, thus moving the system between worlds. Roger Jones, a central figure in the ICL team, explained that **mk_thm** had to go (and even **new_axiom** was made unavailable for the particular project on which they first used HOL). "[W]e sealed off the loopholes," he said. In the university world from which HOL had come, **mk_thm** and **new_axiom** were, of course, facilities, not loopholes. "It depends on your culture," said Jones:

> it depends what you think the proof tool's doing for you. I think academics operate in an environment in which they are not pathologically suspicious of each other, and they're quite prepared to take somebody's word when they come up with a machine-checked proof that they haven't taken any shortcuts. We were operating in a pathologically . . . suspicious environment . . . where you're required to prove that your system does what it's supposed to and where they pay people to check your claim. As well as having the proof tool check your claim, they have evaluators who are there to make sure that you've really done it the way you're supposed to have done it . . . you're not doing things on trust. So the tool's playing an important role there in this environment that it doesn't really play in an academic environment, which is, it is sort of putting its hand on its heart and saying, "Yes, that guy really did do his proof properly. You don't have to take his word for it, you can take my word for it."[138]

For some members of the community of developers and users of auto-mated provers, the removal of **mk_thm** was puzzling. If one was con-cerned about abuse of **mk_thm** or **new_axiom** in a putative proof, one could simply use Unix's "grep" facility (which searches files) to find where they had been used in the proof.[139] Roger Jones concedes that this is possi-ble. "However," he says, "a much better solution is to remove the facilities, then you don't have the trouble of checking whether [they have] been used, and you don't have to worry about whether your checks can be circumvented. . . . What we did was easier than 'grepping,' and makes a much better story for the evaluators" of a claimed proof of security:

Our proof was going to be evaluated, leading to certification. The proof log was in the order of 10Mb in length. . . . So we really needed to convince them [the evaluators] that they could trust the proof tool to check the proof. We couldn't do that unless we believed it ourselves. So we had to make it true that there were no known defects in the soundness of the proof checker. Grepping the proof scripts was simply not an option, since it would not allow us to claim that the proof checker could be relied upon.[140]

The demands of the world of security-critical computing thus became a matter not just of how and why the theorem prover was used but brought about an alteration to its internal structure. That is a point of some interest, because it illustrates not just the importance of questions of trust but also another point. The different notions of what constitutes proof that have been discussed in this chapter cannot be organized into a simple, universally agreed hierarchy of rigor. Differences between an academic and an industrial environment, and possibly even differences between European "purism" and American "pragmatism" are important, but they are neither simple nor one-dimensional. There is, for example, a sense in which ICL's "industrialists" made their version of HOL more, not less, rigorous than the academic original. Machines, proofs, and the cultures within which both circulate *are* interrelated, but not in straight-forward ways. It is to this interrelation that the final chapter turns.

9

Machines, Proofs, and Cultures

The preceding chapters have examined our knowledge of the properties of computer systems, especially their dependability, and the nature of deductive proof, especially automated proof. This final chapter begins by returning to dependability. In 1969 Tony Hoare wrote that "the cost of error in certain types of program may be almost incalculable—a lost spacecraft, a collapsed building, a crashed aeroplane, or a world war." In 1981 he commented that an "unreliable programming language generating unreliable programs constitutes a far greater risk to our environment and to our society than unsafe cars, toxic pesticides, or accidents at nuclear power stations." He was not alone in his concern. The fear of catastrophe in a critical system haunted the 1968 Garmisch meeting where the "software crisis" was diagnosed. J. C. R. Licklider, former director of the Information Processing Techniques Office in the Defense Department's Advanced Research Project Agency, warned in 1969 that basing software-controlled nuclear missiles around American cities to defend them against Soviet missile attack was a "potentially hideous folly" because of the certainty of faulty software: "All the large software systems that exist contain 'bugs.'" In the realm of security, similarly, warnings of the vulnerability to intrusion of critical systems have been issued for decades. "You can't trust code that you did not totally create yourself," Ken Thompson, a key figure in the development of the Unix operating system, told the members of the Association for Computing Machinery in 1984 after showing them how almost undetectable Trojan horses could be inserted deep in the infrastructure of computer systems.[1]

How well-founded were and are these fears? In 1994 I tried to find out, at least for the domain of safety, by seeking to determine how many people had died in computer-related accidents worldwide up to the end of 1992. I worked from the reports by a large number of correspondents, compiled since 1976 by Peter Neumann of SRI International, first in the newsletter *Software Engineering Notes* and eventually in the widely read on-line *Risks Digest*.[2] I winnowed out cases where further investigation suggested no significant causal role for the computer and sought alternative sources of information for categories of accident, notably industrial accidents, that appeared likely to be underreported in *Risks* (which is based primarily on press reports). The resultant data set contained around 1,100 deaths.[3] Over 90 percent of these deaths were caused by faulty human-computer interaction (often the result of poorly designed interfaces or of organizational failings as much as of mistakes by individuals). Physical faults such as electromagnetic interference were implicated in a further 4 percent of deaths, while the focus of Hoare's and Licklider's warnings, software "bugs," caused no more than 3 percent, or thirty, deaths: two from a radiation-therapy machine whose software control system contained design faults, and twenty-eight from faulty software in the Patriot antimissile system that caused a failed interception in the 1991 Gulf War.[4]

Leave aside the multiple ways in which the finding of thirty software-caused accidental deaths could be challenged: have I missed cases? Would Patriot have successfully intercepted the attacking missile in the absence of the particular software fault?[5] Nor is it necessary to point to the even greater difficulties of empirical investigation of security failures and of the multiplicity of other forms that lack of dependability can take (for example, the most serious security failures are arguably those that go undetected). More important to the assessment of Hoare's, Licklider's, and Thompson's assertions is the basic fact that a warning is not a prediction. How dependable the computer is, or how dangerous, is affected by how we use it and the latter is affected by the reception of warnings such as these.

Hoare was advocating greater rigor in language and compiler design and the adoption of the proof-based verification techniques discussed in the previous chapters. Licklider was warning his contemporaries not to place nuclear missiles under the computer's sole control; the specific plan against which he was warning was indeed abandoned, albeit for other reasons.[6] Thompson called for security flaws to be taken seriously and for an end to what he felt to be overindulgent attitudes to violations of security: the actions of "hackers," he argued, were "vandalism at best and probably trespass and theft at worst."[7]

Warnings like these, or the many warnings of the potential seriousness of the Y2K "Millennium bug" problem, or Neumann's extensive collection of risks reports, are best seen not as prophecy but—to borrow a term from the sociology of deviance—as moral entrepreneurship. As the sociologist Howard Becker pointed out, "Rules are not made automatically. Even though a practice may be harmful in an objective sense to the group in which it occurs, the harm needs to be discovered and pointed out. People must be made to feel that something ought to be done about it. Someone must call the public's attention to these matters, supply the push necessary to get things done, and direct such energies as are aroused in the proper direction to get a rule created."[8]

The warnings of the moral entrepreneurs of computerized risk in many respects have been listened to. Studying safety-critical computing in the United Kingdom in the mid-1990s, my colleague Maggie Tierney and I found considerable reluctance among engineers to implement the most critical functions in software.[9] They were wary of software and, perhaps more importantly, they knew that regulatory agencies shared that wariness. While I have not investigated the equivalent issue for military security—where implementation details are classified information—I suspect that the same is true there: that the networks truly critical to security, such as those controlling nuclear forces and nuclear early warning, are kept physically separate from less critical networks and from the Internet.[10] Security's moral entrepreneurs have also perhaps been heeded, at least as far as the most critical military systems are concerned.

The Hoare Paradox

Like all discourse on risk, therefore, discussion of computerized risk has a reflexive aspect. This does not refer to the complex matters examined by Ulrich Beck and those who have followed him, but to a simple point: perception of a situation as dangerous often leads to action that reduces those dangers; perception of it as safe can have the opposite effect.[11] To an extent, danger is a self-negating prophecy.[12] This is plausibly part of the explanation of one of the most puzzling phenomena of computer dependability, a phenomenon I like to call the Hoare paradox.[13] Although software seldom has had proof applied to it (the industrial uptake of the proof-based methods described here remains limited, hardware model-checking aside), its dependability is often adequate to the tasks for which it is actually used. Faulty software appears to have killed remarkably few people; security failures have generally been embarrassing rather than catastrophic; in areas such as telephony and avionics, real-time systems, containing millions or tens of millions of lines of program, function tolerably well. The highly automated, fly-by-wire[14] Boeing 777 airliner, for example, has been in service since 1995 without, at the time of writing, a single crash or other serious mishap.

"How Did Software Get So Reliable without Proof?" asked Hoare in 1994.[15] The question is an interesting one, because it turns the conventional query—why do accidents and other failures happen—on its head and asks why they don't, given the depth of the software development problems identified in the 1960s and the limited (though real) progress made subsequently in alleviating them. Although the exercise is necessarily speculative, it is worth considering both Hoare's answers and some additional possibilities. Part of the explanation, Hoare suggested, is that though there has been little direct application of proof to software, the "structured programming" methods advocated by Dijkstra and others were widely adopted. The rapid growth in the power of hardware, together with its declining relative cost, meant that the most dangerous unstructured practices were no longer needed for reasons of machine efficiency. Theoretical reasoning, though seldom taking the form of program verification, influenced the "infrastructure" within which programs were constructed and run: above all, perhaps, the design of programming languages and of the compilers for them.[16] The effects of such "bugs" as remained were mitigated by the practice of "defensive programming," which anticipates error states and seeks to prevent them from leading to system failures, and by the provision of constantly running audit programs, which check for anomalies.

Another part of the explanation, however, may be that the success of Hoare and of software's other moral entrepreneurs in inculcating a sense that software is dangerous has helped keep it safe by leading those involved to avoid, wherever possible, making software safety-critical or security-critical and to lavish particular attention on it if criticality was impossible to avoid. If correct, this last conjecture is worth emphasizing. The Y2K episode—the first real upsurge of public concern about computerized risk—may, because of the very limited actual problems that manifested themselves, lead to complacency and thus to greater future danger in safety-critical and security-critical computing.

A further possible reason why software-based systems are often reasonably reliable is suggested by Harry Collins's discussion of how human users interact with an electronic calculator or an expert system in artificial intelligence: we "repair" its output, said Collins, in other words we "rectify its deficiencies," often "without noticing that we do so."[17] (Collins gives the example of converting his height—5 feet 9 inches—to centimeters. As a skilled human user, he knows that an answer appropriate to the implicit accuracy of the input is 175 centimeters, not the spuriously precise 175.26 that appears on his calculator's display. That latter answer is not "wrong," but there is a sense in which it is inappropriate.[18])

It may be quite mistaken to think of human-computer interaction solely in terms of human error. Much more of such interaction is probably repair: rebooting; avoiding or working around situations that trigger failures; interpreting output in the light of other information sources and appropriate context; critically judging the credibility of output; disregarding erroneous output, and so on. The spurious warning of impending nuclear attack discussed in chapter 2 is a dramatic example of users repairing—in that case by disregarding—defective computer system output, but many software systems are made reasonably dependable in practice by more mundane instances of repair.

Authority and Induction

The rarity of formal verification of programs and designs means that formal deductive knowledge of the properties of software systems has been limited. In consequence, there is perhaps reason to think that another part of the explanation of the Hoare paradox may be that informal deductive knowledge and the other sources of knowledge, authority and induction, are more effective than might abstractly be thought. The processes of peer review of designs and programs briefly described in chapter 2 have been adopted in a wide range of contexts in which dependability is important and are applied at key transitions, such as from requirements analysis to specification, specification to design, design to code, and so on. In Hoare's words: "The individual designer or programmer has to accept the challenge not only of making the right decisions, but also of presenting to a group of colleagues the arguments and reasons for confidence in their correctness."[19]

The knowledge that processes of review produce—even in their partly mathematicized form in the cleanroom (chapter 2)—is explicitly intersubjective knowledge, not objective knowledge in any abstract sense. Proof, for example, is present at best in what a formalist would regard as a thoroughly attenuated and unsatisfactory sense. Being intersubjective, this knowledge is only as robust as the social relations that generate it: pressure quickly to approve a design or a program could easily subvert it. It is, however, more robust than the reasoning of the individual programmer or designer. As the authors of a study of the industrial effectiveness of review, Ann Jackson and Daniel Hoffman, put it: "two or three pairs of eyes see much better than one pair."[20]

The process of review appears both to change people and to generate knowledge of them. The typical "proof technique" in review is partitioning "all the possible states and input values into a collection of cases" and then arguing "each case in turn." The experience of review—having to do this in a way explicable to someone else and seeing others do it—appears to help participants learn how to do this partitioning, which in turn helps to improve the dependability of their programming.[21] Who possesses and who does not possess that kind of skill can quickly become evident during reviews. Reported Hoffman: "It is usually easy to distinguish between readers [those who 'talk' the inspection team through the design or program and the arguments for its correctness], creator or not, who do and do not have a clear grasp of the code."[22]

Testing, too, may work in part by generating knowledge of people as well as knowledge of things. Inductive, test-based knowledge of the properties of computer systems appears, in Hoare's words, "more effective than it has any right to be": that is, more effective than might be presumed from the small proportion of the state space of a system that can be explored by realistic amounts of testing. Suggested Hoare: "The real value of tests is not that they detect bugs in the code, but that they detect inadequacy in the methods, concentration and skills of those who design and produce the code. Programmers who consistently fail to meet their testing schedules are quickly isolated and assigned to less intellectually demanding tasks."[23] If the dependability with which different designers and programmers perform different aspects of their work differs substantially,[24] then testing and review may work in part by leading to the most critical parts of projects being assigned to the most dependable people.

It is important to note that the sociotechnical processes underpinning the modest effectiveness of review and testing are local. They involve the generation of trust in particular, personally known people. The knowledge of people they produce does not, for example, take the form of their membership in or exclusion from a professional body. The local nature of this knowledge makes it fragile—more fragile, for example, than its equivalents in scientific communities. If programmers are in short supply, a local reputation for poor dependability can be left behind by shifting firms. The interweaving of knowledge of things and knowledge of people can be expected to be effective only in situations where there is sufficient continuity of personnel.

It is also important to recognize that systematic review and testing may simply not be applied. When Tierney and I examined safety-critical computing in the mid-1990s, we found situations in which these disciplines were not practiced. Even in sectors which did in general seek to practice them, time pressure and budget constraints could easily undercut that commitment. As an interviewee reported:

In general, things tend to go wrong when timescale is short. When engineers disappear to go on other projects, and when corners start to be cut to get things out the door. When engineers degenerate into the hacking mode. And they stop keeping logs of the testing. "Is it tested?" "Yes." "Where's the evidence?" "Well, it works, doesn't it?" It's a culture, it has to be encouraged, that isn't fully there yet, and it's a culture that comes from the top.[25]

Part of the explanation of the reasonable dependability of much deployed software may indeed simply be selection: the worst systems, developed in the least disciplined ways, often end up being cancelled before deployment. Even in the 1990s expensive cancellation remained the fate of many ambitious software projects.

Nor should the modest effectiveness of testing and review be seen as eliminating the need for formal deductive reasoning. Unless there is a breakthrough in the automation of software verification akin to the success of model checking in hardware design, it is not realistic to expect proof to be applied to each and every line of program, even in a critical system, especially if the program is produced by conventional methods and only subsequently subjected to formal verification. The process is too difficult, too expensive, and too slow; in any case specifications and interfaces (including human interfaces) will in many cases be where extra attention is likely to be most helpful. Proof-based techniques, however, may still bring considerable benefits if integrated into the software development process rather than being applied post hoc. Designs often have crucial aspects involving matters with which unaided human intuition or informal deductive reasoning appear ill-equipped to grapple, matters such as "redundancy management, partitioning, and the synchronization and coordination of distributed components."[26] The flight-control software for the Boeing 777, for example, was largely subject only to conventional process of testing and review—that is all that is required by the regulatory agencies in civil aviation—and the aircraft's record appears to indicate their effectiveness.[27] Formal verification, however, was apparently applied to the redundancy management system, a critical SIFT-like part of the design.[28]

The proof-based techniques discussed in this book remain essential resources for the task of gaining knowledge of the properties of computer systems. That task will inevitably grow in significance in the years to come, as computing becomes ever more ubiquitous and more critical to safety and to security, and as the interaction between large numbers of heterogeneous computing elements brings even further to the fore matters where intuitive understanding is fallible. All that the Hoare paradox suggests is that the deployed systems of the final decades of the twentieth century were more dependable than had been feared, and perhaps that sociotechnical sources of knowledge of them were more trustworthy than their purely technical analysis had suggested. But the bases of that dependability appear to be local and contingent, and they may well be undermined as the computing infrastructure inherited from the twentieth century is replaced by the new world of pervasive, distributed computing. Electronic commerce, where security is a key concern, is only one of many areas where dependability is likely to become a major issue. To turn away from proof-based technologies, just when they are most needed, would therefore be an act of folly.

Cultures of Proving

The practical need for proof thus remains. But what is proof? Different technical communities offer subtly different answers to this key question: they can be said to constitute different "cultures of proving." The phrase is drawn from an article by Eric Livingston,[29] but greater emphasis is placed on the plurality of cultures here than by him. He considers essentially one culture, that of mathematics,[30] while the wider domain dealt with here contains significant diversity in its cultures of proving. Compare, for example, the two extremes among the cultures described here. One is Harlan Mills's cleanroom, discussed in chapter 2. There, proof was an explicitly human and intersubjective activity, a refinement of the processes of review.

A cleanroom proof was an argument that convinced another human being: specifically, a designer's or programmer's argument that convinced fellow team members or other reviewers of the correctness of a design or program, for example, by convincing them that account had been taken of all possible cases and that the program or design would behave correctly in each case. The claim, "it is obvious," counted as a proof, if to the reviewing team what was claimed was indeed self-evident. Even the use of mathematical notation was not an essential part of proof, except, in the words of Mills and colleagues, "in its effect on the person who is the experimental subject." That cleanroom proof explicitly aimed to produce "subjective conviction" was no argument against it, because that was "the only type of reasoned conviction possible."[31] Mistakes were always possible, but systematic reasoning made human beings less error-prone, and systematic review by other people reduced mistakes even further. The trustworthy agent in cleanroom proof—not a perfect agent, but good enough in practice, according to the cleanroom's proponents—was explicitly an interacting group of human beings.

At the other extreme, the trustworthy agent of proof is taken to be the machine. The ambiguities characteristic of human deductive reasoning have to be resolved, and its tacit features made explicit, before it can be mechanized. Furthermore, human beings are prone to lapses of concentration and to wishful thinking, while machines are not: the automated theorem prover or mechanical proof checker is, in John Rushby and Friedrich von Henke's words, an "implacable skeptic."[32] Although machines can play a variety of roles in proof (arithmetical calculation, algebraic manipulation, case-by-case checking of the kind used in the proof of the four-color theorem, and so on), one particular role of the machine has dominated in the areas discussed in this book: the machine as performer of formal proof. A formal proof is a sequence of formulae in which each formula is either an axiom (a formula which is simply stipulated) or is constructed from previous formulae by application of the rules of inference of the formal system being used. These rules are syntactic in nature and apply to formulae as patterns of symbols. A pervasive example is the rule known as *modus ponens:* if p is a formula in the sequence, and $p \rightarrow q$ ("p implies q") is a formula in the sequence, then q can be added to the sequence. The rule is formal and syntactic; its application involves no appeal, at least no direct appeal, to the meaning of p and q.[33]

The notion of formal proof predates the digital computer. For example, Whitehead and Russell's *Principia Mathematica* (the source, for instance, of the theorems on which Simon, Shaw, and Newell's Logic Theory Machine was put through its paces) dates from 1910–1913. Its three large volumes were testimony to its authors' dedication to the task of founding mathematics solely on logical principles, but they were also testimony to the sheer practical difficulty of formal proof as conducted by human beings. Only limited parts of mathematics were treated directly, and so painstakingly slow was the process that theorems a mathematician would regard as elementary to the point of triviality lay hundreds of pages into the *Principia:* notoriously, that $1 + 1 = 2$ is not proved until well into the second volume.[34] When David Hilbert discussed formal proof in 1925, it was not to suggest that mathematicians should actually perform such proofs. Instead, formal proof was a tool of Hilbert's "metamathematics," a way of making proof itself a mathematical object about which one could reason mathematically.[35] As late as 1986 Eric Livingston could observe that "The representation of [mathematical] work in a formal logistic system is never carried out as a check on either one's own or on one's colleagues' work."[36]

Although that was, and indeed still is, the case within the culture of ordinary mathematics, by 1986 members of a different culture of proving—of mechanical, formal proving—were already using the machine to do that checking. The historical significance of the machine, of the digital computer, for proving is that it has turned formal proof from a tool of metamathematics to a practical possibility. In formal proof, logical deduction takes the form of syntactic pattern matching, with no requirement for "understanding" of the meaning of the formulae being processed. Formal proof's implementation on a digital computer may present practical difficulties (the theorem-proving bugs discussed in chapter 8 are evidence of this), but that it was in principle feasible was never in dispute. Formal systems consist of formulae, considered as strings of symbols, and of syntactic rules for manipulating those symbols. To check that a sequence of formulae is constructed according to syntactic rules of inference is a technologically tractable task. Finding a sequence that is a formal proof of a particular putative theorem is more difficult, but in many cases not impossible, although in the majority of the situations discussed in this book guidance from a human user ("tuning" search strategies, selecting lemmas, sometimes choosing substitution instances, and so on) is part of the process of machine proving.

Although its institutional "home" is primarily in computer science, the disciplinary culture in which formal, mechanized proving has its roots is logic rather than computing or mathematics. As seen in chapter 3, for example, logicians played an important part in the early history of automated theorem proving. Although there were other strands involved (in particular, the pioneers of artificial intelligence such as Simon, Newell, and Gelernter), the formal systems used came from logic as did many of the key ideas. Both logic and mathematics concern deductive knowledge but they are, at least to a certain extent, distinct disciplines. Although mathematical logicians are to be found in some—not all—mathematics departments, much research work in logic (including several of the developments in automated theorem proving described in chapter 3) has been conducted in philosophy departments.

At the University of Edinburgh, for example, until relatively recently only elementary logic (truth tables, quantifiers, and so on) was taught in the Mathematics Department, and students who wished to learn more advanced logic had to take a course offered by a member of the Philosophy Department, which was in a different faculty (arts rather than science). Colleagues at other universities have reported that sometimes even distinguished mathematical logicians have not been considered "real mathematicians" by their mathematical colleagues, and Ph.D. students in formal logic have encountered the attitude that their studies are not "real" mathematics.[37] Those interviewed for this book frequently drew a distinction between mathematics and logic, saying things like "I was going to be a mathematician, so I didn't learn any logic."[38]

In the words of the eminent mathematical logician Alfred Tarski, "a great achievement of modern logic" was to replace "the old psychological notion of proof, which could hardly ever be made clear and precise, by a new simple notion of a purely formal character." Up until Frege's work at the end of the nineteenth century, the concept of proof was of:

an intellectual activity that aimed at convincing oneself and others of the truth of a sentence discussed. . . . No restrictions were put on arguments used in proofs, except that they had to be intuitively convincing. . . . [A] need began to be felt for submitting the notion of proof to a deeper analysis that would result in restricting the recourse to intuitive evidence. . . . The analysis was carried out by logicians . . . it led to the introduction of a new notion, that of a *formal proof,* which turned out to be an adequate substitute and an essential improvement over the old psychological notion.[39]

The culture of proving that treats the machine as the trustworthy agent of proof is philosophically orthodox: the canonical meaning of proof in modern philosophy is formal proof. Nevertheless, commitment to philosophical orthodoxy is probably only a minor motivator of the use of formal proof by the communities discussed here (though it does, for example, appear to have played a part in Fetzer's rejection of DeMillo, Lipton, and Perlis's heterodox "social" view of proof). In most cases, it is more plausible that commitment is to the machine as trustworthy agent, and formal proof is then employed because of its technological tractability. Consider the 1991 British Interim Defence Standard,

00-55, governing safety-critical software in defense equipment, which explicitly distinguished between formal proof and what it called "rigorous argument," in other words proof "at the level of a mathematical argument in the scientific literature that will be subjected to peer review." That the ministry judged the latter to provide "a lower level of design assurance" than formal proof is not, I think, to be explained by the capture of the Ministry of Defence by philosophers.[40]

Instead, what the ministry envisaged was proofs produced by automated theorem provers and then subjected to checking by independently written programs. Automated proving and independent mechanized proof checking were conceivable if formal proof was used (although, in practice, as seen in chapter 8, such independent checking has not been commonplace), but for generic rigorous argument they were scarcely thinkable. For example, the assertion "It is obvious" is to be found not just in the cleanroom but is frequent in everyday mathematical usage, and unless the referent is a matter of algorithmic checking, or unless it is painstakingly translated into formal criteria, "It is obvious" is not a claim that a machine can evaluate. With no mechanized provers capable of constructing or even of checking the full range of rigorous arguments, those who have wanted mechanically checked proofs generally have had to insist that proofs be formal. That the commitment of agencies such as the Ministry of Defence and the National Security Agency was to mechanization, rather than to formality per se, becomes clear from the treatment of what has been in practice the most important exception to the rule that the automation of proof demands its formality: mechanized decision procedures. To agencies such as NSA these have been perfectly acceptable, even if they do not generate formal proofs.

There is, therefore, no necessary identity between "mechanized" and "formal." For example, John Rushby, whose work was discussed in chapter 8, is perfectly relaxed about the nonformalism of mechanized decision procedures that do not produce formal proofs, even if the implementation of those decision procedures is not subject to formal verification. Artificial intelligence offers quite a different motivation for breaking the equation of the mechanical and the formal. To those who, like Bledsoe (see chapter 3), wanted to create machines that proved in ways similar to how human mathematicians proved, formality in proof was not a desirable goal. Similar reasoning underpins Alan Robinson's changed view of proof, discussed later. Human deductive reasoning does not appear to be a matter of step-by-step syntactic transformation, or at least not just that, so a machine with a claim to be a "artificial mathematician" might well have to depart from formal proof.

Edsger W. Dijkstra, in contrast, is the most celebrated proponent of nonmechanized formalism. He and other proponents of what he calls "calculational" proofs believe that mathematics, including the mathematics of computer science, should be performed formally, that is, "by manipulating uninterpreted formulae accordingly to explicitly stated rules." To do otherwise is, in Dijkstra's view, to be "medieval," yet the Enlightenment that Dijkstra counterposes to medievalism is a nonmechanical Enlightenment.[41] As seen in chapter 6, Dijkstra said that he is "not interested in mechanization" of proof. There is, indeed, a significant (and to the outsider, a surprising) current of ambivalence about mechanization in the culture of elite, theoretical computer science. The iconic representation of this ambivalence is in the matter of writing.

At the start of this research, I assumed that the easiest way to contact computer scientists to set up interviews was via electronic mail. That was indeed true in many cases, but I gradually came to realize that some computer scientists were not users of electronic mail. Dijkstra has only recently begun to use it; Tony Hoare has not been an enthusiast; Peter Naur told me of his view that it promoted hasty and ill-thought-out messages.[42] Within this strand of the culture of computer science, the fountain pen, to others an archaic technology, has become something of an icon. Dijkstra's beautifully handwritten lecture notes and correspondence have become famous. One of Dijkstra's students even hand-wrote and published in handwritten form his Ph.D. thesis (figure 9.1).[43]

David Gries sees a connection between formality and the iconic matter of handwriting: "Contrast your own handwriting with the remarkably clear foils produced by the speakers this week," he told a symposium on formal methods. "Look at their handwritten lectures and papers. . . . Realizing that absolute clarity and unambiguity are necessary if formal manipulations are to be performed, and realizing that computers are not yet helpful in this regard, the speakers have consciously worked to improve their writing. And it shows. Moreover, they all carry fountain pens and, to the astonishment of their colleagues, like to talk about them."[44] More is at stake here than aesthetics (although the latter is clearly important). If proof is the nonmechanized manipulation literally by hand of uninterpreted symbols, then poor handwriting can be a source of error. Explaining a mistake in one of his proofs, Dijkstra said, "I . . . hadn't spaced my formula nicely, and as a result had erroneously parsed it."[45]

Foreword

The general Ph.D. Thesis is written for a very specific audience: the members of the Ph.D. Committee and a few close colleagues of the author. Hence, it is a rare occurrence when a Ph.D. Thesis is suitable reading for a much wider audience. The thesis of Jan L.A. van de Snepscheut is such an exception, and I applaud its inclusion in Springer's "Lecture Notes in Computer Science".

It is a text that can be read with many eyes, even with eyes looking beyond its subject matter proper. This is due to the style in which its proofs have been conducted: the proofs are in a form of annotated formal calculations we owe to W.H.J. Feijen, a form which makes the proofs as pleasant to read as they were to write down. The mere fact that this text is the first large-scale application of Feijen's discipline is, all by itself, a sufficient justification for its wider dissemination.

For those with more technical interests it has more technical charms. It is, for instance, not a mere exercise in some sort of algebra: its close connection between formalism and physical reality ranks it among the jewels of applied science. It is the first formal attack on the technically important notion of delay-insensitivity. On a more detailed level, the text is full of nuggets of mathematical technology: I mention the algorithm (plus its correctness proof) for the minimization of finite automata and the way in which the traditional problems of concatenation have been avoided by distinguishing between "components" and "commands".

Finally, I applaud its inclusion in the Lecture Notes because it is a well-written manuscript in every sense of the words.

Edsger W. Dijkstra

Figure 9.1
Foreword by Edsger W. Dijkstra to the handwritten book by Jan L. A. van de Snepscheut, *Trace Theory and VLSI Design* (Berlin: Springer 1985), pp. iii–iv.

Even those for whom the canonical notion of proof is both formal and mechanical do not form an entirely unitary culture, and the issues that divide them give evidence for David Bloor's contention that even matters of formal logic and its inference rules can be subject to sociological analysis.[46] In chapter 8 some of the choices the developers of automated provers face were seen. Which formal logic should be implemented? Should it be classical or constructive? Should the law of excluded middle be permitted? Should the fact that a contradiction implies any proposition whatsoever be regarded as an elementary theorem, or as a paradox to be avoided by the construction of a logic in which deduction is guided by relevance? Although the majority of those studied here took a relatively ecumenical and pluralistic attitude to questions such as these, not all did, and in any case the view (noted in chapter 8) that the choice of logic is a pragmatic matter, even in part "a marketing decision," is itself a socially and historically situated view.[47]

At least as important as issues of the choice of formal system—and if anything more divisive in practice—are the issues that arise in implementing a formal system on a machine. What is necessary to support the claim that a mechanized prover has performed a formal proof? Ought it to produce a full, formal proof object which can be submitted to an independent proof-checking program? Ought one seek to verify formally that a theorem-proving program has itself been implemented correctly? Is an LCF-style "secure cordon" architecture safer than other theorem-proving designs?

Surrounding this class of issues is at least a faint trace of an explicitly cultural divide between European and American computer science. "[T]he Atlantic Ocean has Two Sides," Edsger W. Dijkstra famously pointed out, and in automated theorem proving and formal methods more generally there is at least some evidence of European purism and American pragmatism. Said David Gries: "What one does see in Americans—and I am one—is a more hurried emphasis on facts and mechanical tools." Indeed, the very persona of Dijkstra—"a cultured European in a land of cowboys"—encapsulates how the divide is often seen.[48] Actual, technical differences do not follow cultural stereotypes in any straightforward sense (for example, the commitment of Boyer and Moore to rigor is at least as great as any of their European counterparts), but it is true that the main American mechanical theorem-proving systems used in verification—notably PVS and the Boyer-Moore system—are more highly automated than their European counterparts such as HOL. In particular the American systems have employed unverified decision procedures which Robin Milner, arguably the central European figure, regarded, as seen in chapter 8, as "like selling your soul to the Devil."[49]

More clear-cut in its effects than any overall differences between the wider cultures of Europe and the United States is the way in which the practicalities of building and of using theorem provers divide the culture of mechanized proving into largely disjoint, though interacting, local subcultures. Major theorem-proving systems like those discussed in chapter 8 are integrated suites of often complex programs; they represent person-decades of demanding work, substantial intellectual and, in the more commercial contexts, monetary investments. Accordingly, the main theorem provers have tended to change by evolutionary modification rather than by revolutionary discarding of what exists and starting again with a clean sheet of paper. The leading sites of theorem proving—SRI, the Boyer-Moore group at Austin, Argonne, and so on—have thus developed distinctive local "styles" of prover.

Learning to use these provers effectively also involves a major investment of time. Though a person skilled in the use of one prover can rapidly grasp the rudiments of another, developing the understanding and the skills necessary to use it to do hard proofs efficiently is not quick: as seen in chapter 8, Avra Cohn, for example, estimates that a year's work might be needed to learn to use HOL truly effectively,[50] and HOL is arguably one of the simpler provers for ease of use. Users as well as developers therefore typically switch provers only reluctantly.

One needs to be cautious, therefore, in how one interprets the relationship between theorem-proving preferences and attitudes to "philosophical" questions such as the choice of formal logics or the acceptability of unverified decision procedures. There *are* cases where philosophical preference can be seen as clearly prior to technological implementation, and as shaping the latter: Constable's constructivism discussed in chapter 8 is one. In other cases, however, people appear to have started to modify or to use a particular prover simply because it was the dominant system at their particular location. Having thus developed commitments to a particular prover, they are then led to see the virtues of the particular version of proof it performs. The consequent local subcultures of mechanized proving change, as all cultures do, and affect each other. If, for example, a particular proving technique is successfully applied in one it may well be adopted in others, at least if it can be added to existing systems rather than demanding their radical overhaul.

These subcultures nevertheless manifest relative coherence and continuity through time. They are recognizably part of an overall culture of mechanized proving. Their sense of common participation in a joint enterprise no doubt helps explain why different theorem-proving preferences have seldom spilled over into public controversy, but the anchoring of subcultures in investments in their theorem provers has been the most important way in which that overall culture has been structured. In contrast, local traditions on matters not anchored in differences between theorem provers have tended to be less persistent. For example, the divide discussed in chapter 7 between the Boyer-Moore group and SRI on matters of design proof, code proof, and hardware proof is now much less sharp than it was in the early 1980s.

Model checking, discussed in chapter 7, potentially offers yet another variant of the culture of mechanized proving, one that has spread from academia to industry more quickly than automated theorem proving of the type described in chapters 3 and 8. What model checking enables one to do is to construct two abstract machines, one representing the specification of a system, the other its implementation, and "to compare *all possible* behaviors of the two machines."[51] The status of model checking is not entirely agreed. "I agree [that] it's proof," said automated theorem proving researcher Alan Bundy, "but some don't agree. They see it as massive testing."[52]

Furthermore, complex questions are raised by the simplifications that may be necessary to keep numbers of states finite and model checking tractable. "Technically, I'm not convinced that 'model checking' is the same as proof," said British formal methods specialist Cliff Jones. "The finiteness restriction means that in all but special cases model checking cannot provide a positive result about all inputs."[53] To date, the status of the various forms of model checking as proof has scarcely mattered because in its industrial applications it appears to be treated more as a debugging tool, for finding design faults, rather than as a verification tool, for demonstrating that a design is a correct implementation of its specification. If model checking starts to be used more heavily in verification, however, then a crucial new strand—more than just another local subculture—will be added to mechanized proving.

The cultures of mechanized proving do not exist in isolation from the wider society. Model checking's automaticity is one reason for its acceptance, but also important was the Pentium divide bug, described in chapter 7, which demonstrated vividly to the microprocessor industry that societal acceptance of even minor design faults could not be taken for granted. The single most important connection, however, between mechanized proving and the wider culture was the Cold War, the concerns for computer security it generated, and the desire of bodies like the National Security Agency for systems that were proved to be secure. National security was for many years the dominant source of funds for the development of automated provers, at least in the United States. The American "pragmatism" in theorem proving referred to above results in good part from the demands of this milieu: as seen in chapter 5, NSA and other defense interests wanted not elegant exercises in computer science but provers that could verify complex designs.

The demands of security, furthermore, offer an interesting window on the matter of trust. Automated theorem provers do not entirely eliminate the need for trusted human users. As seen in chapter 8, key American systems of the 1980s were judged to have "some areas of unsoundness" that might require user expertise to "avoid" or "finesse." Furthermore, in using these and other systems to perform verifications, human users frequently found they needed to assume lemmas (intermediate steps toward a proof) that their automated system could not prove. Trust in users' competence and in their commitment to rigor could therefore not be circumvented altogether: recall, for instance, J Strother Moore's list, quoted in chapter 8, of examples of individuals whose commitment to soundness he trusted. The demands of security, however, deepen the question of trust beyond issues of competence and commitment to rigor. The possibility has to be considered (and if possible guarded against technologically in the design of theorem provers, such as by the elimination of HOL's **mk_thm**) that a user could be untrustworthy in a far more profound sense and might try to subvert security by constructing spurious proofs of its implementation. The demands of a world in which trust is problematic thus highlight its usually unnoticed extent and foundational role outside of that world.

Mathematics

Although ordinary academic mathematics shares with mechanized theorem proving (outside of the sphere of security) a culture in which members are trusted not to produce deliberately deceptive "proofs," it is worth reflecting upon the wider contrast between its culture and that of mechanized proving. The nature of proof in ordinary mathematics is, as noted in chapter 1, a topic that has received little attention in the modern social studies of science. Nevertheless, one thing that can be said with some confidence is that proof as ordinarily conducted in mathematics is not formal proof in the sense used here. If one opens the pages of a standard mathematics research journal one is most unlikely to find a formal proof in that sense.[54]

A textbook of proving for mathematics students notes that "[T]he fundamentals of mathematical proof have rarely been taught in a systematic way. Most students of mathematics are expected to develop their understanding of proof and the associated theorem-proving skills by a process of 'osmosis' through encounters with the various techniques and methods. . . . [T]he notion of 'formal proof' is covered well in many books on mathematical logic, but the proofs that mathematicians write are not formal proofs in this sense."[55] Sociologist Eric Livingston commented: "[M]athematical rigor consists of the local work of producing and exhibiting, for and among mathematicians, a 'followable' . . . line of mathematical argumentation." "Following" a proof is more than reading it line-by-line, and certainly more than checking that each line is a syntactically correct transformation of previous lines. It is following the reasoning to which the written proof is a guide. "[P]rovers," wrote Livingston, "look for the coherence of reasoning—the gestalt—of which the . . . proof consists."[56]

Given that ordinary mathematical proofs are not usually sequences of applications of syntactic inference rules like *modus ponens,* what are they? Apart from one interview with the leading British mathematician Sir Michael Atiyah (drawn on below), the only mathematicians interviewed at length for this book were those involved in the proof of the four-color theorem or skeptics about computerized proof and so their views cannot be assumed to be representative. Nevertheless, comments by two of them on the nature of mathematical proof are of some interest. Asked "How would you explain to me what a proof is?" one interviewee answered:

Certainly it's a very sensible question to ask, and I think it's not answerable in short terms. I think what you have to do is to show . . . the best examples you can think of, of proofs which establish something that's not quite obvious, but establish [it] so that if you've understood what [the proof has] done, you're completely convinced. You know that's right, it couldn't be wrong, it's right. And I think if they've seen a few examples of this kind, they can begin to understand what a proof is, even though you don't try to state it in words.

As a professor of mathematics, "you hope" that eventually students "will cotton on" to what proof is. "And the good mathematicians, I think, do. Those who don't, I'm afraid, don't become mathematicians."[57]

Daniel I. A. Cohen, a critic of the Appel-Haken solution, gave a broadly similar answer. Though he teaches in a computer science department, he was trained as a mathematician and said he "would never use a computer" in proof, "because I would lose touch [with] understanding," and mathematics "is supposed to . . . give you understanding. That's what's wrong with predicate calculus . . . understanding cannot be part of logic, because it's . . . a psychological event. There has to be a psychological event that takes place." Reflecting upon how he taught what proof is to Harvard mathematics graduate students, Cohen said:

> [he] demonstrated it, like I demonstrate ice-skating. Even without using a word I can demonstrate ice-skating; and now I push you onto the ice—you'll fall a few times, but eventually you can skate. Now, that's how I'm doing it. That's what we're doing here. We're learning to skate—sensitivity, taste, aesthetics, we're learning to paint, we're not learning to type, we're not learning how to do long division. For long division, I can give you the set of rules. But anything you can learn by a complete set of rules isn't worth knowing, leave it to androids.[58]

What both these sets of comments have in common is that they are ostensive: mathematical proof is not defined other than by pointing to instances of proofs. The interviewees are no doubt untypical, and an interview is not an easy situation in which to construct a formal definition, but I suspect a deeper difficulty. If mathematical proof is not to be defined as formal proof—and the disadvantage of such a definition is that it would imply that what most mathematicians do is not proof—then what alternative is there to ostention? The *Oxford Dictionary of Philosophy*'s "procedure that brings conviction" hardly helps.[59] Gödel's incompleteness theorem appears to suggest the impossibility of constructing a finite list of all mathematical proof procedures: it "demands the . . . conclusion that there can be no definitive answer to the question 'What is a valid proof?' "[60]

Of mathematical proof, then, it can be said (in the words of a more general sociological analysis of science) that there is "no specification or template or algorithm fully formed in the present, capable of fixing the future correct use of the term, of distinguishing in advance all the things to which it will eventually be correctly applicable."[61] Emphatically, though, this does not imply that "anything goes," that any arbitrary argument can count as a mathematical proof. What it suggests, rather, is that the members of the relevant specialist mathematical community, in interaction with each other, come to a collective judgment as to what counts as a mathematical proof. "[W]hen people look at [mathematics] from a purely logical, philosophical point of view they just see a little side of it," said Michael Atiyah. "[A] step in a mathematical argument is not a one-line syllogism, it is in fact an encapsulation of a hundred years of mathematics which has been shortcut into one word. . . . [T]here's a certain amount of sociology in mathematics . . . [T]here is a certain amount of sociology for proof—what is acceptable at any given moment as a statement that people think they understand. . . . [I]t changes over time."[62] The last is certainly what the history of mathematics suggests. "Standards of rigor have changed in mathematics," wrote Israel Kleiner, "and not always from less rigor to more. The notion of proof is not absolute. Mathematicians' views of what constitutes an acceptable proof have evolved."[63]

The Hilbert-Brouwer dispute over the acceptability of proofs invoking the law of the excluded middle, touched on in chapter 8, is perhaps the most obvious case of variability in the kinds of arguments that are accepted by mathematicians as constituting proof, but other examples can be found in the work of Kleiner and historians such as Judith Grabiner, Joan Richards, and Massimo Mazzotti.[64] Nor has debate over proof ceased. The 1990s saw sharp debate among mathematicians about rigor and proof, debate focused most clearly by a 1993 article by Arthur Jaffe and Frank Quinn warning of threats to mathematical rigor, especially in work such as in string theory at the intersection of physics and mathematics. Jaffe and Quinn warned that although this work can produce "new insights into mathematics," the physicists doing it "are still working in the speculative and intuitive mode of theoretical physics. Many have neither training for nor interest in rigor," while those mathematicians involved "are unused to dealing with the difference in cultures" and do not fully recognize the "hazards" involved. Jaffe and Quinn's paper sparked fierce debate in which mathematicians criticized them from all sides, both for allegedly overgreat sympathy for physics and physical reasoning and for an allegedly sclerotic overemphasis on rigor. Although most of this debate was conducted at a general level, in one case at least clearly divergent assessments of a particular proof emerged.[65]

The basis of a sociology of ordinary "rigorous-argument" mathematical proof is thus that there is no abstract, context-free way of demarcating what constitutes a proof; that there is no higher criterion than the judgment of the adequacy of a putative proof by the members of the relevant specialist mathematical community; and that judgments can both vary at any given time and change through time. That the general outline of a sociology of mathematical proof is clear, however, is not to say that the detail is satisfactory: for example, no more than a few case studies have been seen of what causes judgments to change. Eric Livingston is one of the few sociologists who has grasped that there is something profoundly interesting and puzzling about ordinary mathematical proof, yet even he has not published the ethnographic work needed to provide clear insight into the processes by which, in the absence of any definitive abstract criterion, some arguments and not others achieve the status of "proof."[66]

Note that, as suggested in chapter 1, such a study would not be a "zero-sum" investigation of social processes within the mathematical community overriding mathematical considerations. It would be a study of how those considerations are shaped, refined—and almost certainly improved—in processes of social interaction. Ethnography may be necessary for such a study because face-to-face communication appears to be of great importance in mathematics, at least since around 1900. For example, one study of scientific communication by John Walsh and Todd Bayma suggests that travel is more important in mathematics than in other disciplines:

Interviewer: It seems that mathematicians travel more than other fields.
Mathematician: Yes. They have to. The way mathematicians write and talk are two different things. We write very proper, formal, very abstract. We think informally, intuitively. None of that is in the publication. When we get together we ask, "What does that mean?" I pity the fool who is off by himself reading the journals. The dean asking him, "Why can't you do it?" Unless you're in a new area of your own. You don't write insight, intuition, what got left out because of lack of room. That is very critical. Travel is our lab.[67]

Mathematics is ordinarily thought of as a solitary activity, and as Thomas Tymoczko has argued the notion of a "single isolated" mathematician implicitly underpins much of the philosophy of mathematics.[68] In contrast, I would conjecture that mathematics may be the most social of the non-experimental disciplines, the one in which the intensity of professional interaction is the greatest (at least, this would be an interesting hypothesis to test empirically, perhaps by measuring the proportion of time spent in professional interaction). There is no full analogue within mathematics to experiments in the natural sciences, or, for example, to historians' use of primary sources; so where can mathematical ideas and mathematical proofs better be tested than in interaction with other mathematicians? DeMillo, Lipton, and Perlis's view of automated theorem proving may be flawed (see below), but there is surely merit to their emphasis on the role of social processes in mathematical proof. Proof, arguably, is intrinsically a public, social act: in Tymoczko's words, "a message, a communication among mathematicians." That is not to say that mathematicians do not prove results to themselves, in private—

obviously, they do—but the "private act" of proving "derives from the public act and not vice versa," in much the same way as the private use of speech or writing (in talking to one's self, or writing a note to be read only by one's self) derives from their public use.[69]

As Yuri I. Manin put it: "Proof is not just an argument convincing an imaginary opponent. Not at all. Proof is the way we communicate mathematical truth." Nor is the only criterion that a proof convinces one of the correctness of a result: a "good" proof is supposed also to convey insight. Beyond all the reservations about Appel and Haken's use of the computer lay a further dissatisfaction with a proof that was often seen as not helping one understand why the four-color theorem was true. In Manin's words, "A good proof is a proof that makes us wiser. If the heart of the proof is a voluminious [sic] search or a long string of identities, it is probably a bad proof. If something is so isolated that it is sufficient to get the result popped up on the screen or a computer, then it is probably not worth doing. Wisdom lives in connections."[70]

If in learning to prove one is learning "aesthetics," if a proof is a "message," if a "good proof . . . makes us wiser," then the rigorous-argument proofs of ordinary mathematics are "polimorphic actions," in the terminology of Harry Collins and Martin Kusch, actions in which human beings "draw on their understanding of their society,"[71] in this case of the mathematical community. A sense of audience is crucial to this form of proving: a sense of what listeners or readers will know, and of what will be enlightening; of what the audience will understand, and what they will not; of what needs to be spelt out, and what can be covered by phrases such as "it is obvious that . . .," or "we can show similarly that . . ." or "without loss of generality, we can assume that . . ."; and so on. Formal proof, in contrast, is arguably "mimeomorphic action," in Collins and Kusch's terms, action "where exact reproduction of the behavior by someone who did not understand the action would always appear to reproduce the action to someone who did understand the action."[72] If this is correct, then one can see why the rigorous-argument proving of ordinary mathematics is hard to tear out of its social context, and thus one of the reasons why it is hard to automate and why, in contrast, formal proof has been relatively readily susceptible to mechanization.

Unity or Diversity?

Two key cultures of proving have been identified: that of formal, mechanized proof and that of ordinary mathematics. Although other variants exist (the cleanroom; Dijkstra's nonmechanical formalism), and neither culture is unitary, these two cultures are central. What is the relationship between what they do? There is widespread conviction among those whose work is studied here, and in mathematics and logic more generally, that the "rigorous-argument" proofs of ordinary mathematics, in principle, could be replaced by formal proofs. The former are often seen as sketches of formal proofs: arguments with gaps that could, in principle, be filled by series of applications of laws of logical inference. Until the development of the automated systems described in this book, the possibility of the replacement of rigorous-argument proofs by formal proofs was more an article of faith than an empirical fact. In 1957 the logician Peter Nidditch wrote that: "Since no mathematician has ever constructed a complete [formal] proof, his reputed capacity for doing so has no better status than an occult quality."[73] In the decades since then, however, many rigorous arguments in ordinary mathematics have been replaced successfully by formal proofs, using automated theorem provers and proof checkers, especially the AUTOMATH and MIZAR systems touched on in chapter 3. There are still many rigorous-argument proofs in mathematics that cannot currently be replaced by formal proofs. For example, the translation of Andrew Wiles's proof of Fermat's last theorem into a form in which it is checked using an automated system is unlikely in the near term, but there appears to be no convincing reason in principle why this replacement will not eventually be possible.

In particular, the extent to which Gödel's incompleteness theorem forms a barrier should not be overstated. What Gödel showed was that any consistent formal system powerful enough to encompass arithmetic must contain a formula for which there is no formal proof or disproof within the system. The theorem, however, allows for the possibility that the formula might be provable formally using a more powerful formal system, even though that more powerful system will itself contain further incompleteness. Thus, as seen in chapter 8, the Paris-Harrington theorem, a Gödelian incompleteness in elementary number theory, was proved by logician Kenneth Kunen using the Boyer-Moore prover, which supports a form of induction more powerful than that permitted in the standard axiomatization of arithmetic.

What is most remarkable about these many replacements of the rigorous arguments of mathematics with formal, mechanized proofs is a fact that seldom attracts comment.[74] In practice, it is a conservative process. Applied to programs, hardware designs, and system designs, efforts at formal, mechanical proof frequently find faults and deficiences that have not been detected by other means; that, indeed, is a key aspect of their practical importance. Applied to rigorous arguments within mathematics, however, efforts at mechanized proof nearly always suggest at most the need to remedy matters that a mathematician would regard as basically trivial, such as typographic errors or failures to state the full range of conditions necessary for a theorem to hold. (Part of the reason for the contrast is that a slip that may be trivial in ordinary mathematics may be fatal in computer programming or in hardware design.)

Research for this book has been unable to find a case in which the application of mechanized proof threw doubt upon an established mathematical theorem and only one case in which it showed the need significantly to modify an accepted rigorous-argument proof.[75] This is testimony to the robustness of the "social processes" of proof within mathematics described by DeMillo, Lipton, and Perlis. Individual mathematicians may make errors, and papers with proofs that are subsequently found to require significant revision may find their way into the literature, but well-established results in fields where the Lakatosian proof-refining, definition-adjusting processes have reached a stable state, with proofs that have been checked and rechecked many times by human mathematicians, do not crumble upon the application of formal, mechanized proof.

The conservative nature of formal, mechanized proof, when applied to established rigorous-argument proof, can indeed be taken as evidence for the view that a rigorous-argument proof is a sketch that can be translated into a formal proof. Nevertheless, a subtly different interpretation is possible and was put forward by the mathematical logician Jon Barwise in a comment on the dispute begun by James Fetzer's critique of program verification. Barwise rightly noticed that the fierce controversy masked considerable areas of agreement among Fetzer and his critics. Not only did they agree that mathematical proof could be applied only to a mathematical model, not to physical objects, but Fetzer, as an "orthodox" philosopher, and his critics, as proponents of automated theorem proving, took the canonical notion of proof to be formal proof. In this tacit agreement, said Barwise, both sides "stumble over a landmine left by the retreating formalists"; both believed that a "real proof" was a formal one. "[A]t the risk of stepping on the toes of my fellow mathematical logicians," Barwise argued that it was not. Formal proof was only a model of real proof, indeed a "severely impoverished" model:

[T]here are many perfectly good proofs that are not modeled in any direct way by a formal proof in any current deductive system. For example, consider proofs where one establishes one of several cases and then observes that the others follow by symmetry considerations. This is a perfectly valid (and ubiquitous) form of mathematical reasoning, but I know of no system of formal deduction that admits of such a general rule. They can't, because it is not, in general, something one can determine from local, syntactic features of a proof. . . . [I]t could be that the best proofs (in the sense of being most enlightening or easiest to understand) of a program's correctness will use methods, like symmetry considerations, that are not adequately modeled in the logician's notion of formal proof, and so which would not be deemed correct by some automated proof checker designed around the formalist's model.[76]

Instead of seeing rigorous argument as a sketch of real, formal proof, Barwise thus argued that formal proof is a partially adequate model of real, rigorous-argument proof. These subtly different interpretations of the translatability of rigorous-argument proof into formal proof, and different views of what constitutes "real" proof, indicate that though not inherently opposed, rigorous-argument proof and formal proof are available to be counterposed. In the area discussed here, their counterposing often implicitly or explicitly indicates a preference for formal proof. For example, the 1991 British Interim Defence Standard governing safety-critical software in defense equipment explicitly stated a preference for formal proof. Nevertheless, that judgment is not universal. DeMillo, Lipton, and Perlis's attack on program proof rested upon the claim that rigorous argument is superior to formal proof, and Martyn Thomas's defense of the claim of proof for VIPER (chapter 7) was also based upon a defense of rigorous argument against formal proof.

Even among central figures in automated proving one can sometimes find a preference for rigorous argument expressed. In the article describing their verification of the clock convergence algorithm, John Rushby and Friedrich von Henke wrote of their desire "to obtain a genuine proof—that is, a chain of argument that will convince a human reviewer rather than a mere grunt of assent from a mechanical theorem prover." According to Rushby and von Henke, automated proofs should be conducted in such a way that from them there can be extracted a description that is "very close to a proof that can accompany a journal-style presentation of the verification." Their belief that "genuine proof" was rigorous argument, they argued, had consequences for how an automated prover should be constructed. Techniques such as resolution "work in ways that do not lend themselves to the extraction of a proof." Furthermore, some automated systems "require, or strongly encourage, a bottom up development in which only previously proven lemmas can be cited in a new proof. This is not the way real mathematics is performed: one generally prefers to know whether a proposed lemma is adequate to its intended use before attempting to prove it." The relative attractiveness of rigorous-argument proof and formal proof, for Rushby and von Henke, was thus not merely a matter of overall preference but a factor that ought to influence the detailed design of a theorem prover.[77]

Even Alan Robinson, developer of resolution, has become a proponent of rigorous argument rather than of formal proof. Over the years that followed his early-1960s breakthrough, Robinson gradually became disillusioned with the automation of formal proof. The results on the complexity of theorem proving described in chapter 3 left him convinced that "you're not going to get very far just by crunching out searches." For a while he hoped that by theoretical work he could "do another coup like resolution." Gradually, however, "I really got pushed back into philosophy . . . again, by asking myself, 'What the hell is a proof anyway?' " He became convinced that formal proofs performed by automated theorem provers, including those implementing his own technique of resolution, missed what he called "the heart of this problem," which is "first of all to say what it is about a proof that makes it intelligible," and, secondly, to automate that rigorous-argument reasoning. He pointed to examples, often geometric in nature, of arguments that are difficult to formalize without losing their simplicity or compelling nature. His favorite example is the mutilated chessboard problem (figure 9.2), the solution of which is an argument of this kind. It has been formalized, indeed proved with automated theorem provers, but Robinson's claim is that such formalizations and mechanizations are less convincing than the simple argument in the caption of figure 9.2.[78]

Whatever the relationship in principle between formal proof and rigorous argument, in practice the cultures of formal, mechanized proof and of ordinary mathematics generate significantly different corpuses of "proven" knowledge. In the former culture, "we allow . . . as proofs . . . derivations that are too big, or too combinatorially complicated, to be checked by a person,"[79] while ordinary mathematics allows as proofs many arguments that have not been, and currently could not be, formalized (in the sense in which the term is used within the culture of mechanized proving) and checked mechanically. Statements of preference for rigorous-argument proof over formal proof, or vice versa, usually stop short of denying that the less favored alternative is proof and of asserting that the corpus of knowledge verifiable only by its application is

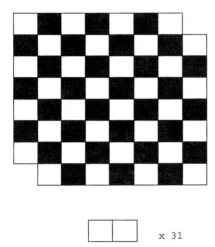

x 31

Figure 9.2
The mutilated chessboard. Two diagonally opposite corner squares are excised from a chessboard. Can the remaining 62 squares be covered entirely by 31 dominoes, each of which covers two squares? The answer is "no." An unmutilated chessboard has an equal number of squares (32) of each color. The two excised squares must be the same color, so there remain two squares more of one color than of the other. Whenever we lay a domino, it covers one square of each color. After laying 30 dominoes, the last two uncovered squares must be the same color, and the 31st domino therefore cannot cover them. See Max Black, *Critical Thinking: An Introduction to Logic and Scientific Method* (New York: Prentice-Hall, 1946), pp. 142 and 394.

therefore defective and its contents not theorems. Nevertheless, that denial can be found. DeMillo, Lipton, and Perlis argued, in effect, that because program verifications were formal proofs, and because what mathematicians did was rigorous argument not formal proof, program verifications were therefore not proofs and their results not theorems.

In 1957 the logician Peter Nidditch came close to the opposite claim, when he argued that what mathematicians do is not fully valid proof:

In the whole literature of mathematics there is not a single valid proof in the logical sense. . . . The number of original books or papers on mathematics in the course of the last 300 years is of the order of 10^6; in these, the number of even close approximations to really valid proofs is of the order of 10^1. . . . In the relatively few places where a mathematician has seriously tried to give a valid proof, he has always overlooked at least some of the rules of inference and logical theorems of which he has made use and to which he has made no explicit reference. . . .

In addition, in these places, the mathematician has failed to pay sufficient critical attention to purely mathematical points of detail.[80]

In a broadly similar vein, Roger Jones, a key figure in the development of the ProofPower version of the HOL automated theorem prover discussed in chapter 8, comments that even as an undergraduate, taking a joint degree in mathematics and philosophy, "If I weren't already annoyed by the vagueness of what constitutes a mathematics proof, I would still have been utterly infuriated by the fact that they'd change the rules of the game at every turn. . . . I was . . . always dissatisfied with the notion of proof that was used by mathematicians. . . . I'm a dyed-in-the-wool logicist to this day. . . . [M]athematics . . . is, effectively, reducible to logic."[81]

Nidditch's and Jones's comments are critiques of ordinary rigorous-argument mathematical proof from the viewpoint of logic. Dijkstra offers a similar critique from the viewpoint of his nonmechanical formalism. One of his famous, widely circulated handwritten memoranda, dating from 1988, was caustically entitled "Real Mathematicians Don't Prove." For Dijkstra the struggle in computing between formalists and "real programmers" (who "don't reason about their programs, for reasoning isn't macho") was part of a wider battle pervading "the rest of mathematics" between formalists and " 'informalists'—only they don't call themselves by that negative name: presumably they present themselves as 'the real mathematicians'—who constantly interpret their formulae and 'reason' in terms of the model underlying that interpretation." By rejecting formalism, with its clear distinction between "provability" and "the fuzzy metaphysical notion of 'truth,' " mathematics remained "still a discipline with a sizeable pre-scientific component, in which the spirit of the Middle Ages is allowed to linger on." Among its "medieval characteristics" was that "how to *do* mathematics is not taught explicitly but only by osmosis, as in the tradition of the guilds."[82]

It should be emphasized, however, that explicit attacks from one culture of proving on another are unusual. Among those studied in this book, it is more common to allow both the rigorous arguments of ordinary mathematics and formal, mechanized deductions as proofs, and little effort is devoted to arguing for the superiority of one over the other. This ecumenicism extends even to more detailed matters such as the choice of formal logic to be implemented in a theorem prover: the modern divide between "classical" and "constructive" theorem proving is marked by almost none of the philosophical bitterness to be found in the earlier Hilbert-Brouwer controversy. To borrow a metaphor productively employed by historian of physics Peter Galison, the domain of proof by and about computers has something of the characteristics of what anthropologists call a "trading zone": a site where diverse cultures coordinate their practical activities while maintaining distinct understandings of the meaning of what they do and of what they exchange.

For example, Galison shows that different groups of specialists in the simulation technique known as Monte Carlo modeling had different understandings of the key notion of "randomness," but they still were able to communicate well enough to work together productively. Discrepant understandings, a lack of conceptual unity, are not a weakness, Galison argued: "It is the *disorder* of the scientific community—the laminated, finite, partially independent strata supporting one another; it is the *dis*-unification of science—the intercalation of *different* patterns of argument—that is responsible for its strength and coherence."[83]

Proof by and about computers is not, at least not yet, a trading zone as developed as some of those described by Galison. Thus, at one of the sites he has studied, the World War II MIT Radiation Laboratory which was responsible for radar development, the different technical cultures involved (such as theoretical physics and radio engineering) were transformed in ways that went beyond the translation of terms from the one into the language of the other.[84] In contrast, it is still more accurate to talk of mathematicians' rigorous-argument proofs being "translated" into formal, mechanical ones rather than of the former being transformed by mechanization. But even in this less intense trading zone, Galison's central insight that diversity brings strength is surely correct. This is especially the case when one moves away from mathematics (where important theorems will often have been proved in several different ways anyway, so that mechanized, formal proof is simply a small addition to the diversity) to critical computer systems, where mechanized proof is potentially a vital addition to existing approaches to verification such as testing and review. DeMillo, Lipton, and Perlis were right to contrast the strong social processes of mathematics with the weak ones of computer-system verification, but in attacking the latter they drew precisely the wrong conclusion. Where social processes are weak, the mechanized sceptic is the more valuable.

Furthermore, in some areas of the trading zone constituted by proof by and about computers, the intensity of interchange is increasing. The rapid uptake of model checking in hardware design is a good example. It is unlikely that many engineers who use model checking fully understand the intellectual roots of much of the latter field in formal temporal logic: they do not need to. When cultures meet, pidgins, "contact languages," impoverished by the standards of their parent languages but adequate for the purposes of communication, can suffice.[85] It is still too early to say whether the adoption of model checking (and possibly also of theorem-proving techniques) will transform hardware design and verification, but it is a possibility.

Logic, too, may eventually be transformed by its central role in this trading zone. Modern formal logic was to a substantial extent shaped by the desire adequately to model processes of deduction within mathematics: for example, an acknowledged weak point of Whitehead and Russell's *Principia Mathematica* was its "axiom of reducibility," a somewhat ad hoc addition to its central logical structure, needed to preserve the validity of much of ordinary mathematical reasoning, such as the basic theorem of real analysis that "every bounded set of real numbers has a least upper bound."[86] For a deductive system to have appeared to require the outlawing of routine mathematical practices and proofs would have carried a high price. Constructivism (see chapter 8) paid that price, with many mathematicians sharing Hilbert's fear that it would leave them with only "wretched remnants" of their subject.[87]

There is reason to think, however, that formal logic, long shaped by the exigencies of its relationship to mathematics, is now starting to march to the beat of a different drummer: computer science. Constructivism's popularity in computer science, which contrasts sharply with its limited attractiveness to mathematicians, can be explained by the fact that, to a significant number of computer scientists, constructivism appears a productive not a restrictive enterprise, in particular allowing the extraction of programs from proofs. Nonclassical logics, unsuitable for modeling mathematical reasoning, are no longer simply philosophers' playthings but are being used to model the operations of machines in situations in which those involved often believe that the use of classical logic would be cumbersome or incorrect. "Specifying and reasoning about the behaviour of computer programs takes us into the realm of logic," said Samson Abramsky, one of the many logicians now working in computer science. To begin with, "logic could be taken 'as it was'—static and timeless," suitable for modeling the apparently timeless truths of mathematics. "Getting an adequate account" of the world of distributive, interactive computing, however, "may require a fundamental reconceptualization of logic itself."[88] That conclusion is speculative, but it is worth reemphasizing that it was temporal logic, not standard predicate logic, that inspired model checking. It may well be that the modeling of machines will require richer logics than the modeling of mathematics, and that logic itself will be changed fundamentally by its involvement in this trading zone.

What Machines Don't Do

There are, therefore, intellectual as well as practical reasons for welcoming both proof about machines and machine proof. Yet—if only for the Turklean reason that the computer matters as an "evocative object," not just practically—it is important also to remain aware of the machine's limitations. By this, I do not mean what machines might, or might not, eventually be able to do: I am happy to leave that issue to philosophers like Hubert Dreyfus, and I am warier than he of the capacity of technologists to confound theorists of all stripes by achieving things believed impossible.[89] Rather, I am concerned with what mechanized proving systems of the kind discussed here, and easily anticipatable developments of them, can and cannot do. Examining this will, for example, enable us to unpack a key ambiguity in the phrase "machine proof."

Five closely related limitations are important. First, machines operate within formal systems; they do not change formal systems, nor choose between them, nor modify definitions, in Lakatosian manner, to suit the demands of evolving proofs. Human beings do those things. Second, many of the judgments that mathematicians make—between a "deep" theorem and a trivial deduction, between a proof that is "elegant" or "natural" and one that lacks these qualities—escape the capacities of current machines.[90] Third, the mechanized provers discussed here at most simulate individual mathematicians working in isolation.[91] Among the mechanized activities examined here, perhaps the closest analogue of the interaction between human mathematicians is the running of a proof produced by one program through a different proof-checking program. Line-by-line syntactic checking of this sort, however, is only a small part of the way mathematical knowledge and mathematical proofs are evaluated, transmitted, and modified communally.

All of these first three matters are the subjects of current research. An Edinburgh colleague Alan Bundy, for example, has started work on an automated system that he hopes will perform Lakatosian definition-modification.[92] Multiagent systems for the automation of mathematical reasoning, involving a number of different programs that run independently but which communicate with each other, are under development, though whether they will be able to achieve anything approaching the richness of interaction between human mathematicians remains to be seen.[93] A fourth and more profound issue, however, is that it is human judgment not the machine or any algorithm that decides whether a formal specification captures how a system should behave, or whether a formal expression captures the mathematical theorem or object system it is intended to.

The latter is more of an issue than might at first sight appear: Randy Pollack reported two months of theorem proving in the λ-calculus based upon a set of definitions that contained an undetected typographical error. The theorems proved, while correct derivations, were not proofs about the intended object system.[94] Commented Pollack:

What we usually call a "formal system," say first-order logic, or primitive recursive arithmetic, exists on blackboards, in textbooks, in our intentions; it is *informal*. Even when printed in a textbook its meaning depends on much that is unstated, and may be interpreted differently by different readers. . . . The job of a proof system implementor is to produce a correct [mechanized] implementation, but since intention is *informal* and implementation is formal, there is a gap between different categories.[95]

As Robin Milner put it, "the glue," connecting formal proof to the world of mathematics or of technology, "is informal."[96] Whether a formal specification is appropriate, or whether a formal expression captures the intended "meaning" of a theorem or of an intended object system, are informal matters checkable neither by any current machine nor by any machine that can easily be anticipated.

Finally, and most importantly, even within a given formal system, the machine does not serve as the ultimate criterion of correctness. The point is most easily made by analogy with arithmetic. Electronic calculators perform arithmetic more reliably than nearly all individual human beings, yet when machine output diverges from collective convictions, as happens more often than naive users might imagine, it is human arithmetic that is the criterion by which the machine is judged, not vice versa.[97] It was never in doubt, for example, that the Pentium divide bug led to error, not to new discoveries in arithmetic.

The theorem-proving bugs discussed in chapter 8 are the equivalent phenomenon for machine proof. At least in the area of computer system verification, an automated prover may be more reliable than an individual human prover, but when the results of machine proof diverge from our collective convictions, it is we who judge which will prevail. A theorem-proving bug may enable one to "prove" that $1 = 0$, but we do not thereby admit that result into the corpus of mathematics. Rather, we search for the fault in the design or in the implementation of the theorem prover that has led to what we know is error. In a more complex case we may be prepared, after examining the reasons for the discrepancy between the machine's results and ours, to entertain the possibility of deeming the machine to be right and previous human consensus to be wrong. Even in that kind of case, however, it is we, not the machine, who make the judgment.

Normativity—the capacity to distinguish between correct and erroneous deductions—remains vested ultimately in the human collectivity. As David Bloor has argued, the isolated human individual has no way of distinguishing between being right and believing one is right.[98] The individual machine is no better placed, nor would we human beings be if we elected to treat it as canonical.[99] If normativity were vested in the operations of the machine, the possibility of identifying those operations as being in error, of us talking meaningfully about theorem-proving "bugs," would not exist for those operations would define correct deduction.

The key question was asked long ago by philosopher Ludwig Wittgenstein: what if the machine breaks? What of the possibility of its parts "bending, breaking off, melting, and so on?"[100] When that happens, the machine's role as the servant of the human collectivity becomes clear. Its actions are not the ultimate criterion of what is correct arithmetic or valid proof. There is a sense, then, in which it is incorrect to say that a calculator performs arithmetic or that a computer performs proof. It is *we*, sociologist of science Harry Collins points out, who turn an electronic calculator "from a box which produces series of flashes on a liquid crystal display into something which 'does arithmetic.' "[101] Similarly, it is we who allow or disallow what a machine does as constituting proof. In that sense, it is we who turn a workstation running a program manipulating binary digits representing strings of symbols into a proving machine.

It is possible that a culture may emerge that will treat the machine as canonical. With electronic calculators that has already happened to a degree. Among the courses that I teach is one in elementary statistics. Recently, I set my students an exercise that involved them working out an expected frequency by performing the calculation: $(400/1200) \times 588$. Many of them turned to their calculators and produced results such as 195.9998. They did not pause to perform by hand the canceling and simple division that shows the result to be exactly 196. A more experienced group, if they had used calculators at all, would immediately have suspected round-off error and treated the hand calculation, not the machine one, as canonical.

To date, automated theorem provers have remained the preserve of the mathematically sophisticated: they are hard to use, requiring not just facility with the formal system they implement, but considerable "hands on" experience before they can be used effectively to perform hard proofs. Model checkers, however, are something of a departure in this respect. Their use is much more "push button," and that is a large part of the reason for their industrial acceptance. Those who use them may thus be tempted to treat them as oracles, especially under commercial pressure to certify a design as correct and to do so quickly. Their current predominant industrial use as debuggers, as machines that find mistakes in designs rather than certify their absence, does not produce that danger. It is perfectly possible, however, that model checkers will start to be used as verifiers as well as debuggers and in that context they could become dangerously canonical.

There is also another way in which undue trust can be placed in the results of proving machines. This is what I have called elsewhere "the certainty trough" (see figure 9.3).[102] Those at intermediate social distances from the production of technical knowledge (for example,

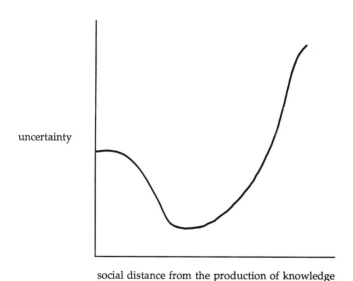

Figure 9.3
The certainty trough.

managers without direct "hands-on" involvement) sometimes appear to evince greater certainty than those who take part directly in its production. The strongest claims for the proof of VIPER, for example, were made not by those directly involved in the proof, but by those responsible for "selling" the technology, literally or metaphorically, and by those reporting on the proof in the press; the strongest warnings of its limitations came from one of those most intimately involved, Avra Cohn.[103]

Those who lack intimacy with the machine cannot be expected a priori to have insight into its limitations. The choice of trope for human-machine interaction therefore becomes important. My preference is for the metaphor reached for independently by computer scientist Robin Milner and by sociologist Harry Collins: the computer is a "prosthetic limb," said Milner; a "social prosthesis," said Collins.[104] Abstracted from its connotations of wholeness and deficiency,[105] the prosthetic trope is helpful because it distributes agency accurately.[106] The machine helps one to perform proofs one could not otherwise perform and, at least in the circumstances of computer system verification, to perform them with greater dependability than individually one might be able to. But it is important to emphasize that the machine helps us: it is our servant, not our master; it cannot make the informal judgments that are crucial to its appropriate use; and it is we who allow its operations to count as correct deductions or who deem them to be in error. Even in the most formal and most mechanical of domains, trust in the machine cannot entirely replace trust in the human collectivity.

The proving machine, whether in the form of the automated theorem prover, the model checker, some hybrid of the two, or some other variant, is destined to become a permanent part of our technological and perhaps also of our mathematical culture. Present and future generations will need to make decisions about the proper status and role of such machines. Treated as social prostheses they are benign; treated as oracles they become dangerous. If this book on the interactions among machines, proofs, and cultures helps this choice to be made wisely, it will have served a purpose.

Notes

Chapter 1

1. For a sample, albeit far from comprehensive, from this literature, see *The Science Studies Reader,* ed. Mario Biagioli (New York: Routledge, 1999).

2. See, especially, Trevor J. Pinch and Wiebe E. Bijker, "The Social Construction of Facts and Artefacts: or How the Sociology of Science and the Sociology of Technology might Benefit Each Other," *Social Studies of Science* 14 (1984): 399–441.

3. D. MacKenzie, "How Do We Know the Properties of Artefacts? Applying the Sociology of Knowledge to Technology," in *Technological Change: Methods and Themes in the History of Technology,* ed. Robert Fox (Amsterdam: Harwood, 1996), 247–263.

4. This is the classic topic of Thomas S. Kuhn, *The Structure of Scientific Revolutions* (Chicago: University of Chicago Press, second edition, 1970).

5. Steven Shapin, *A Social History of Truth: Civility and Science in Seventeenth-Century England* (Chicago: University of Chicago Press, 1994).

6. For a sophisticated treatment, avoiding both naive assertions of the independence of induction and simplistic claims about the nature of its dependence upon theory, see Peter Galison, *Image and Logic: A Material Culture of Microphysics* (Chicago: University of Chicago Press, 1997).

7. See David Bloor, *Knowledge and Social Imagery* (London: Routledge & Kegan Paul, 1976); Bloor, *Wittgenstein: A Social Theory of Knowledge* (London: Macmillan, 1983); Bloor, *Wittgenstein: Rules and Institutions* (London: Routledge, 1997); Barry Barnes, David Bloor, and John Henry, *Scientific Knowledge: A Sociological Analysis* (London: Athlone and Chicago: Chicago University Press, 1996), chapter 7; Eric Livingston, *The Ethnomethodological Foundations of Mathematics* (London: Routledge & Kegan Paul, 1986); Livingston, "Cultures of Proving," *Social Studies of Science* 29 (1999): 867–888; Sal Restivo, *Mathematics in Society and History: Sociological Inquiries* (Dordrecht: Kluwer, 1992); *Math Worlds: Philosophical and Social Studies of Mathematics and Mathematics Education,* eds. Sal Restivo, Jean Paul

Van Bendegem, and Roland Fischer (Albany, New York: State University of New York Press, 1993); Claude Rosental, "Histoire de la Logique Floue: Une Approche Sociologique des Practiques de Démonstration," *Revue de Synthèse 4 (1998): 575–602;* Bettina Heintz, *Die Innenwelt der Mathematik: Zur Kultur und Praxis einer beweisenden Disziplin* (Vienna: Springer, 2000). Among earlier contributions is the work of Charles S. Fisher: see, e.g., Fisher, "The Last Invariant Theorists: A Sociological Study of the Collective Biographies of Mathematical Specialists," *European Journal of Sociology* 8 (1967): 216–244, and Fisher, "Some Social Characteristics of Mathematicians and Their Work," *American Journal of Sociology* 78 (1973): 1094–1118. There is also a wide range of relevant work in the history of mathematics, among which one of the most ambitious pieces is Herbert Mehrtens, *Moderne-Sprache-Mathematik. Eine Geschichte des Streits um die Grundlagen der Disziplin und des Subjekts formaler Systeme* (Frankfurt: Suhrkamp, 1990).

8. For references, see note 7. See also: Trevor J. Pinch, "What Does a Proof Do if It Does Not Prove? A Study of the Social Conditions and Metaphysical Divisions leading to David Bohm and John von Neumann failing to communicate in Quantum Physics," in *The Social Production of Scientific Knowledge: Sociology of the Sciences, Volume 1, 1977,* eds. Everett Mendelsohn, Peter Weingart, and Helga Nowotny (Dordrecht: Reidel, 1977), 171–215; Heintz, *Innenwelt;* Rosental, "Histoire"; Claude Rosental, "Les Travailleurs de la Preuve sur Internet: Transformations et Permanences du Fonctionnement de la Recherche," *Actes de la Recherche en Sciences Sociales* 134 (2000): 37–44; Rosental, "La Production de Connaissances Certifiées en Logique: Un Processus Collectif d'Accréditation d'un Théorème," *Cahiers Internationaux de Sociologie* 91 (2000): 343–374.

9. Imre Lakatos, "Essays in the Logic of Mathematical Discovery" (Ph.D. thesis, Cambridge University, 1961); Lakatos, *Proofs and Refutations: The Logic of Mathematical Discovery,* eds. John Worrall and Elie Zahar (Cambridge: Cambridge University Press, 1976).

10. Karl Mannheim, *Ideology and Utopia: An Introduction to the Sociology of Knowledge* (New York: Harcourt, Brace & World, n.d.; first published in 1936), pp. 25, 43, 79, 293, and 298. Q.v. David Bloor, "Wittgenstein and Mannheim on the Sociology of Mathematics," *Studies in the History and Philosophy of Science* 4 (1973): 173–191.

11. Whenever it is not too anachronistic, I shall in general use the terminology of *Dependability: Basic Concepts and Terminology in English, French, German, Italian and Japanese,* ed. J.C. Laprie (Vienna: Springer, 1992). A failure is "when the delivered service no longer complies with the specification, the latter being an agreed description of the system's expected function and / or service"; an error is "that part of the system state which is liable to lead to subsequent failure"; and a fault is "[t]he adjudged or hypothesized cause of an error" (ibid., p. 4, emphasis in original deleted). Note that in this terminology a mistake in programming or in hardware design is a "fault" not an "error"; to avoid confusion with physical faults I shall refer to it as a "design fault." The definition of "failure" by Laprie and colleagues is too narrow, since it excludes the case—important

in practice—of failures caused by mistaken specifications. See John Rushby, "Critical System Properties: Survey and Taxonomy," *Reliability Engineering and System Safety* 43 (1994): 189–219, at p. 193.

12. Edsger W. Dijkstra, "Structured Programming," in *Software Engineering Techniques: Report on a Conference Sponsored by the NATO Science Committee, Rome, Italy, 27th to 31st October 1969,* eds. J. N. Buxton and B. Randell (Brussels: NATO Scientific Affairs Division, 1970), 84–88, at p. 85, emphasis in original deleted.

13. Julia King, "Engineers to IS: Drop that Title!" *ComputerWorld* 28 (22) (30 May 1994): 1 and 119; Barry Boehm, "The ACM-IEEE Initiative on Software Engineering as a Profession," *ACM Software Engineering Notes* 19 (4) (October 1994): 1–2, at p. 1. See also, more generally, Wanda J. Orlikowski and Jack J. Baroudi, "The Information Systems Profession: Myth or Reality?" *Office: Technology & People* 4 (1989): 13–30, and Stuart Shapiro, "Boundaries and Quandaries: Establishing a Professional Context for IT," *Information Technology & People* 7 (1994): 48–68.

14. For this analogy, see Leslie Lamport, Letter to editor, *Communications of the ACM* 22 (1979): 624.

15. A "theorem" is a mathematical statement for which there is a proof. Pythagoras's theorem is that the square of the length of the hypotenuse of a right-angled triangle is equal to the sum of the squares of the other two sides. (The hypotenuse is the side opposite the right angle.)

16. This point is spelled out most clearly in Avra Cohn, "The Notion of Proof in Hardware Verification," *Journal of Automated Reasoning* 5 (1989): 127–139.

17. In a small number of cases, it was either inappropriate to name the interviewee, or he or she preferred not to be named. These cases are referenced as "interview data."

18. The closest existing general historical treatment is Gabriele Lolli, *La Macchina e le Dimostrazioni* (Bologna: il Mulino, 1987). Witold Marciszewski and Roman Murawski, *Mechanization of Reasoning in a Historical Perspective* (Amsterdam: Rodopi, 1995), focuses primarily on developments prior to those discussed here. References to other historical work relevant to particular chapters will be found in those chapters.

19. See, e.g., *A House Built on Sand: Exposing Postmodernist Myths about Science,* ed. Noretta Koertge (New York: Oxford University Press, 1998) and the consequent debate in *Social Studies of Science* 29 (April 1999).

20. I draw the "zero-sum" metaphor from David Bloor and David Edge, "Knowing Reality Through Society," *Physics World* 11 (3) (March 1998): 23, now reprinted in *Social Studies of Science* 30 (2000): 158–160. See also D. MacKenzie, "The Zero-Sum Assumption: Reply to Sullivan," *Social Studies of Science* 29 (1999): 223–234, and Noretta Koertge, "The Zero-Sum Assumption and the Symmetry Thesis," *Social Studies of Science* 29 (1999): 777–784.

21. Anthony Giddens, *The Consequences of Modernity* (Cambridge: Polity, 1990).

22. Ulrich Beck, *Risk Society: Towards a New Modernity* (London: Sage, 1992). See also, for example, *The Risk Society and Beyond,* eds. Barbara Adam, Ulrich Beck, and Joost van Loon (London: SAGE, 2000).

23. Beck, *Risk Society,* pp. 20, 21, and 23–24, emphases in original deleted. Beck overstates the historical novelty of high-modern risks, but that issue does not need discussion here.

24. Paul Taylor, "The Beneficial Effects of the Millennium Bug," *Financial Times* (January 7, 2000): 15.

25. Charles Perrow, *Normal Accidents: Living with High-Risk Technologies* (Princeton, N.J.: Princeton University Press, revised edition, 1999), discusses the Y2K problem, which turned out to be a much less severe "test of the robustness of societies" (p. 393, emphasis deleted) than it appeared it might when Perrow was writing.

26. See, especially Brian Wynne, "Misunderstood Misunderstanding: Social Identities and Public Uptake of Science," *Public Understanding of Science* 1 (1992): 281–304.

27. Theodore M. Porter, *Trust in Numbers: The Pursuit of Objectivity in Science and Public Life* (Princeton, N.J.: Princeton University Press, 1995), pp. viii–ix; Porter, "Quantification and the Accounting Ideal in Science," *Social Studies of Science* 22 (1992): 633–651, at pp. 640 and 644. On premodern measures Porter is drawing upon Witold Kula, *Measures and Men,* trans. Richard Szreter (Princeton, N.J.: Princeton University Press, 1986). The contrast of Gemeinschaft and Gesellschaft comes from Ferdinand Tönnies, *Community and Association (Gemeinschaft und Gesellschaft),* trans. Charles P. Loomis (London: Routledge & Kegan Paul, 1955).

28. Giddens, *Consequences of Modernity,* p. 27.

29. Steven Shapin, *A Social History of Truth: Civility and Science in Seventeenth-Century England* (Chicago: University of Chicago Press, 1994), pp. 15, 42, 414 and 417, emphases in original deleted.

30. Porter, *Trust in Numbers,* chapter 9.

31. Shapin, *Social History of Truth,* p. xxv.

32. Steven Shapin and Simon Schaffer, *Leviathan and the Air-Pump: Hobbes, Boyle, and the Experimental Life* (Princeton, N.J.: Princeton University Press, 1985); Porter, *Trust in Numbers,* pp. 225–26; Boyle, as quoted by Shapin, *Social History of Truth,* p. 322; ibid.

33. Porter, *Trust in Numbers,* p. 225; see also p. 227: "Theory, especially of a mathematical sort, has at least the virtues mentioned by Hobbes: the reasoning is explicit, and what appears on the printed page is largely self-contained."

34. Shapin, *Social History of Truth*, p. xxvi.

35. See Bloor, *Wittgenstein, Rules and Institutions*.

36. David Hume, *A Treatise of Human Nature*, ed. Ernest C. Mossner (Harmondsworth, England: Penguin, 1969), 231. I am grateful to Ursula Martin for directing me to this passage.

37. For a useful sketch of the emergence of "mechanical objectivity," see Lorraine Daston and Peter Galison, "The Image of Objectivity," *Representations* 40 (fall 1992): 81–128.

38. Sherry Turkle, *The Second Self: Computers and the Human Spirit* (London: Granada, 1984), pp. 3, 13, and 326.

39. H. M. Collins, *Artificial Experts: Social Knowledge and Intelligent Machines* (Cambridge, Mass.: MIT Press, 1990) and Harry Collins and Martin Kusch *The Shape of Actions: What Humans and Machines Can Do* (Cambridge, Mass.: MIT Press, 1998). See also Peter Slezak, "Scientific Discovery by Computer as Empirical Refutation of the Strong Programme," *Social Studies of Science* 19 (1989): 563–600, together with the responses in that issue of the journal. Slezak (p. 564 and passim) cites Lenat's AM (see chapter 3 below), but much of the debate sparked by his paper focused on science, not mathematics.

40. See, for example (although its sociological implications are not developed), Israel Kleiner, "Rigor and Proof in Mathematics: A Historical Perspective," *Mathematics Magazine* 64 (1991): 291–314.

41. I draw the term from Eric Livingston, "Cultures of Proving," but Livingston's analysis in this article is not comparative: he focuses on ordinary human proof.

42. See also, e.g., Philip J. Davis and Reuben Hersh, *The Mathematical Experience* (Boston: Birkhäuser, 1981); *New Directions in the Philosophy of Mathematics*, ed. Thomas Tymoczko (Boston: Birkhäuser, 1985); Philip Kitcher, *The Nature of Mathematical Knowledge* (New York: Oxford University Press, 1983); *Revolutions in Mathematics*, ed. Donald Gillies (Oxford: Clarendon, 1992).

43. Unless otherwise indicated, the sources of quotations in this synopsis will be found in the endnotes to the chapters that follow.

44. Gottfried Leibniz, "Elements of a Calculus," in *Leibniz: Logical Papers—A Selection*, trans. and ed. G. H. R. Parkinson (Oxford: Clarendon, 1966), 17–24, at p. 18.

45. H. M. Collins, "The Place of the 'Core-Set' in Modern Science: Social Contingency with Methodological Propriety in Science," *History of Science* 19 (1981): 6–19.

46. Lakatos, *Proofs and Refutations*.

47. Edsger W. Dijkstra, interviewed by A. J. Dale, Austin, Texas, April 6, 1994.

48. Edsger W. Dijkstra, "On the Cruelty of Really Teaching Computer Science: The SIGCSE Award Lecture," *ACM SIGCSE Bulletin* 21 (1) (February 1989), xxiv–xxxix, p. xxxiii.

49. Peter Galison, "Einstein's Clocks: The Place of Time," *Critical Inquiry* 26 (Winter 2000): 355–389, esp. p. 375.

50. D. MacKenzie, "The Fangs of the VIPER," *Nature* 352 (August 8, 1991): 467–468, reprinted as chapter 7 of MacKenzie, *Knowing Machines: Essays on Technical Change* (Cambridge, Mass.: MIT Press, 1996).

51. Bloor, *Wittgenstein: Rules and Institutions*, p. 2.

Chapter 2

1. Anon., " 'Missile Attack' Terror Described," *Oakland Tribune* (December 11, 1960): 15. I am grateful to Scott Sagan for a copy of this article.

2. General Laurence S. Kuter, U.S. Air Force Oral History Interview (Maxwell Air Force Base, Alabama: Albert F. Simpson Historical Research Center, K239.0512–810). Again, I am grateful to Scott Sagan for a copy of this interview.

3. John Hubbell, "You Are Under Attack!" *Readers Digest* 78 (May 1961): 47–51.

4. Hubbell, "You Are Under Attack!" Hubbell's article contains one clear error—the return time of a radar echo from the moon is around 2½ seconds, not the 75 seconds quoted by Hubbell—but it remains the best available account of the incident. An archival search conducted for me by Barry Spink of the Air Force Historical Research Agency, Maxwell Air Force Base, Alabama, turned up no definitive analysis. I am grateful to Tony King of GEC Marconi, Edinburgh, and to colleagues of his at GEC, Chelmsford, for helpful technical discussions of Hubbell's account.

5. Paul E. Ceruzzi, *Beyond the Limits: Flight Enters the Computer Age*, (Cambridge, Mass.: MIT Press, 1989), pp. 202–203.

6. Maurice V. Wilkes, *Memoirs of a Computer Pioneer* (Cambridge, Mass.: MIT Press, 1985), p. 145; see Martin Campbell-Kelly and William Aspray, *Computer: A History of the Information Machine* (New York: Basic Books, 1996), p. 185, and Maurice V. Wilkes, David J. Wheeler, and Stanley Gill, *The Preparation of Programs for an Electronic Digital Computer* (Cambridge, Mass.: Addison-Wesley, 1951).

7. Frederick P. Brooks, Jr., *The Mythical Man-Month: Essays on Software Engineering* (Reading, Mass.: Addison-Wesley, 1975), pp. 7–8.

8. Edsger W. Dijkstra, interviewed by A. J. Dale, Austin, Texas, April 6, 1994.

9. Ceruzzi, *Beyond the Limits*, p. 249.

10. Ceruzzi, *Beyond the Limits*, p. 193; Eldon C. Hall, *Journey to the Moon: The*

History of the Apollo Guidance Computer (Reston, Virginia: American Institute of Aeronautics and Astronautics, 1996).

11. Ceruzzi, *Beyond the Limits*, pp. 210–211; Hall, *Journey to the Moon*.

12. David G. Hoag, "The History of Apollo Onboard Guidance, Navigation, and Control," *Journal of Guidance, Control, and Dynamics* 6 (1983): 4–13, at 10; Hall, *Journey to the Moon*, pp. 157 and 169.

13. Hall, *Journey to the Moon*, p. 170, emphasis in original.

14. J Strother Moore, interviewed by Margaret Tierney, Austin, Texas, November 12, 1991; Moore, electronic mail message to author, April 23, 1999.

15. There was a separate Abort Guidance System on the Lunar Module which, while it could not have landed the module, could have returned it to rendezvous with the Command Module.

16. Hall, *Journey to the Moon*, p. 180; Ceruzzi, *Beyond the Limits*, pp. 212–218.

17. Kent C. Redmond and Thomas M. Smith, *Project Whirlwind: The History of a Pioneer Computer* (Bedford, Mass.: Digital Press, 1980). For the history of SAGE, see Paul N. Edwards, *The Closed World: Computers and the Politics of Discourse in Cold War America* (Cambridge, Mass.: MIT Press, 1996), chapter 3, Thomas P. Hughes, *Rescuing Prometheus* (New York: Pantheon, 1998), chapter 2, and Kent C. Redmond and Thomas M. Smith, *From Whirlwind to MITRE: The R & D Story of the SAGE Air Defense Computer* (Cambridge, Mass.: MIT Press, 2000).

18. Redmond and Smith, *Project Whirlwind*, pp. 192–193 and 203.

19. J. C. R. Licklider, "Underestimates and Overexpectations," in *ABM: An Evaluation of the Decision to Deploy an Antiballistic Missile System*, eds. Abram Chayes and Jerome B. Wiesner (New York: Harper and Row, 1969), 118–129, at p. 121. Licklider, a psychologist by training, was a pioneer in the field of human-computer interaction, and while at ARPA he had been involved in evaluating SDC's work in this area: see Arthur L. Norberg and Judy E. O'Neill, *Transforming Computer Technology: Information Processing for the Pentagon, 1962–1986* (Baltimore: John Hopkins, 1996) and Edwards, *Closed World*.

20. J. I. Schwartz, transcription of talk, in *Software Engineering Techniques: Report on a Conference Sponsored by the NATO Science Committee, Rome, Italy, 27th to 31st October 1969*, eds. J. N. Buxton and B. Randell (Brussels: NATO Science Committee, 1970), 41–43, at p. 41; Campbell-Kelly and Aspray, *Computer*, p. 193. For the history of the programming of SAGE, see Claude Baum, *The System Builders: The Story of SDC* (Santa Monica, Calif.: System Development Corporation, 1981) and John F. Jacobs, *The SAGE Air Defense System: A Personal History* (Bedford, Mass.: MITRE Corporation, 1986).

21. Andrew L. Friedman with Dominic S. Cornford, *Computer Systems Development: History, Organization and Implementation* (Chichester, West Sussex: Wiley, 1989).

22. Baum, *System Builders,* p. 38; Campbell-Kelly and Aspray, *Computer,* p. 193.

23. Baum, *System Builders,* p. 36.

24. Licklider, "Underestimates and Overexpectations," p. 121.

25. Robert R. Everett, "Editor's Note," *Annals of the History of Computing* 5 (1983): 350.

26. Campbell-Kelly and Aspray, *Computer,* pp. 197–199; Eloína Peláez, "A Gift from Pandora's Box: The Software Crisis" (Ph.D. thesis, University of Edinburgh, 1988), chapter 3; Barry W. Boehm, "Software and Its Impact: A Quantitative Assessment," *Datamation* 19(5) (May 1973): 48–59, at p. 57.

27. Emerson W. Pugh, Lyle R. Johnson, and John H. Palmer, *IBM's 360 and Early 370 Systems* (Cambridge, Mass.: MIT Press, 1991), p. 344; see Campbell-Kelly and Aspray, *Computer,* p. 200.

28. Frederick P. Brooks, Jr., *The Mythical Man-Month: Essays on Software Engineering* (Reading, Mass.: Addison-Wesley, 1975), p. 4.

29. Brooks, *Mythical Man-Month,* pp. 20 and 24.

30. Barry Boehm, presentation to Conference on the History of Software Engineering, Schloss Dagstuhl, Wadern, Germany, August 26, 1996; Boehm, undated letter to author.

31. Peláez, "Pandora's Box," p. 101.

32. Boehm, "Software and Its Impact," p. 48

33. See Werner L. Frank, "The History of Myth No. 1," *Datamation* 29 (5) (May 1983): 252–256.

34. M. E. Mengel, "Present and Projected Computer Manpower Needs in Business and Industry," *Proceedings of the First Conference on Training Personnel for the Computing Machine Field,* ed. Arvid W. Jacobson (Detroit: Wayne University Press, 1955), 4–9, at pp. 5–6, estimated that in 1954 a fifth of the 500 largest manufacturing companies in the United States were using computers and they employed an estimated 400 programmers in total. Mengel (p. 6) suggested a rather larger number of staff—perhaps 1,000—were employed as "analyzers," and total computing staff numbers in manufacturing were estimated at 2,325. The definition of "computer" he used, however, was wide and included card-programmed calculators.

35. The figure (254,537) is quoted by Philip Kraft, *Programmers and Managers: The Routinization of Computer Programming in the United States* (New York: Springer, 1977), p. 15.

36. Peláez, "Pandora's Box," p. 173; Ross, personal communication at Conference on the History of Software Engineering, Schloss Dagstuhl, Wadern, Germany, August 26, 1996.

37. Bauer, quoted by Peláez, "Pandora's Box," p. 173.

38. F. L. Bauer, letter to author, November 10, 1998.

39. John Buxton, interviewed by Eloína Peláez, as quoted in Peláez, "Pandora's Box," p. 174.

40. I am grateful to Brian Randell for finding the conference's precise location by searching his collection of photographs, many of which he copied for me. The published report—*Software Engineering: Report on a Conference Sponsored by the NATO Science Committee, Garmisch, Germany, 7th to 11th October 1968,* eds. Peter Naur and Brian Randell (Brussels: NATO Scientific Affairs Division, 1969)—is remarkably full, detailing the chief discussions among participants as well as reproducing position papers, but, despite enlisting the help of Randell and of Fritz Bauer, I have been unable to locate other than the most sketchy unpublished records.

41. *Software Engineering,* eds. Naur and Randell, p. 138.

42. John Buxton, interviewed by Eloína Peláez, as quoted in Peláez, "Pandora's Box," p. 175.

43. *Software Engineering,* eds. Naur and Randell, pp. 138–139.

44. *Software Engineering,* eds. Naur and Randell, p. 120.

45. *Software Engineering,* eds. Naur and Randell, p. 121.

46. David Gries, "Remarks at the Banquet Celebrating Edsger W. Dijkstra's Sixtieth Birthday," *Software Engineering Notes* 15(3) (July 1990): 21–24, at p. 22.

47. It is briefly described in Edsger W. Dijkstra, "The Structure of the 'THE'-Multi-Programming System," *Communications of the ACM* 11 (1968): 341–346.

48. Edsger W. Dijkstra, interviewed by Eloína Peláez, as quoted in Peláez, "Pandora's Box," p. 175. In matters like weather, memory plays notorious tricks, but Randell's photographs do indeed show sunshine.

49. *Software Engineering,* eds. Naur and Randell, p. 13.

50. Peláez, "Pandora's Box," chapter 7.

51. Albert Endres (in 1968 at the IBM Programming Center at Böblingen, Germany) in contribution to discussion at Conference on the History of Software Engineering, Schloss Dagstuhl, Wadern, Germany, 26 August 1996.

52. Douglas Ross, Edsger W. Dijkstra, Brian Randell, and John Buxton, as interviewed by Eloína Peláez, quoted in Peláez, "Pandora's Box," p. 184.

53. Buxton and Randell, *Software Engineering Techniques,* p. 9; see Peláez, "Pandora's Box," p. 185.

54. Edsger W. Dijkstra, "Programming considered as a Human Activity." *IFIP*

Congress 65: Proceedings (London: Macmillan, 1965), 213–217, at p. 214; Dijkstra, "'Why Is Software So Expensive?' An Explanation to the Hardware Designer," in Dijkstra, *Selected Writings on Computing: A Personal Perspective* (New York: Springer, 1982), 338–348, at pp. 341–342. See also Dijkstra, "Structured Programming," in Buxton and Randell, *Software Engineering Techniques*, pp. 84–88.

55. For early discussions of segmentation and modularity in programming, see Stuart Shapiro, "Computer Software as Technology: An Examination of Technological Development" (Ph.D. thesis, Carnegie-Mellon University, 1990), pp. 90–93.

56. Edsger W. Dijkstra, "Go To Statement Considered Harmful," *Communications of the ACM* 11 (1968): 147–148, at p. 147; see Peláez, "Pandora's Box," pp. 204–220. I am grateful to Mike Mahoney for a helpful email discussion of **go to.**

57. Dijkstra, "Structured Programming," pp. 85–86.

58. Peter Naur, "Go To Statements and Good ALGOL Style," *BIT* 3 (1963): 204–205, reprinted in Naur, *Computing: A Human Activity* (Reading, Mass.: Addison-Wesley 1992), 327–328.

59. Dijkstra, "Go To Statement Considered Harmful," p. 147.

60. John R. Rice, "The Go To Statement Reconsidered," *Communications of the ACM* 11 (1968): 538.

61. F. T. Baker, "Chief Programmer Team Management of Production Programming," *IBM Systems Journal* 1 (1972): 56–73; F. Terry Baker and Harlan D. Mills, "Chief Programmer Teams," *Datamation* 19(12) (Dec. 1973): 58–61, at p. 58; Friedman, *Computer Systems Development*, pp. 133–134.

62. Baker, "Chief Programmer Team," p. 57.

63. Michael S. Mahoney, "The Roots of Software Engineering," *CWI Quarterly* 3 (1990): 325–334 at p. 330; Naur and Randell, *Software Engineering*, p. 139.

64. Kraft, *Programmers and Managers*, p. 59.

65. Friedman, *Computer Systems Development*, esp. pp. 141–167.

66. Kraft, *Programmers and Managers*, p. 9.

67. See e.g., Edsger W. Dijkstra, "The Humble Programmer," *Communications of the ACM* 15 (1972): 859–866.

68. Dijkstra, "Why Is Software So Expensive?" pp. 341 and 344.

69. Dijkstra, *Selected Writings on Computing*, p. 126; see Peláez, "Pandora's Box," p. 241.

70. Friedman, *Computer Systems Development*, p. 174.

71. C. A. R. Hoare, "How Did Software Get So Reliable Without Proof?" typescript, University of Oxford Computing Laboratory, December 1995.

72. For example, in the 1981 official history of the System Development Corporation, the SAGE programming manager talks of "today's much smaller staffs" (Baum, *The System Builders*, p. 38).

73. Robert L. Glass, "Real Time: The 'Lost World' of Software Debugging and Testing," *Communications of the ACM* 23 (1980): 264–271, p. 269.

74. Frederick P. Brooks, Jr., "No Silver Bullet: Essence and Accidents of Software Engineering," *Computer* 20 (April 1987): 10–19. See also Shapiro, "Computer Software."

75. Baum, *The System Builders*, p. 8.

76. Glass, "Real Time," p. 266.

77. Fred Gruenberger, "Program Testing and Validating," *Datamation* 14 (7) (July 1968): 39–47, at p. 43

78. William C. Hetzel, "A Definitional Framework," in *Program Test Methods: Computer Program Test Methods Symposium, 1972, University of North Carolina,* ed. Hetzel (Englewood Cliffs, NJ: Prentice-Hall, 1973), 7–10, at p. 7. I am grateful to Susan Gerhart for helpful discussions of the history of testing in the 1970s.

79. Fred Gruenberger, "Program Testing: The Historical Perspective," in Hetzel, *Program Test Methods*, 11–14, at p. 11.

80. A strategy advocated by J. C. Huang, "An Approach to Program Testing," *Computing Surveys* 7(3) (September 1975): 113–128. Among influential early testing papers are John B. Goodenough and Susan L. Gerhart, "Toward a Theory of Test Data Selection," *IEEE Transactions on Software Engineering* SE-1 (1975): 156–173, and Thomas J. McCabe, "A Software Complexity Measure," *IEEE Transactions on Software Engineering* SE-2 (1976): 308–320.

81. Glenford J. Myers, *The Art of Software Testing* (New York: Wiley, 1979), p. 73.

82. See T. A. Thayer, M. Lipow, and E. Nelson, *Software Reliability: A Study of Large Project Activity* (Amsterdam: North-Holland, 1978).

83. David L. Parnas, A. John van Schouwen and Shu Po Kwan, "Evaluation of Safety-Critical Software," *Communications of the ACM* 33 (1990): 636–648, at p. 644.

84. Bev Littlewood and Lorenzo Strigini, "Validation of Ultrahigh Dependability for Software-Based Systems," *Communications of the ACM* 36 (1993): 69–80, at p. 72.

85. Generators used in practice are "pseudorandom" rather than strictly random (that is, they rely upon underlying deterministic mechanisms) but the point is not of great importance compared to other issues surrounding random testing. For a good description of the variety of meanings of "random," see Peter Galison, *Image and Logic: A Material Culture of Microphysics* (Chicago: University of Chicago Press, 1997), chapter 8.

86. Joe W. Duran and Simeon C. Ntafos, "An Evaluation of Random Testing," *IEEE Transactions on Software Engineering* SE-10 (1984): 438–444.

87. Statistical theory is itself historically and socially situated (see, for example, D. MacKenzie, *Statistics in Britain, 1865–1930: The Social Construction of Scientific Knowledge* [Edinburgh: Edinburgh University Press, 1981]), and there are, for example, a variety of different approaches to statistical inference. As noted below, however, the differences between these approaches are not of overwhelming importance to the matters discussed here.

88. Parnas, Schouwen, and Kwan, "An Evaluation," p. 647.

89. A common procedure is to test individual program modules separately.

90. Richard Hamlet, "Random Testing," *Encyclopedia of Software Testing*, ed. John J. Marciniak (Chichester: Wiley, 1994), vol. 2, 970–978, at p. 977. The objection is less of a problem for a Bayesian approach to random testing (see below) in that beliefs, prior to testing, about the reliability of the two programs would be expected to be quite different.

91. Ricky W. Butler and George B. Finelli, "The Infeasibility of Quantifying the Reliability of Life-Critical Real-Time Software," IEEE *Transactions on Software Engineering* 19 (1993): 3–12, at p. 10.

92. Littlewood and Strigini, "Validation," p. 73, emphasis in original.

93. See, e.g., Elaine J. Weyuker, "On Testing Non-testable Programs," *Computer Journal* 25 (1982): 465–470.

94. D. M. Hunns and N. Wainwright, "Software-based Protection for Sizewell B: The Regulator's Perspective," *Nuclear Engineering International* 36 (446) (September 1991): 38–40, at p. 39.

95. Dijkstra, "Structured Programming," p. 85, emphasis in original deleted.

96. Dick Hamlet, "Foundations of Software Testing: Dependability Theory," *Software Engineering Notes* 19(5) (December 1994): 128–139, at p. 130.

97. M. E. Fagan, "Design and Code Inspections to Reduce Errors in Program Development," *IBM Systems Journal* 15 (1976): 182–211, at pp. 190 and 194–195.

98. Ian Sommerville, *Software Engineering* (Wokingham, England: Addison-Wesley, fifth edition 1996), p. 487.

99. Fagan, "Design and Code Inspection," pp. 190, 191, and 197–198, emphasis in original.

100. Considerations of space prevent systematic discussion of other verification techniques such as static analysis. For a brief description of the latter and an account of its development in the United Kingdom, see D. MacKenzie and Graham Spinardi, "The Technological Impact of a Defence Research Establishment," in *Defence Science and Technology: Adjusting to Change*, eds. Richard Coopey,

Matthew R.H. Uttley, and Graham Spinardi (Reading, England: Harwood, 1993), 85–124, at pp. 105–107.

101. Peláez, "Pandora's Box," chapter 1; Dennis Shasha and Cathy Lazere, *Out of their Minds: The Lives and Discoveries of 15 Great Computer Scientists* (New York: Copernicus, 1995), pp. 16–17.

102. Peter Naur, ed., "Report on the Algorithmic Language ALGOL 60," *Communications of the ACM* 3 (1960): 299–314.

103. There is an outline history of programming language semantics in Peter Lucas, "On the Formalization of Programming Languages: Early History and Main Approaches," *The Vienna Development Method: The Meta-Language*, eds. D. Bjørner and C.B. Jones (Berlin: Springer, 1978), 1–23.

104. See Herman H. Goldstein and John von Neumann, "Planning and Coding Problems for an Electronic Computing Instrument," *John von Neumann: Collected Works*, vol. 5, ed. A.H. Taub (Oxford: Pergamon, 1963), 80–151, esp. p. 98; anon. [Alan M. Turing, possibly with Cicely Popplewell], Programmers' Handbook for Manchester Electronic Computer Mark II (n.p.: n.d., but c. 1950), p. 11, in National Archive for the History of Computing, Manchester University, NAHC/TUR/C1 (I am grateful to Jon Agar, Associate Director of the National Archive for the History of Computing, for locating this for me; I also owe to him the information that Popplewell may be a coauthor: Agar, electronic mail message to author, September 24, 1998). See also F. L. Morris and C. B. Jones, "An Early Program Proof by Alan Turing," *Annals of the History of Computing* 6 (1984): 139–143, and C. B. Jones, "The Search for Tractable Ways of Reasoning about Programs" (Manchester: University of Manchester, Department of Computer Science, 1992, UMCS-92-4-4), pp. 3–7.

105. David J. Israel, "A Short Sketch of the Life and Career of John McCarthy," in *Artificial Intelligence and Mathematical Theory of Computation: Papers in Honor of John McCarthy*, ed. Vladimir Lifschitz (Boston: Academic Press, 1991), 1–5.

106. J. McCarthy, "Towards a Mathematical Science of Computation," in *Information Processing 1962: Proceedings of IFIP Congress 62*, ed. Cicely M. Popplewell (Amsterdam: North Holland, 1963), 21–28, at pp. 21–22; see also McCarthy, "A Basis for a Mathematical Theory of Computation, Preliminary Report," in Proceedings of Western Joint Computer Conference, 9–11 May 1991, Los Angeles, 225–238; Michael S. Mahoney, "Computers and Mathematics: The Search for a Discipline of Computer Science," in *The Space of Mathematics: Philosophical, Epistemological, and Historical Explorations*, eds. Javier Echeverria, Andoni Ibarra, and Thomas Mormann (Berlin: de Gruyter, 1992), 349–363, at p. 354.

107. John McCarthy, "Computer Programs for Checking Mathematical Proofs," *Proceedings of Symposia in Pure Mathematics, Vol. 5* (Providence, Rhode Island: American Mathematical Society, 1962), 219–227; John McCarthy and James Painter, "Correctness of a Compiler for Arithmetic Expressions," in *Mathematical Aspects of Computer Science: Proceedings of Symposia in Applied Mathematics, Vol. 19*

(Providence, Rhode Island: American Mathematical Society, 1967), 33–41. The date of the meeting to which the latter paper was read was April 1966: see Jones, "Search for Tractable Ways," pp. 8–9.

108. See Jones, "Search for Tractable Ways."

109. Peter Naur, "Proof of Algorithms by General Snapshots," *BIT* 6 (1966): 310–316, at pp. 310, 311, 312, and 315.

110. Peter Naur, "Formalisation in Program Development," *BIT* 22 (1982): 437–453, at pp. 437 and 440.

111. Peter Naur, personal communication to author, Schloss Dagstuhl, Wadern, Germany, August 28, 1996.

112. Peter Naur, *Computing: A Human Activity* (New York and Reading, Mass.: ACM Press/Addison-Wesley, 1992), p. viii.

113. Jones, "Search for Tractable Ways," p. 9.

114. Robert W. Floyd, "Assigning Meanings to Programs," in *Mathematical Aspects of Computer Science: Proceedings of Symposia in Applied Mathematics, Vol. 19* (Providence, Rhode Island: American Mathematical Society, 1967), 19–32, at pp. 19–20.

115. C. A. R. Hoare, interviewed by A.J. Dale, Oxford, February 22, 1994; Hoare, electronic mail message to author, June 10, 1999.

116. Hoare interview; C. A. R. Hoare, *Essays in Computing Science*, ed. C.B. Jones (New York: Prentice Hall, 1989), pp. 1–3 and 11; C. A. R. Hoare, "Quicksort," *Computer Journal* 5 (1962): 10–15; C. A. R. Hoare, "The Axiomatic Method" (typescript, n.p., December 1967), part 1, pp. 4–5. I am grateful to Professor Hoare for letting me see this last item; the dating of it to December 1967 follows Jones, "Search for Tractable Ways," p. 11.

117. Hoare interview; C. A. R. Hoare, "An Axiomatic Basis for Computer Programming," *Communications of the ACM* 12 (1969): 576–583, at p. 576.

118. Hoare, "An Axiomatic Basis," pp. 577 and 579.

119. In later versions, the brackets were usually placed around the precondition and postcondition, so the triple became $\{P\} \; Q \; \{R\}$.

120. "Side effects" are effects that a command exerts on the "processing environment" other than those expressed in the command's name and parameters. See. e.g., Richard E. Fairley, *Software Engineering Concepts* (New York: McGraw-Hill, 1985), p. 155.

121. Hoare, "An Axiomatic Basis," pp. 577–579.

122. Hoare interview.

123. Hoare, *Essays in Computing Science*, pp. 7–8 and 17; Hoare, "An Axiomatic Basis," pp. 579–580.

124. Brooks, *Mythical Man-Month,* p. 9.

125. Hoare, "An Axiomatic Basis," p. 579.

126. See Friedman, *Computer Systems Development,* and Shapiro, "Computer Software."

127. Ralph L. London, "Computer Programs Can Be Proved Correct," in *Theoretical Approaches to Non-Numerical Problem Solving: Proceedings of the IV Systems Symposium at Case Western Reserve University* (Berlin: Springer, 1970), 281–302, at pp. 281, 287, and 288.

128. Susan L. Gerhart and Lawrence Yelowitz, "Observations of the Fallibility of Modern Programming Methodologies," *IEEE Transactions on Software Engineering* SE-2 (1976): 195–207.

129. Harlan D. Mills, "The New Math of Computer Programming," *Communications of the ACM* 18 (1975): 43–48, at p. 44.

130. The Böhm-Jacopini theorem is that "every Turing machine is reducible into . . . a program written in a language which admits as formation rules only composition and iteration." See Corrado Böhm and Giuseppe Jacopini, "Flow Diagrams, Turing Machines and Languages With Only Two Formation Rules," *Communications of the ACM* 9 (1966): 366–371, at p. 366.

131. Harlan D. Mills, "Structured Programming: Retrospect and Prospect," *IEEE Software* (November 1986): 58–66, at p. 60.

132. Mills, "Structured Programming," p. 60. My attention was first drawn to this use of the Böhm-Jacopini theorem by a talk by Tony Hoare, "How Did Software get so Reliable Without Proof?" Heriot Watt University, Edinburgh, March 21 1994. Barry Boehm confirmed to me in a personal communication (Schloss Dagstuhl, August 26, 1996) that Mills did indeed use the Böhm-Jacopini theorem in this way within IBM. The structure theorem is stated in Harlan D. Mills, "The New Math," p. 45.

133. Richard C. Linger, Harlan D. Mills, and Bernard I. Witt, *Structured Programming: Theory and Practice* (Reading, Mass.: Addison-Wesley, 1979), pp. 1–3.

134. Mills, "Structured Programming," p. 63.

135. Linger, Mills, and Witt, *Structured Programming,* 3–4.

136. P. A. Hausler, R. C. Linger, and C. J. Trammell, "Adopting Cleanroom Software Engineering with a Phased Approach," *IBM Systems Journal* 33 (1994): 89–109, pp. 90 and 94.

137. Linger, Mills, and Witt, *Structured Programming,* 2–3.

138. Mills, "Structured Programming," p. 65.

139. John R. Garman, "The 'Bug' Heard 'Round the World," *Software Engineering*

Notes 6 (5) (October 1981): 3–10; Alfred Spector and David Gifford, "Case Study: The Space Shuttle Primary Computer System," *Communications of the ACM* 27 (1984): 872–900; Committee for Review of Oversight Mechanisms for Space Shuttle Flight Software Processes, National Research Council, *An Assessment of Space Shuttle Flight Software Development Processes* (Washington, D.C.: National Academy Press, 1993); Edward J. Joyce, "Is Error-Free Software Achievable?" *Datamation* (February 15, 1989): 53–56, at p. 53.

140. Stacy J. Prowell, Carmen J. Trammell, Richard C. Linger, and Jesse H. Poore, *Cleanroom Software Engineering: Technology and Process* (Reading, Mass.: Addison-Wesley, 1999), p. 72.

141. See the attack by testing proponent Boris Beizer, reported in Nicholas Zvegintov, "Testing vs. Cleanroom: The Software Methods Controversy," *Managing System Development* 16 (4) (April 1996): 1–3.

142. Dan Hoffman, personal communication to author, Schloss Dagstuhl, Wadern, Germany, August 29, 1996. Hoffman does not himself share the criticism, believing the cleanroom approach to proof to be "quite satisfactory": electronic mail message to author, June 9, 1999.

143. Edsger W. Dijkstra, in Richard A. DeMillo, Edsger W. Dijkstra, Panel Discussion Moderated by Robert Paige, Purdue University, April 16, 1993. I am grateful to Professor DeMillo for a videotape of this discussion. Panagiotis Manolios and J Strother Moore, "On the Desirability of Mechanizing Calculational Proofs" (forthcoming in *Information Processing Letters*) argue that "proof errors" (p. 5) can in fact be found in Dijkstra's work.

144. McCarthy, "Programs for Checking."

145. Robert W. Floyd, "The Verifying Compiler," in *Carnegie Mellon University Annual Report* (Pittsburgh, Penn.: Carnegie Mellon University, 1967), 18–19, at p. 18.

146. James Cornelius King, "A Program Verifier" (Ph.D. thesis, Carnegie Mellon University, 1969), pp. i, 2–3, and passim. The proof of the program raising an integer to an integral power is given in King's thesis, pp. 183–189.

Chapter 3

1. Edward A. Feigenbaum, interviewed by Pamela McCorduck, as quoted in McCorduck, *Machines Who Think: A Personal Inquiry into the History and Prospects of Artificial Intelligence* (San Francisco: Freeman, 1979), p. 116. Simon cannot recall the remark, but commented that "If, indeed, I did say that, I should have included Cliff Shaw among the inventors": Herbert A. Simon, *Models of my Life* (New York: Basic Books, 1991), p. 206.

2. For political science at the University of Chicago in the interwar years, see Barry D. Karl, *Charles E. Merriam and the Study of Politics* (Chicago: Chicago University Press, 1974).

3. Herbert A. Simon, *Administrative Behavior* (New York: Macmillan, 1947), p. 79; see also, especially, Simon, "A Behavioral Model of Rational Choice," *Quarterly Journal of Economics* 69 (1955): 99–118.

4. Simon, *Models*, p. 198; Edmund Berkeley, *Giant Brains, or Machines that Think* (London: Chapman & Hall and New York: Wiley, 1949).

5. Herbert A. Simon, "Modern Organization Theories," *Advanced Management* 15 (October 1950): 2–4, at p. 3. Simon suggests (electronic mail message to author, June 22, 1998) that another source of his interest in "using a computer to simulate human thinking" might have been his reading of the classic 1943 paper by Warren McCulloch and Walter Pitts arguing that propositional logic could be used to model the operation of nerve cells: McCulloch and Pitts, "A Logical Calculus of the Ideas Immanent in Nervous Activity," *Bulletin of Mathematical Biophysics* 5 (1943): 115–133. Simon's 1950 paper, however, which appears to be his first published discussion of computers, makes no reference to the work of McCulloch and Pitts.

6. Simon, *Models*, pp. 199–201; McCorduck, *Machines who Think*, p. 117. The card-programmed calculator is described in Charles J. Bashe, Lyle R. Johnson, John H. Palmer, and Emerson W. Pugh, *IBM's Early Computers* (Cambridge, Mass.: MIT Press, 1986), pp. 68–72.

7. Simon, *Models*, pp. 203–205; Herbert A. Simon, interviewed by A.J. Dale, Pittsburgh, Pennsylvania, April 21, 1994.

8. Herbert A. Simon, electronic mail message to author, January 10, 1997; Alfred North Whitehead and Bertrand Russell, *Principia Mathematica* (Cambridge: Cambridge University Press, 1910–13; second edition, 1925–27).

9. G. Polya, *How to Solve It* (Princeton, New Jersey: Princeton University Press, 1945).

10. Simon, *Models*, p. 205.

11. Simon, *Models*, pp. 206–207.

12. A. Newell, J. C. Shaw and H. Simon, "Empirical Explorations of the Logic Theory Machine: A Case Study in Heuristic," *Proceedings of the Western Joint Computer Conference, 1957*, 218–239, at pp. 218 and 221. The text of the Logic Theorem Machine program can be found in Allen Newell and Herbert A. Simon, "The Logic Theory Machine: A Complex Information Processing System," *IRE Transactions* IT2 (1956): 61–79, at pp. 74–78.

13. Suppose the desired theorem is $a \rightarrow c$ ("a implies c"). If there is an axiom or previously proved theorem that has the form $a \rightarrow b$, then $b \rightarrow c$ becomes a subgoal. If there is an axiom or theorem of the form $b \rightarrow c$, $a \rightarrow b$ becomes a subgoal (Newell, Shaw, and Simon, "Logic Theory Machine," p. 222).

14. Newell, Shaw, and Simon, "Logic Theory Machine" (1957), p. 225.

15. Simon, *Models*, p. 202.

16. As far as I am aware, the phrase "combinatorial explosion" was first used in this context by Alan Robinson in "Theorem-Proving on the Computer," *Journal of the ACM* 10 (1963): 163–174, at p. 163. Awareness of the problem, however, certainly predated this paper.

17. The Dartmouth workshop is described in several places, for example in McCorduck, *Machines Who Think,* chapter 5, and Daniel Crevier, *AI: The Tumultuous History of the Search for Artificial Intelligence* (New York: Basic Books, 1993), chapter 2.

18. The General Problem Solver is discussed in A. Newell and H. A. Simon, "GPS: A Program that Simulates Human Thought," in *Computers and Thought,* eds. E. A. Feigenbaum and J. Feldman (New York: McGraw-Hill, 1963), 279–293.

19. See, for example, James Fleck, "Development and Establishment in Artificial Intelligence," in *Scientific Establishments and Hierarchies: Sociology of the Sciences, Volume VI, 1982,* eds. Norbert Elias, Herminio Martins, and Richard Whitley (Dordrecht, Netherlands: Reidel, 1982), 169–217, at 177.

20. McCorduck, *Machines Who Think,* p. 108; Newell and Simon, "Logic Theory Machine" (1956).

21. Marvin Minsky, interviewed by Pamela McCorduck, as quoted in McCorduck, *Machines Who Think,* p. 106. See also M.L. Minsky, "Heuristic Aspects of the Artificial Intelligence Problem" (Massachusetts Institute of Technology, Lincoln Laboratory, Group Report 34–55, December 17, 1956). The theorem is proposition 5 of book 1 of Euclid's *Elements,* and it appears (see Hubert L. Dreyfus, "Alchemy and Artificial Intelligence" [Santa Monica, CA: RAND, 1965, P-3224], p. 4) that the proof was the alternative one given by Pappus, for which see *The Thirteen Books of Euclid's Elements,* ed. T. L. Heath (Cambridge: Cambridge University Press, 1908), vol. 1, 254–255.

22. H. Gelernter, J. R. Hansen, and D. W. Loveland, "Empirical Explorations of the Geometry Theorem Machine," in *Proceedings of the Western Joint Computer Conference 1960,* 143–147, at p. 143.

23. Simon interview; H. L. Gelernter and N. Rochester, "Intelligent Behavior in Problem-Solving Machines," *IBM Journal of Research and Development* 2 (1958): 336–345. Truth tables were perhaps best known through Ludwig Wittgenstein's description of them in his *Tractatus Logico-Philosophicus* (London: Routledge & Kegan Paul, 1955; first published in 1921), pp. 93–95. That the method of truth tables is equivalent to proof of theorems in propositional logic using the *Principia's* inference rules was shown by Emil L. Post, "Introduction to a General Theory of Elementary Propositions," *American Journal of Mathematics* 43 (1921): 163–185.

24. Hao Wang, "Toward Mechanical Mathematics," *IBM Journal of Research and Development* 4 (1960): 2–21, at p. 3. There is a useful historical discussion of the "logic approach" and the "human-oriented or human simulation approach" to

automated theorem by a practitioner with experience of both in Donald W. Loveland, "Automated Theorem-Proving: A Quarter-Century Review," *Contemporary Mathematics* 29 (1984): 1–45, quotations from p. 3, emphasis deleted.

25. See, for example, Gottfried Leibniz, "Elements of a Calculus," in *Leibniz: Logical Papers—A Selection,* trans. and ed. G. H. R. Parkinson (Oxford: Clarendon Press, 1966), 17–24.

26. William Kneale and Martha Kneale, *The Development of Logic* (Oxford: Clarendon, 1962), p. 328.

27. The classic exposition of formal, mathematical logic as it stood immediately prior to the work of Gödel, discussed below, is D. Hilbert and W. Ackermann, *Grundzüge der Theoretischen Logik* (Berlin: Springer, 1928).

28. See Witold Marciszewski and Roman Murawski, *Mechanization of Reasoning in a Historical Perspective* (Amsterdam: Rodopi, 1995); Martin Gardner, *Logic, Machines, and Diagrams* (New York: McGraw-Hill, 1958); and William Aspray, "Logic Machines," in *Computing before Computers,* ed. Aspray (Ames, Iowa: Iowa State University Press, 1990), 99–121.

29. Wang, "Toward Mechanical Mathematics," p. 18.

30. A prime number is an integer greater than 1 that can be divided without remainder by no positive integers other than itself and 1. The integers 2, 3, and 5 for example, are all prime numbers; 4 and 6 are not.

31. In first-order predicate logic, quantified variables range over individual entities, not over functions or predicates. An example of a statement not directly expressible in first-order predicate logic is the principle of mathematical induction (see chapter 8), the formal expression of which involves quantification over predicates.

32. A. Robinson, "Proving a Theorem (as Done by Man, Logician, or Machine)," reprinted in *Automation of Reasoning: Classical Papers on Computational Logic,* eds. Jörg Siekmann and Graham Wrightson (Berlin: Springer, 1983), vol. 1, 74–76, at 75; M. Davis, "The Prehistory and Early History of Automated Deduction," ibid., vol. 1, 1–28, at p. 16; Jacques Herbrand, "Recherches sur la Théorie de la Démonstration" (Ph.D. thesis: University of Paris, 1930), reprinted in Herbrand, *Écrits Logiques* (Paris: Presses Universitaires de France, 1968), 35–153, at pp. 138–139.

33. Robinson, "Proving a Theorem," p. 75. For a fine biography of Robinson, see Joseph W. Dauben, *Abraham Robinson: The Creation of Nonstandard Analysis. A Personal and Mathematical Odyssey* (Princeton, N.J.: Princeton University Press, 1995).

34. An "algorithm" is "a recipe which tells one what to do at each step so that no intelligence is required to follow it": Alfred Tarski, *A Decision Method for Elementary Algebra and Geometry* (Berkeley, Calif.: University of California Press, second edition, 1951), p. 1.

35. M. Presburger, "Über die Vollständigkeit eines gewissen Systems der Arithmetik ganzer Zahlen, in welchem die Addition als einzige Operation hervortritt," in *Sprawozdanie z I Kongresu Matematyków Krajów Slowianski Warszawa 1929* (Warsaw: Sklad Glówny, 1930), 92–101.

36. Martin Davis, interviewed by A. J. Dale, New York, April 29, 1994; M. Davis, "A Computer Program for Presburger's Algorithm," paper presented to Cornell Summer Institute for Symbolic Logic, 1957, in *Automation of Reasoning*, eds. Siekmann and Wrightson, vol. 1, 41–48.

37. Martin Davis, "The Prehistory and Early History of Automated Deduction," in *Automation of Reasoning*, eds. Siekmann and Wrightson, vol. 1, 1–28, at p. 15.

38. There is a useful discussion of the contrast in Daniel J. O'Leary, "*Principia Mathematica* and the Development of Automated Theorem Proving," in *Perspectives on the History of Mathematical Logic*, ed. Thomas Drucker (Boston: Birkhauser, 1991), 47–53.

39. Hao Wang, "Computer Theorem Proving and Artificial Intelligence," *Contemporary Mathematics* 29 (1984): 49–70, at p. 50; Wang, "The Formalization of Mathematics, "*Journal of Symbolic Logic* 19 (1954): 241–266, at p. 266; Wang, "Toward Mechanical Mathematics," p. 18.

40. Wang, "Computer Theorem Proving," p. 51; Wang, "Toward Mechanical Mathematics"; Wang, "Proving Theorems by Pattern Recognition—I," *Communications of the ACM*, 3 (1960): 220–234. The decidable fragment of predicate logic on which Wang focused—AE predicate logic—contains only propositions "which can be transformed into a form in which no existential quantifier ['there exists'] governs any universal quantifier ['for all']": Wang, Computer Theorem Proving," p. 52.

41. Wang, "Toward Mechanical Mathematics," p. 4.

42. Simon interview.

43. B. Dunham, R. Fridshal, and G. L. Sward, "A Non-Heuristic Program for Proving Elementary Logical Theorems," in *Proceedings of International Federation for Information Processing Congress, 1959*, 282–285, at pp. 283 and 285.

44. E. W. Beth, "On Machines which prove Theorems," *Simon Stevin Wis- en Natuurkundig Tijdschrift* 32 (1958): 49–60, at p. 59.

45. Wang, "Computer Theorem Proving," p. 60.

46. D. Prawitz, H. Prawitz, and N. Voghera, "A Mechanical Proof Procedure and Its Realization in an Electronic Computer," *Journal of the ACM* 7 (1960): 102–128.

47. P. C. Gilmore, "A Proof Method for Quantification Theory: Its Justification and Realization," *IBM Journal of Research and Development* 4 (1960): 28–35.

48. Gilmore, "Proof Method for Quantification Theory"; Prawitz et. al., "A Mechanical Proof Procedure."

49. Pat Hayes, electronic mail message to author, April 20, 1999.

50. A propositional logic formula is satisfiable if there is an assignment of truth values to its component propositions that makes the overall formula true; it is valid (a tautology) if every such assignment makes the overall formula true.

51. Dag Prawitz, "An Improved Proof Procedure," *Theoria* 26 (1960): 102–139, at p. 103; Prawitz, "Preface to 'A Mechanical Proof Procedure . . .'," in *Automation of Reasoning,* eds. Siekmann and Wrightson, vol. 1, 200–201; Prawitz, electronic mail message to author, October 16, 1999.

52. See Putnam's paper read to the 1959 New York Institute of Philosophy: "Minds and Machines," in *Dimensions of Mind,* ed. Sidney Hook (New York: Collier, 1961), 138–164.

53. Martin Davis, interviewed by A. J. Dale, New York, April 29, 1994.

54. Martin Davis and Hilary Putnam, *Feasible Computational Methods in the Propositional Calculus* (Troy, New York: Rensselaer Polytechnic Institute, October 1958). One of the Davis-Putnam rules, the "affirmative-negative rule," was developed independently by Dunham, Fridshal, and Sward, "A Non-Heuristic Program." The Davis-Putnam procedure was eventually implemented with a slight variation to one of the rules by Martin Davis and two colleagues (including Donald Loveland, who had also worked on the Geometry Machine) on the IBM 704 computer at the Institute of Mathematical Sciences at New York University. See M. Davis, G. Logemann, and D. Loveland, "A Machine Program for Theorem Proving," *Communications of the ACM* 5 (1962): 394–397.

55. Martin Davis and Hilary Putnam, "A Computing Procedure for Quantification Theory," *Journal of the ACM* 7 (1960): 201–215, at p. 202, emphasis in original.

56. Davis, "Prehistory and Early History," p. 18; Davis, "Eliminating the Irrelevant from Mechanical Proofs," *Proceedings of Symposia in Applied Mathematics* 15 (1963): 15–30.

57. Alan Robinson, interviewed by A. J. Dale, Edinburgh, February 15 and 16, 1994.

58. William F. Miller, letter to author, June 18, 1993.

59. Robinson interview.

60. J. A. Robinson, "Theorem-Proving on the Computer," *Journal of the ACM* 10 (1963): 163–174, at p. 167. This paper was submitted to the *Journal of the ACM* in November 1962.

61. See, for example, Alan Bundy, *The Computer Modelling of Mathematical Reasoning* (London: Academic Press, 1983), chapter 5.

62. As Bundy, *Computer Modelling*, p. 74 notes, the first formula, $A \vee p$, is equivalent to $\neg A \rightarrow p$ (see figure 3.1). The second formula, $B \vee \neg p$, is equivalent to $p \rightarrow B$. So from the two formulae we can deduce $\neg A \rightarrow B$, which is equivalent to $A \vee B$.

63. J. A. Robinson, "A Machine-Oriented Logic based on the Resolution Principle," *Journal of the Association for Computing Machinery* 12 (1965): 23–41, at pp. 23 and 24; see also the abstract, Robinson, "A Machine-Oriented First Order Logic," *Journal of Symbolic Logic* 28 (1963): 302.

64. Robinson interview.

65. J. A. Robinson, "Logic and Logic Programming," *Communications of the Association for Computing Machinery* 35 (1992): 41–65; Bernard Meltzer, letter to author, August 7, 2000; Fleck, "Development and Establishment." I was delighted to discover from Meltzer that his nascent Metamathematics Unit, which was not universally popular in Edinburgh University (a prominent mathematician was a particular opponent), was housed temporarily by the Sociology Department (Meltzer, letters to author, August 7 and 27, 2000).

66. See, e.g., Bundy, *Computer Modelling*, pp. 73–74.

67. D. W. Loveland, *Automated Theorem Proving: A Logical Basis* (Amsterdam: North-Holland, 1978).

68. Robinson, "Logic and Logic Programming," p. 45.

69. Robert Moore, "The Use of Logic in Intelligent Systems," in *Intelligent Machinery: Theory and Practice,* ed. Ian Benson (Cambridge: Cambridge University Press, 1986), 31–47, at p. 34.

70. Patrick J. Hayes, interviewed by A. J. Dale, Urbana-Champaign, Illinois, April 16, 1994.

71. Hayes, electronic mail message.

72. Crevier, *AI,* p. 64.

73. John McCarthy, "Programs with Common Sense," *Proceedings of the Teddington Conference on the Mechanization of Thought Processes* (London: Her Majesty's Stationery Office, 1959): 77–84, at p. 78, italicization in original deleted. See, e.g. McCarthy and P. J. Hayes, "Some Philosophical Problems from the Standpoint of Artificial Intelligence," in *Machine Intelligence 4,* eds. B. Meltzer and D. Michie. (Edinburgh: Edinburgh University Press, 1969), 463–502.

74. Seymour Papert, interviewed by A. J. Dale, Cambridge, Mass., June 7, 1994.

75. M. Minsky, S. Papert, and staff, *Proposal to ARPA for Research on Artificial Intelligence at M.I.T., 1971–1972,* MIT Artificial Intelligence Memo No. 245, 1971, pp. 13–14. I owe the reference to Fleck, "Development and Establishment," p. 212.

76. Carl Hewitt, quoted in Crevier, *AI,* p. 193.

77. Hayes interview.

78. D. Bruce Anderson and Patrick J. Hayes, "An Arraignment of Theorem-Proving or The Logicians' Folly" (University of Edinburgh: Department of Computational Logic, memo no. 54, n.d., but c. 1972).

79. P. J. Hayes, "A Critique of Pure Treason," *Computational Intelligence* 3 (1987): 179–185, at p. 183; Marvin Minsky, "Logical vs Analogical or Symbolic vs Connectionist or Neat vs Scruffy," in *Artificial Intelligence at MIT: Expanding Frontiers,* eds. P.H. Winston and S.A. Shellard (Cambridge, Mass.: MIT Press, 1990), 219–243. See also Crevier, *AI,* p. 168 and passim.

80. Pat Hayes, electronic mail message to author, September 1, 1993.

81. Pat Hayes, electronic mail message to author, May 26, 1999. For ARPA's relations to artificial intelligence, see Jon Guice, "Controversy and the State: Lord ARPA and Intelligent Computing," *Social Studies of Science* 18 (1998): 103–138.

82. R. A. Kowalski, "The Early Years of Logic Programming," *Communications of the ACM* 31 (1988): 38–42, at p. 39; Kowalski, interviewed by A. J. Dale, London, January 6, 1994.

83. P. J. Hayes, "Computation and Deduction," *Proceedings of the 2nd MFCS Symposium* (Prague: Czechoslovak Academy of Sciences, 1973), 105–118.

84. Kowalski, "Early Years"; Kowalski, "Predicate Logic as Programming Language," *Information Processing 74: Proceedings of IFIP 1974* (Amsterdam: North-Holland, 1974), 569–574; A. Colmerauer, "Metamorphosis Grammars," in *Natural Language Communication with Computers,* ed. Leonard Bolc (New York: Springer, 1978), 133–189.

85. Crevier, *AI,* p. 195.

86. Sir James Lighthill, "Artificial Intelligence: A General Survey," in *Artificial Intelligence: A Paper Symposium* (London: Science Research Council, 1973), 1–21, at p. 10.

87. There is a useful outline of the history of complexity theory in Richard N. Karp, "Combinatorics, Complexity, and Randomness," *Communications of the ACM* 29 (1986): 98–109.

88. S. A. Cook, "The Complexity of Theorem-Proving Procedures," in *Proceedings of the Third Annual ACM Symposium on Theory of Computing* (New York: Association for Computing Machinery, 1971), 151–158. For an exposition, see C. Cherniak, "Computational Complexity and the Universal Acceptance of Logic," *Journal of Philosophy* 81 (1984): 739–758.

89. The problem of satisfiability is the "dual" (see chapter 4) of that of determining tautologyhood because the negation of a tautology is not satisfiable: no assignment of truth values to its component parts makes the formula true.

90. An exception is the Russian-born theorist Leonid Levin, a student of A. N. Kolmogorov. In parallel with Cook, Levin developed a broadly similar analysis of computational complexity. He told authors Dennis Shasha and Cathy Lazere that: "The fact that almost all mathematical conjectures that have been famous conjectures for many centuries have been solved is strong evidence that the solution is polynomial not exponential. Mathematicians often think that historical evidence is that NP is exponential [$NP \neq P$]. Historical evidence is quite strongly in the other direction." Shasha and Lazere, *Out of Their Minds: The Lives and Discoveries of 15 Great Computer Scientists* (New York: Copernicus, 1995), at p. 156. Cook also reminds one (ibid.) that the issue is an open one.

91. Michael J. Fischer and Michael O. Rabin, "Super-Exponential Complexity of Presburger Arithmetic," *SIAM-AMS Proceedings* 7 (1974): 27–41; Michael O. Rabin, "Theoretical Impediments to Artificial Intelligence," *Information Processing 74: Proceedings of IFIP Congress 74* (London: North-Holland, 1974), 615–619, at p. 617; Rabin, as interviewed by Shasha and Lazere, quoted in Shasha and Lazere, *Out of Their Minds,* p. 82.

92. Robert S. Boyer and J Strother Moore, *A Computational Logic* (New York: Academic Press, 1979), p. 6.

93. Pat Hayes, electronic mail message to author, May 26, 1999.

94. Woody Bledsoe, "I Had a Dream: AAAI Presidential Address, 19 August 1985," *AI Magazine* 7 (1986): 57–61, at p. 57, emphasis in original; A. O. Boyer and R. S. Boyer, "A Biographical Sketch of W. W. Bledsoe," in *Automated Reasoning: Essays in Honor of Woody Bledsoe,* ed. R. S. Boyer (Dordrecht: Kluwer, 1991), 1–29.

95. W. W. Bledsoe, "Non-Resolution Theorem Proving," *Artificial Intelligence* 9 (1977): 1–35, at p. 2, emphasis in original.

96. C. Hewitt, "Description and Theoretical Analysis (using Schemas) of Planner: A Language for proving Theorems and Manipulating Models in a Robot" (Ph.D. thesis, Massachusetts Institute of Technology, 1971).

97. Bledsoe, "Non-Resolution Theorem Proving," p. 12.

98. Loveland, "Automated Theorem-Proving," p. 24, emphasis in original.

99. A formal system is complete with respect to an interpretation of it if every statement that is true on the interpretation is provable within the system.

100. W. W. Bledsoe, "Splitting and Reduction Heuristics in Automatic Theorem Proving," *Artificial Intelligence* 2 (1971): 55–77, at p. 55.

101. A. P. Morse, *A Theory of Sets* (New York: Academic Press, 1965).

102. Bledsoe, "Splitting and Reduction Heuristics," p. 66, emphasis in original.

103. W. W. Bledsoe, R. S. Boyer, and W. H. Henneman, "Computer Proofs of Limit Theorems," *Artificial Intelligence* 3 (1972): 27–60, at pp. 28 and 35; details of the procedure are on pp. 35–38.

104. Larry Wos, "Automated Reasoning Answers Open Questions," *Notices of the American Mathematical Society* 40 (1993): 15–26, at p. 16, emphasis in original.

105. Larry Wos, electronic mail message to author, May 11, 1993.

106. Lawrence Wos, George A. Robinson, Daniel F. Carson, and Leon Shalla, "The Concept of Demodulation in Theorem Proving," *Journal of the ACM* 14 (1967): 698–709; G. Robinson and L. Wos, "Paramodulation and Theorem-Proving in First-Order Theories with Equality," in *Machine Intelligence 4*, eds. B. Meltzer and D. Michie (Edinburgh: Edinburgh University Press, 1969), 135–150.

107. A Boolean algebra is an algebraic structure expressing, for example, the properties of set-theoretic operations like the union of sets. The Robbins problem concerned the replacement of one of three equations forming an axiomatization of Boolean algebra by a simpler equation suggested by Herbert Robbins. Was the resultant algebra equivalent to Boolean algebra? In other words: "Are all Robbins algebras Boolean?" See Gina Kolata, "With Major Math Proof, Brute Computers Show Flash of Reasoning Power," *New York Times* (December 10, 1996): C1 and C8; William McCune, "Solution of the Robbins Problem," *Journal of Automated Reasoning* 19 (1997): 263–276; and McCune, Robbins Algebras are Boolean (http://www-unix.mcs.anl.gov/~mccune/papers/robbins/). For the earlier work on open problems, see Steve Winker and L. Wos, "Automated Generation of Models and Counterexamples and its Application to Open Questions in Ternary Boolean Algebra," in *Proceedings of the Eighth International Symposium on Multiple-valued Logic, Rosemont, Illinois* (New York: IEEE and ACM, 1978), 251–256; S. K. Winker, L. Wos, and E. L. Lusk, "Semigroups, Antiautomorphisms, and Involutions: A Computer Solution to an Open Problem, I," *Mathematics of Computation* 37 (1981): 533–545; Steve Winker, "Generation and Verification of Finite Models and Counterexamples using an Automated Theorem Prover answering two open Questions," *Journal of the ACM* 29 (1982): 273–284; L. Wos, "Solving Open Questions with an Automated Theorem-Proving Program," in *Proceedings of Sixth Conference on Automated Deduction, New York, June 7–9, 1982*, ed. D. W. Loveland (New York: Springer, 1982), 1–31; L. Wos, S. Winker, R. Veroff, B. Smith, and L. Henschen, "Questions Concerning Possible Shortest Single Axioms for the Equivalential Calculus: An Application of Automated Theorem Proving to Infinite Domains," *Notre Dame Journal of Formal Logic* 24 (1983): 205–223.

108. Kolata, "Major Math Proof."

109. McCorduck, *Machines who Think*, p. 145.

110. Herbert A. Simon and Allen Newell, "Heuristic Problem Solving: The Next Advance in Operations Research," *Operations Research* 6 (1958): 1–10, at pp. 7–8.

111. J. R. Guard, F. C. Oglesby, J. H. Bennett, and L. G. Settle, "Semi-Automated Mathematics," *Journal of the ACM* 16 (1969): 49–62.

112. Robert Bumcrot, "On Lattice Complements," *Proceedings of the Glasgow Mathematical Association* 7 (1965): 22–23.

113. Guard et al., "Semi-Automated Mathematics," p. 58.

114. Hubert L. Dreyfus, *Alchemy and Artificial Intelligence* (Santa Monica, Calif.: Rand Corporation, December 1965, P-3244), at p. 4 and p. 10, quoting a manuscript review (which I have not seen) by Ashby of *Computers and Thought*, eds. Edward A. Feigenbaum and Julian Feldman (New York: McGraw-Hill, 1963); W. Ross Ashby, *Design for a Brain* (New York: Wiley, 1952). Herbert Gelernter pointed out the error in Ashby's attribution of Minsky's hand proof to the Geometry Machine in Gelernter, "Commentary by the Author," in *Automation of Reasoning*, eds. Siekmann and Wrightson, vol. 1, 118–121.

115. K. Gödel, "Über formal unentscheidbare Sätze der Principia Mathematica und verwandter Systeme I," *Monatshefte für Mathematik und Physik* 38 (1931): 173–198. There is an English translation in *From Frege to Gödel*, ed. van Heijenoort, 596–616.

116. Strictly, Gödel required not just simple consistency (the absence of proofs within *S* of both a proposition and its negation) but the stronger property called ω-consistency, that is that there is no predicate *Q* within *S* such that each of this infinite collection of propositions is provable:

Not all positive integers have property Q.

1 has property Q.

2 has property Q.

3 has property Q.

. . .

I draw this explanation of ω-consistency from Barkley Rosser, "An Informal Exposition of Proofs of Gödel's Theorem and Church's Theorem," *Journal of Symbolic Logic* 4 (1939): 53–60, at pp. 54–55. In 1936, Rosser showed that the assumption of the ω-consistency of *S* could be weakened to its simple consistency: Rosser, "Extensions of Some Theorems of Gödel and Church," *Journal of Symbolic Logic* 1 (1936): 87–91.

117. To be more precise, Gödel demonstrated that the provability of *A* shows *S* is simply inconsistent; the provability of not-*A* shows *S* is ω-inconsistent: Gödel, "Über formal unentscheidbare Sätze," p. 189.

118. Exactly what is to count as a "finistic" proof was a matter of some controversy. Roughly, however, a finitist proof makes "no reference either to an infinite number of structural properties of formulas or to an infinite number of operations with formulas": Ernest Nagel and James R. Newman, *Gödel's Proof* (New York: New York University Press, 1966), p. 33. See ibid., pp. 95–96, for a brief account of how the second incompleteness theorem follows from the first.

119. John W. Dawson, Jr., "The Reception of Gödel's Incompleteness Theorems," in *Perspectives on the History of Mathematical Logic*, ed. Thomas Drucker (Boston: Birkhauser, 1991), 84–100, at p. 94.

120. Kurt Gödel to Hao Wang, December 7, 1967, as quoted in Wang, *From Mathematics to Philosophy* (London: Routledge & Kegan Paul, 1974), pp. 8–9. Solomon Feferman, however, suggests that Gödel was not always a convinced Platonist (Feferman, "Penrose's Gödelian Argument," *Psyche* 2 [1] [1996]: 21–32), and so the letter to Wang may involve a degree of retrospective reconstruction.

121. Nagel and Newman, *Gödel's Proof*, p. 101. See ibid., p. 93, for a rather more precise account of this reasoning than I have given.

122. J. R. Lucas, "Minds, Machines and Gödel," *Philosophy* 36 (1961): 112–127, at pp. 112–113; this is the published version of a 1959 paper to the Oxford Philosophical Society. Among those whom Lucas believed had anticipated the argument without stating it clearly enough was, for example, Paul C. Rosenbloom, *The Elements of Mathematical Logic* (New York: Dover, 1950), especially pp. 160–161.

123. Lucas, "Minds, Machines and Gödel," at pp. 124–125 and 126–127.

124. Roger Penrose, "Précis of *The Emperor's New Mind: Concerning Computers, Minds, and the Laws of Physics*," *Behavioral and Brain Sciences* 13 (1990), 643–705, at p. 648, emphases in original; Penrose, *The Emperor's New Mind: Concerning Computers, Minds and the Laws of Physics* (Oxford: Oxford University Press, 1989). See also Penrose, *Shadows of the Mind: A Search for the Missing Science of Consciousness* (Oxford: Oxford University Press, 1994).

125. Paul Benacerraf, "God, the Devil, and Gödel," *Monist* 51 (1967), 9–32, at pp. 19–20 and 21; Judson Webb, "Metamathematics and the Philosophy of Mind," *Philosophy of Science* 35 (1968): 156–78, at pp. 167–168. For a brief review of the debate sparked by Lucas's paper, see Judith V. Grabiner, "Artificial Intelligence: Debates about its Use and Abuse," *Historia Mathematica* 11 (1984): 471–480, at p. 473.

126. Martin Davis, "Is Mathematical Insight Algorithmic?" *Behavioral and Brain Sciences* 13 (1990): 659–660, emphases in original (this special issue of *Behavioral and Brain Sciences* [volume 13, no. 4] contains a wide range of critiques of Penrose, and a response by him); Geoffrey LaForte, Patrick J. Hayes, and Kenneth M. Ford, "Why Gödel's Theorem Cannot Refute Computationalism," *Artificial Intelligence* 104 (1998): 265–286, at p. 285. See also Alan Bundy, "On the Nature of Mathematical Judgement: Reply to Penrose" (University of Edinburgh: Department of Artificial Intelligence research paper no. 498, n.d.).

127. LaForte, Hayes, and Ford, "Why Gödel's Theorem Cannot Refute Computationalism," pp 277, 280, 281–282, and 285.

128. See chapter 1.

129. See, e.g., Kenneth R. Foster and Haim H. Bau, "Symbolic Manipulation Programs for the Personal Computer," *Science* 243 (February 3, 1989): 679–684. For a critical comment on such systems, seeking to "inspire caution" in their users, see David R. Stoutemyer, "Crimes and Misdemeanors in the Computer

Algebra Trade," *Notices of the American Mathematical Society* 38 (1991): 778–785, at p. 784.

130. Lenat, as quoted by Shasha and Lazere, *Out of Their Minds,* p. 229.

131. Douglas Bruce Lenat, "AM: An Artificial Intelligence Approach to Discovery in Mathematics as Heuristic Search" (Ph.D. thesis, Stanford University, 1976).

132. I am quoting here from the published version of Lenat's thesis, Douglas B. Lenat, "AM: Discovery in Mathematics as Heuristic Search," part one of Randall Davis and Douglas B. Lenat, *Knowledge-Based Systems in Artificial Intelligence* (New York: McGraw-Hill, 1982), at pp. 4 and 101. Further citations are to this version.

133. Lenat, "AM," pp. 11–12 and 125.

134. Lenat, as quoted by Shasha and Lazere, *Out of Their Minds,* p. 231; G.H. Hardy, "Obituary, S. Ramanujan," *Nature* 105 (June 17, 1920): 494–495, at p. 494; Robert Kanigel, *The Man who Knew Infinity: A Life of the Genius Ramanujan* (London: Abacus, 1992); Lenat, "AM," p. 101.

135. Randall Davis, as quoted by Crevier, *AI,* p. 179.

136. Lenat, "AM," p. 113.

137. Crevier, *AI,* pp. 148–149.

138. Wang, "Computer Theorem Proving," p. 50.

139. Keith Hanna, interviewed by A. J. Dale, Canterbury, England, January 18, 1994; Alan Bundy, personal communication, December 14, 1998; Graeme Ritchie, electronic mail message to author, August 30, 1999.

140. G. D. Ritchie and F. K. Hanna, "AM: A Case Study in AI Methodology," *Artificial Intelligence* 23 (1984): 249–268, at pp. 249, 261, 263, 264, and 267.

141. Douglas B. Lenat and John Seely Brown, "Why AM and EURISKO Appear to Work," *Artificial Intelligence* 23 (1984): 269–294, at p. 289. In a "bag," as distinct from a set, multiple occurrences of a member are not merged, but (in distinction from a list) their order is ignored: "One may visualize a paper bag filled with cardboard letters," wrote Lenat. The representation of "number" constructed by AM is that of a bag all of the elements of which are the same letter T. The LISP operation APPEND then "becomes addition (for instance, (T T) appended to (T T T) gives (T T T T T)). . . . [B]ag-operations restricted to Bags-of-T's *are* arithmetic functions." See Lenat, "AM," pp. 20 and 77, and Lenat and Brown "Why AM and EURISKO Appear to Work," p. 288, emphasis in original.

142. Lenat and Brown, "Why AM and EURISKO Appear to Work," p. 290.

143. Douglas B. Lenat and R. V. Guha, *Building Large Knowledge-Based Systems:*

Representation and Inference in the Cyc Project (Reading, Mass.: Addison-Wesley, 1990), p. xviii.

144. For a discussion of subsequent work on the automation of discovery, see Simon Colton, Alan Bundy, and Toby Walsh, "Automatic Concept Formation in Pure Mathematics," paper presented to Sixteenth International Joint Conference on Artificial Intelligence, 1999.

145. Lighthill, "Artificial Intelligence," p. 7.

146. N. G. de Bruijn, "AUTOMATH, A Language for Mathematics," in *Automation of Reasoning*, eds. Siekmann and Wrightson, vol. 2, 159–200, at p. 159.

147. E. G. H. Landau, *Grundlagen der Analysis* (Leipzig: Akademische Verlag, 1930); L. S. van Benthem Jutting, "Checking Landau's 'Grundlagen' in the Automath System" (Ph.D. thesis, Technische Hogeschool Eindhoven, 1977).

148. Philip J. Davis and Reuben Hersh, "Rhetoric and Mathematics," in *The Rhetoric of the Human Sciences*, eds. John S. Nelson et al. (London: University of Wisconsin Press, 1987), 53–68, at pp. 63–64.

149. Paper versions of MIZAR work are published in the journal *Formalized Mathematics* (Warsaw University, Bialystok campus); the QED proposal was first circulated by Robert S. Boyer and Rusty Lusk (a member of the Argonne group) in March 1993: electronic mail message from Lusk to multiple recipients, March 14, 1993. See anon., "The QED Manifesto," in *Automated Deduction: CADE-12*, ed. Alan Bundy (London: Springer, 1994), 238–251.

Chapter 4

1. The observer was Donald J. Albers: see Albers, "Polite Applause for a Proof of One of the Great Conjectures of Mathematics: What Is a Proof Today?," *Two-Year Mathematics Journal* 12 (1981): 82; Kenneth O. May, "The Origin of the Four-Color Conjecture," *Isis* 56 (1965): 346–348, at p. 346, n. 1; W.T. Tutte as quoted in Hans-Günther Bigalke, *Heinrich Heesch: Kristallgeometrie, Parkettierungen, Vierfarbenforschung* (Basle: Birkhäuser, 1988), p. 225, capitalization in original. The phrase "man-eating problem" is taken from an interview with Wolfgang Haken, by A. J. Dale, Urbana-Champaign, Illinois, April 16, 1994. I owe the reference to Albers's article to *The History of Mathematics: A Reader*, eds. John Fauvel and Jeremy Gray (Basingstoke, England: Macmillan, 1987), pp. 598 and 618.

2. Albers, "Polite Applause"; F. F. Bonsall, "A Down-to-Earth View of Mathematics," *American Mathematical Monthly*, 89 (1982): 8–15, at pp. 13–14; K. Appel and W. Haken, "The Four Color Proof Suffices," *The Mathematical Intelligencer* 8(1) (1986): 10–20, at p. 12. Halmos's remarks are from a tape recording of his address to the Columbus, Ohio, summer meeting of the Mathematical Association of America in 1990, as quoted by Reuben Hersh, *What is Mathematics, Really?* (London: Cape, 1997), p. 54.

3. May, "Origin," p. 346. The following account of the conjecture's origins is drawn from May, supplemented by Rudolf Fritsch and Gerda Fritsch, *Der Vierfarbensatz: Geschichte, topologische Grundlagen und Beweisidee* (Mannheim: Wissenschaftsverlag, 1994), chapter 1; an English translation of this now available: Fritsch and Fritsch, *The Four-Color Theorem: History, Topological Foundations, and Idea of Proof*, trans. Julie Peschke (New York: Springer, 1998). Among other treatments are Norman L. Biggs, E. Keith Lloyd, and Robin J. Wilson, *Graph Theory 1736–1936* (Oxford: Clarendon Press, 1976); Kenneth Appel and Wolfgang Haken, *Every Planar Map is Four Colorable: Contemporary Mathematics 98* (Providence, Rhode Island: American Mathematical Society, 1989), pp. 1–9; and Bigalke, *Heesch*.

4. Biggs, Lloyd, and Wilson, *Graph Theory*, p. 216.

5. Augustus De Morgan to William Rowan Hamilton, October 23, 1852, in Robert P. Graves, *Life of Sir William Rowan Hamilton* (London: Longmans Green, 1882–89) 3, 422–423, at p. 423, emphasis in original.

6. Frederick Guthrie, "Note on the Colouring of Maps," *Proceedings of the Royal Society of Edinburgh* 10 (1880): 727–728, at p. 728.

7. De Morgan to Hamilton, October 23, 1852.

8. Hamilton to De Morgan, October 26, 1852, in Graves, *Life of Sir William Rowan Hamilton* 3, 423–424, at p. 423.

9. A. Cayley, [On the Colouring of Maps], *Proceedings of the London Mathematical Society* 9 (1878): 148; Cayley, "On the Colouring of Maps," *Proceedings of the Royal Geographical Society* n.s. 1 (1879): 259–261.

10. A. B. Kempe, "On the Geographical Problem of the Four Colours," *American Journal of Mathematics* 2 (1879): 193–200; Kempe, "How to Colour a Map with Four Colours," *Nature* 21 (February 26, 1880): 399–400.

11. A reader wishing a mathematically more rigorous (but still accessible) treatment should turn to Fritsch and Fritsch, *Four-Color Theorem*. In my exposition of the proof of the four-color conjecture I will be drawing on a variety of popular treatments, notably K. Appel and W. Haken, "The Solution of the Four-Color-Map Problem," *Scientific American* 237 (October 1977): pp. 108–121; Keith Devlin, *Mathematics: The New Golden Age* (London: Penguin, 1988), pp. 148–176; and Ian Stewart, *Concepts of Modern Mathematics* (New York: Dover, 1995), pp. 169–173 and 300–305. These sources present the early work on the problem in the framework of the eventual successful solution, while I have tried to remain closer to the original presentations.

12. Fritsch and Fritsch, *Four-Color Theorem*, p. 44.

13. Appel and Haken, "The Solution of the Four-Color-Map Problem," p. 111.

14. Cayley, "On the Colouring" (*Royal Geographical Society*), p. 259.

15. See Appel and Haken, "The Solution of the Four-Color-Map Problem," p. 111.

16. Cayley, "On the Colouring" (*Royal Geographical Society*), p. 260.

17. Martin Gardner, "A Quarter-Century of Recreational Mathematics," *Scientific American* 279 (August 1998): 48–55, p. 52.

18. Here I am drawing on Devlin, *Mathematics,* pp. 154–155.

19. Kempe, "Geographical Problem," p. 200.

20. Here my presentation follows Appel and Haken, "The Solution of the Four-Color-Map Problem," p. 112.

21. For its history, see Biggs, Lloyd, and Wilson, *Graph Theory.*

22. Augustin-Louis Cauchy, "Recherches sur les Polyèdres," *Journal de l'École Polytechnique* 9(16) (1813): 68–86.

23. Imre Lakatos, *Proofs and Refutations: The Logic of Mathematical Discovery,* eds. John Worrall and Elie Zahar (Cambridge: Cambridge University Press, 1976), pp. 7–8; the simple proof is taken from Devlin, *Mathematics,* pp. 158–160.

24. Lakatos, *Proofs and Refutations.*

25. Leonhard Euler, letter to Christian Goldbach, November 1750, in Biggs, Lloyd and Wilson, *Graph Theory,* 76–77; Leonhard Euler, "Demonstratio Nonnullarum Insignium Proprietatum quibus Solida Hedris Planis Inclusa sunt Praedita," in Euler, *Commentationes Geometricae* (Lausanne: Orell Füssli, 1953), vol. 1, 94–108; Biggs, Lloyd and Wilson, *Graph Theory,* pp. 77–78.

26. Lakatos, *Proofs and Refutations,* p. 7.

27. Lakatos, *Proofs and Refutations,* pp. 106 and 87 n.

28. William E. Story, "Note on the Preceding Paper," *American Journal of Mathematics* 2 (1879): 201–204; see Kenneth Appel's review of Fritsch and Fritsch, *Four-Color Theorem, Mathematical Intelligencer* 4(1) (2000): 73–74.

29. Biggs, Lloyd, and Wilson, *Graph Theory,* p. 102.

30. Kempe, "Geographical Problem," p. 197.

31. Ibid., pp. 197–198. See below, note 47.

32. I am here drawing on the presentation of the Kempe chain argument in Biggs, Lloyd, and Wilson, *Graph Theory,* p. 95.

33. To Kempe, at least, it appears to have been obvious. To the modern mathematician, however, it is not a self-evident truth but a consequence of Jordan's curve theorem, which states that any simple closed curve on a plane divides the latter into two disjoint connected regions. The proof of this theorem is far from trivial,

and the mathematical reputation of the intuitionist mathematician L. E. J. Brouwer (discussed in chapter 8) rested in part on his improved proof: Brouwer, "Beweis des Jordanschen Kurvensatzes," *Mathematische Annalen* 69 (1910): 169–175.

34. Kempe, "Geographical Problem," p. 195. In this passage I have relabeled colors so that they correspond to Heawood's counterexample (see below) and also changed Kempe's lower-case letters into upper-case ones.

35. P. J. Heawood, "Map-colour Theorem," *Quarterly Journal of Mathematics* 24 (1890): 332–339, at pp. 337–338 (emphasis in original). I have changed Heawood's numerical labels for countries into alphabetical ones.

36. Heawood, "Map-colour theorem," p. 338.

37. A. B. Kempe, untitled note, *Proceedings of the London Mathematical Society* 21 (1889–90): 456. See also [Report of Meeting, 9 April 1891], *Proceedings of the London Mathematical Society* 22 (1890–91): 263.

38. Appel and Haken, "The Solution of the Four-Color-Map Problem," p. 111.

39. P. G. Tait, "On the Colouring of Maps," *Proceedings of the Royal Society of Edinburgh* 10 (1880): 501–503, and "Remarks on the Previous Communication," ibid., 729; [Note by the Headmaster of Clifton College], *Journal of Education* 11 (1889): 277. See Biggs, Lloyd, and Wilson, *Graph Theory,* pp. 103, 105, and 159.

40. George D. Birkhoff, "The Reducibility of Maps," *American Journal of Mathematics* 35 (1913): 115–128, esp. p. 125.

41. K. Appel and W. Haken, "Every Planar Map is Four Colorable. Part 1: Discharging," *Illinois Journal of Mathematics* 21 (1977): 429–490, at p. 431.

42. Haken interview.

43. Appel and Haken, "Every Planar Map is Four Colorable," p. 430.

44. See, e.g., Appel and Haken, "The Solution of the Four-Color-Map Problem," p. 112. In this and the next paragraph I follow the discussion in Devlin, *Mathematics,* pp. 163–166.

45. Appel and Haken, "The Solution of the Four-Color-Map Problem," p. 108.

46. Appel and Haken, "The Solution of the Four-Color-Map Problem," p. 108.

47. Let country i in a normal map have e_i neighbors and thus e_i borders or edges. Each edge separates two countries. So E, the total number of edges in the map, is $\frac{1}{2} \sum e_i$. Since in a normal map three edges meet at each vertex, and each edge connects two vertices, the total number of vertices (V) is $\frac{2}{3}E$. So, summing over the countries in the map:

$$\sum (6 - e_i) = \sum 6 - \sum e_i$$
$$= 6F - 2E \text{ (where F is the total number of countries or "faces")}$$
$$= 6F - 6E + 4E = 6F - 6E + 6V = 6 (V - E + F)$$

Euler's theorem now applies: $V - E + F = 2$. (To see this, imagine gathering together and folding the map so that it becomes a sphere, the unbounded country becoming an ordinary "enclosed" region: Fritsch and Fritsch, *Four-Color Theorem*, pp. 44–45; Devlin, *Mathematics*, p. 163. Further "rubber sheet" stretching can then turn the spherical map into a polyhedron.) Hence: $\Sigma(6 - e_i) = 12$. If each country had six or more neighbors, in other words if $e_i \geq 6$ for all i, $\Sigma(6 - e_i)$ could be at most zero. So there must be at least one country in any normal map with five or fewer neighbors. I draw this simple proof from Lynn Arthur Steen, "Solution of the Four Color Problem," *Mathematics Magazine* 49 (September 1976): 219–222, at p. 219.

48. Appel and Haken, "The Solution of the Four-Color-Map Problem," p. 114. Countries with one neighbor are excluded by the definition of a normal map. A country with no neighbors must occupy the entire infinite plane, which then obviously requires only one color.

49. Fritsch and Fritsch, *Four-Color Theorem*, p. 28–30; Bigalke, *Heesch*, pp. 114, 115–116, 152. I am grateful to Rudolf Fritsch for a helpful electronic mail discussion of the regular parquet problem.

50. Bigalke, *Heesch;* Haken interview.

51. Appel and Haken, "The Solution of the Four-Color-Map Problem," pp. 113–114. In fact, the sum of charges must be precisely 12, since the charge on any vertex is $6 - e_i$, where e_i is the number of neighbors of the country corresponding to vertex i, and $\Sigma(6 - e_i) = 12$, as shown in note 47 above.

52. Appel and Haken, "The Solution of the Four-Color-Map Problem," p. 113; Devlin, *Mathematics*, pp. 172–173.

53. For the proof of reducibility, see Birkhoff, "The Reducibility of Maps," pp. 125–126.

54. Philip Franklin, "The Four Color Problem," *American Journal of Mathematics* 44 (1922): 225–236; Oystein Ore and Joel Stemple, "Numerical Calculations on the Four-Color Problem," *Journal of Combinatorial Theory* 8 (1970): 65–78.

55. Heinrich Heesch, *Untersuchungen zum Vierfarbenproblem* (Mannheim: Bibliographisches Institut, 1969), chapter 1; Fritsch and Fritsch, *Four-Color Theorem*, chapter 6; Thomas L. Saaty and Paul C. Kainen, *The Four-Color Problem: Assaults and Conquests* (New York: McGraw Hill, 1977), pp. 76–79; Appel and Haken, *Every Planar Map is Four Colorable*, pp. 9–13.

56. Suppose one begins by identifying colorings of the ring that can be extended, preserving four-colorability, to the interior of the ring: these are called "initially good colorings." Then one identifies colorings of the ring (called "good" colorings) that can be transformed into initially good colorings by a finite number of Kempe interchanges whatever the Kempe chain connectivity of the graph outside the ring. Next one identifies colorings that can be transformed into colorings that have already been shown to be good, and so on until one

can obtain no more good colorings. A configuration is D-reducible if all the colorings of its ring are good. I owe this description of D-reducibility to an electronic mail message from Kenneth Appel, November 11, 1996. For a more rigorous account, see Heesch and Heesch, *Four-Color Theorem,* pp. 187–207.

57. Appel and Haken, *Every Planar Map is Four Colorable,* p. 10.

58. Fritsch and Fritsch, *Four-Color Theorem,* pp. 27–28 and 30–31; Bigalke, *Heesch,* pp. 172 and 180. Karl Dürre describes the underlying basis of his work in his thesis: Dürre, "Untersuchungen an Mengen von Signierungen" (Ph.D. thesis, Technische Universität Hannover, 1969).

59. The graph with the reducer in place of the original configuration has fewer vertices than the original. If the latter is a minimal five-chromatic graph, the graph with the reducer must therefore be four-colorable. In seeking to show C-reducibility, one checks whether all the colorings of the ring of the original configuration compatible with the reducer are "good" with respect to the original configuration (that is, can be extended, preserving four-colorability, to the original interior of the ring after a finite number of Kempe interchanges). If so, whatever the coloring of the graph outside the ring, one of these ring colorings must be compatible with it (else the graph with the reducer would not be four-colorable), and since they are all extensible to the original interior of the ring, the original graph must be four-colorable. So the original graph cannot be a minimal five-chromatic graph: the original configuration is C-reducible. Any D-reducible configuration is thus C-reducible, but not necessarily *vice versa.* I owe this account of the logic of C-reducibility to an electronic mail message from Kenneth Appel, November 11, 1996. For a more rigorous account, see Fritsch and Fritsch, *Four-Color Theorem,* pp. 208–217.

60. Yoshio Shimamoto, letter to author, November 11, 1996.

61. Fritsch and Fritsch, *Four-Color Theorem,* p. 28; Shimamoto letter.

62. Shimamoto letter; Y. Shimamoto, "On the Four-Color Conjecture" (typescript, n.d. but c. October 6, 1971). I am grateful to Professor John Mitchem of San Jose State University for a copy of this unpublished paper. A "critical" graph is a five-chromatic graph that is vertex-critical (if any vertex is removed, the remaining subgraph no longer requires five colors) and edge-critical (if any edge is removed, the remaining subgraph no longer requires five colors). See Shimamoto, "Conjecture," pp. 2–3.

63. Shimamoto letter.

64. Shimamoto, "Conjecture," p. 21.

65. Shimamoto letter.

66. Haken interview.

67. Bigalke, *Heesch,* pp. 211–212.

68. Bigalke, *Heesch,* p. 212.

69. Shimamoto letter.

70. Hassler Whitney and W. T. Tutte, "Kempe Chains and the Four Colour Problem," *Utilitas Mathematica* 2 (1972): 241–281, at p. 241.

71. Haken interview.

72. Whitney and Tutte, "Kempe Chains," p. 242.

73. Quoted in Bigalke, *Heinrich Heesch,* p. 213.

74. Whitney and Tutte, "Kempe Chains," p. 243.

75. Haken interview.

76. Haken interview.

77. W. T. Tutte, "Map-Coloring Problems and Chromatic Polynomials," *American Scientist* 62 (1974): 702–705; Kenneth Appel, interviewed by A. J. Dale, Durham, New Hampshire, 6 June 1994.

78. Haken interview.

79. For an accessible account of the Poincaré conjecture, see Ian Stewart, *From Here to Infinity* (Oxford: Oxford University Press, 1996), pp. 121–124. For a sociological study of mathematicians involved in trying to prove the Poincaré conjecture, see Charles S. Fisher, "Some Social Characteristics of Mathematicians and Their Work," *American Journal of Sociology* 78 (1973): 1094–1118.

80. Loosely, the knot problem is to provide an algorithm to decide whether a knot—a tangled-up loop of "rope"—can be untangled without being cut. For knot theory, see Stewart, *From Here to Infinity,* chapters 9 and 10.

81. Haken interview; Wolfgang Haken, "Theorie der Normalflächen: Ein Isotopiekriterium für den Kreisknoten," *Acta Mathematica* 105 (1961): 245–375.

82. Moritz Epple, private communication.

83. Haken interview.

84. Appel and Haken, "Every Planar Map Is Four Colorable," p. 433.

85. Haken interview.

86. Shimamoto letter; Bigalke, *Heesch,* pp. 180–181 and passim; Fritsch and Fritsch, *Four-Color Theorem,* pp. 29–30.

87. Haken interview. Osgood's thesis was "An Existence Theorem for Planar Triangulations with Vertices of Degree Five, Six, and Eight" (Ph.D. thesis, University of Illinois at Urbana-Champaign, 1974).

88. Appel interview.

89. K. Appel, as quoted by John Koch, interviewed by A. J. Dale, Wilkes-Barre, Penn., May 3, 1994.

90. Haken interview.

91. W. R. Stromquist, "Some Aspects of the Four Color Problem" (Ph.D. thesis, Harvard University, 1975).

92. Appel and Haken, "Four-Color Proof Suffices," p. 13.

93. Koch interview.

94. Appel interview; John A. Koch, "Computation of Four Color Irreducibility" (Ph.D. thesis, University of Illinois at Urbana-Champaign, 1976).

95. Kenneth Appel, electronic mail message to author, November 11, 1996.

96. The article appeared as F. Allaire and E. R. Swart, "A Systematic Approach to the Determination of Reducible Configurations in the Four-Color Conjecture," *Journal of Combinatorial Theory* series B 25 (1978): 339–362.

97. K. Appel, W. Haken, and J. Koch, "Every Planar Map is Four-Colorable. Part II: Reducibility," *Illinois Journal of Mathematics* 21 (1977): 491–567, at pp. 491–492.

98. Appel and Haken, "Four-Color Proof Suffices," p. 13.

99. Appel interview.

100. Haken interview.

101. Appel interview.

102. Haken interview and Kenneth Appel, electronic mail message to author, November 6, 1996.

103. Appel interview.

104. Appel, Haken, and Koch, "Every Planar Map is Four-Colorable. Part II," p. 494; Neil Robertson, Daniel P. Sanders, Paul Seymour, and Robin Thomas, "A New Proof of the Four-Colour Theorem," *Electronic Research Announcements of the American Mathematical Society* 2 (1996): 17–25 (http://www.ams.org/era), at p. 18.

105. Appel and Haken, "The Solution of the Four-Color-Map Problem," p. 121.

106. Appel and Haken, "Every Planar Map is Four Colorable. Part I"; Appel, Haken, and Koch, "Every Planar Map is Four Colorable. Part II."

107. This microfiche was later printed in Appel and Haken, *Every Planar Map is Four Colorable*, pp. 275–739.

108. K. Appel, W. Haken, and J. Mayer, "Triangulation à v_5 Séparés dans le Problème des Quatre Couleurs," *Journal of Combinatorial Theory* series B 27 (1979): 130–150. For a brief biography of Mayer, see Fritsch and Fritsch, *Four-Color Theorem*, pp. 32–33.

109. Haken interview.

110. Simon Singh, *Fermat's Last Theorem: The Story of a Riddle that Confounded the World's Greatest Minds for 358 Years* (London: Fourth Estate, 1997), pp. 278–279.

111. To be more precise, a coloring of the ring that can be extended to the vertices inside the ring is (see note 56 above) "initially good." A coloring of the ring is "good" if a finite number of Kempe interchanges transforms it into an "initially good" coloring; if it is neither "initially good" nor "good," it is "bad." I am grateful to Kenneth Appel for discussing this point with me (electronic mail message to author, September 9, 1998).

112. Haken interview. The general checks applied by Allaire (though not these details) are described in Francis Ronald Allaire, "On Reducible Configurations for the Four Colour Problem" (Ph.D. thesis, University of Manitoba, 1977), p. 94.

113. K. Dürre, H. Heesch, and F. Miehe, *Eine Figurenliste zur Chromatischen Reduktion* (Hannover: Institut für Mathematik der Technischen Universität Hannover, preprint no. 73, 1977).

114. Haken interview.

115. Appel and Haken, *Every Planar Map is Four Colorable*, p. 92.

116. Haken interview.

117. Haken interview.

118. A copy of this was given to A. J. Dale by Professor Haken.

119. Appel interview; for Tutte's support, see, especially, Gina Bari Kolata, "The Four-Color Conjecture: A Computer-Aided Proof," *Science* 193 (August 13, 1976): 564–565.

120. Appel interview. For Tutte's earlier views, see Tutte, "Map-Coloring Problems," p. 703.

121. Appel interview; [PHS], "Solved," *The Times* [London] (July 23, 1976): 14; anon., "Eureka!" *Time* (20 September 1976): 68–69, at p. 69. See also, for example, Stephen Klaidman, "At Least that's Settled!" *Washington Post* (September 18, 1976): D1 and D4.

122. Appel interview.

123. Haken interview.

124. Ian Stewart, *Concepts of Modern Mathematics* (Harmondsworth, Middlesex: Penguin, 1981), p. 304, as quoted in S. G. Shanker, "The Appel-Haken Solution of the Four-Colour Problem," in *Ludwig Wittgenstein: Critical Assessments*, ed. Shanker (London: Croom Helm 1986), vol. 3, 395–412, at p. 407.

125. Appel and Haken, "Four Color Proof Suffices."

126. See Steve Woolgar and Geoff Russell, "The Social Basis of Computer Viruses" (Uxbridge: Brunel University Centre for Research into Innovation, Culture and Technology, typescript, 1990). For an introduction to the concept of an urban legend, see Jan Harold Brunvand, *The Vanishing Hitchhiker: American Urban Legends and their Meanings* (London: Pan, 1983).

127. See the amended version of the original articles in Appel and Haken, *Every Planar Map is Four Colorable*, pp. 31–170.

128. Edward Swart, interviewed by A. J. Dale, Guelph, Ontario, 1 June 1994.

129. H. M. Collins, "The Place of the 'Core-Set' in Modern Science: Social Contingency with Methodological Propriety in Science," *History of Science* 19 (1981): 6–19.

130. Allaire, "On Reducible Configurations," p. 94; E. R. Swart, "The Philosophical Implications of the Four-Color Problem," *American Mathematical Monthly* 87 (1980): 697–707, at p. 698.

131. Swart, "Philosophical Implications," p. 700.

132. Allaire, On Reducible Configurations, p. 94.

133. U. Schmidt, "Überprüfung des Beweises für den Vierfarbensatz" (Diplomarbeit, Technische Hochschule Aachen, 1982). I have not been able to inspect this work, which is not available from the library of the Technische Hochschule Aachen, and owe my knowledge of it to Appel and Haken, "Four-Color Proof Suffices," pp. 19–20.

134. S. Saeki, "Verification of the Discharging Procedure in the Four Color Theorem" (Master's thesis, University of Tokyo, Department of Information Science, 1985). Again, I have been unable to inspect Saeki's thesis and owe my knowledge of it to Appel and Haken, *Every Planar Map is Four Colorable*, p. 27, which also records that a mistake in a formula in Appel and Haken's probabilistic analysis (not in the proof per se) was also found by M. Aigner. Appel, Wolfgang and Dorothea Haken themselves rechecked their work prior to its republication in book form in 1989, seeking as far as possible to perform by computer the "bookkeeping" checks that had been done by hand in their original work. They found only nonserious mistakes.

135. Haken worked on the FORTRAN discharging program but not on the assembly-language reducibility programs.

136. Koch interview. Appel (electronic mail message to author, December 17, 1996) comments that Koch may be overstating Haken's scepticism.

137. This emerged clearly from interviews conducted with members of this community by A. J. Dale in 1993–1994.

138. David Gries, interviewed by A. J. Dale, Ithaca, New York, April 27, 1994.

139. Haken interview; Andrew Wiles, "Modular Elliptic Curves and Fermat's Last Theorem," *Annals of Mathematics* 142 (1995): 443–551.

140. Appel and Haken, "The Four-Color Proof Suffices," p. 13.

141. Appel interview.

142. F. Allaire, "Another Proof of the Four Colour Theorem–Part I," *Proceedings of the 7th Manitoba Conference on Numerical Mathematics and Computing* (1977), 3–72. To my knowledge, Part II of this article has not appeared in print, but it was presented to the conference (Swart, "Philosophical Implications," p. 707, n.5).

143. Robertson et al., "A New Proof," p. 17; Neil Robertson, telephone discussion with author, October 4, 1996. The definitive published version of their proof is Neil Robertson, Daniel Sanders, Paul Seymour, and Robin Thomas, "The Four-Colour Theorem," *Journal of Combinatorial Theory* series B 70 (1997): 2–44.

144. Thomas Tymoczko, "The Four-Color Problem and its Philosophical Significance," *The Journal of Philosophy* 76 (1979): 57–83, pp. 58, 75 and 78.

145. Thomas Tymoczko, "Computers, Proofs and Mathematicians: A Philosophical Investigation of the Four-Color Proof," *Mathematics Magazine* 53 (1980): 131–138, at p. 131.

146. Elsie Cerutti and P. J. Davis, "FORMAC Meets Pappus: Some Observations on Elementary Analytic Geometry by Computer," *American Mathematical Monthly* 76 (1969): 895–905, at p. 904.

147. Paul Teller, "Computer Proof," *The Journal of Philosophy* 77 (1980): 797–803, pp. 798 and 802–803, emphasis in original.

148. Shanker, "The Appel-Haken Solution," pp. 395, 409, and 410, emphases in original.

149. Daniel I. A. Cohen, "The Superfluous Paradigm," in *The Mathematical Revolution Inspired by Computing*, eds. J. H. Johnson and M. J. Loomes, (Oxford: Clarendon, 1991), 323–329, at p. 328.

150. C. W. H. Lam, L. Thiel, and S. Swiercz, "The Non-Existence of Finite Projective Planes of Order 10," *Canadian Journal of Mathematics* 41 (1989): 1117–1123. As they explain (ibid., p. 1117), a "finite projective plane of order n, with $n > 0$, is a collection of $n^2 + n + 1$ lines," and an equal number of points, "such that every line contains $n + 1$ points, every point is on $n + 1$ lines, . . . any two distinct lines intersect at exactly one point, and . . . any two distinct points lie on exactly one line." William McCune's 1996 automated proof of the Robbins conjecture in Boolean algebra (discussed in chapter 3), is not relevant to the current discussion because it is sufficiently simple to be understood and checked by human mathematicians.

151. Lam et al., "Non-existence," pp. 1120–1122.

152. Peter Galison, personal communication. A milestone in the banishing of

physical argument was Dirichlet's principle in analysis, originally supported in mid-nineteenth century by such argument. "Nowadays we do not accept such physical considerations in our [mathematical] papers," comments A. F. Monna, *Dirichlet's Principle: A Mathematical Comedy of Errors and Its Influence on the Development of Analysis* (Utrecht: Oosthoek, Scheltema and Holkema, 1975), p. 98.

153. John Horgan, "The Death of Proof," *Scientific American* 269 (October 1993): 75–82, at p. 75.

154. Steven G. Krantz, "The Immortality of Proof," *Notices of the American Mathematical Society* 41 (1994): 10–13, at pp. 10, 12 and 13.

155. Tom Hales, electronic mail message to multiple recipients, August 19, 1998; David Hilbert, "Mathematical Problems," *Bulletin of the American Mathematical Society* 8 (1902): 437–479, p. 467 (this is the English translation of Hilbert's lecture to the International Congress of Mathematicians, Paris, 1900); Wu-Yi Hsiang, "On the Density of Sphere Packings in E^3, II—The Proof of Kepler's Conjecture" (Berkeley, Calif.: Center for Pure and Applied Mathematics, University of California, Berkeley, September 1991, PAM-535). Hales's message, and other materials on the work of Hales and his student Samuel P. Ferguson, can be found at http://www.math.lsa.umich.edu/~hales. I owe the orange-stacking analogy to Keith Devlin, "Proof Is Out There," *The Guardian* (September 24, 1998): "online" section, 7.

156. Swart interview. See also Swart, "Philosophical Implications."

157. John Slaney, "The Crisis in Finite Mathematics: Automated Reasoning as Cause and Cure," in *Proceedings of the 12th International Conference on Automated Deduction*, ed. Alan Bundy (London: Springer, 1994), 1–13, at pp. 1, 2 and 12.

158. Singh, *Fermat's Last Theorem;* Henri Darmon, "A Proof of the Full Shimura-Taniyama-Weil Conjecture Is Announced," *Notices of the American Mathematical Society* 46 (1999): 1397–1401.

159. Neil Robertson, electronic mail messages to author, November 20, 1996 and February 5, 1998; H. Hadwiger, "Über eine Klassifikation der Streckenkomplexe," *Vierteljahrsschrift der Naturf. Gesellschaft in Zürich* 88 (1943): 133–142; Neil Robertson, Paul Seymour, and Robin Thomas, "Hadwiger's Conjecture for K_6-free Graphs," *Combinatorica* 13 (1993): 279–361. Hadwiger's conjecture is that loopless graphs without K_{k+1}-minors are k-colorable. A "minor" of a graph G is produced by contracting some of the edges of a subgraph of G to vertices; thus a K_{k+1}-minor is made up of k + 1 subgraphs that are connected, pairwise-disjoint, and any two of which are linked by an edge of G. The four-color theorem is equivalent to Hadwiger's conjecture with k = 4. Neil Robertson (to whom I owe this account) and his colleagues proved Hadwiger's conjecture for k = 5 by demonstrating that any minimal counterexample had to include a vertex (an "apex") which if removed would leave a planar graph (electronic mail message, February 5, 1998). Since that planar graph must be four-colorable, the apex can be given the fifth color.

160. Lynn Arthur Steen, "Living with a New Mathematical Species," *Mathematical Intelligencer* 8(2) (1986): 33–40, at p. 34.

161. Steven Krantz, letter to author, May 26, 1994.

162. Robertson et al., "A New Proof," p. 17.

Chapter 5

1. General Accounting Office, Information Security: Computer Attacks at Department of Defense Pose Increasing Risks (Washington, D.C.: General Accounting Office, May 1996, GAO/AIMD-96-84), pp. 22–25; General Accounting Office, Information Security: Computer Attacks at Department of Defense Pose Increasing Risks, Testimony of Jack L. Brock, Jr., before the Permanent Subcommittee on Investigations, Committee on Governmental Affairs, U.S. Senate (Washington, D.C.: General Accounting Office, 1996, GAO/T-AIMD-96-92); Christopher Elliott, "Found: Spy who Hacked into Pentagon During A Levels," *The Guardian* (March 22, 1997): 1.

2. Christopher Elliott, "Schoolboy Hacker 'Better than KGB,'" *The Guardian* (March 22, 1997): 4.

3. Bill O'Neill, "Hackers for Hire," *The Guardian* (February 26, 1998): "online" section, 5.

4. Paul Mann, "Cyber Threat Expands with Unchecked Speed," *Aviation Week & Space Technology* (July 8, 1996): 63–64, at p. 63; General Accounting Office, GAO/AIMD-96-84, at pp. 18–19 and 27.

5. For a good description of batch operation and of the shift to time-sharing, see Arthur L. Norberg and Judy E. O'Neill, *A History of the Information Processing Techniques Office of the Defense Advanced Research Projects Agency* (Minneapolis, Minn.: Charles Babbage Institute, October 1992), chapter I and appendix I; an amended version of this report has been published as *Transforming Computer Technology: Information Processing for the Pentagon, 1962–1986* (Baltimore, Maryland: Johns Hopkins University Press, 1996).

6. Karl L. Wildes and Nilo A. Lindgren, *A Century of Electrical Engineering and Computer Science at MIT, 1882–1982* (Cambridge, Mass.: MIT Press, 1985), p. 348. Project MAC had wider aims, captured in the alternative version of the acronym, Machine-Aided Cognition (MAC), for which see, e.g., Norberg and O'Neill, *Transforming Computer Technology*, and Paul N. Edwards, *The Closed World: Computers and the Politics of Discourse in Cold War America* (Cambridge, Mass.: MIT Press, 1996).

7. See, for example, the paper by Jack B. Dennis (of Project MAC), "Segmentation and the Design of Multiprogrammed Computer Systems," *Journal of the ACM* 12 (1965): 589–602, esp. pp. 597–599.

8. Norberg and O'Neill, *A History;* Kent C. Redmond and Thomas M. Smith,

Project Whirlwind: The History of a Pioneer Computer (Bedford, Mass.: Digital Press, 1980); Claude Baum, *The System Builders: The Story of SDC* (Santa Monica, Calif.: System Development Corporation, 1981); Edwards, *Closed World.*

9. James Bamford, *The Puzzle Palace: A Report on America's Most Secret Agency* (Boston: Houghton Mifflin, 1982); Keith Devlin, "You Win Sum," *The Guardian* (January 15, 1998): "online" section, 11.

10. Interview data.

11. Herman H. Goldstine, *The Computer from Pascal to von Neumann* (Princeton, N.J.: Princeton University Press, 1972), pp. 253, 306–307, 314.

12. Bamford, *Puzzle Palace,* p. 340.

13. Willis H. Ware, electronic mail message to author, October 17, 1996.

14. Willis H. Ware, "Security and Privacy in Computer Systems," in *AFIPS Conference Proceedings, Volume 30: 1967 Spring Joint Computer Conference* (Washington, D.C.: Thompson Books, 1967), 279–282, at p. 279.

15. Bernard Peters, "Security Considerations in a Multi-Programmed Computer System," in *AFIPS Conference Proceedings, Volume 30: 1967 Spring Joint Computer Conference* (Washington, D.C.: Thompson Books, 1967), 283–286, at p. 283.

16. Emerson W. Pugh, Lyle R. Johnson, and John H. Palmer, *IBM's 360 and Early 370 Systems* (Cambridge, Mass.: MIT Press, 1991), pp. 362–363.

17. Peters, "Security Considerations," p. 283.

18. Peters, "Security Considerations," pp. 283 and 285, emphasis in original.

19. Willis H. Ware, electronic mail message to author, October 17, 1996.

20. *Security Controls for Computer Systems: Report of Defense Science Board Task Force on Computer Security,* ed. Willis H. Ware (Santa Monica, CA: RAND Corporation, February 1970, R-609). Originally classified "confidential," the report was declassified in October 1975. The quotations in the text are from Ware's foreword to the version reissued by RAND in October 1979, and from p. 18 of the latter; subsequent citations are also to this later version.

21. *Security Controls,* ed. Ware, pp. 8, 29 and 36.

22. Roger Schell, telephone interview by Garrel Pottinger, October 10, 1993.

23. Willis H. Ware, electronic mail message to author, October 21, 1996.

24. James P. Anderson, *Computer Security Technology Planning Study* (Bedford, Mass.: Air Force Systems Command, Electronic Systems Division, October 1972, ESD-TR-73-51), vol. 1, pp. 3 and 33.

25. Roger R. Schell, "Computer Security: The Achilles' Heel of the Electronic Air Force?" *Air University Review* 30(2) (January–February 1979): 16–33, at pp. 28–29.

26. Garrel Pottinger, "Proof Requirements in the Orange Book: Origins, Implementation, and Implications" (typescript, February 1994), p. 39.

27. Anderson, *Computer Security,* vol. 1, p. 15.

28. W. L. Schiller, "Design of a Security Kernel for the PDP-11/45" (Bedford Mass.: Air Force Systems Command, Electronic Systems Division, December 1973, ESD-TR-73-294); Schell, "Computer Security," p. 28; Wildes and Lindgren, *A Century,* p. 300.

29. Schell, "Computer Security," p. 31.

30. Paul A. Karger, Mary Ellen Zurko, Douglas W. Bonin, Andrew H. Mason, and Clifford E. Kahn, "A Retrospective on the VAX VMM Security Kernel," *IEEE Transactions on Software Engineering* 17 (1991), 1147–1165, at p. 1159, emphasis in original.

31. Schell interview; Schell, "Computer Security," p. 29.

32. *Security Controls,* ed. Ware, p. 48.

33. C. Weissman, "Security Controls in the ADEPT-50 Time-Sharing System," in *Proceedings of AFIPS Fall Joint Computer Conference* (Arlington, Va.: AFIPS Press, 1969): 119–133, at p. 122.

34. Anderson, *Computer Security,* vol. 1, p. 4.

35. K. G. Walter, W. F. Ogden, W. C. Rounds, F. T. Bradshaw, S. R. Ames, and D. G. Shumway, "Primitive Models for Computer Security" (Bedford, Mass.: Air Force Systems Command, Electronic Systems Division, January 1974, ESD-TR-74-117).

36. Ludwig von Bertalanffy, *General System Theory: Foundations, Development, Applications* (London: Allen Lane, 1971), p. 3; first published New York: Braziller, 1968.

37. D. E. Bell and L. J. LaPadula, "Secure Computer Systems: Mathematical Foundations" (Bedford, Mass: Air Force Systems Command, Electronic Systems Division, November 1973, ESD-TR-73-278), vol. 1; Leonard J. LaPadula, electronic mail message to author, October 29, 1996; M. D. Mesarović, D. Macko, and Y. Takahara, *Theory of Hierarchical, Multilevel, Systems* (New York: Academic Press, 1970), esp. p. 66.

38. D. E. Bell and L. J. LaPadula, "Secure Computer Systems: A Mathematical Model" (Bedford, Mass: Air Force Systems Command, Electronic Systems Division, November 1973, ESD-TR-73-278), vol. 2, p. 15.

39. Anderson, *Computer Security,* vol. 2, p. 62.

40. Bell and LaPadula, "Secure Computer Systems: A Mathematical Model," vol. 2, p. 17; D. E. Bell and L. J. LaPadula, "Secure Computer System: Unified Exposition and Multics Interpretation" (Bedford, Mass: Air Force Systems Command, Electronic Systems Division, March 1976, ESD-TR-75-306), p. 17.

41. Changes of state also had to satisfy the rule of discretionary security (where individuals can extend access to a document to anyone permitted by the mandatory security rules to view it). More formally (Bell and LaPadula, "Unified Exposition," p. 94), the Basic Security Theorem is: "Σ (R,D,W,z_0) is a secure system iff [if and only if] z_0 is a secure state and W satisfies the conditions of theorems A_1, A_2, and A_3 for each action." Σ represents a system; R represents requests (e.g., for access); D represents decisions in response to requests; W represents the rules governing changes of state; z_0 represents an initial state of the system; and A_1, A_2 and A_3 are theorems concerning the characteristics of W that are necessary and sufficient to maintain the simple security property, *-property, and discretionary security property.

42. Bell and LaPadula, "Unified Exposition," pp. 20–21.

43. Bell and LaPadula, "Unified Exposition," pp. 64–70.

44. Schell, "Computer Security," p. 29.

45. Peters, "Security Considerations," p. 285.

46. Carl E. Landwehr, "The Best Available Technologies for Computer Security," *Computer* 16 (1983): 86–100, at p. 96.

47. Anderson, *Computer Security*, vol. 1, p. 10, emphasis in original deleted.

48. Donald I. "Good, Toward a Man-Machine System for Proving Program Correctness" (Ph.D. thesis, University of Wisconsin, 1970); Good, personal communication.

49. Donald I. Good, interviewed by A. J. Dale, Austin, Texas, April 8, 1994; Good, interviewed by M. Tierney, Austin, Texas, November 12, 1991; W. W. Bledsoe and Peter Bruell, "A Man-Machine Theorem Proving System," in *Advance Papers of Third International Joint Conference on Artificial Intelligence 1973*, ed. W. W. Bledsoe, 56–65; D. I. Good, "Proof of a Distributed System in Gypsy," in *Formal Specification: Proceedings of the Joint IBM/University of Newcastle upon Tyne Seminar, 7–10 September 1983*, ed. M. J. Elphick (Newcastle upon Tyne, England: University of Newcastle upon Tyne, Computing Laboratory, 1983) 44–89, at p. 61.

50. See Janet Abbate, *Inventing the Internet* (Cambridge, Mass.: MIT Press, 1999).

51. Good, "Proof of a Distributed System," pp. 45–46; Donald I. Good, "Mechanical Proofs about Computer Programs," *Philosophical Transactions of the Royal Society of London* A312 (1984): 389–409.

52. Richard J. Feiertag, "A Technique for Proving Specifications are Multilevel Secure" (Menlo Park, Calif.: SRI Computer Science Laboratory, January 1980, CSL-109).

53. Lawrence Robinson and Karl N. Levitt, "Proof Techniques for Hierarchically Structured Programs," *Communications of the ACM* 20 (1977): 271–283.

54. Peter G. Neumann, Robert S. Boyer, Richard J. Feiertag, Karl N. Levitt, and

Lawrence Robinson, "A Provably Secure Operating System: The System, Its Applications, and Proofs" (Menlo Park, Calif.: SRI Computer Science Laboratory, May 1980, CSL 116).

55. Richard J. Feiertag and Peter G. Neumann, "The Foundations of a Provably Secure Operating System (PSOS)," in *National Computer Conference, 1979* (New York: AFIPS, 1979), 329–343, p. 333.

56. Peter Neumann, interviewed by A. J. Dale, Menlo Park, Calif., March 25, 1994.

57. Neumann et. al., "Operating System," Technical Summary, p. 2.

58. Landwehr, "Technologies for Computer Security," p. 96.

59. In packet-switching, a message is broken up into separate blocks or "packets," which can take different routes through a network: see Abbate, *Inventing the Internet*, esp. pp. 17–20.

60. Landwehr, "Technologies for Computer Security," p. 97.

61. Marvin Schaefer, "Symbol Security Condition Considered Harmful," in *Proceedings of the 1989 IEEE Symposium on Security and Privacy*, 20–46, p. 22.

62. George F. Jelen, "Information Security: An Elusive Goal" (Cambridge, Mass.: Harvard University Center for Information Policy Research, June 1985, P-85-8), pp. III–84 to III–91. See also Abbate, *Inventing the Internet*, pp. 138–140.

63. D. Elliott Bell, "Concerning 'Modeling' of Computer Security," *1988 IEEE Symposium on Security and Privacy*, 8–13, at p. 12.

64. D. E. Bell, "Secure Computer Systems: A Refinement of the Mathematical Model" (Bedford, Mass.: Air Force Systems Command, Electronic Systems Division, April 1974, ESD-TR-73-278, vol. III), pp. 29 and 31.

65. This example is taken from Garrel Pottinger, Proof Requirements in the Orange Book, pp. 45–46.

66. I draw these examples from Feiertag and Neumann, "Foundations," p. 333.

67. A term used, for example, by G. H. Nibaldi, "Proposed Technical Evaluation Criteria for Trusted Computer Systems" (Bedford, Mass.: MITRE Corporation, October 1979, M79-225), p. 9.

68. Butler W. Lampson, "A Note on the Confinement Problem," *Communications of the ACM* 16 (1973): 613–615, pp. 613 and 614, emphases in original deleted.

69. Schiller et al., "Design of a Security Kernel," p. 7; Carl E. Landwehr, "Formal Models for Computer Security," *Computing Surveys* 13 (September 1981): 247–278, at p. 252.

70. Bell and LaPadula, "Unified Exposition," pp. 67–70.

71. See, e.g., Marvin Schaefer, Barry Gold, Richard Linde, and John Scheid, "Program Confinement in KVM/370," in *ACM 77: Proceedings of the Annual Conference* (New York: Association for Computing Machinery, 1977), 404–410, at p. 406; J. Thomas Haigh, Richard A. Kemmerer, John McHugh, and William D. Young, "An Experience Using Two Covert Channel Analysis Techniques on a Real System Design," *IEEE Transactions on Software Engineering* 13 (1987): 157–168, at p. 159.

72. See, e.g., Jonathan K. Millen, "Security Kernel Validation in Practice," *Communications of the ACM* 19 (1976): 243–250, at p. 250.

73. J. M. Rushby, "Certifiably Secure Systems: Technologies, Prospects and Proposals" (typescript, August 8, 1982), p. 3, reports that "KSOS and UCLA D[ata] S[ecure] U[nix] appear at least an order of magnitude slower than standard UNIX, while KVM/370, in many ways the most successful of these projects, is currently reported to be three to four times slower than VM/370 and seven to eight times slower for I[input]/O[utput] operations)."

74. Schaefer, Gold, Linde, and Scheid, "Program Confinement in KVM/370," p. 409.

75. This is no longer straightforwardly the case with "public key encryption," but that was a later development.

76. See David Kahn, *The Codebreakers* (London: Sphere, 1973) and Bamford, *Puzzle Palace.*

77. Jelen, "Information Security," pp. I–11, III–4 (emphasis in original), and passim.

78. Jelen, "Information Security," p. I–11. The inverted commas around "low politics" are in the original.

79. Norberg and O'Neill, *Transforming Computer Technology.*

80. Anderson, *Computer Security,* vol. 1, p. 4, first parentheses in original.

81. Jelen, "Information Security," pp. i, II–74 to II–75.

82. Walker's formal role was director, Information Systems, Office of the Assistant Secretary of Defense for Communications, Command, Control, and Intelligence (C^3I).

83. Jelen, "Information Security," p. II–75; Stephen T. Walker, interviewed by Garrel Pottinger, Glenwood, Maryland, 24 March 1993.

84. Jelen, "Information Security," p. II–79.

85. Walker interview.

86. "A Plan for the Evaluation of Trusted Computer Systems," typescript, February 22, 1980, reprinted in Jelen, "Information Security," pp. V–2 to V–9.

87. Walker interview; Walker, quoted by Jelen, "Information Security," p. II–81.

88. Jelen, "Information Security," p. II–81, citing Jelen's interview with Admiral Bobby R. Inman.

89. Stephen T. Walker, electronic mail message to author, August 22, 1996.

90. Frank C. Carlucci, Department of Defense Directive 5215.1, "Computer Security Evaluation Center" (October 25, 1982), reproduced in Jelen, "Information Security," pp. V–11 to V–17.

91. Nibaldi, "Proposed Technical Evaluation Criteria," pp. 30, 33–34, 36, and 37.

92. Steven T. Walker, "Thoughts on the Impact of Verification Technology on Trusted Computer Systems (and vice versa)," *Software Engineering Notes* 5(3) (July 1980): 8.

93. William D. Young and John McHugh, "Coding for a Believable Specification to Implementation Mapping," in *IEEE Symposium on Security and Privacy, 1987* (Washington D.C.: IEEE Computer Society, 1987), 140–148, at p. 140.

94. Department of Defense, *Trusted Computer System Evaluation Criteria* (Washington, D.C.: Department of Defense, December 1985, DOD 5200.28-STD), pp. 19, 26, 40, and 50, emphases in original deleted.

95. Robert S. Boyer and J Strother Moore, "Program Verification," *Journal of Automated Reasoning* 1(1985): 17–23, at p. 22.

96. Neumann interview.

97. Pottinger, "Proof Requirements in the Orange Book."

98. Terry C. Vickers Benzel, "Verification Technology and the A1 Criteria," *Software Engineering Notes* 10(4) (August 1985): 108–109, at p. 109.

99. Donald I. Good, interviewed by Eloína Peláez, Austin, Texas, May 16, 1991.

100. Walker interview.

101. Clark Weissman, electronic mail message to Garrel Pottinger, December 18, 1993; Weissman, electronic mail message to author, August 7, 1996.

102. Clark Weissman, "BLACKER: Security for the DDN. Examples of A1 Security Engineering Trades," in *Proceedings of the 1992 IEEE Symposium on Research in Security and Privacy*, 286–292, p. 289. This paper was presented by Weissman to the 1988 IEEE Symposium, but "not published at that time because of a four year rescission of publication release" (ibid., p. 286).

103. John McLean, electronic mail messages to author, February 2, 1998, and May 22, 1998.

104. Carl E. Landwehr, Constance L. Heitmeyer, and John McLean, "A Security Model for Military Message Systems," *ACM Transactions on Computer Systems* 2 (1984): 198–222; John McLean, "A Comment on the 'Basic Security Theorem' of Bell and LaPadula," *Information Processing Letters* 20 (1985): 67–70, at p. 69.

105. McLean, "Comment," p. 70.

106. John McLean, electronic mail message to author, January 18, 1998.

107. John McLean, contribution to Computer Security Forum 5(14), June 22, 1986. I am grateful to Carl Landwehr and to Ted Lee, the then convenor of the forum, for access to the relevant parts of its archive.

108. John McLean, "Reasoning about Security Models," *Proceedings of the 1987 IEEE Symposium on Security and Privacy,* 123–131, at p. 130.

109. Leonard LaPadula and David Bell, contributions to Computer Security Forum 5(18), June 23 and 27, 1986; David Elliott Bell, "Concerning 'Modeling' of Computer Security," *Proceedings of the 1988 IEEE Symposium on Security and Privacy,* 8–13, pp. 9 and 11.

110. Jonathan Millen, contribution to Computer Security Forum 5(18), June 23 1986; Leonard J. LaPadula, comments at Computer Security Foundations Workshop, Franconia, New Hampshire, June 13–14, 1988 (I am grateful to John McLean for a copy of his notes on this event); Ted Lee, contribution to Computer Security Forum 5 (29), October 16, 1986; Don Good, contribution to Computer Security Forum 5(27), October 16, 1986.

111. Imre Lakatos, *Proofs and Refutations: The Logic of Mathematical Discovery,* eds. John Worrall and Elie Zahar (Cambridge: Cambridge University Press, 1976), pp. 14, 24, and 30.

112. Lakatos, *Proofs and Refutations,* p. 94 and passim; Good, contribution.

113. David Bloor, "Polyhedra and the Abominations of Leviticus," *British Journal for the History of Science* 11 (1979): 245–272; Mary Douglas, *Natural Symbols: Explorations in Cosmology* (London: Barrie & Rockliff, 1970).

114. John McLean, electronic mail messages to author, January 18, 1998, and June 5, 1998, and letter to author, May 8, 1998.

115. J. A. Goguen and J. Meseguer, "Security Policies and Security Models," in *Proceedings of the 1982 Berkeley Conference on Computer Security,* 11–22, at p. 11, emphasis in original deleted.

116. Under noninterference, a user with a low-security clearance can copy the contents of one high-security file into another such file, since the outcome of the copying would not interfere with the low-security user. On the Bell-LaPadula model, in contrast, this operation would be prohibited, because it involves a "read" of the high-security file. I am grateful to John McLean for bringing this to my attention in an electronic mail message, January 17, 1998.

117. Dana Scott, "Outline of a Mathematical Theory of Computation," in *Proceedings of the Fourth Annual Conference on Information Systems and Sciences, Princeton University* (1970), 169–176, at p. 176.

118. Richard Platek, interviewed by Garrel Pottinger, Ithaca, New York, February 4, 1993.

119. Daryl McCullough, "Specifications for Multi-Level Security and a Hook-Up Property," in *Proceedings of the 1987 IEEE Symposium on Security and Privacy*, 161–166, at 162. Nondeducibility security is outlined in David Sutherland, "A Model of Information," in *Proceedings of the 9th National Computer Security Conference, September 1986*, 175–183.

120. John McLean, "Security Models," in *Encyclopedia of Software Engineering*, ed. John. J. Marciniak (New York: Wiley, 1994), vol. 2, 1136–1145 at, p. 1141. According to C. T. Sennett, "Formal Methods for Computer Security" (Malvern, Worcs.: Defence Research Agency, 1995, typescript), p. 2: "by providing a means to define even more rigid security controls this approach [noninterference] exacerbated the conflict between security and functionality."

121. McLean, "Security Models," p. 1142. A useful discussion of determinism and nondeterminism appears in Dennis Shasha and Cathy Lazere, *Out of Their Minds: The Lives and Discoveries of 15 Great Computer Scientists* (New York: Copernicus, 1995), pp. 73–79.

122. McCullough, "Specifications for Multi-level Security," p. 163; McLean, "Security Models," p. 1142.

123. McCullough, "Specifications for Multi-Level Security," p. 161; Daryl McCullough, "Noninterference and the Composability of Security Properties," *Proceedings of the 1988 IEEE Symposium on Security and Privacy*, 177–186.

124. McCullough, "Noninterference," pp. 182–183. Noninterference requires that a high-level input must not affect the state of the system as visible to a low-level user, but "does not guarantee that a *pair,* consisting of a high-level input followed immediately by a low-level input, will have the same effect on the low-level behavior as the low-level input alone." Demanding that pairs have the latter property constitutes "restrictiveness" (McCullough, "Noninterference," p. 184, emphasis in original).

125. John McLean, electronic mail message to author, January 27, 1998; McLean, "A General Theory of Composition for a Class of 'Possibilistic' Properties," *IEEE Transactions on Software Engineering* 22 (1996): 53–67; McLean, "Security Models" esp. p. 1143; McLean, "Security Models and Information Flow," in *Proceedings of the 1990 IEEE Symposium on Security and Privacy*, 180–187; James W. Gray, III, "Toward a Mathematical Foundation for Information Flow Security," in *Proceedings of the 1991 IEEE Symposium on Security and Privacy*, 21–34.

126. Daryl McCullough, electronic mail message to author, February 4, 1998.

127. Rita C. Summers, *Secure Computing: Threats and Safeguards* (New York: McGraw-Hill, 1997), p. 140.

128. Weissman, "BLACKER," pp. 288–289 and 291; Weissman, electronic mail messages to Pottinger and MacKenzie.

129. National Research Council, System Security Study Committee, *Computers at Risk: Safe Computing in the Information Age* (Washington D.C.: National Academy Press, 1991), p. 195.

130. See the Evaluated Product List, www.radium.ncsc.mil/tpep/ A further high-assurance system, developed for government use, was Honeywell's LOCK (Logical Coprocessing Kernel). The Goguen-Meseguer noninterference model was used in LOCK's development: Todd Fine, J. Thomas Haigh, Richard C. O'Brien, and Dana L. Toups, "Noninterference and Unwinding for LOCK," paper read to Computer Security Foundations Workshop, Franconia, New Hampshire, June 11, 1989. For a description of LOCK, see National Research Council, *Computers at Risk*, pp. 251–252. LOCK is now known as the Secure Network Server and the Honeywell division responsible for it is now the Secure Computing Corporation.

131. Steven Lipner, electronic mail message to Garrel Pottinger, October 22, 1993.

132. Karger, et al., "A Retrospective," p. 1147; Lipner electronic mail message.

133. Karger et. al., "A Retrospective," p. 1163; Lipner electronic mail message.

134. Charles Bonneau, telephone interview by Garrel Pottinger, November 20, 1993.

135. National Research Council, *Computers at Risk*, p. 143, capitalization in original deleted.

136. Bonneau interview.

137. National Research Council, *Computers at Risk*, p. 154.

138. Walker interview.

139. Vickers Benzel, "Verification Technology," p. 108.

140. Karger et al., "A Retrospective," p. 1156.

141. *Common Criteria for Information Technology Security Evaluation* (multiple publishers including Cheltenham, Glouc.: U.K. IT Security and Certification Scheme, 1996).

142. Pottinger, Proof Requirements in the Orange Book, pp. 16–17.

143. David D. Clark and David R. Wilson, "A Comparison of Commercial and Military Computer Security Policies," *Proceedings of 1987 IEEE Symposium on Security and Privacy*, 184–194.

144. K. J. Biba, "Integrity Considerations for Secure Computer Systems" (Bedford, Mass.: Air Force Systems Command, Electronic Systems Division, 1977, ESD-TR-76-372).

145. National Research Council, *Computers at Risk*.

Chapter 6

1. Richard A. DeMillo, Richard J. Lipton, and Alan J. Perlis, "Social Processes and Proofs of Theorems and Programs," *Proceedings of the Fourth ACM Symposium on Principles of Programming Languages* (January 1977), 206–214, at p. 206, cited below as "Social Processes" (*POPL*).

2. Edsger W. Dijkstra, "On a Political Pamphlet from the Middle Ages," *Software Engineering Notes* 3(2) (April 1978): 14–16, capitalization in original deleted; Letters to Editor from Leonard F. Zettel Jr., H. Lienhard, Allan G. Pomerantz, and Daniel Glazer, *Communications of the ACM* 22 (1979): 621–623.

3. Richard A. DeMillo, interviewed by A. J. Dale, Chicago, September 25, 1994.

4. DeMillo interview.

5. Richard A. DeMillo, "Formal Semantics and the Logical Structure of Programming Languages" (Ph.D. thesis, Georgia Institute of Technology, Atlanta, 1972).

6. DeMillo interview; Edsger W. Dijkstra, "The Structure of the 'THE'-Multiprogramming System," *Communications of the ACM* 11(1968): 341–346; Dijkstra, "Cooperating Sequential Processes," in *Programming Languages*, ed. F. Genuys (New York: Academic Press, 1968), 43–112; Richard J. Lipton, "On Synchronization Primitive Systems" (Ph.D. thesis, Carnegie Mellon University, Pittsburgh, 1973); Lipton, interviewed by A. J. Dale, Princeton, N.J., May 4, 1994.

7. DeMillo interview. Topological sorting is arranging objects in a "partially ordered" set in a sequence that reflects their partial ordering, a procedure that is useful in many contexts in computer science. An example given by Knuth is arranging the words in a glossary of technical terms "so that no term is used before it has been defined." See Donald E. Knuth, *The Art of Computer Programming. Vol. 1: Fundamental Algorithms* (Reading, Mass.: Addison-Wesley, 1968), pp. 259–265.

8. A. N. Habermann, "Alan J. Perlis, 1922–1990," *Acta Informatica* 28 (1990–1991): 409–410.

9. *Software Engineering Techniques: Report on a Conference Sponsored by the NATO Science Committee, Rome, Italy, 27th to 31st October 1969*, eds. J. N. Buxton and B. Randell (Brussels: NATO, 1970), pp. 21–22.

10. DeMillo interview.

11. Lipton interview.

12. DeMillo recalled this conversation as taking place in the year that President Nixon resigned.

13. DeMillo interview.

14. DeMillo interview.

15. Habermann, "Perlis"; DeMillo interview.

16. They used italics for formal proof and Roman letters within inverted commas for informal proof.

17. DeMillo, Lipton, and Perlis, "Social Processes" (*POPL*), pp. 206–208, emphasis in original.

18. DeMillo, Lipton, and Perlis, "Social Processes" (*POPL*), p. 209.

19. The axiom of choice asserts that if A is a family of nonempty sets, there is a function f such that $f(S)$ is a member of S for every set S in A. The function selects or "chooses" a member of each set, hence the axiom's name.

20. The continuum hypothesis is that the cardinal number of the set of real numbers (that is, of the continuum of points on a line) is the infinite cardinal number next largest to that of the set of natural numbers $(0, 1, 2, \ldots)$. A cardinal number expresses how many members a set has: two sets the members of which can be put in one-to-one correspondence have the same cardinal number.

21. The other axioms of Zermelo-Fraenkel set theory do not imply either the axiom of choice or its negation, and the continuum hypothesis is independent from the axioms of set theory together with the axiom of choice. See Paul J. Cohen, "The Independence of the Continuum Hypothesis," *Proceedings of the National Academy of Sciences* (USA) 50 (1963): 1143–1148 and 51 (1964): 105–110.

22. DeMillo, Lipton, and Perlis, "Social Processes" (*POPL*), p. 209.

23. DeMillo, Lipton, and Perlis, "Social Processes" (*POPL*), pp. 206, 209, and 210–211, emphases in original.

24. DeMillo interview; R. A. DeMillo, S. C. Eisenstat, and R. J. Lipton, "Can Structured Programs be Efficient?" *SIGPLAN Notices* (October 1976): 10–18, at p. 10, emphasis in original.

25. See, e.g., Richard A. DeMillo, Richard J. Lipton, and Frederick G. Sayward, "Hints on Test Data Selection: Help for the Practicing Programmer," *Computer* 11 (4) (April 1978): 34–41; Timothy A. Budd, Richard A. DeMillo, Richard J. Lipton, and Frederick G. Sayward, "Theoretical and Empirical Studies on Using Program Mutation to Test the Functional Correctness of Programs," in *ACM Symposium on Principles of Programming Languages, Jan. 1980*, 220–223. In mutation testing, both the original program and "mutants" (which differ from the original only in the presence of small errors, such as alteration of a single character) are run on the same test data. Good test data are data on which the output

of most mutants differs from that of the original; such mutants as discarded as "dead." "Mutation analysis relies on the notion that if the test data discovers the single change that has been made to produce the mutant program then the test data will discover more major faults in the program. Thus, if the test data has not discovered any major faults, and a high proportion of the mutants have been killed, then the program is likely to be sound" (P. David Coward, "Software Testing Techniques," in *The Software Life Cycle*, eds. Darrel Ince and Derek Andrews [London: Butterworths, 1990], 386–402, pp. 398–399).

26. DeMillo (DeMillo interview) dates the original idea of mutation testing to the fall of 1976, two years after they started to formulate their critique of formal verification.

27. *SIGPLAN Notices* (May 1976): 64–68. Tanenbaum argued that proofs of program correctness might mislead because specifications might be incorrect, proofs may contain errors, the causal effects of instructions might not be as expected, and real, physical hardware might not behave as assumed in the mathematical model underlying the proof. He did not develop these points into a philosophical case against program verification as Fetzer did, but he illustrated them with plausible examples of what might go wrong.

28. DeMillo interview.

29. DeMillo interview; J. J. Horning, "Resolved: 'Program Verification is a Useful Activity,'" (typescript, August 25, 1977), pp. 1, 6, and 7. I am grateful to Jim Horning for a copy of his unpublished notes for this debate.

30. DeMillo interview; J. Barkley Rosser, "Highlights of the History of the Lambda Calculus," *Annals of the History of Computing* 6 (1984): 337–349, at pp. 344–345. A mimeographed version of Rosser's (and S. C. Kleene's) notes of Gödel's spring 1934 Princeton lectures appeared as Kurt Gödel, "On Undecidable Propositions of Formal Mathematical Systems," in *The Undecidable: Basic Papers on Undecidable Propositions, Unsolvable Problems and Computable Functions*, ed. Martin Davis (Hewlett, New York: Raven, 1965), 41–71. This version, however, contains only expository footnotes, not discursive marginalia.

31. DeMillo interview; Richard A. DeMillo, Richard J. Lipton, and Alan J. Perlis, "Social Processes and Proofs of Theorems and Programs," *Communications of the ACM* 22 (1979): 271–280, pp. 271, 272, 273, and 275, emphasis in original.

32. DeMillo interview.

33. W. D. Maurer, Letter to Editor, *Communications of the ACM* 22 (1979): 625–629, at p. 627. For Maurer's work, see, for example, Maurer, "Some Correctness Principles for Machine Language Programs and Microprograms," *Proceedings of Seventh Workshop on Microprogramming, Palo Alto, Calif., September 30–October 2, 1974* (New York: Association for Computing Machinery, 1974), 225–234.

34. Leslie Lamport, Letter to Editor, *Communications of the ACM* 22 (1979): 624.

35. Dijkstra, "On a Political Pamphlet," p. 14.

36. Edsger W. Dijkstra, "On the Cruelty of Really Teaching Computer Science: The SIGCSE Award Lecture," *ACM SIGCSE Bulletin* 21(1) (February 1989): xxiv–xxxix, p. xxxiii.

37. Richard A. DeMillo, Edsger W. Dijkstra, panel discussion moderated by Robert Paige, Purdue University, April 16, 1993. I am grateful to Richard DeMillo for a copy of the videotape of this discussion.

38. DeMillo, Dijkstra, panel discussion.

39. Edsger W. Dijkstra, "EWD563: Formal Techniques and Sizeable Programs," paper prepared for Symposium on the Mathematical Foundations of Computing Science, Gdansk, 1976, as reprinted in Dijkstra, *Selected Writings on Computing: A Personal Perspective* (New York: Springer, 1982), 205–214, at pp. 211–212.

40. DeMillo, Dijkstra, panel discussion.

41. DeMillo interview.

42. Susan Gerhart, interviewed by A. J. Dale, Houston, Texas, April 10, 1994.

43. James H. Fetzer, "Program Verification: The Very Idea," *Communications of the ACM* 31 (1988): 1048–1063.

44. James H. Fetzer, interviewed by A. J. Dale, Duluth, Minnesota, April 17, 1994. For Wilkins's work, see, e.g., B. T. Wilkins, *Hegel's Philosophy of History* (Ithaca, NY: Cornell University Press, 1974).

45. Fetzer interview.

46. Fetzer interview; James H. Fetzer and Donald E. Nute, "Syntax, Semantics, and Ontology: A Probabilistic Causal Calculus," *Synthese* 40 (1979): 453–495.

47. Fetzer interview.

48. Fetzer interview. The textbook was Michael Marcotty and Henry F. Ledgard, *Programming Language Landscape: Syntax, Semantics, and Implementation* (Chicago: Science Research Associates, second edition, 1986). The work of DeMillo, Lipton, and Perlis is cited ibid., p. 532.

49. Fetzer interview; Peter J. Denning, "Reply from the Editor in Chief," *Communications of the ACM* 32 (1989): 289–290, at p. 289.

50. Fetzer, "Program Verification," pp. 1049–1053 and 1061.

51. Fetzer, "Program Verification," pp. 1059 and 1060; James H. Fetzer, "Philosophical Aspects of Program Verification," in *Program Verification: Fundamental Issues in Computer Science,* eds. Timothy R. Colburn, James H. Fetzer, and Terry L. Rankin (Dordrecht: Kluwer, 1993), 403–427, at p. 418.

52. Fetzer, "Program Verification," p. 1062, emphasis in original.

53. Mark Ardis, Victor Basili, Susan Gerhart, Donald Good, David Gries, Richard

Kemmerer, Nancy Leveson, David Musser, Peter Neumann, and Friedrich von Henke, "Editorial Process Verification," *Communications of the ACM* 32 (1989): 287–288, at p. 288.

54. Lawrence Paulson, Avra [Cohn], and Michael Gordon, Letter to Editor, *Communications of the ACM* 32 (1989): 375. Cohn's surname is misspelt as "Cohen" in the published version of this letter. William R. Bevier, Michael K. Smith, and William D. Young, Letter to Editor, *Communications of the ACM* 32 (1989): 375–376.

55. Fetzer interview.

56. Fetzer interview.

57. Ardis et al., "Editorial Process Verification," p. 287; James H. Fetzer, Response from the Author, *Communications of the ACM* 32 (1989): 288–289, emphases in original.

58. Peter J. Denning, "Reply from the Editor in Chief," *Communications of the ACM* 32 (1989): 289–290, at p. 289.

59. Leslie Lamport, "I told you so," electronic mail message to multiple recipients, March 15, 1989.

60. Paulson et. al., Letter; Avra Cohn, "The Notion of Proof in Hardware Verification," *Journal of Automated Reasoning* 5 (1989): 127–139; Bevier et al., Letter, p. 376.

61. John Dobson and Brian Randell, "Program Verification: Public Image and Private Reality," *Communications of the ACM* 32 (1989): 420–422, capitalization in original deleted; James C. Pleasant, Letter to Editor, *Communications of the ACM* 32 (1989): 374–375, at p. 374.

62. Aaron Watters, Letter to Editor, *Communications of the ACM* 32 (1989): 509–510.

63. Watters, Letter.

Chapter 7

1. Thomas R. Nicely, "Enumeration to 10^{14} of the Twin Primes and Brun's Constant," *Virginia Journal of Science* 46 (1996): 195–204; Viggo Brun, "La Série $^1/_5$ + $^1/_7$ + $^1/_{11}$ + $^1/_{13}$ + $^1/_{17}$ + $^1/_{19}$ + $^1/_{29}$ + $^1/_{31}$ = [sic] $^1/_{41}$ + $^1/_{43}$ + $^1/_{59}$ + $^1/_{61}$ + ... ou les Dénominateurs sont 'Nombres Premiers Jumeaux' est Convergente ou Finie," *Bulletin des Sciences Mathématiques* 43 (1919): 124–128; Barry Cipra, "How Number Theory Got the Best of the Pentium Chip," *Science* 267 (January 13, 1995): 175.

2. Nicely, "Enumeration," p. 196.

3. The sieve of Eratosthenes is an algorithm for identifying prime numbers by

systematically eliminating composite (nonprime) numbers. List the natural numbers greater than one: 2, 3, 4, 5, . . . Leave in 2, but delete all its multiples (4, 6, 8, . . .). Move to the next remaining number, 3, leave it in, but delete all its multiples, and so on.

4. Nicely, "Enumeration," pp. 196–197 and 203.

5. Floating-point arithmetic is arithmetic in which the position of the decimal point (or its computer equivalent, the binary point) is not fixed but (at least in most computer implementations) the number of digits available for use is fixed. A decimal floating-point number, for example, is one expressed in terms of powers of 10, so that, for example, 123 is expressed 1.23×10^2 and 0.00123 as 1.23×10^{-3}.

6. Nicely, "Enumeration," p. 197.

7. Nicely, "Enumeration," pp. 197–198; Tim Coe, Terje Mathisen, Cleve Moler, and Vaughan Pratt, "Computational Aspects of the Pentium Affair," *IEEE Computational Science & Engineering* (spring 1995): 18–30, pp. 19–20.

8. Coe et al., "Pentium Affair," pp. 20–21; K. D. Tocher, "Techniques of Multiplication and Division for Automatic Binary Computers," *Quarterly Journal of Mechanics and Applied Mathematics* 11 (1958): 364–384; James E. Robertson, "A New Class of Digital Division Methods," *IRE Transactions on Electronic Computers* 7 (1958): 218–222. Sweeney's work (unpublished as far as I am aware) is referred to in Daniel E. Atkins, "Higher-Radix Division Using Estimates of the Division and Partial Remainders," *IEEE Transactions on Computers* C-17 (1968): 925–934, at p. 925.

9. Nicely, "Enumeration," p. 198; H. P. Sharangpani and M. L. Barton, "Statistical Analysis of Floating Point Flaw in the Pentium™ Processor (1994)" (n.p.: Intel Corporation, 1994); Andy Grove, "My Perspective on Pentium," comp.sys.intel, November 27, 1994.

10. Michael S. Malone, *The Microprocessor: A Biography* (New York: Springer, 1995), pp. 236–243; Mark Tran and Nicholas Bannister, "IBM Pulls Plug on Pentium Shipments," *The Guardian* (December 13, 1994): 16; Nicholas Bannister, "Intel Left with Egg on Its Face as Pentium Flaw Costs £306m," *The Guardian* (January 19, 1995): 16.

11. Jack Goldberg, "A History of Research in Fault Tolerant Computing at SRI International," in *The Evolution of Fault-Tolerant Computing: In the Honor of William C. Carter*, eds. A. Avizienis, H. Kopetz, and J. C. Laprie (Vienna: Springer, 1987), 101–119.

12. See J. E. Tomayko, "Achieving Reliability: The Evolution of Redundancy in American Manned Spacecraft Computers," *Journal of the British Interplanetary Society* 38 (1985): 545–552.

13. Albert L. Hopkins, Jr., Jaynarayan H. Lala, and T. Basil Smith, III, "The Evo-

lution of Fault Tolerant Computing at the Charles Stark Laboratory, 1955–1985," in *The Evolution of Fault Tolerant Computing*, eds. Avizienis et. al., 121–140, pp. 128–130; for the history of the Draper Laboratory, see D. MacKenzie, *Inventing Accuracy: A Historical Sociology of Nuclear Missile Guidance* (Cambridge, Mass.: MIT Press, 1990).

14. John H. Wensley, "SIFT—Software Implemented Fault Tolerance," in *Proceedings of 1972 Fall Joint Computer Conference* (Montvale, N.J.: AFIPS Press, 1972), 243–253; John H. Wensley, Leslie Lamport, Jack Goldberg, Milton W. Green, Karl N. Levitt, P. M. Melliar-Smith, Robert E. Shostak, and Charles B. Weinstock, "SIFT: Design and Analysis of a Fault-Tolerant Computer for Aircraft Control," *Proceedings of the IEEE* 66 (1978): 1240–1255.

15. P. M. Melliar-Smith and Richard L. Schwartz, "The Proof of SIFT," *Software Engineering Notes* 7(1) (January 1982): 2–5; Jack Goldberg, "SIFT: A Provable Fault-Tolerant Computer for Aircraft Flight Control," in *Information Processing 80*, ed. S. H. Lavington (Amsterdam: North-Holland, 1980), 151–156.

16. Wensley et al., "SIFT," p. 1240.

17. Wensley et al., "SIFT," p. 1240, emphasis in original.

18. Peter Galison, "Einstein's Clocks: The Place of Time," *Critical Inquiry* 26 (winter 2000): 355–389, see esp. p. 375.

19. Leslie Lamport, as quoted in Dennis Shasha and Cathy Lazere, *Out of their Minds: The Lives and Discoveries of 15 Great Computer Scientists* (New York: Copernicus, 1995), p. 124.

20. Galison, "Einstein's Clocks," pp. 358, 361, and 378.

21. Charles B. Weinstock, "SIFT: System Design and Implementation," in *Proceedings of the Tenth International Symposium on Fault-Tolerant Computing, October 1980*, 75–77, at p. 75; Melliar-Smith and Schwartz, "Proof of SIFT," p. 2.

22. John Rushby, "More on the AFTI/F-16," *Software Engineering Notes* 16(3) (July 1991): 22–23, at p. 22.

23. Weinstock, "SIFT," p. 77.

24. Shasha and Lazere, *Out of their Minds*, p. 132.

25. I am here following the exposition in Weinstock, "SIFT," p. 77. On the general problem of Byzantine faults, see also Leslie Lamport, Robert Shostak, and Marshall Pease, "The Byzantine Generals Problem," *ACM Transactions on Programming Languages and Systems* 4 (1982): 382–401.

26. Rob Shostak, electronic mail message to author, June 2, 1999.

27. Leslie Lamport and P. M. Melliar-Smith, "Synchronizing Clocks in the Presence of Faults," *Journal of the ACM* 32 (1985): 52–78.

28. Consider a four-clock system, in which at most one clock is faulty. The goal of the interactive convergence algorithm is to keep the good clocks within some skew, δ, of each other. Assume A and B are good clocks. If clock C is also a good clock, then the estimates that A and B form of its clock value can differ at most by 2ε, where ε is the upper limit of the error in any good clock's estimate of the reading of a good clock. If C is faulty, the estimates that A and B form of its clock value can differ by $2\Delta + \delta$, where Δ is the threshold value beyond which skews are set to zero. (C could report to A a value different from A's of as much as Δ without being ignored; it could also report to B a value different from B's by Δ; and A's and B's clocks themselves could differ by δ.) With at least three good clocks, and at most one faulty clock, the "egocentric means" calculated by A and B can differ by no more than

$$\frac{6\varepsilon + (2\Delta + \delta)}{4}$$

The algorithm, therefore, will keep the good clocks within δ of each other so long as

$$\frac{6\varepsilon + (2\Delta + \delta)}{4} \leq \delta$$

and this will be the case provided that

$$\delta \geq 2\varepsilon + \frac{2\Delta}{3}$$

In the general case of n clocks, of which m are faulty, the egocentric means of two good clocks can differ from each other by at most

$$\frac{(n - m)2\varepsilon + m(2\Delta + \delta)}{n}$$

and the algorithm will maintain the good clocks within δ of each other provided that

$$\delta \geq 2\varepsilon + \frac{2m\Delta}{n - m}$$

This sketch of the proof of the interactive convergence algorithm is drawn from John M. Rushby and Friedrich von Henke, "Formal Verification of Algorithms for Critical Systems," *IEEE Transactions on Software Engineering* 19 (1993): 13–23, at p. 15. As Rushby and Von Henke point out, it ignores important complications, such as the fact that the different processors "do not perform the algorithm simultaneously and instantaneously" (ibid.).

29. Wensley et. al., "SIFT," p. 1250.

30. Melliar-Smith and Schwartz, "Proof of SIFT," p. 3.

31. P. Michael Melliar-Smith and Richard L. Schwartz, "Formal Specification

and Mechanical Verification of SIFT: A Fault-Tolerant Flight Control System," *IEEE Transactions on Computers* C-31 (1982): 616–630, at p. 621.

32. Melliar-Smith and Schwartz, "Formal Specification and Mechanical Verification of SIFT," p. 629.

33. Melliar-Smith and Schwartz, "Formal Specification and Mechanical Verification of SIFT," pp. 622 and 629. "The mean time between failures" of an individual unit of SIFT, "containing processor, store, and interfaces," was less than 1,000 hours: ibid., p. 618.

34. Richard A. DeMillo, interviewed by A. J. Dale, Chicago, September 25, 1994.

35. SRI International, "Overview of SRI Accomplishments," appendix A of *Peer Review of a Formal Verification/Design Proof Methodology* (Washington, D.C.: NASA, 1985, NASA Conference Publication 2377), 25–31, at p. 26.

36. Leslie Lamport, interviewed by A. J. Dale, Palo Alto, Calif., March 29, 1994.

37. SRI International, "Overview of SRI Accomplishments," p. 31.

38. SRI International, "Overview of SRI Accomplishments," pp. 26–27.

39. SRI International, "Overview of SRI Accomplishments," p. 27.

40. I am grateful to J Strother Moore for making this feature clear to me in an electronic mail message, February 25, 1993.

41. Lamport interview.

42. SRI International, "Overview of SRI Accomplishments," pp. 27 and 31.

43. Ricky Butler, interviewed by A. J. Dale, Hampton, Virginia, May 6, 1994.

44. Donald I. Good, interviewed by Margaret Tierney, Austin, Texas, November 12, 1991.

45. DeMillo interview.

46. Richard Schwartz, electronic mail message to author, June 9, 1999; DeMillo interview.

47. Research Triangle Institute, "Proceedings of a Formal Verification/Design Proof Peer Review" (Research Triangle Park, North Carolina: Research Triangle Institute, January 1984, RTI/2094/13–01F), pp. 39–40.

48. *Peer Review* (1985), p. 23.

49. Richard Schwartz, interviewed by A. J. Dale, March 30, 1994; Schwartz, electronic mail messages to author, June 18, 1997 and June 9, 1999.

50. J Strother Moore, interviewed by A. J. Dale, Austin, Texas, April 7, 1994.

51. J. Wensley, "August Systems Industrial Control Computers," in *Resilient*

Computing Systems, ed. T. Anderson (London: Collins, 1985), 232–246; C. J. Goring, "The History and Development of Computer Based Safety Systems for Offshore Oil and Gas Production Platforms from the Sixties to the Present Day," in *Safety of Computer Control Systems 1990: Safety, Security and Reliability Related Computers for the 1990s,* ed. B. K. Daniels (Oxford: Pergamon Press, 1990), 145–150, at p. 148.

52. J Strother Moore, "System Verification," *Journal of Automated Reasoning* 5 (1989): 409–410, at p. 410.

53. Robert S. Boyer, interviewed by Eloína Peláez, Austin, Texas, May 20, 1991; Boyer, electronic mail message to author, June 4, 1997.

54. Robert S. Boyer, interviewed by A. J. Dale, Austin, Texas, April 8, 1994; Boyer, "Locking: A Restriction of Resolution" (Ph.D. thesis, University of Texas at Austin, 1971).

55. J Strother Moore, interviewed by Margaret Tierney, Austin, Texas, November 12, 1991.

56. Moore, interviewed by Tierney.

57. Robert S. Boyer and J Strother Moore, "On Why It Is Impossible to Prove that the BDX930 Dispatcher Implements a Time-Sharing System," unpaginated section 17 of K. N. Levitt, D. F. Hare, P. M. Melliar-Smith, R. L. Schwartz, R. E. Shostak, M. W. Green, R. Boyer, J Moore, M. S. Moriconi, and W. D. Elliott, *Investigation, Development, and Evaluation of Performance Proving for Fault-Tolerant Computers: Interim Report Covering the Period September 1978 to June 1982* (Menlo Park, Calif.: SRI International, June 1983).

58. Boyer and Moore, "On Why It Is Impossible to Prove."

59. Robert S. Boyer and J Strother Moore, "Proving Theorems about LISP Functions," *Journal of the ACM* 22 (1975): 129–144.

60. J Strother Moore, electronic mail message to author, February 25, 1993, italics substituted for capitalization in original.

61. Robert S. Boyer and J Strother Moore, "A Formal Semantics for the SRI Hierarchical Program Design Methodology," p. 27. This June 1977 document forms section 16 of K N. Levitt et al., *Interim Report.*

62. Boyer and Moore, "The B930 Adventure," section 18 of Levitt et al., *Interim Report.*

63. Boyer and Moore, "On Why It Is Impossible to Prove."

64. Donald I. Good, "Provable Programs and Processors," in *Proceedings of National Computer Conference, 1974,* 357–363, at p. 357.

65. Donald I. Good, interviewed by A. J. Dale, Austin, Texas, April 8, 1994.

66. Robert S. Boyer and J Strother Moore, "A Theorem Prover for a Computa-

tional Logic," Keynote Address to 10th Conference on Automated Deduction, July 1990, 1–15, at p. 3.

67. Robert S. Boyer and Yuan Yu, "A Formal Specification of Some User Mode Instructions for the Motorola 68020" (Austin, Texas: University of Texas at Austin, February, 1992, Technical Report TR-92-04).

68. Warren A. Hunt, Jr., interviewed by Margaret Tierney, Austin, Texas, November 12, 1991.

69. Warren A. Hunt, Jr., "FM8501: A Verified Microprocessor" (Austin, Texas: Institute for Computer Science and Computer Applications, December, 1985, Technical Report 47), p. 6; this report was Hunt's Ph.D. thesis and was published as Hunt, *FM8501: A Verified Microprocessor* (Berlin: Springer, 1994).

70. Robert S. Boyer and J Strother Moore, *A Computational Logic Handbook* (San Diego, Calif.: Academic Press, 1988), p. 393.

71. Hunt, "FM8501" (1985), p. 6.

72. Hunt interview.

73. Warren A. Hunt, Jr., and Bishop C. Brock, "A Formal HDL and Its Use in the FM9001 Verification," in *Mechanized Reasoning and Hardware Design*, eds. C. A. R. Hoare and M. J. C. Gordon (London: Prentice-Hall, 1992), 35–46, at pp. 35–37 and p. 46.

74. Warren A. Hunt, Jr., electronic mail message to author, May 23, 1995 and telephone conversation with author, June 12, 1997.

75. Robert S. Boyer, electronic mail message to author, March 2, 1995.

76. Moore, "System Verification," p. 410.

77. William R. Bevier, Warren A. Hunt, Jr., J Strother Moore, and William D. Young, "An Approach to Systems Verification," *Journal of Automated Reasoning* 5 (1989): 411–428, at pp. 422–423.

78. Moore, "System Verification," p. 409.

79. William R. Bevier, Michael K. Smith, and William D. Young, Letter to Editor, *Communications of the ACM* 32 (1989): 375–376, at p. 376.

80. Moore, interviewed by Dale; Moore, electronic mail message to author, April 23, 1999.

81. D. MacKenzie, "The Fangs of the VIPER," *Nature* 352 (August 8, 1991): 467–468, reprinted in MacKenzie, *Knowing Machines: Essays on Technical Change* (Cambridge, Mass.: MIT Press, 1996), 159–164.

82. W. J. Cullyer and C. H. Pygott, "Application of Formal Methods to the VIPER Microprocessor," *IEE Proceedings* 134(Pt. E) (1987): 133–141.

83. Cullyer and Pygott, "Application of Formal Methods," pp. 137–138.

84. Cullyer and Pygott, "Application of Formal Methods," p. 138.

85. See Avra Cohn, "A Proof of Correctness of the Viper Microprocessor: The First Level" (University of Cambridge: Computer Laboratory, January 1987, technical Report no. 104).

86. Avra Cohn, "Correctness Properties of the Viper Block Model: The Second Level" (University of Cambridge: Computer Laboratory, May 1988, technical report no. 134), p. 86.

87. John Kershaw, "The Meaning of Proof," *SafetyNet* no. 4 (January/February/March 1989), 4. In twos complement arithmetic, the sign is expressed as a binary digit (0 for positive, 1 for negative), thus representing negative numbers "by their complements with respect to 2." See Robert F. Shaw, "Arithmetic Operation in a Binary Computer," *Review of Scientific Instruments* 21 (1950): 687–693, at pp. 687–688.

88. E.g., Cullyer and Pygott, "Application of Formal Methods."

89. Charter Technologies, Ltd., "VIPER Microprocessor: Development Tools" (Worcester, England: Charter Technologies Ltd., December 1987, unpaginated).

90. *New Scientist,* October 16, 1986; *Electronics Weekly,* October 15, 1986; *Engineer,* February 4, 1988. I am quoting from a file of unpaginated cuttings of coverage of VIPER provided to me, along with much other material on the episode, by Digby Dyke.

91. Cohn, "Correctness Properties," pp. 10–12, emphases in original; see also Avra Cohn, "The Notion of Proof in Hardware Verification," *Journal of Automated Reasoning* 5 (1989): 127–139.

92. Cohn, "The Notion of Proof," pp. 128 and 135, parentheses in original. For a discussion of intelligent exhaustion, and for further work being done in the area of RSRE, see Clive H. Pygott, "NODEN_HDL: An Engineering Approach to Hardware Verification," in *The Fusion of Hardware Design and Verification,* ed. G. J. Milne (Amsterdam: North-Holland, 1988), 211–219.

93. Bishop Brock and Warren A. Hunt, Jr., "Report on the Formal Specification and Partial Verification of the VIPER Microprocessor" (Austin, Texas: Computational Logic, Inc., January 15, 1990, Technical Report 46), pp. 15, 21, and 22.

94. MacKenzie, "Fangs of the VIPER."

95. Eloína Peláez, James Fleck, and Donald MacKenzie, "Social Research on Software," paper presented to meeting of the U.K. Economic and Social Research Council, Programme on Information and Communication Technology, Manchester, December 16–18, 1987, p. 5.

96. Martyn Thomas, "VIPER Law Suit Withdrawn," electronic mail message to multiple recipients, June 5, 1991.

97. See, e.g., C. H. Pygott, "Verification of VIPER's ALU [Arithmetic/Logic Unit]" (Malvern, Worcs.: Royal Signals and Radar Establishment, Technical Report, Divisional memo, draft, 1991); Wai Wong, "Formal Verification of VIPER's ALU" (Cambridge: University of Cambridge Computer Laboratory, typescript, April 15, 1993); J. Joyce, S. Rajan, and Z. Zhu, "A Virtuoso Performance Becomes Routine Practice: a Re-Verification of the VIPER Microprocessor Using a Combination of Interactive Theorem-Proving and B[inary] D[ecision] D[iagram]-Based Symbolic Trajectory Evaluation," typescript abstract of paper presented at Conference on the Mathematics of Dependable Systems, University of London, 1993. I have not seen the first of these items; I owe my knowledge of it to Wong ("Formal Verification," pp. 4 and 60).

98. Kershaw, "Meaning of Proof."

99. Edmund M. Clarke and E. Allen Emerson, "Design and Synthesis of Synchronization Skeletons Using Branching Time Temporal Logic," in *Logics of Programs: Lecture Notes in Computer Science, Volume 131,* ed. D. Kozen (Berlin: Springer 1981), 52–71.

100. See, for example, Aarti Gupta, "Formal Hardware Verification Methods: A Survey," in *Formal Methods in System Design,* ed. Robert Kurshan (Dordrecht: Kluwer, 1993), 151–238.

101. John Harrison, *Theorem Proving with the Real Numbers* (London: Springer, 1998), p. 5.

102. E. Clarke, O. Grumberg, and D. Long, "Model Checking," in *Deductive Program Design,* ed. Manfred Broy (Berlin: Springer, 1996), 305–349, at p. 306.

103. Randal E. Bryant, "Graph-Based Algorithms for Boolean Function Manipulation," *IEEE Transactions on Computers* C-35 (1986): 677–691, at pp. 677, 681, and 689.

104. An alternative technique was developed by the Swedish computer scientist Gunnar Stålmarck (a student of Dag Prawitz). See Gunnar M. N. Stålmarck, "System for Determining Propositional Logic Theorems by applying Values and Rules to Triplets that are Generated from Boolean Formula [sic]" (U.S. patent no. 5,276,897, January 4, 1994); I owe the information that Stålmarck was one of Prawitz's students to an electronic mail message from John Harrison, February 26, 1996.

105. Victor Konrad, "Job Opportunities in Formal Verification at Intel," electronic mail message to multiple recipients, November 22, 1996. For a range of other industrial applications of model checking, see Edmund M. Clarke, Jeannette M. Wing et al., "Formal Methods: State of the Art and Future Directions," *ACM Computing Surveys* 28 (1996): 626–643, esp. pp. 630–633.

106. Edmund Clarke, electronic mail message to author, May 31, 1999.

107. See, for example, John Rushby, "Model Checking and Other Ways of Automating Formal Methods," discussion paper for panel on Model Checking for Concurrent Programs, Software Quality Week, San Francisco, May/June 1995, available at http://www.csl.sri.com/sqw95.html.

108. David E. Long, "Model Checking, Abstraction, and Compositional Verification" (Ph.D. thesis, Carnegie Mellon University, 1993), p. 209; electronic mail message from Edmund Clarke to author, June 2, 1999.

109. K. L. McMillan, "A Methodology for Hardware Verification using Compositional Model Checking" (Berkeley, Calif.: Cadence Berkeley Laboratories, typescript, April 15, 1999), available at http://www-cad.eecs.berkeley.edu/~kenmcmil/papers/1999—03.ps.gz; electronic mail message from McMillan to author, June 7, 1999.

110. J Strother Moore, Thomas W. Lynch, and Matt Kaufmann, "A Mechanically Checked Proof of the AMD5$_K$86™ Floating-Point Division Program," *IEEE Transactions on Computers* 47 (1998): 913–926.

111. J Strother Moore, "Towards a Mechanically Checked Theory of Computation: A Progress Report" (typescript, May 1999), p. 17.

112. *Computer-Aided Reasoning: ACL2 Case Studies*, eds. Matt Kaufmann, Panagiotis Manolios, and J Strother Moore (Boston: Kluwer, 2000), pp. 12–14.

113. John Kershaw, "Foreword," to Brock and Hunt, "Formal Specification and Partial Verification," i–iii, at p. iii.

Chapter 8

1. "Profession of Faith by L. E. J. Brouwer," March 30, 1898 (delivered April 3, 1898), reproduced in English translation in Walter P. van Stigt, *Brouwer's Intuitionism* (Amsterdam: North-Holland, 1990), 390–393.

2. L. E. J. Brouwer, "Intuitionism and Formalism," *Bulletin of the American Mathematical Society* 20 (1913): 81–96, at pp. 83 and 85.

3. I owe this example to Randy Pollack.

4. L. E. J. Brouwer, "The Unreliability of the Logical Principles," in *L. E. J. Brouwer: Collected Works, Volume 1, Philosophy and Foundations of Mathematics*, ed. A. Heyting (Amsterdam: North-Holland, 1975), 107–111, at p. 109.

5. Hermann Weyl, "Uber die neue Grundlagenkrise der Mathematik," *Mathematische Zeitschrift* 10 (1921): 39–79, at p. 56.

6. David Hilbert, "The Foundations of Mathematics," in *From Frege to Gödel: A Source Book in Mathematical Logic, 1879–1931*, ed. Jean van Heijenoort (Cambridge, Mass.: Cambridge University Press, 1967), 464–479, at pp. 475–476. This is the English translation of an address by Hilbert to the Hamburg Mathematical Seminar in July 1927.

7. Solipsism is the philosophical position that the only certainty is one's own existence.

8. L. E. J. Brouwer, "Life, Art and Mysticism," in *Brouwer: Collected Works,* vol. 1, 1–10, at pp. 1, 3, 6, and 9.

9. Van Stigt, *Brouwer's Intuitionism,* p. 32; Brouwer, "Life, Art and Mysticism," as translated ibid., pp. 32–33.

10. Dirk van Dalen, "The War of the Frogs and the Mice, or the Crisis of the *Mathematische Annalen*," *The Mathematical Intelligencer* 12(4) (1990): 17–31, at p. 19., n. 5.

11. Herbert Mehrtens, "Ludwig Bieberbach and 'Deutsche Mathematik,' " in *Studies in the History of Mathematics,* 26, ed. Esther R. Phillips (Washington D.C.: Mathematical Association of America, 1987), 195–241; see p. 232 for "reactionary romanticism." The charges against Brouwer are discussed briefly in van Stigt, *Brouwer's Intuitionism,* p. 107.

12. Barry Barnes, "On the Implications of a Body of Knowledge," *Knowledge: Creation, Diffusion, Utilization* 4 (1982): 95–110; D. MacKenzie, "The Political 'Implications' of Scientific Theories: A Comment on Bowler," *Annals of Science* 42 (1985): 417–420.

13. Errett Bishop, *Foundations of Constructive Analysis* (New York: McGraw-Hill, 1967), p. 2. A useful review of the varieties of constructivism appears in A. S. Troelstra and D. van Dalen, *Constructivism in Mathematics: An Introduction, volume 1* (Amsterdam: North-Holland, 1988), chapter 1.

14. Van Stigt, *Brouwer's Intuitionism,* p. 90. An intuitionist logic was also developed by A. N. Kolmogorov: see Kolmogorov, "O Printsipe Tertium non Datur," *Matematicheskii Sbornik* 32 (1925): 646–667; English translation as Kolmogorov, "On the Principle of Excluded Middle," in *From Frege to Gödel,* 413–437.

15. A. Heyting, *Intuitionism: An Introduction* (Amsterdam: North-Holland, second edition, 1966), pp. 99–100. Heyting first presented his intuitionist logic in "Die formalen Regeln der intuitionistischen Logik," *Sitzungsberichte der preuszischen Akademie von Wissenschaften,* Physikalisch-mathematische Klasse (1930): 42–56.

16. Robert S. Boyer and J Strother Moore, "A Theorem Prover for a Computational Logic," keynote address to Tenth Conference on Automated Deduction (July 1990), 1–15, at p. 9.

17. J Strother Moore, interviewed by A. J. Dale, Austin, Texas, April 7, 1994.

18. See chapter 3, note 31.

19. J Strother Moore, interviewed by M. Tierney, Austin, Texas, November 12, 1991; R. M. Burstall, "Proving Properties of Programs by Structural Induction," *Computer Journal* 12 (1969): 41–48. See also John McCarthy and James Painter,

"Correctness of a Compiler for Arithmetic Expressions," in *Mathematical Aspects of Computer Science: Proceedings of Symposia in Applied Mathematics, Vol. 19* (Providence, Rhode Island: American Mathematical Society, 1967), 33–41.

20. Moore, interviewed by Tierney.

21. Robert S. Boyer, interviewed by A. J. Dale, Austin, Texas, April 8, 1994.

22. J Strother Moore II, "Computational Logic: Structure Sharing and Proof of Program Properties" (University of Edinburgh: Ph.D. thesis, 1973), pp. 222–223; the inverted commas around "creative" are in the original.

23. Robert S. Boyer and J Strother Moore, *A Computational Logic* (New York: Academic Press, 1979), p. 6.

24. Boyer interview; Robert S. Boyer, "Locking: A Restriction of Resolution" (Ph.D. thesis, University of Texas at Austin, 1971).

25. Bertrand Russell, letter to Gottlob Frege, June 16, 1902; an English translation of Russell's letter, which he wrote in German, is in van Heijenoort, *From Frege to Gödel*, 124–125. For Skolem's work, see Thoralf Skolem, "Some Remarks on Axiomatized Set Theory," in van Heijenoort, *From Frege to Gödel*, 290–301, at p. 300, emphases in original (this is a translation of Skolem's address to the Fifth Congress of Scandinavian Mathematicians, Helsinki, August 4–7, 1922); and Skolem, "The Foundations of Elementary Arithmetic Established by Means of the Recursive Mode of Thought, Without the Use of Apparent Variables Ranging over Infinite Domains," in van Heijenoort, *From Frege to Gödel*, 302–333. The latter is a translation of paper written in 1919: Skolem, "Begründung der elementaren Arithmetik durch die rekurrierende Denkweise ohne Anwendung scheinbarer Veränderlichen mit unendlichem Ausdehnungsbereich," *Videnskapsselskapets Skrifter, I. Matematisk-naturvidenskabelig Klasse* 6 (1923): 1–38.

26. R. L. Goodstein, *Recursive Number Theory* (Amsterdam: North-Holland, 1957): see p. ix, where Goodstein thanks Heyting for "the very kind interest he has taken in the preparation of this book, from the first manuscript draft to the finished typescript." Goodstein's *Recursive Analysis* also appeared in the same series (Amsterdam: North-Holland, 1961).

27. Goodstein, *Recursive Number Theory*, p. 13.

28. Skolem, "Foundations of Elementary Arithmetic."

29. Boyer and Moore, "Theorem Prover," p. 4.

30. Boyer interview.

31. Moore, "Computational Logic" (1973), p. 99.

32. That is, if A, B, and C are lists and we are using the LISP's prefix notation, (APPEND A (APPEND B C)) is equal to (APPEND (APPEND A B) C). See Robert S. Boyer and J Strother Moore, "Proving Theorems about LISP Functions,"

Journal of the ACM 22 (1975): 129–144. For how the prover learned from failures, see Alan Bundy, *The Computer Modelling of Mathematical Reasoning* (London: Academic Press, 1983), chapter 11.

33. That is, formulae that did not violate the construction rules of the formal system being used; the quotations in this paragraph are from the Boyer interview.

34. Boyer interview; Moore, interviewed by Tierney. Neither Boyer nor Moore cited specific instances, but for a report of their uncovering "several invalid axioms" in a particular program verification, see Dan Craigen, "A Technical Review of Four Verification Systems: Gypsy, Affirm, FDM and Revised Special" (Ottawa, Ontario: I. P. Sharp Associates, August 1985, FR-85-5401-01), p. 47.

35. Craigen, "Four Verification Systems," p. 64, again cites an example, but this time one found by Dave Musser, a member of the Kemmerer panel discussed below.

36. As Boyer and Moore, *A Computational Logic*, pp. 13, 31–32, and 44, explain, a new function $(f x_1 \ldots x_n)$ is well-founded if it is defined in terms of "recursive calls" taking the form $(f y_1 \ldots y_n)$, when on every call the y_i are "smaller" than the x_i in some measure that is "well-founded": that is, any sequence in which each object is smaller (on the measure) than the one before has to be finite. (To get an intuitive sense of what this means, consider not a recursive function but a recursive program, one that includes a call to itself. Unless the program has, so to speak, less to do each time it is called, it will loop forever.) Insisting that new functions pass the well-foundedness test prevents one, for example, from formulating Russell's paradox in Boyer-Moore logic by prohibiting the function RUSSELL, where (RUSSELL X) = (IF (RUSSELL X) F T). In Boyer-Moore logic (IF A B C) takes the value C if A has the value F ("false"); otherwise it takes the value B. From its definition, (RUSSELL X) must either have the value F or the value T ("true"). If (RUSSELL X) = F, then (IF (RUSSELL X) F T) = T; if (RUSSELL X) = T, then (IF (RUSSELL X) F T) = F. In either case we have a contradiction.

37. Robert S. Boyer and J Strother Moore, "A Computational Logic" (typescript, Computer Science Laboratory, SRI International, May 1978), part 1, p. 2.

38. Moore, "Computational Logic" (1973), p. 203.

39. Robert S. Boyer and J Strother Moore, *A Computational Logic Handbook* (San Diego, Calif.: Academic Press, 1988), pp. xi–xii and 5; Boyer and Moore, "Integrating Decision Procedures into Heuristic Theorem Provers: A Case Study of Linear Arithmetic" in *Machine Intelligence 11: Logic and the Acquisition of Knowledge*, eds. J. E. Hayes et al. (Oxford: Clarendon, 1988), 83–124; Boyer and Moore, "The Addition of Bounded Quantification and Partial Functions to A Computational Logic and its Theorem Prover," *Journal of Automated Reasoning* 4 (1988): 117–172.

40. Robert S. Boyer, interviewed by E. Peláez, Austin, Texas, May 20, 1991.

41. John Rushby, interviewed by A. J. Dale, Menlo Park, Calif., March 29, 1994.

42. Natarajan Shankar, "Proof-Checking Metamathematics" (Ph.D. thesis, University of Texas at Austin, 1986); Shankar, *Metamathematics, Machines, and Gödel's Proof* (Cambridge: Cambridge University Press, 1994).

43. Robert S. Boyer and J Strother Moore, "Proof Checking the RSA Public Key Encryption Algorithm," *American Mathematical Monthly* 91 (1984): 181–189; Robert S. Boyer, electronic mail message to multiple recipients, September 20, 1994. The latter reported Kenneth Kunen's use of the Boyer-Moore system to prove the Paris-Harrington theorem (he proved the theorem itself, not that it could not be proved within elementary number theory). For the Paris-Harrington theorem, see Jeff Paris and Leo Harrington, "A Mathematical Incompleteness in Peano Arithmetic," in *Handbook of Mathematical Logic,* ed. Jon Barwise (Oxford: North Holland, 1977), 1133–1142.

44. Robert E. Shostak, interviewed by A. J. Dale, Menlo Park, Calif., March 28, 1994.

45. Shostak interview; Robert E. Shostak, "On the SUP-INF Method for Proving Presburger Formulas," *Journal of the ACM* 24 (1977): 529–543; Shostak, "An Algorithm for Reasoning about Equality," *Communications of the ACM* 21 (1978): 583–585; Shostak, "A Practical Decision Procedure for Arithmetic with Function Symbols," *Journal of the ACM* 26 (1979): 351–360; Shostak, "Deciding Linear Inequalities by Computing Loop Residues," *Journal of the ACM* 28 (1981): 769–779; Shostak, "Deciding Combinations of Theories," *Journal of the ACM* 31 (1984): 1–12.

46. R. E. Shostak, Richard Schwartz, and P. M. Melliar-Smith, "STP: A Mechanized Logic for Specification and Verification," in *Proceedings of 6th International Conference on Automated Deduction, New York, June 7–9, 1982* (New York: Springer, 1982), 32–49, at p. 34; Richard Schwartz, interviewed by A. J. Dale, Scotts Valley, Calif., March 30, 1994.

47. John Rushby, electronic mail message to author, February 23, 1999.

48. Shostak interview; Shostak et al., "STP"; Karl Levitt and Peter Neumann, "Recent SRI Work in Verification," *ACM SIGSOFT Software Engineering Notes* 6 (3) (July 1981): 27–35, at p. 30; Richard Schwartz, electronic mail message to author, March 2, 1999. The parts of Shostak's work most centrally drawn on were Shostak, "Reasoning about Equality," "Arithmetic with Function Symbols," and "Deciding Combinations."

49. Shostak et al., "STP," p. 34.

50. Richard Schwartz, electronic mail message to author, March 2, 1999.

51. Rushby, electronic mail message.

52. Rushby, electronic mail message; Rushby, interviewed by M. Tierney, Menlo Park, Calif., November 6, 1991. See Michael Melliar-Smith and John Rushby,

"The Enhanced HDM System for Specification and Verification," *ACM SIGSOFT Software Engineering Notes* 10 (4) (August 1985): 41–43.

53. Rushby, interviewed by Tierney.

54. Melliar-Smith and Rushby, "Enhanced HDM," p. 41.

55. Sam Owre, John Rushby, Natarajan Shankar, and Friedrich von Henke, "Formal Verification for Fault-Tolerant Architectures: Prolegomena to the Design of PVS," *IEEE Transactions on Software Engineering* 21 (1995): 107–125.

56. Rushby, interviewed by Dale.

57. L. Lamport and P. M. Melliar-Smith, "Synchronizing Clocks in the Presence of Faults," *Journal of the ACM* 32 (1985): 52–78; John M. Rushby and Friedrich von Henke, "Formal Verification of Algorithms for Critical Systems," *IEEE Transactions on Software Engineering* 19 (1993): 13–23, at pp. 17 and 22; Rushby, electronic mail message. For examples of other verification work using the SRI systems, see David Cyrluk et al., "Mechanized Formal Verification—Seven Papers" (Menlo Park, Calif.: SRI International, January 1995, SRI-CSL-95-03).

58. Robin Milner, interviewed by A. J. Dale, Edinburgh, November 17 and 30, 1993; Martin Campbell-Kelly, "Christopher Strachey, 1916–1975: A Biographical Note," *Annals of the History of Computing* 7 (1985): 19–42.

59. Rod Burstall, interviewed by A. J. Dale, Edinburgh, November 29, 1993; Burstall, electronic mail message to author, February 4, 1999.

60. Milner interview; Dana Scott, interviewed by A. J. Dale, Pittsburgh, Pennsylvania, April 19, 1994; Scott, "1976 ACM Turing Award Lecture: Logic and Programming Languages," *Communications of the ACM* 20 (1977): 634–641; Campbell-Kelly, "Strachey"; P. J. Landin, "A Correspondence Between ALGOL 60 and Church's Lambda-Notation: Part I," *Communications of the ACM* 8 (1965): 89–101, and "Part II," ibid., 158–165. See also Michael S. Mahoney, "Computers and Mathematics: The Search for a Discipline of Computer Science," in *The Space of Mathematics: Philosophical, Epistemological, and Historical Explorations,* eds. Javier Echeverria, Andoni Ibarra and Thomas Mormann (Berlin: de Gruyter, 1992), 349–363, pp. 354–361.

61. I am following here the introduction to the λ-calculus in Haskell B. Curry and Robert Feys, *Combinatory Logic* (Amsterdam: North Holland, 1968), vol. 1, pp. 80–83, at p. 82.

62. Alonzo Church, *The Calculi of Lambda-Conversion* (Princeton: Princeton University Press, 1941), p. 2.

63. J. Barkley Rosser, "Highlights of the History of the Lambda Calculus," *Annals of the History of Computing* 6 (1984): 337–349, at pp. 344–345; Alonzo Church, "An Unsolvable Problem of Elementary Number Theory," *American Journal of Mathematics* 58 (1936): 345–363, at p. 356, and the abstract of this paper, *Bulletin of the American Mathematical Society* 41 (1935): 332–333; A. M. Turing, "On

Computable Numbers, with an Application to the Entscheidungsproblem," *Proceedings of the London Mathematical Society* 42 (1937): 230–265; Turing, "A Correction," *Proceedings of the London Mathematical Society* 43 (1937): 544–546.

64. Scott, "Turing Lecture," p. 637; Campbell-Kelly, "Strachey," p. 39; Dana Scott, "Outline of a Mathematical Theory of Computation," in *Proceedings of the Fourth Annual Conference on Information Systems and Sciences, Princeton University* (1970): 169–176 at p. 175; Dana Scott and Christopher Strachey, "Toward a Mathematical Semantics for Computer Languages," in *Proceedings of the Symposium on Computers and Automata, Polytechnic Institute of Brooklyn, April 13–15, 1971,* 19–46; Rosser, "Highlights," p. 346.

65. Milner interview; Robin Milner, "Logic for Computable Functions: Description of a Machine Implementation" (Stanford, Calif.: Stanford University Artificial Intelligence Project, 1972, AIM-169).

66. Milner interview; M. Gordon, R. Milner, and C. Wadsworth, "Edinburgh LCF" (Edinburgh: University of Edinburgh, Department of Computer Science, 1977, CSR-11-77).

67. Lawrence C. Paulson, *ML for the Working Programmer* (Cambridge: Cambridge University Press, 1991).

68. Robin Milner, "A Theory of Type Polymorphism in Programming," *Journal of Computer and System Sciences* 17 (1978): 348–375, at p. 348; Paulson, *ML,* p. 58. Subsequently, others applied formal, mechanized proof to the ML type inference algorithm: see Catherine Dubois and Valérie Ménissier-Morain, "Certification of a Type Inference Tool for ML: Damas-Milner within Coq," *Journal of Automated Reasoning* 23 (1999): 319–346.

69. Gordon, Milner, and Wadsworth, "Edinburgh LCF," p. 5.

70. L. C. Paulson, *Logic in Computation: Interactive Proof with Cambridge LCF* (Cambridge: Cambridge University Press, 1987), p. 209.

71. Milner interview.

72. Andrew S. Tanenbaum, *Structured Computer Organization* (Englewood Cliffs, New Jersey: Prentice-Hall, 1976), esp. pp. 150–164.

73. Michael J. C. Gordon, interviewed by author, Cambridge, January 10, 1991; Michael J. C. Gordon, interviewed by A. J. Dale, Cambridge, February 2, 1994; Gordon, "Proving a Computer Correct with the LCF_LSM Hardware Verification System" (Cambridge: University of Cambridge Computer Laboratory, 1983, Technical Report 42).

74. Gordon interviewed by MacKenzie; Gordon interviewed by Dale. As stated in note 31 to chapter 3, in first-order predicate logic, quantified variables range over individual entities, not over functions and predicates. In higher-order logics this restriction is removed. Variables can range over functions and predicates, one can generalize about or quantify over properties of predicates, and so on.

75. Hanna and his research associate Neil Daeche noted in 1986 that "a waveform is a function from time to voltage," and hence to be able to assert a property of waveforms requires quantification over functions, and thus not first- but second-order logic. A specification of a logic gate might then involve the assertion that under all conditions a particular relationship must hold between different waveforms, and thus takes one into the domain of third-order logic, and so on. See F. K. Hanna and N. Daeche, "Specification and Verification Using Higher-Order Logic: A Case Study," in *Formal Aspects of VLSI Design*, eds. G. J. Milne and P. A. Subrahmanyam (Amsterdam: North-Holland, 1986), 179–213, at p. 180. An automated system for higher-order logic was also developed by Peter Andrews, a student of Alonzo Church: P. B. Andrews et al., "Automating Higher-Order Logic," *Contemporary Mathematics* 29 (1984): 169–192; Peter Andrews, interviewed by A. J. Dale, Pittsburgh, Pennsylvania, April 20, 1994.

76. Alonzo Church, "A Formulation of the Simple Theory of Types," *Journal of Symbolic Logic* 5 (1940): 56–68.

77. Gordon, interviewed by Dale; Gordon, "HOL: A Machine Oriented Formulation of Higher Order Logic" (Cambridge: Cambridge University Computer Laboratory, 1985, Technical Report 103); Gordon, "Why Higher-Order Logic Is a Good Formalism for Specifying and Verifying Hardware," in *Formal Aspects of VLSI Design*, eds. G. J. Milne and P. A. Subrahmanyam (Amsterdam: North Holland, 1986), 153–177; Gordon, "HOL: A Proof Generating System for Higher-Order Logic," in *VLSI Specification, Verification and Synthesis*, eds. Graham Birtwistle and P. A. Subrahmanyam (Boston: Kluwer, 1988), 73–128; *Introduction to HOL: A Theorem Proving Environment for Higher Order Logic*, eds. M. J. C. Gordon and T. F. Melham (Cambridge: Cambridge University Press, 1993).

78. Gordon, interviewed by Dale; Avra Cohn, interviewed by A. J. Dale, February 2, 1994; Gordon, interviewed by MacKenzie.

79. Communications-Electronics Security Group, "CESG Computer Security Memorandum No. 3: UK Systems Security Confidence Levels" (Cheltenham: Communications-Electronics Security Group, 1989).

80. U.K. IT Security Evaluation and Certification Scheme, "Certified Product List UKSP06" (Cheltenham: Certification Body Secretariat, U.K. IT Security Evaluation and Certification Scheme, April 1995), p. 38; Roger Bishop Jones, "Methods and Tools for the Verification of Critical Properties," in *Proceedings of the 5th Refinement Workshop, London 1992*, eds. Cliff B. Jones et al. (London: Springer, 1992), 88–118; K. Blackburn, "A Report on ICL HOL," in *Automated Deduction CADE-II*, ed. D. Kapur (Berlin: Springer, 1992), 743–747; D. J. King and R. D. Arthan, "Development of Practical Verification Tools," *ICL System Journal* 11 (May 1996): 106–122.

81. Gordon, "HOL: Machine Oriented Formulation," pp. 21–22; A. C. Leisenring, *Mathematical Logic and Hilbert's ε-symbol* (London: MacDonald, 1969). For the axiom of choice, see chapter 6, note 19; its history is described in Gregory H. Moore, *Zermelo's Axiom of Choice: Its Origins, Development, and Influence* (New

York: Springer, 1982); for a brief account, see Barry Barnes, David Bloor, and John Henry, *Scientific Knowledge: A Sociological Analysis* (London: Athlone, 1996), pp. 191–192.

82. See, for example, Per Martin-Löf, *Notes on Constructive Mathematics* (Stockholm: Almqvist and Wiksell, 1970).

83. David Epstein and Silvio Levy, "Experimentation and Proof in Mathematics," *Notices of the American Mathematical Society* 42 (1995): 670–674, at p. 671.

84. Robert Constable, interviewed by A. J. Dale, Ithaca, New York, April 26, 1994; see, e.g., S. C. Kleene, "On the Interpretation of Intuitionistic Number Theory," *Journal of Symbolic Logic* 10 (1945): 109–124.

85. Constable, interviewed by Dale.

86. Robert Constable, "Mathematical Existence: Idea # 2.5 (August 1963), Intelligence Systems" (summer/fall 1963), and "A New Basis for Mathematics" (undated but c. 1963), all unpaginated. I am grateful to Professor Constable for copies of these notebook entries.

87. The continuum hypothesis is described in chapter 6, note 20.

88. Constable, interviewed by Dale.

89. Constable, interviewed by Dale.

90. Constable, interviewed by Dale; Robert L. Constable, "Constructive Mathematics and Automatic Program Writers," in *Information Processing 71: Proceedings of IFIP Congress 71* (Amsterdam: North-Holland, 1972), vol. 1, 229–233.

91. Joseph L. Bates and Robert L. Constable, "Proofs as Programs," *ACM Transactions on Programming Languages and Systems* 7 (1985): 113–136, at p. 114, emphasis in original.

92. Robert L. Constable, letters to author, July 16, 1993 and February 17, 1999.

93. Constable, interviewed by Dale; Constable, interviewed by author, Ithaca, New York, November 3, 1997; Constable letter (1999).

94. Constable letter (1999); R. L. Constable et al., *Implementing Mathematics with the Nuprl Proof Development System* (Englewood Cliffs, New Jersey: Prentice-Hall, 1986).

95. Constable, interviewed by MacKenzie; Gordon, "HOL: Machine Oriented Formulation," pp. 17–18; Robert [Randy] Pollack, "How to Believe a Machine-Checked Proof," in *Twenty-Five Years of Constructive Type Theory*, eds. Giovanni Sambin and Jan M. Smith (Oxford: Clarendon, 1998), 205–220, at p. 215.

96. Douglas J. Howe, "The Computational Behaviour of Girard's Paradox," in *Proceedings of 2nd Symposium on Logic in Computer Science, Ithaca, June 22–25, 1987* (Washington, D.C.: IEEE Computer Society, 1987), 205–214; Chetan R. Murthy

and James R. Russell, "A Constructive Proof of Higman's Lemma," in *Proceedings of the 5th Annual IEEE Symposium on Logic in Computer Science, June 4–7, 1990* (Washington, D.C.: IEEE Computer Society, 1990), 257–267; Miriam Leeser, "Using Nuprl for the Verification and Synthesis of Hardware," *Philosophical Transactions of the Royal Society of London* A339 (1992): 49–68; Robert Constable, electronic mail message to author, November 27, 1998; Constable letter, 1999; Constable, Jason Hickey and Christoph Kreitz, "Assuring the Integrity of Highly Decentralized Communications Systems" (grant proposal to ARPA, n.p., n.d.).

97. Paul B. Thistlewaite, Michael A. McRobbie, and Robert K. Meyer, *Automated Theorem-Proving in Non-Classical Logic* (London: Pitman, 1988), p. 4. For a sociological discussion of relevance logic, see David Bloor, *Wittgenstein: A Social Theory of Knowledge* (London: Macmillan, 1983), pp. 124–136.

98. J. Alan Robinson, interviewed by A. J. Dale, Edinburgh, February 15 and 16, 1994.

99. That is, it permits impredicative definition: a definition is impredicative if it makes reference to a collection containing the entity being defined.

100. Constable interviewed by Dale; Constable interviewed by MacKenzie.

101. Robin Milner, reply to question at meeting of Awareness Club in Computer Assisted Formal Reasoning, Edinburgh, March 21, 1994. The paraphrase in the text is taken from my notes on this event.

102. See, for example, Kurt Gödel, "Zur intuitionistischen Arithmetik und Zahlentheorie," with English translation as "On Intuitionistic Arithmetic and Number Theory," *in Kurt Gödel: Collected Works, Volume I: Publications 1929–1936*, eds. Solomon Feferman, John W. Dawson, Jr., Stephen C. Kleene, Gregory H. Moore, Robert M. Solovay, and Jean van Heijenoort (New York: Oxford University Press, 1986), 286–295. To take another example, Constable's collaborator Doug Howe has shown how to give a classical, set-theoretic, reinterpretation of Nuprl, thus making possible the consistent addition to Nuprl of theorems proved by HOL; Constable, letter to MacKenzie, November 27, 1998.

103. Michael Fourman, personal communication to author, December 9, 1991.

104. Milner interview; Rosser, "Highlights," p. 339; Paulson, *ML*, p. 336. I owe the information that the Milner algorithm is used only in HOL88, and not, e.g., in HOL90, to an electronic mail message from John Harrison, June 23, 1999.

105. Constable, interviewed by Dale.

106. Richard A. Kemmerer, "A Brief Summary of a Verification Assessment Study" (Santa Barbara, Calif.: Department of Computer Science, University of California at Santa Barbara, July 25, 1996, typescript), p. 7. I am grateful to Professor Kemmerer for making available to me this unrestricted summary of the study.

107. Craigen, "Four Verification Systems," p. 74.

108. Robinson interview.

109. Harrison, *Theorem Proving*, p. 8.

110. Richard Kemmerer, interviewed by A. J. Dale, Santa Barbara, Calif., April 1, 1994.

111. Kemmerer, "Brief Summary," p. 7.

112. Rushby interview; Rushby and von Henke, "Formal Verification," p. 20.

113. Siva Anantharam, "Robbins Conjecture has been proved by Computer," electronic mail message to rewriting group, May 18, 1995; Anantharam, "The Robbins Conjecture is still open," electronic mail message to rewriting group, August 28, 1995; Anantharam, electronic mail messages to author, December 4 and 5, 1998; Harrison, *Theorem Proving*, p. 7, note 8. The error was caused by erroneous behavior of the program (written in the C programming language) following the exhaustion of the "heap" (memory space) allocated to it. I do not count, as an instance of a theorem-proving bug causing a fallacious proof, Shimamoto's proof of the four-color conjecture described in chapter 4, because the program being used was not a general-purpose theorem prover, and, in any case, the precise cause of the error remains unclear.

114. Pollack, "How to Believe," pp. 206–207.

115. *Interim Defence Standard 00–55 (PART 2)/Issue 1: The Procurement of Safety Critical Software in Defence Equipment. Part 2: Guidance* (Glasgow: Ministry of Defence, April 5, 1991), pp. 28–29. See also, for example, C. B. Jones, K. D. Jones, P. A. Lindsay and R. Moore, *Mural: A Formal Development Support System* (London: Springer, 1991), p. 305, which advocates independent mechanized proof checking; the idea is attributed to Malcolm Newey.

116. Mike Gordon, electronic mail message to author, January 27, 1999; see, e.g., Wai Wong, "Recording HOL Proofs" (typescript, July 30, 1993).

117. Constable, interviewed by MacKenzie.

118. John Rushby, "Formal Methods and the Certification of Critical Systems" (Menlo Park, Calif.: SRI International, 1993, SRI-CSL-93-07), p. 85.

119. Boyer interview.

120. Boyer interview; Moore, interviewed by Dale.

121. Moore, interviewed by Dale.

122. Robert S. Boyer and J Strother Moore, "Program Verification," *Journal of Automated Reasoning* 1 (1985): 17–23, at p. 23.

123. Boyer and Moore, "Theorem Prover," p. 7; J Strother Moore, electronic mail message to multiple recipients, September 25, 1995; Boyer interview; Moore, interviewed by Dale; Boyer, electronic mail message to author, February

20, 1999. See also Matt Kaufmann and J S. Moore, "An Industrial Strength Theorem Prover for a Logic Based on Common Lisp," *IEEE Transactions on Software Engineering* 23 (1997): 203–213; and Kaufmann, Panagiotis Manolios, and Moore, *Computer-Based Reasoning: An Approach* (Boston: Kluwer, 2000).

124. Boyer interview; Moore interviewed by Dale.

125. Randy Pollack, electronic mail message to author, October 27, 1994. I am grateful to Pollack for conducting this counting exercise on my behalf. A signature "consists of type checking information about each item declared in a structure" within ML (Paulson, *ML*, p. 235).

126. Stuart Anderson, personal communication; Harrison, *Theorem Proving*, pp. 7–8.

127. Boyer, interviewed by Dale; Randy Pollack, electronic mail messages to author, October 27, 1994 and February 8, 1999.

128. Rushby interview.

129. Moore, interviewed by Dale.

130. Milner interview.

131. Constable, interviewed by Dale; Constable, interviewed by MacKenzie. See the later paper, William E. Aitken, Robert L. Constable, and Judith L. Underwood, "Metalogical Frameworks II: Developing a Reflected Decision Procedure," *Journal of Automated Reasoning* 22 (1999): 171–221.

132. Gordon, interviewed by Dale.

133. Ludwig Wittgenstein, *Remarks on the Foundations of Mathematics* (Oxford: Blackwell 1967), p. 75e.

134. **new_axiom** is available only in HOL's draft mode, not in its proof mode. As the main textbook of HOL puts it, "Draft mode is analogous to 'super user mode' in Unix in that it gives access to dangerous facilities": Gordon and Melham, *Introduction to HOL*, p. 15.

135. Moore, interviewed by Dale.

136. Steven T. Walker, interviewed by Garrel Pottinger, Glenwood, Maryland, March 24, 1993.

137. Gordon, interviewed by MacKenzie.

138. Roger Jones, interviewed by A. J. Dale, Winnersh, Berks, U.K., March 8, 1994; Jones, electronic mail messages to author, February 4, 1999 and May 30, 1999.

139. Two readers of the draft of this book made that point to me in personal communications.

140. Roger Jones, electronic mail messages to author, August 17 and 20, 2000.

Chapter 9

1. C. A. R. Hoare, as quoted in chapter 2 above; J. C. R. Licklider, "Underestimates and Overexpectations," in *ABM: An Evaluation of the Decision to Deploy an Antiballistic Missile System,* eds. Abram Chayes and Jerome B. Wiesner (New York: Harper and Rowe, 1969), 118–129, at p. 123; Ken Thompson, "Reflections on Trusting Trust," *Communications of the ACM* 27 (1984): 761–763, p. 763. For "Trojan horses," see chapter 5.

2. Current and back issues of *Risk Digest* are accessible at http://catless.ncl.ac.uk/Risks/ See also Peter G. Neumann, *Computer-Related Risks* (Reading, Mass.: Addison-Wesley, 1995).

3. In one of the episodes, a set of failures in radiation therapy in the North Staffordshire Royal Infirmary, a precise number of deaths cannot be determined.

4. D. MacKenzie, "Computer-Related Accidental Death: An Empirical Exploration," *Science and Public Policy* 21 (1994): 233–248, reprinted as chapter 9 of MacKenzie, *Knowing Machines: Essays on Technical Change* (Cambridge, Mass.: MIT Press, 1996).

5. The Gulf War performance of Patriot was the subject of fierce debate reported in D. MacKenzie, "How Good a Patriot Was It?" *The Independent* (16 December 1991), 13, and in Harry Collins and Trevor Pinch, *The Golem at Large: What You Should Know about Technology* (Cambridge: Cambridge University Press, 1998), chapter 1.

6. For a brief historical review and references, see David N. Schwartz, "Past and Present: The Historical Legacy," in *Ballistic Missile Defense,* eds. Ashton B. Carter and David N. Schwartz (Washington, D.C.: Brookings, 1984), 330–349.

7. Thompson, "Trust," p. 763.

8. Howard S. Becker, *Outsiders: Studies in the Sociology of Deviance* (New York: Free Press, 1973), p. 162.

9. See, e.g., D. MacKenzie and M. Tierney, "Safety-Critical and Security-Critical Computing in Britain: An Exploration," *Technology Analysis & Strategic Management* 8 (1996): 355–379.

10. According to William B. Scott, "USSC Initiates New Tactics to Safeguard Military Computers," *Aviation Week & Space Technology* (June 12, 2000): 54–55, at p. 55, "very few classified network (Siprnet) incidents have been recorded. Most were mistakes made by insiders." Unfortunately, one's confidence in this claim is reduced by anon., "Who Knows?" *Aviation Week & Space Technology* (December 6, 1999): 27, which quotes an unnamed Pentagon official as saying "We don't monitor the Siprnet," apparently because of the presumption that it is secure. Monitoring of it, however, was commencing.

11. See, e.g., John Adams, *Risk* (London: UCL Press, 1995).

12. For the classic sociological discussion of the obverse phenomenon, self-validating belief, see Robert K. Merton, "The Self-Fulfilling Prophecy," *Antioch Review* (Summer 1948): 193–210.

13. See D. MacKenzie, "A View from the Sonnenbichl: On the Historical Sociology of Software and System Dependability," paper presented to ICHC 2000: Mapping the History of Computing—Software Issues, Paderborn, Germany, April 5–8, 2000.

14. In a fly-by-wire aircraft, actions by pilots are inputs to a set of computer systems controlling engine states and the positions of control surfaces, rather than, for example, directly altering the positions of those control surfaces via hydraulic or electromechanical connections.

15. C. A. R. Hoare, "How Did Software Get So Reliable Without Proof?" Presentation to Awareness Club in Computer Assisted Formal Reasoning, Edinburgh, March 21, 1994; Hoare, "How Did Software Get So Reliable Without Proof?" typescript, December 1995.

16. I draw the term "infrastructure" from a discussion with Victoria Stavridou at the conference ICHC 2000: Mapping the History of Computing—Software Issues, Paderborn, Germany, April 5–8, 2000. The general point expressed here also draws upon wider discussions in that meeting. See also Hoare, "How did Software Get so Reliable?" (1995), pp. 16–17.

17. See Harry Collins, *Artificial Experts: Social Knowledge and Intelligent Machines* (Cambridge, Mass.: MIT Press, 1990), pp. 60 and 65, emphasis in original deleted. See also Harry Collins and Martin Kusch, *The Shape of Actions: What Humans and Machines can do* (Cambridge, Mass.: MIT Press, 1998), pp. 121–122 and passim.

18. Collins, *Artificial Experts,* pp. 62–65.

19. Hoare, "How Did Software Get So Reliable" (1995), p. 5.

20. Ann Jackson and Daniel Hoffman, "Inspecting Module Interface Specifications," *Software Testing, Verification and Reliability* 4 (1994): 101–117, p. 112.

21. Jackson and Hoffman, "Inspecting," p. 112.

22. Daniel Hoffman, electronic mail message to author, May 1, 2000.

23. Hoare, "How Did Software Get So Reliable?" (1994), "How Did Software Get So Reliable?" (1995), p. 8.

24. Gerald M. Weinberg, *The Psychology of Computer Programming* (New York: Van Nostrand Reinhold, 1971), p. 135, suggests that individual variation in performance in particular aspects of programming may be as large as 30:1, but that this variation is greatly reduced (perhaps to 3:1 or 2:1) when "differences average out over a project that requires all sorts of attitudes and skills."

25. Interview data.

26. John Rushby, *Formal Methods and the Certification of Critical Systems* (Menlo Park, Calif.: SRI International, 1993, SRI-CSL-93-07), p. 178.

27. See *Software Considerations in Airborne Systems and Equipment Certification* (Washington, DC: RTCA, 1992, RTCA/DO-178B).

28. Interview data.

29. Eric Livingston, "Cultures of Proving," *Social Studies of Science* 29 (1999): 867–888.

30. Eric Livingston, *The Ethnomethodological Foundations of Mathematics* (London: Routledge & Kegan Paul, 1986), pp. 181–189, interestingly compares the cultures of proving of mathematics and of physics, but as David Bloor points out, the comparison is not developed: see Bloor, "The Living Foundations of Mathematics," *Social Studies of Science* 17 (1987): 337–358, p. 352.

31. Richard C. Linger, Harlan D. Mills, and Bernard I. Witt, as quoted in chapter 2 above.

32. John Rushby and Friedrich von Henke, as quoted in chapter 8 above.

33. See Barry Barnes, David Bloor, and John Henry, *Scientific Knowledge: A Sociological Analysis* (London: Athlone, and Chicago: University of Chicago Press, 1996), pp. 196–199, for a sociological discussion of *modus ponens*.

34. Alfred North Whitehead and Bertrand Russell, *Principia Mathematica* (Cambridge: Cambridge University Press, 1910–1913, second edition, 1925–1927), vol. 2, p. 83.

35. David Hilbert, "On the Infinite," in *From Frege to Gödel: A Source Book in Mathematical Logic, 1879–1931,* ed. Jean van Heijenoort (Cambridge, Mass.: Harvard University Press, 1967), 367–392. This is the English translation of an address delivered by Hilbert to the Westphalian Mathematical Society on June 4, 1925.

36. Livingston, *Ethnomethodological Foundations,* p. 30. For example, as noted in chapter 8, Natarajan Shankar had by 1986 used the Boyer-Moore theorem prover to perform a formal, mechanical proof of Gödel's incompleteness theorem, the "ordinary," informal, rigorous-argument proof which is the focus of Livingston's book.

37. Personal communications from, among others, Bill Aspray and Michael Mahoney.

38. Interview data.

39. Alfred Tarski, "Truth and Proof," *Scientific American* 220 (6) (June 1969): 63–77, at pp. 70 and 75, emphasis in original. On the general issue of the critique of "psychologism" by philosophers, see Martin Kusch, *Psychologism: A Case Study in the Sociology of Philosophical Knowledge* (London: Routledge, 1995).

40. U.K. Ministry of Defence, *Interim Defence Standard 00–55: The Procurement of*

Safety Critical Software in Defence Equipment (Glasgow: Ministry of Defence, Directorate of Standardisation, 1991), part 2, p. 28. The term "rigorous argument," used in this sense, can also be found in Cliff B. Jones, *Software Development: A Rigorous Approach* (Englewood Cliffs, N.J.: Prentice-Hall, 1980), pp. 13–14.

41. Edsger W. Dijkstra and Carel S. Scholten, *Predicate Calculus and Program Semantics* (New York: Springer, 1990), p. 1; Edsger W. Dijkstra, "Real Mathematicians Don't Prove," handwritten memo, EWD1012 (Austin, Texas, January 24, 1988), pp. 4 and 7. I am grateful to Professor Dijkstra for a copy of this memo. That Dijkstra's "calculational" proofs are not "formal," but "rigorous arguments in a strict format . . . but where the notion of proof is 'convincing enough for your fellow mathematicians,' " is argued by Panagiotis Manolios and J Strother Moore, "On the Desirability of Mechanizing Calculational Proofs," forthcoming in *Information Processing Letters,* typescript p. 4.

42. Peter Naur, personal communication to author, Schloss Dagstuhl, Wadern, Germany, August 28, 1996.

43. Jan L. A. van de Snepscheut, *Trace Theory and VLSI Design* (Berlin: Springer, 1985).

44. David Gries, "Influences (or Lack Thereof) of Formalism in Teaching Programming and Software Engineering," in *Formal Development of Programs and Proofs,* ed. Edsger W. Dijkstra (Reading, Mass.: Addison-Wesley, 1990), 229–236, at p. 230.

45. Edsger W. Dijkstra, in Richard A. DeMillo, Edsger W. Dijkstra, Panel Discussion moderated by Robert Paige, Purdue University, April 16, 1993.

46. David Bloor, *Wittgenstein: A Social Theory of Knowledge* (London: Macmillan, 1983); Barnes, Bloor, and Henry, *Scientific Knowledge,* chapter 7.

47. That is not to deny that the technical development of logic in the twentieth century has played a major part in the emergence of a pluralist attitude.

48. Edsger W. Dijkstra, "EWD611: On the Fact that the Atlantic Ocean Has Two Sides," in Dijkstra, *Selected Writings on Computing: A Personal Perspective* (New York: Springer, 1982), 268–276; Gries, "Influences," p. 230; Dennis Shasha and Cathy Lazere, *Out of their Minds: The Lives and Discoveries of 15 Great Computer Scientists* (New York: Copernicus, 1995), p. 67.

49. Milner, as quoted in chapter 8 above.

50. Avra Cohn, interviewed by A. J. Dale, Cambridge, February 2, 1994.

51. John Rushby, "Using Model Checking to Help Discover Mode Confusions and Other Automation Surprises," paper presented to the Third Workshop on Human Error, Safety, and System Development, Liege, Belgium, June 7–8, 1999, p. 2, emphasis in original.

52. Alan Bundy, personal communication.

53. Cliff Jones, electronic mail message to author, September 3, 2000.

54. In 1996, while at a meeting at the conference center of the German Mathematical Society at Oberwolfach in the Black Forest, I examined the current issues of all the mathematical journals in its well-stocked library, and found not a single formal proof in the sense in which I am using the term here.

55. Rowan Garnier and John Taylor, *100% Mathematical Proof* (Chichester, England: Wiley, 1996) p. vii.

56. Livingston, *Ethnomethodological Foundations,* p. 16; Livingston, "Cultures of Proving," p. 880.

57. Interview data.

58. Daniel I. A. Cohen, interviewed by A. J. Dale, New York, May 2, 1994; Cohen, undated letter to author.

59. Simon Blackburn, *Oxford Dictionary of Philosophy* (Oxford: Oxford University Press, 1996), p. 306.

60. Gregory J. Chaitin, "Randomness and Mathematical Proof," *Scientific American* 232 (May 1975): 47–52, at p. 51.

61. Barnes, Bloor, and Henry, *Scientific Knowledge,* p. 55.

62. Sir Michael Atiyah, interviewed by A. J. Dale, London, February 23, 1994.

63. Israel Kleiner, "Rigor and Proof in Mathematics: A Historical Perspective," *Mathematics Magazine* 64 (1991): 291–314, at p. 314.

64. See, for example, Judith V. Grabiner, "Is Mathematical Truth Time-Dependent?" *American Mathematical Monthly* 81 (1974): 354–365; Joan L. Richards, *Mathematical Visions: The Pursuit of Geometry in Victorian England* (Boston: Academic Press, 1988); Richards, "Rigor and Clarity: Foundations of Mathematics in France and England, 1800–1840," *Science in Context* 4 (1991): 297–319; Massimo Mazzotti, "The Geometers of God: Mathematics and Reaction in the Kingdom of Naples," *Isis* 89 (1998): 674–701: Mazzotti, "The Geometers of God: Mathematics in a Conservative Culture, Naples 1780–1840" (PhD thesis, University of Edinburgh, 1999).

65. Arthur Jaffe and Frank Quinn, "'Theoretical Mathematics': Toward a Cultural Synthesis of Mathematics and Theoretical Physics," *Bulletin of the American Mathematical Society* (new series) 29 (1993): 1–13, at pp. 3, 4 and 6; see the subsequent discussion ibid., 30 (1994): 159–211. The particular proof in contention is of William Thurston's "geometrization theorem" for what are called Haken three-manifolds. See Jaffe and Quinn, p. 8, and William P. Thurston, "On Proof and Progress in Mathematics," *Bulletin of the American Mathematical Society* (new series) 30 (1994): 161–177, at pp. 174–176.

66. Livingston, *Ethnomethodological Foundations,* and Livingston, "Cultures of

Proving," *point* to the need for detailed ethnographic work, but in practice largely discuss proofs as written texts and infer, rather than observe, the relationship between these texts and the "lived work" (*Ethnomethodological Foundations,* p. 23) of the production and reception of proofs.

67. John P. Walsh and Todd Bayma, "Computer Networks and Scientific Work," *Social Studies of Science* 26 (1996): 661–703, p. 666–667. I am grateful to David Rowe for a helpful discussion of the oral culture of twentieth-century mathematicians.

68. Thomas Tymoczko, "Making Room for Mathematicians in the Philosophy of Mathematics," *Mathematical Intelligencer* 8 (3) (1986): 44–50, at p. 44, emphasis in original deleted. See also, for example, Philip Kitcher, *The Nature of Mathematical Knowledge* (New York: Oxford University Press, 1983).

69. Thomas Tymoczko, "Gödel, Wittgenstein and the Nature of Mathematical Knowledge," *Philosophy of Science Association, PSA 1984,* vol. 2, 449–468, at p. 465; Tymoczko, "Making Room for Mathematicians," p. 48.

70. Yuri I. Manin, "Good Proof Are Proofs that Make Us Wiser," interview by Martin Aigner and Vasco A. Schmidt, *Berlin Intelligencer,* eds. Vasco A. Schmidt, Martin Aigner, Jochen Brüning, and Günter M. Ziegler (Heidelberg: Springer, 1998), 16–19, at p. 17.

71. Collins and Kusch, *Shape of Actions,* p. 1.

72. Collins and Kusch, *Shape of Actions,* pp. 21–23, emphasis in original deleted.

73. P. H. Nidditch, *Introductory Formal Logic of Mathematics* (London: University Tutorial Press, 1957), p. 6.

74. This was brought into sharper focus for me by conversations with philosopher Jody Azzouni at a meeting at Roskilde University in 1998.

75. Jacques Désiré Fleuriot, "A Combination of Geometry Theorem Proving and Nonstandard Analysis, with Applications to Newton's Principia" (Ph.D. thesis, University of Cambridge, 1999), chapter 5, finds a flaw in one of Newton's proofs that had, as far as I am aware, not previously been noticed by the many commentators on Newton. It appears to be a flaw on the criteria Newton himself applied, not just on the retrospective application of modern criteria. I exclude here Rushby and von Henke's mechanical reproof of Lamport's clock convergence algorithm, described in chapter 8, because that was a proof within computer science rather than mathematics. I do not think that the absence of examples is the result of my ignorance: Bob Boyer, William McCune, and Andrzej Trybulec, who were kind enough in 1998 to answer requests from me for examples, were unable to provide me with any.

76. Jon Barwise, "Mathematical Proofs of Computer System Correctness," *Notices of the American Mathematical Society* 36 (1989): 844–851, at p. 849.

77. John M. Rushby and Friedrich von Henke, "Formal Verification of Algorithms

for Critical Systems," *IEEE Transactions on Software Engineering* 19 (1993): 13–23, at pp. 20–21.

78. Alan Robinson, interviewed by A. J. Dale, Edinburgh, February 15–16, 1994; Robinson, "Formal and Informal Proofs," in *Automated Reasoning: Essays in Honor of Woody Bledsoe,* ed. Robert S. Boyer (Dordrecht: Kluwer, 1991), 267–282. According to Robinson (ibid., p. 271), the problem was first put forward by Max Black, *Critical Thinking: An Introduction to Logic and Scientific Method* (New York: Prentice-Hall, 1946), p. 142, and the outline of the solution is given at the end of Black's book (p. 394). The mutilated chess board was posed as a hard problem for automated provers by John McCarthy, "A Tough Nut for Proof Procedures" (Stanford, Calif.: Stanford Artificial Intelligence Project, 1964, memo no. 16). An example of its formal, automated solution is William McCune, "Another Crack in a Tough Nut," *Association for Automated Reasoning Newsletter* no. 31 (1995): 1–3.

79. Robert Pollack, "How to Believe a Machine Checked Proof," in *Twenty-Five Years of Constructive Type Theory,* eds. Giovanni Sambin and Jan M. Smith (Oxford: Clarendon 1998), 205–220, at p. 214.

80. Nidditch, *Formal Logic,* pp. v, 1, 6; emphasis in original.

81. Roger Jones, interviewed by A. J. Dale, Winnersh, Berks, U.K., March 8, 1994; Jones, electronic mail message to author, May 30, 1999.

82. Dijkstra, "Real Mathematicians Don't Prove," pp. 3, 4, 7, 8, and 9, emphasis in original.

83. Peter Galison, *Image and Logic: A Material Culture of Microphysics* (Chicago: University of Chicago Press, 1997), at pp. 708–709, 778–779, and 844, emphases in original.

84. Galison, *Image and Logic,* pp. 820–827.

85. Galison, *Image and Logic,* pp. 831–832 and passim.

86. See Whitehead and Russell, *Principia Mathematica,* second edition, vol. 1, pp. xiv and 59. I draw the example of the least upper bound from Christopher Menzel, "Type Theory," in *The Cambridge Dictionary of Philosophy,* ed. Robert Audi (Cambridge: Cambridge University Press, 1995), 816–818, at p. 818. The problem, roughly, is that the property that constitutes being a least upper bound of a set of real numbers is of higher type than the property of being a real number and so, without the axiom of reducibility, the bound cannot itself be a real number.

87. David Hilbert, as quoted in chapter 8 above.

88. Samson Abramsky, "From Computation to Interaction: Towards a Science of Information," forthcoming in *Computer Journal,* typescript p. 14.

89. Hubert L. Dreyfus, *What Computers Can't Do: The Limits of Artificial Intelligence* (New York: Harper & Row, revised edition, 1979).

90. See Herbert Breger, "Tacit Knowledge in Mathematical Theory," in *The Space of Mathematics: Philosophical, Epistemological, and Historical Explorations*, eds. Javier Echeverria, Andoni Ibarra, and Thomas Mormann (Berlin: de Gruyter, 1992), 79–90.

91. In that sense, one could argue that efforts to automate mathematics have so far automated not actual mathematicians but how the latter are often conceived philosophically.

92. Alan Bundy, electronic mail message to author, August 23, 2000.

93. Some intriguing experiments in this direction are reported in Simon Colton, Alan Bundy, and Toby Walsh, "Agent Based Cooperative Theory Formation in Pure Mathematics," presented to symposium on Creative & Cultural Aspects and Applications of AI & Cognitive Science, Birmingham, England, April 2000.

94. Randy Pollack, interviewed by A. J. Dale, Edinburgh, November 15, 1993.

95. Randy Pollack, electronic mail message to author, April 30, 1999, emphases in original.

96. Robin Milner, interviewed by A. J. Dale, Edinburgh, November 17, 1993.

97. Collins, *Artificial Experts,* chapter 5; D. MacKenzie, "Negotiating Arithmetic, Constructing Proof: The Sociology of Mathematics and Information Technology," *Social Studies of Science* 23 (1993): 37–65, reprinted as chapter 8 of MacKenzie, *Knowing Machines: Essays on Technical Change* (Cambridge, Mass.: MIT Press, 1996).

98. Bloor, *Wittgenstein: Rules and Institutions.*

99. Thus J. J. C. Smart is wrong to imagine that "a nonnormative notion of correctness that could be applied to a computer" can be found in the computer remaining "an effectively closed system" free from "random external or internal influences." Computers that are closed systems, free from such influences, can "prove" $1 = 0$. As Bloor points out, Smart's apparently nonnormative solution simply displaces normativity. See Smart, "Wittgenstein, Following a Rule, and Scientific Psychology," in *The Scientific Enterprise,* ed. Edna Ullmann-Margalit (Dordrecht: Kluwer, 1992), pp. 129–130; Bloor, *Wittgenstein: Rules and Institutions,* p. 138.

100. Ludwig Wittgenstein, *Philosophical Investigations* (Oxford: Blackwell, 1963), p. 77e.

101. Collins, *Artificial Experts.* The quoted phrase, summarizing Collins's analysis, is not from the book but from Barry Barnes's review of it, "Social Prosthesis," *The Times Higher Education Supplement* (February 15, 1991): 21.

102. See, for example, D. MacKenzie, "The Certainty Trough," in *Exploring Expertise: Issues and Perspectives,* eds. Robin Williams, Wendy Faulkner, and James Fleck (Basingstoke: Macmillan, 1998), 325–329. Literally, it is an uncertainty trough,

but I choose the phrase "certainty trough" to emphasize that in many contexts it is undue certainty, not uncertainty, that is problematic.

103. Avra Cohn, "The Notion of Proof in Hardware Verification," *Journal of Automated Reasoning* 5 (1989): 127–139.

104. Milner, as quoted in chapter 8 above; Collins, *Artificial Experts,* p. 14.

105. For an elegant essay on these, see Sarah S. Jain, "The Prosthetic Imagination: Enabling and Disabling the Prosthesis Trope," *Science, Technology, & Human Values* 24 (1999): 31–54.

106. See also, e.g., Collins and Kusch, *Shape of Actions,* pp. 121 and 124–125.

Index